Lecture Notes in Computer Science 1381

Edited by G. Goos, J. Hartmanis and J. van Leeuwen

Springer

Berlin
Heidelberg
New York
Barcelona
Budapest
Hong Kong
London
Milan
Paris
Santa Clara
Singapore
Tokyo

Chris Hankin (Ed.)

Programming
Languages and Systems

7th European Symposium on Programming,
ESOP'98
Held as Part of the Joint European Conferences
on Theory and Practice of Software, ETAPS'98
Lisbon, Portugal, March 28 – April 4, 1998
Proceedings

Springer

Series Editors

Gerhard Goos, Karlsruhe University, Germany
Juris Hartmanis, Cornell University, NY, USA
Jan van Leeuwen, Utrecht University, The Netherlands

Volume Editor

Chris Hankin
The Imperial College of Science and Technology, Department of Computing
180 Queen's Gate, London SW7 2BZ, UK
E-mail: clh@doc.ic.ac.uk

Cataloging-in-Publication data applied for

Die Deutsche Bibliothek - CIP-Einheitsaufnahme

Programming languages and systems : proceedings / 7th European
Symposium on Programming, ESOP '98, held as part of the Joint
European Conferences on Theory and Practice of Software, ETAPS
'98, Lisbon, Portugal, March 28 - April 4, 1998. Chris Hankin (ed.). -
Berlin ; Heidelberg ; New York ; Barcelona ; Budapest ; Hong Kong
; London ; Milan ; Paris ; Santa Clara ; Singapore ; Tokyo : Springer,
1998
   (Lecture notes in computer science ; Vol. 1381)
   ISBN 3-540-64302-8

CR Subject Classification (1991): D.3, F.3, F.4, D.1-2

ISSN 0302-9743
ISBN 3-540-64302-8 Springer-Verlag Berlin Heidelberg New York

© Springer-Verlag Berlin Heidelberg 1998
Printed in Germany

Typesetting: Camera-ready by author
SPIN 10631992   06/3142 – 5 4 3 2 1 0   Printed on acid-free paper

Foreword

The European conference situation in the general area of software science has long been considered unsatisfactory. A fairly large number of small and medium-sized conferences and workshops take place on an irregular basis, competing for high-quality contributions and for enough attendees to make them financially viable. Discussions aiming at a consolidation have been underway since at least 1992, with concrete planning beginning in summer 1994 and culminating in a public meeting at TAPSOFT'95 in Aarhus.

On the basis of a broad consensus, it was decided to establish a single annual federated spring conference in the slot that was then occupied by TAPSOFT and CAAP/ESOP/CC, comprising a number of existing and new conferences and covering a spectrum from theory to practice. ETAPS'98, the first instance of the European Joint Conferences on Theory and Practice of Software, is taking place this year in Lisbon. It comprises five conferences (FoSSaCS, FASE, ESOP, CC, TACAS), four workshops (ACoS, VISUAL, WADT, CMCS), seven invited lectures, and nine tutorials.

The events that comprise ETAPS address various aspects of the system development process, including specification, design, implementation, analysis and improvement. The languages, methodologies and tools which support these activities are all well within its scope. Different blends of theory and practice are represented, with an inclination towards theory with a practical motivation on one hand and soundly-based practice on the other. Many of the issues involved in software design apply to systems in general, including hardware systems, and the emphasis on software is not intended to be exclusive.

ETAPS is a natural development from its predecessors. It is a loose confederation in which each event retains its own identity, with a separate programme committee and independent proceedings. Its format is open-ended, allowing it to grow and evolve as time goes by. Contributed talks and system demonstrations are in synchronized parallel sessions, with invited lectures in plenary sessions. Two of the invited lectures are reserved for "unifying" talks on topics of interest to the whole range of ETAPS attendees. The aim of cramming all this activity into a single one-week meeting is to create a strong magnet for academic and industrial researchers working on topics within its scope, giving them the opportunity to learn about research in related areas, and thereby to foster new and existing links between work in areas that have hitherto been addressed in separate meetings.

ETAPS'98 has been superbly organized by José Luis Fiadeiro and his team at the Department of Informatics of the University of Lisbon. The ETAPS steering committee has put considerable energy into planning for ETAPS'98 and its successors. Its current membership is:

André Arnold (Bordeaux), Egidio Astesiano (Genova), Jan Bergstra (Amsterdam), Ed Brinksma (Enschede), Rance Cleaveland (Raleigh), Pierpaolo Degano (Pisa), Hartmut Ehrig (Berlin), José Fiadeiro (Lisbon), Jean-Pierre Finance (Nancy), Marie-Claude Gaudel (Paris), Tibor

Gyimothy (Szeged), Chris Hankin (London), Stefan Jähnichen (Berlin), Uwe Kastens (Paderborn), Paul Klint (Amsterdam), Kai Koskimies (Tampere), Tom Maibaum (London), Hanne Riis Nielson (Aarhus), Fernando Orejas (Barcelona), Don Sannella (Edinburgh, chair), Bernhard Steffen (Dortmund), Doaitse Swierstra (Utrecht), Wolfgang Thomas (Kiel)

Other people were influential in the early stages of planning, including Peter Mosses (Aarhus) and Reinhard Wilhelm (Saarbrücken). ETAPS'98 has received generous sponsorship from:

Portugal Telecom
TAP Air Portugal
the Luso-American Development Foundation
the British Council
the EU programme "Training and Mobility of Researchers"
the University of Lisbon
the European Association for Theoretical Computer Science
the European Association for Programming Languages and Systems
the Gulbenkian Foundation

I would like to express my sincere gratitude to all of these people and organizations, and to José in particular, as well as to Springer-Verlag for agreeing to publish the ETAPS proceedings.

Edinburgh, January 1998   Donald Sannella
                                           ETAPS Steering Committee chairman

7th European Symposium on Programming – ESOP'98

ESOP is devoted to fundamental issues in the specification, analysis, and implementation of programming languages and systems. The emphasis is on research which bridges the gap between theory and practice.

Traditionally, this has included the following non-exhaustive list of topics: software specification and verification (including algebraic techniques and model checking), programming paradigms and their integration (including functional, logic, concurrent and object-oriented), semantics facilitating the formal development and implementation of programming languages and systems, advanced type systems (including polymorphism and subtyping), program analysis (including abstract interpretation and constraint systems), program transformation (including partial evaluation and term rewriting), and implementation techniques (including compilation).

The programme committee received 59 submissions from which 17 papers were accepted. This proceedings volume also includes an invited contribution by Gert Smolka.

Programme Committee:

J. de Bakker (The Netherlands)	P. Lee (USA)
L. Cardelli (UK)	H.R. Nielson (Denmark)
A. Deutsch (France)	M. Odersky (Australia)
R. Giegerich (Germany)	A. Pettorossi (Italy)
R. Glück (Denmark)	A. Porto (Portugal)
R. Gorrieri (Italy)	D. Sands (Sweden)
C. Hankin (UK, chair)	D. Schmidt (USA)
P. Hartel (UK)	

I would like to thank the members of the programme committee and their sub-referees; the sub-referees are listed below. I also wish to express my gratitude to Hanne Riis Nielson, for passing on the wisdom she gained in chairing ESOP'96, and Don Sannella and José Luis Fiadeiro for the excellent job that they have done in organising ETAPS'98.

ESOP'98 was organised in cooperation with ACM SIGPLAN.

London, January 1998   Chris Hankin

Referees for ESOP'98

S. Abramov	R. Focardi	G. Malcolm	S. Romanenko
J. Alferes	N. Francez	J. Maraist	A. Sabelfeld
S.M. Ali	M. Gaspari	L. Margara	E. Scholz
L. Augustsson	G. Gonthier	C. Mascolo	J.P. Secher
M. Beemster	A. Gordon	E. Meijer	R. Segala
W. Bibel	A. Gravell	A. Middeldorp	E. Sekerinski
B. Blanchet	C. Haack	D. Miller	P. Sestoft
F.S. de Boer	T. Hallgren	T. Mogensen	O. Shivers
E. Boerger	M. Hanus	A. Montresor	H. Sondergaard
M. Bonsangue	J. Hatcliff	L. Moreau	C. Stone
A. Bossi	N. Heintze	J.J. Moreno Navarro	A. Stoughton
M. Bugliesi	J. Hughes	J. Mountjoy	C. Szyperski
M. Bulyonkov	M. Huth	M. Muench	A. Takano
M. Butler	H. Ibraheem	A.P. Nemytykh	P. Thiemann
L. Caires	B. Jacobs	F. Nielson	B. Thompson
M. Carlsson	J. Jeuring	R. O'Callahan	M.G.J. van den Brand
S. Cimato	T. Johnsson	E. Ohlebusch	W. van Oortmerssen
K. Claessen	J. Jørgensen	C. Okasaki	W. Vree
C. Colby	B. Jung	C. Palamidessi	H.R. Walters
J.C. Cunha	A. Klimov	F. Pfenning	J. Warners
M. Dam	O. Kullmann	D. Plump	M. Wermelinger
L. Dami	E. Lamma	M. Proietti	A. Werner
R. Davies	C. Laneve	P. Purdom	P. Wickline
S. Etalle	M. Leuschel	S. Renault	G. Zavattaro
M.C.F. Ferreira	S. Maclean	J.G. Riecke	

Table of Contents

Invited Papers

Concurrent Constraint Programming Based on Functional Programming (Extended Abstract) 1
G. Smolka

Regular Papers

A Bisimulation Method for Cryptographic Protocols 12
M. Abadi and A. D. Gordon

A Polyvariant Binding-Time Analysis for Off-line Partial Deduction 27
M. Bruynooghe, M. Leuschel and K. Sagonas

Verifiable and Executable Logic Specifications of Concurrent Objects in $\mathcal{L}_\pi$ 42
L. Caires and L. Monteiro

Complexity of Concrete Type-Inference in the Presence of Exceptions .. 57
R. Chatterjee, B. G. Ryder and W. A. Landi

Synchronisation Analysis to Stop Tupling 75
W.-N. Chin, S.-C. Khoo and T.-W. Lee

Propagating Differences: An Efficient New Fixpoint Algorithm for Distributive Constraint Systems 90
C. Fecht and H. Seidl

Reasoning about Classes in Object-Oriented Languages: Logical Models and Tools 105
U. Hensel, M. Huisman, B. Jacobs and H. Tews

Language Primitives and Type Discipline for Structured Communication-Based Programming 122
K. Honda, V. T. Vasconcelos and M. Kubo

The Functional Imperative: Shape! 139
C. B. Jay and P. A. Steckler

Code Motion and Code Placement: Just Synonyms? 154
J. Knoop, O. Rüthing and B. Steffen

Recursive Object Types in a Logic of Object-Oriented Programs 170
K. R. M. Leino

Mode-Automata: About Modes and States for Reactive Systems 185
F. Maraninchi and Y. Rémond

From Classes to Objects via Subtyping 200
D. Rémy

Building a Bridge between Pointer Aliases and Program Dependences .. 221
J. L. Ross and M. Sagiv

A Complete Declarative Debugger of Missing Answers 236
S. Ruggieri

Systematic Change of Data Representation: Program Manipulations
and a Case Study 252
W. L. Scherlis

A Generic Framework for Specialization (Abridged Version) 267
P. Thiemann

Author Index 283

Concurrent Constraint Programming
Based on Functional Programming

(Extended Abstract)

Gert Smolka

Programming Systems Lab
DFKI and Universität des Saarlandes
Postfach 15 11 50, D-66041 Saarbrücken, Germany
smolka@dfki.de, http://www.ps.uni-sb.de/~smolka/

1 Introduction

We will show how the operational features of logic programming can be added as conservative extensions to a functional base language with call by value semantics. We will address both concurrent and constraint logic programming [9, 2, 18]. As base language we will use a dynamically typed language that is obtained from SML by eliminating type declarations and static type checking. Our approach can be extended to cover all features of Oz [6, 15].

The experience with the development of Oz tells us that the outlined approach is the right base for the practical development of concurrent constraint programming languages. It avoids unnecessary duplication of concepts by reusing functional programming as core technology. Of course, it does not unify the partly incompatible theories behind functional and logic programming. They both contribute at a higher level of abstraction to the understanding of different aspects of the class of programming languages proposed here.

2 The Base Language DML

As base language we choose a dynamically typed language DML that is obtained from SML by eliminating type declarations and static type checking. Given the fact that SML is a strictly statically typed language this surgery is straightforward. To some extent it is already carried out for the definition of the dynamic semantics in the definition of SML [4].

There are several reasons for choosing SML. For the extensions to come it is essential that the language has call by value semantics, sequential execution order, and assignable references. Moreover, variants, records and exceptions are important. Finally, SML has a compact formal definition and is well-known.

Since SML does not make a lexical distinction between constructors and variables, we need to retain constructor declarations. Modules loose their special status since they can be easily expressed with records functions.

Since DML is dynamically typed, the primitive operations of the language will raise suitable exceptions if some of their arguments are ill-typed. Equality in DML is defined for all values, where equality of functions is defined analogous to references.

Every SML program can be translated into an DML program that produces exactly the same results. Hence we can see SML as a statically typed language that is defined on top of DML. There is the interesting possibility of a programming system that based on DML offers a variety of type checking disciplines. Code checked with different type disciplines can be freely combined.

To provide for the extensions to come, we will organize the operational semantics of DML in a style that is rather different from the style used in the definition of SML [4].

3   Values

We distinguish between primitive values and compound values. Primitive values include numbers, nullary constructors, and names. Names represent primitive operations, reference cells, and functions. Compound values are obtained by record and variant construction.

We organize values into a first-order structure over which we obtain sufficiently rich first-order formulas. This set-up gives us a relation $\alpha \models \phi$ that holds if an assignment α satisfies a formula ϕ. An *assignment* is a mapping from variables to values. The details of such a construction can be found in [17].

4   States

A *state* is a finite function σ mapping addresses a to so-called units u. *Units* are either primitive values other than names or representations of records, variants, reference cells, functions, and primitive operations:

$$\{l_1 = a_1, \ldots, l_k = a_k\}$$
$$c(a)$$
$$\mathtt{ref}(a)$$
$$\mathtt{fun}(Match,\ Env)$$
$$\mathtt{primop}$$

A match *Match* is a sequence of clauses $(p_1 \mathtt{=>} e_1 \mid \ldots \mid p_k \mathtt{=>} e_k)$. An environment *Env* is a finite function from program variables to addresses.

For technical convenience we will identify addresses, names and variables occurring in formulas. We say that an assignment α satisfies a state σ and write $\alpha \models \sigma$ if for every address a in the domain of σ the following holds:

1. If $\sigma(a)$ is a primitive value v, then $\alpha(a) = v$.
2. If $\sigma(a)$ is a reference cell, a function, or $\mathtt{primop}$, then $\alpha(a) = a$.
3. If $\sigma(a) = \{l_1 = a_1, \ldots, l_k = a_k\}$, then $\alpha(a) = \{l_1 = \alpha(a_1), \ldots, l_k = \alpha(a_k)\}$.
4. If $\sigma(a) = c(a')$, then $\alpha(a) = c(\alpha(a'))$.

Note that every state is satisfiable and that all assignments satisfying a state σ agree on the domain of σ.

Our states and environments are different from the corresponding notions in the definition of SML. There environments map program variables to values and states map addresses to values. In our set-up environments map program variables to addresses and states map addresses to units. This means that our states represent both stateful and stateless information. Moreover, our states make structure sharing explicit. The sharing information is lost when we move from a state to a satisfying assignment. Given a state σ, the unique restriction of an assignment satisfying σ to the domain of σ is an environment in the sense of the definition of SML.

The relation $\sigma \models \phi$ is defined to hold if and only if every assignment that satisfies σ also satisfies ϕ. If the free variables of ϕ are all in the domain of σ, then we have either $\sigma \models \phi$ or $\sigma \models \neg\phi$. This means that a state has complete information about the values of its addresses. We require that the first-order language be rich enough so that for every σ there exists a formula ϕ such that

$$\alpha \models \sigma \iff \alpha \models \phi$$

for all assignments α. Note that σ determines ϕ up to logical equivalence. We use ϕ_σ to denote a constraint with the above property and say that ϕ_σ represents the *logic content of σ*.

5 Thread and Store

The operational semantics of DML distinguishes between a thread and a store. The thread is a functional evaluator that operates on the store. The states of the store are the states defined above. The store should be thought of as an abstract data type that is accessed by the thread only through a number of predefined operations. An example of such an operation is record selection, which takes an address a and a label l and returns an address or an exception packet.

An interesting primitive operation is the equality test $a_1 = a_2$. It returns true if $\sigma \models a_1 = a_2$ and false if $\sigma \models \neg a_1 = a_2$. Note that this definition yields structural equality for records and variants.

We write $\sigma \to \sigma'$ to say that there is an operation on the store that will replace the state σ with a state σ'. The following *monotonicity property* holds for DML and all extensions we will consider:

$$\sigma \models \phi \wedge \sigma \to \sigma' \Rightarrow \sigma' \models \phi$$

provided all free variables of ϕ are in the domain of σ.

6 Logic Variables

We now extend DML with logic variables, one of the essentials of logic programming. Logic variables are a means to represent in a state partial information

about the values of addresses. Logic variables are modelled with a new unit
lvar. The definition of states is extended so that a state may map an address
also to lvar or an address. We only admit states σ whose *dereference relation*
$a \to_\sigma a'$ is terminating, where $a \to_\sigma a'$ holds iff $\sigma(a) = a'$. The case $\sigma(a) = a'$
may appear when a logic variable is bound. We use $\sigma^*(a)$ to denote the unique
normal form of a with respect to the dereference relation $\to_\sigma$. The definition of
the relation $\alpha \models \sigma$ is extended as follows:

1. If $\sigma(a) = $ lvar, then there is no constraint on $\alpha(a)$.
2. If $\sigma(a) = a'$, then $\alpha(a) = \alpha(a')$.

States can now represent partial information about the values of their addresses.
This means that σ does not necessarily determine the truth value of a formula
ϕ whose free variables are in the domain in σ.

Our states contain more information than necessary. For instance, if $\sigma(a) = a_1$
and $\sigma(a_1) = a_2$, then the difference between σ and $\sigma[a_2/a]$ cannot be observed
at the level of the programming language. In general, we impose the semantic
requirement that for a state σ and addresses a_1 and a_2 such that $\sigma \models a_1 = a_2$
the difference between a_1 and a_2 must not be observable. As it comes to space
complexity, it is nevertheless important to model structure sharing.

The existing operations of DML are extended to the new states as follows.
If an operation needs more information about its arguments than the state provides, then the operation returns the control value blocked. If there is only one
thread, then computation will terminate. If there are several threads, the thread
will retry the operation in the hope that other threads have contributed the
missing information (see next section).

A match (e.g., (x::xr => e_1 | nil => e_2)) blocks until the store contains
enough information to commit to one of the clauses or to know that none applies.
Of particular interest is the equality test $a_1=a_2$, which we defined to return true
if $\sigma \models a_1 = a_2$ and false if $\sigma \models \neg a_1 = a_2$. Since in the presence of logic variables
σ may entail neither $a_1 = a_2$ nor $\neg a_1 = a_2$, the equality test $a_1=a_2$ may block.
There is an efficient incremental algorithm [17] that checks for entailment and
disentailment of equations $a_1 = a_2$.

We say that an operation is *granted* by σ if it does not block on σ. All
extensions we will consider will satisfy the *generalized monotonicity condition*:

$$\text{if } \sigma \text{ grants } o \text{ and } \sigma \to \sigma', \text{ then } \sigma' \text{ grants } o.$$

The operation

$$\text{lvar: unit -> 'a}$$

creates a fresh logic variable and returns its address. The operation

$$\text{isvar: 'a -> bool}$$

returns true if its argument a dereferences to a logic variable (i.e., $\sigma(\sigma^*(a)) = $
lvar) and false otherwise. The *variable binding operation*

$$\text{<-: 'a * 'a -> 'a}$$

expects that its left argument is a logic variable, binds it to its right argument, and returns the right argument. More precisely, if <- is applied to (a_1, a_2) and $\sigma^*(a_1) = a_3$, $\sigma(a_3) = \text{lvar}$ and $\sigma^*(a_2) = a_4$, we distinguish two cases:

1. If $a_3 = a_4$, then there is no side effect and a_4 is returned.
2. If $a_3 \neq a_4$, then the store is updated to $\sigma[a_4/a_3]$ and a_4 is returned.

The operation

$$\text{wait: 'a -> 'a}$$

is an identity function that blocks until its argument is bound to a nonvariable unit. This operation is useful for concurrent programming.

7 Multiple Threads

It is straightforward to extend DML with multiple threads. We use interleaving semantics, that is, the operations threads perform on the store do not overlap in time. Threads can be created with the expression

$$\textbf{spawn } e$$

which spawns a new thread evaluating e and returns (). Often it is convenient to use the derived form

$$\textbf{thread } e$$

which expands to

```
let val x = lvar() in (spawn x <- e); x end
```

where x is a program variable that does not occur free in e. For instance, if we want to evaluate the constituents of the application $e(e_1, e_2)$ concurrently, we can simply write

$$(\textbf{thread } e) \ (\textbf{thread } e_1, \ \textbf{thread } e_2)$$

since the necessary synchronization comes for free.

The combination of logic variables and reference cells provides for powerful synchronization techniques. For this we need an operation

$$\text{exchange: 'a ref * 'a -> 'a}$$

which updates the reference cell given as first argument to hold the second argument and returns the previous content of the cell. Now a function

$$\text{mutex: (unit -> 'a) -> 'a}$$

that applies the function given as argument under mutual exclusion can be written as follows:

```
local val r = ref()
in
    fun mutex(a) =
        let val c = lvar()
        in  wait(exchange(r,c));
            let val v = a() in c <- (); v end
        end
end;
```

A function

```
channel: unit -> {put: 'a -> unit, get: unit -> 'a}
```

that returns an asynchronous channel (i.e., a concurrent queue) can be written as follows:

```
fun channel() =
    let val init = lvar()
        val putr = ref init
        val getr = ref init
        fun put(x) =
            let val new = lvar()
                val old = exchange(putr,new)
            in old <- x::new; () end
        fun get() =
            let val new = lvar()
                val x::c = exchange(getr,new)
            in new <- c ; x end
    in {put=put, get=get} end
```

The put function puts items on the channel and the get function gets items from the channel. The get function blocks until there is an item on the channel. The blocking is caused by the match

```
val x::c = exchange(getr,new)
```

To obtain fairness, the simple requirement that every thread that is not blocked will eventually advance suffices. In the two examples above starvation is excluded since the blocked threads are implicitly queued by means of logic variables. Note that both example functions encapsulate the logic variables they introduce. Our simple fairness requirement rests on the generalized monotonicity condition stated above (i.e., the property that a thread can advance cannot be invalidated by the operations performed by other threads). Languages that take channels as concurrency primitive (e.g., Pict [7]) require the more complicated fairness condition that our channels implement with logic variables.

The outlined style of concurrent programming originated with Oz and is explored in [15, 1]. The paper [15] relates to a previous version of Oz that did not have sequential composition. The book [1] is based on the current version of Oz and explores concurrent programming with object-oriented abstractions. The interested reader may also consult [19], which outlines a distributed version of Oz currently under development.

8 Unification

Next we define unification. We say that σ' is obtained from σ by a *narrowing step* if there are addresses a and a' in the domain of σ such that $\sigma(a) = \texttt{lvar}$, $\sigma^*(a') \neq a$, and $\sigma' = \sigma[a'/a]$. Note that the variable binding operation <- performs a narrowing step if it succeeds. We say that σ' is obtained from σ by *unification of a_1 and a_2* if σ' can be obtained from σ by a minimal number of narrowing steps such that $\sigma' \models a_1 = a_2$ holds. If there is such a σ', we say that a_1 and a_2 are *unifiable in σ*. If σ' is obtained from σ by unification of a_1 and a_2, then $\phi_{\sigma'}$ is logically equivalent to $\phi_\sigma \wedge a_1 = a_2$. Moreover, a_1 and a_2 are unifiable in σ if and only if $\phi_\sigma \wedge a_1 = a_2$ is satisfiable. This *logical characterisation of unification* is a design principle and will also hold for the constraint extensions introduced in later sections.

The *unification operation*

$$==: \text{'a} * \text{'a} \rightarrow \text{'a}$$

expects that its two arguments a_1 and a_2 be unifiable. If this is the case, it narrows the state accordingly and returns a_2. Otherwise, it returns an exception packet.

Our states combine first-order constraints with higher-order functions and reference cells. Unification only concerns the part of a state that represents first-order constraints. Investigations of unification and constraint solving that relate to the unification defined here can be found in [3, 17].

9 Choices

An essential feature of logic programming is a built-in mechanism for search. To add this feature to DML, we introduce choice expressions of the form

$$\text{choice } e_1 | \ldots | e_k$$

A choice is evaluated by replacing it with one of its alternatives e_i. To make this practical, the choices are tried from left to right employing chronological backtracking as in Prolog. We arrange things such that a speculative computation terminates with failure if a unification operation fails. If there is only one thread, this gives us the search mechanism of pure Prolog.

If there are multiple threads, we require that a choice is only committed once all other threads are either blocked or can only advance by committing a choice.

10 Spaces

The outlined Prolog-like search is not satisfactory in a concurrent setting since search is done at the top level and cannot be encapsulated into concurrent agents. It also fails to provide means for programming search engines like all solution search. This long standing problem of logic programming is solved by Oz with a new concept called spaces. A space is a box consisting of a store and threads. Computation in a space is speculative and does not have a direct effect outside. Computation in a space proceeds until the space becomes either failed or stable. Stability means that no thread can advance except by committing a choice. There is an operation that blocks until a space is failed or stable and then reports the result. For stable spaces there are two possibilities: either there is a pending choice or not. If there is no pending choice, the space can be merged with the parent space to obtain the result of the speculative computation. If there is a pending choice, the space can be cloned and be committed to the respective alternatives.

Spaces turn out to be a simple and flexible means for programming search engines. A first version is described in [11, 14]. A recent paper on spaces and their use is [10].

11 Finite Domain Constraints

Finite domain constraints are constraints over integers that in conjunction with constraint programming yield a powerful tool for solving combinatorial problems like scheduling [2, 18, 12]. To include them in our framework, we introduce a new unit $\text{lvar}(D)$ that represents a logic variable that is constrained to take a value in D, where D must be a finite set of integers. Variable binding and unification are adapted so that they respect finite domain constraints. The primitive operations of DML treat finite domain variables like unconstrained variables. There is a new primitive operation

```
fdvar: findom -> int
```

that returns a fresh logic variable constrained to the finite domain given as argument. Unification is extended to handle constrained logic variables according to their logical meaning. For instance, the expression

```
let val x = fdvar[1,2] val y = fdvar[0,2] in x == y end
```

is equivalent to the expression 2.

More expressive constraints like $2 * x = y$ are realized with concurrent agents called *propagators*. For instance, if the store knows that $x \in \{1, \ldots, 10\}$ and $y \in \{1, \ldots, 9\}$, a propagator for the constraint $2 * x = y$ can narrow the domains of x and y to $x \in \{1, 2, 3, 4\}$ and $y \in \{2, 4, 6, 8\}$. This form of inference is called *constraint propagation*. In general, there will be many propagators that communicate through the store. The power of a constraint programming system depends on the class of propagators it offers. Depending on the constraints they realize, propagators often use nontrivial algorithms. A ubiquitous constraint is "$x_1, \ldots, x_k$ are all different". For instance, if the store knows

$$x \in \{1,2,3\} \quad y \in \{1,2,3\} \quad z \in \{1,2,3\} \quad u \in \{1,2,3,4,5\} \quad v \in \{1,3,4\}$$

a propagator for "x, y, z, u, v are all different" can narrow the domains to

$$x \in \{1,2,3\} \quad y \in \{1,2,3\} \quad z \in \{1,2,3\} \quad u \in \{5\} \quad v \in \{4\}$$

which determines the values of u and v. There is a complete propagation algorithm for the all different constraint that has quadratic complexity in the number variables and possible values [8].

12 Feature Constraints

Feature constraints are constraints over records that have applications in computational linguistics and knowledge representation. There is a parameterized primitive operation

```
tellfeature#label: record * 'a -> unit
```

that constrains its first argument to be a record that has a field with the label *label* and with the value that is given as second argument. For instance,

```
tellfeature#age(x,y)
```

posts the constraint that x is a record of the form {age=y, ...}.

To accommodate feature constrains, we use units of the form

$$\texttt{lvar}(w, \{l_1 = a_1, \ldots, l_k = a_k\})$$

that represent logic variables that are constrained to records as specified. A record satisfies the above specification if it has at most w fields and at least a field for every label l_i with a value that satisfies the constraints for the address a_i. The metavariable w stands for a nonnegative integer or ∞, where $k \leq w$.

There is also a primitive operation

```
tellwidth: record * int -> unit
```

that constrains its first argument to be a record with as many fields as specified by the second argument.

The operation `tellfeature` is in fact a unification operation. It narrows the store in a minimal way so that the logic content of the new state is equivalent to the logic content of the old state conjoined with the feature constraint told. For instance, the expression

```
let val x = lvar()
in  tellwidth(x,1); tellfeature#a(x,7); x end
```

is equivalent to the expression {a=7}.

Feature constraints and the respective unification algorithms are the subject of [17]. Feature constraints are related to Ohori's [5] inference algorithm for polymorphic record types.

13 Conclusion

The main point of the paper is the insight that logic and concurrent constraint languages can be profitably based on functional core languages with call by value semantics. This avoids unnecessary duplication of concepts. SML wins over Scheme since it has richer data structures and factored out reference cells.

Our approach does not unify the theories behind functional and logic programming. It treats the extensions necessary for concurrent constraint programming at an abstract implementation level. To understand and analyse concurrent constraint programming, more abstract models are needed (e.g., [9, 2, 13, 15, 16]).

It seems feasible to extend the SML type system to logic variables and constraints. Such an extension would treat logic variables similar to reference cells. Feature constraints could possibly be treated with Ohori's polymorphic record types [5].

The approach presented here is an outcome of the Oz project. The development of Oz started in 1991 from logic programming and took several turns. Oz subsumes all concepts in this paper but has its own syntax and is based on a relational rather than a functional core. The relational core makes Oz more complicated than necessary. The insights formulated in this paper can be used to design a new and considerably simplified version of Oz. Such a new Oz would be more accessible to programmers experienced with SML and would be a good vehicle for teaching concurrent constraint programming.

Acknowledgments

Thanks to Martin Müller and Christian Schulte for comments on a draft of the paper, and thanks to all Oz developers for inspiration.

References

1. M. Henz. *Objects for Concurrent Constraint Programming.* Kluwer Academic Publishers, Boston, Nov. 1997.
2. J. Jaffar and M. J. Maher. Constraint logic programming: A survey. *The Journal of Logic Programming*, 19/20:503–582, May-July 1994.
3. J.-L. Lassez, M. J. Maher, and K. Marriott. Unification revisited. In J. Minker, editor, *Foundations of Deductive Databases and Logic Programming*. Morgan Kaufmann Publishers, San Mateo, CA, USA, 1988.
4. R. Milner, M. Tofte, R. Harper, and D. MacQueen. *The Definition of Standard ML (Revised)*. The MIT Press, Cambridge, MA, 1997.
5. A. Ohori. A polymorphic record calculus and its compilation. *ACM Trans. Prog. Lang. Syst.*, 17(6):844–895, 1995.
6. Oz. The Oz Programming System. Programming Systems Lab, DFKI and Universität des Saarlandes: http://www.ps.uni-sb.de/oz/.
7. B. C. Pierce and D. N. Turner. Pict: A programming language based on the pi-calculus. In *Proof, Language and Interaction: Essays in Honour of Robin Milner*. The MIT Press, Cambridge, MA, 1997.

8. J.-C. Regin. A filtering algorithm for constraints of difference in CSPs. In *Proceedings of the National Conference on Artificial Intelligence*, pages 362–367, 1994.

9. V. A. Saraswat. *Concurrent Constraint Programming*. The MIT Press, Cambridge, MA, 1993.

10. C. Schulte. Programming constraint inference engines. In G. Smolka, editor, *Proceedings of the 3rd International Conference on Principles and Practice of Constraint Programming*, volume 1330 of *Lecture Notes in Computer Science*, pages 519–533, Schloss Hagenberg, Linz, Austria, Oct. 1997. Springer-Verlag.

11. C. Schulte and G. Smolka. Encapsulated search in higher-order concurrent constraint programming. In M. Bruynooghe, editor, *Proceedings of the International Logic Programming Symposium*, pages 505–520, Ithaca, New York, USA, Nov. 1994. The MIT Press, Cambridge, MA.

12. C. Schulte, G. Smolka, and J. Würtz. Finite domain constraint programming in Oz, a tutorial, 1998. Programming Systems Lab, DFKI and Universität des Saarlandes: `ftp://ftp.ps.uni-sb.de/oz/documentation/FDTutorial.ps.gz`.

13. G. Smolka. A foundation for concurrent constraint programming. In J.-P. Jouannaud, editor, *Constraints in Computational Logics*, volume 845 of *Lecture Notes in Computer Science*, pages 50–72. Springer-Verlag, Berlin, Sept. 1994.

14. G. Smolka. The definition of Kernel Oz. In A. Podelski, editor, *Constraints: Basics and Trends*, volume 910 of *Lecture Notes in Computer Science*, pages 251–292. Springer-Verlag, Berlin, 1995.

15. G. Smolka. The Oz Programming Model. In J. van Leeuwen, editor, *Computer Science Today*, volume 1000 of *Lecture Notes in Computer Science*, pages 324–343. Springer-Verlag, Berlin, 1995.

16. G. Smolka. Problem solving with constraints and programming. *ACM Computing Surveys*, 28(4), Dec. 1996. Electronic Section.

17. G. Smolka and R. Treinen. Records for logic programming. *The Journal of Logic Programming*, 18(3):229–258, Apr. 1994.

18. P. Van Hentenryck, V. Saraswat, et al. Strategic directions in constraint programming. *ACM Computing Surveys*, 28(4):701–726, Dec. 1997. ACM 50th Anniversary Issue. Strategic Directions in Computing Research.

19. P. Van Roy, S. Haridi, P. Brand, G. Smolka, M. Mehl, and R. Scheidhauer. Mobile objects in Distributed Oz. *ACM Transactions on Programming Languages and Systems*, 19(5), Sept. 1997.

A Bisimulation Method for Cryptographic Protocols

Martín Abadi[1] and Andrew D. Gordon[2]

[1] Digital Equipment Corporation, Systems Research Center
[2] University of Cambridge, Computer Laboratory

Abstract. We introduce a definition of bisimulation for cryptographic protocols. The definition includes a simple and precise model of the knowledge of the environment with which a protocol interacts. Bisimulation is the basis of an effective proof technique, which yields proofs of classical security properties of protocols and also justifies certain protocol optimisations. The setting for our work is the spi calculus, an extension of the pi calculus with cryptographic primitives. We prove the soundness of the bisimulation proof technique within the spi calculus.

1 Introduction

In reasoning about a reactive system, it is necessary to consider not only the steps taken by the system but also the steps taken by its environment. In the case where the reactive system is a cryptographic protocol, the environment may well be hostile, so little can be assumed about its behaviour. Therefore, the environment may be modelled as a nondeterministic process capable of intercepting messages and of sending any message that it can construct at any point. This approach to describing the environment is fraught with difficulties; the resulting model can be somewhat arbitrary, hard to understand, and hard to reason about.

Bisimulation techniques [Par81,Mil89] provide an alternative approach. Basically, using bisimulation techniques, we can equate two systems whenever we can establish a correspondence between their steps. We do not need to describe the environment explicitly, or to analyse its possible internal computations.

Bisimulation techniques have been applied in a variety of areas and under many guises. Their application to cryptographic protocols, however, presents new challenges.

- Consider, for example, a secure communication protocol $P(M)$, where some cleartext M is transmitted encrypted under a session key. We may like to argue that $P(M)$ preserves the secrecy of M, and may want to express this secrecy property by saying that $P(M)$ and $P(N)$ are equivalent, for every M and N. This equivalence may be sensible because, although $P(M)$ and $P(N)$ send different messages, an attacker that does not have the session key cannot identify the cleartext. Unfortunately, a standard notion of bisimulation would require that $P(M)$ and $P(N)$ send identical messages. So we should relax the definition of bisimulation to permit indistinguishable messages.

– In reasoning about a protocol, we need to consider its behaviour in reaction to inputs from the environment. These inputs are not entirely arbitrary. For example, consider a system $P(M)$ which discloses M when it receives a certain password. Assuming that the password remains secret, $P(M)$ should be equivalent to $P(N)$. In order to argue this, we need to characterise the set of possible inputs from the environment, and to show that it cannot include the password.

– Two messages that are indistinguishable at one point in time may become distinguishable later on. In particular, the keys under which they are encrypted may be disclosed to the environment, which may then inspect the cleartext that these keys were concealing. Thus, the notion of indistinguishability should be sensitive to future events.

Conversely, the set of possible inputs from the environment grows with time, as the environment intercepts messages and learns values that were previously secret.

In short, a definition of bisimulation for cryptographic protocols should explain what outputs are indistinguishable for the environment, and what inputs the environment can generate at any point in time. In this paper we introduce a definition of bisimulation that provides the necessary account of the knowledge of the environment. As we show, bisimulation can be used for reasoning about examples like those sketched informally above. More generally, bisimulation can be used for proving authenticity and secrecy properties of protocols, and also for justifying certain protocol optimisations.

We develop our bisimulation proof technique in the context of the spi calculus [AG97a,AG97b,AG97c,Aba97], an extension of the pi calculus [MPW92] with cryptographic primitives. For simplicity, we consider only shared-key cryptography, although we believe that public-key cryptography could be treated through similar methods. Within the spi calculus, we prove the soundness of our technique. More precisely, we prove that bisimulation yields a sufficient condition for testing equivalence, the relation that we commonly use for specifications in the spi calculus.

We have developed other proof techniques for the spi calculus in earlier work. The one presented in this paper is a useful addition to our set of tools. Its distinguishing characteristic is its kinship to bisimulation proof techniques for other classes of systems. In particular, bisimulation proofs can often be done without creativity, essentially by state-space exploration.

The next section is a review of the spi calculus. Section 3 describes our proof method and Section 4 illustrates its use through some small examples. Section 5 discusses related work. Section 6 concludes.

2 The Spi Calculus (Review)

This section reviews the spi calculus, borrowing from earlier presentations. It gives the syntax and informal semantics of the spi calculus, introduces the main notations for its operational semantics, and finally defines testing equivalence.

2.1 Syntax

We assume an infinite set of *names* and an infinite set of *variables*. We let c, m, n, p, q, and r range over names, and let w, x, y, and z range over variables. When they represent keys, we let k and K range over names too.

The set of *terms* is defined by the grammar:

$L, M, N ::=$	terms
n	name
(M, N)	pair
0	zero
$suc(M)$	successor
$\{M\}_N$	encryption
x	variable

Intuitively, $\{M\}_N$ represents the ciphertext obtained by encrypting the term M under the key N using a shared-key cryptosystem such as DES [DES77]. In examples, we write 1 as a shorthand for the term $suc(0)$.

The set of *processes* is defined by the grammar:

$P, Q, R ::=$	processes
$\overline{M}\langle N\rangle.P$	output
$M(x).P$	input (scope of x is P)
$P \mid Q$	composition
$(\nu n)P$	restriction (scope of n is P)
$!P$	replication
$[M \text{ is } N]\, P$	match
$\mathbf{0}$	nil
$let\ (x, y) = M\ in\ P$	pair splitting (scope of x, y is P)
$case\ M\ of\ 0: P\ suc(x): Q$	integer case (scope of x is Q)
$case\ L\ of\ \{x\}_N\ in\ P$	decryption (scope of x is P)

We abbreviate $\overline{M}\langle N\rangle.\mathbf{0}$ to $\overline{M}\langle N\rangle$. We write $P[M/x]$ for the outcome of replacing each free occurrence of x in process P with the term M, and identify processes up to renaming of bound variables and names. Intuitively, processes have the following meanings:

- An *output process* $\overline{M}\langle N\rangle.P$ is ready to output N on M, and then to behave as P. The output happens only when there is a process ready to input from M. An *input process* $M(x).Q$ is ready to input from M, and then to behave as $Q[N/x]$, where N is the input received.
- A *composition* $P \mid Q$ behaves as P and Q running in parallel.
- A *restriction* $(\nu n)P$ is a process that makes a new, private name n, which may occur in P, and then behaves as P.
- A *replication* $!P$ behaves as infinitely many replicas of P running in parallel.
- A *match* $[M \text{ is } N]\, P$ behaves as P provided that M and N are the same term; otherwise it is stuck, that is, it does nothing.
- The *nil* process $\mathbf{0}$ does nothing.

- A *pair splitting* process *let* $(x, y) = M$ *in* P behaves as $P[N/x][L/y]$ if M is a pair (N, L), and it is stuck if M is not a pair.
- An *integer case* process *case* M *of* $0 : P$ $suc(x) : Q$ behaves as P if M is 0, as $Q[N/x]$ if M is $suc(N)$ for some N, and otherwise is stuck.
- A *decryption* process *case* L *of* $\{x\}_N$ *in* P attempts to decrypt L with the key N. If L has the form $\{M\}_N$, then the process behaves as $P[M/x]$. Otherwise the process is stuck.

For example, $P \triangleq m(x).case\ x\ of\ \{y\}_K\ in\ \overline{m}\langle\{0\}_y\rangle$ is a process that is ready to receive a message x on the channel m. When the message is a ciphertext of the form $\{y\}_K$, process P sends 0 encrypted under y on the channel m. This process may be put in parallel with a process $Q \triangleq \overline{m}\langle\{K'\}_K\rangle$, which sends the name K' encrypted under K on the channel m. In order to restrict the use of K to P and Q, we may form $(\nu K)(P \mid Q)$. The environment of $(\nu K)(P \mid Q)$ will not be able to construct any message of the form $\{y\}_K$, since K is bound. Therefore, the component P of $(\nu K)(P \mid Q)$ may output $\{0\}_{K'}$, but not $\{0\}_z$ for any z different from K'. Alternatively, the component P of $(\nu K)(P \mid Q)$ may produce no output: for example, were it to receive 0 on the channel m, it would get stuck.

We write $fn(M)$ and $fn(P)$ for the sets of names free in term M and process P respectively, and write $fv(M)$ and $fv(P)$ for the sets of variables free in M and P respectively. A term or process is *closed* if it has no free variables.

2.2 Operational Semantics

An *abstraction* is an expression of the form $(x)P$, where x is a bound variable and P is a process. Intuitively, $(x)P$ is like the process $p(x).P$ minus the name p. A *concretion* is an expression of the form $(\nu m_1, \ldots, m_k)\langle M\rangle P$, where M is a term, P is a process, $k \geq 0$, and the names $m_1, \ldots, m_k$ are bound in M and P. Intuitively, $(\nu m_1, \ldots, m_k)\langle M\rangle P$ is like the process $(\nu m_1) \ldots (\nu m_k)\overline{p}\langle M\rangle P$ minus the name p, provided p is not one of $m_1, \ldots, m_k$. We often write concretions as $(\nu \vec{m})\langle M\rangle P$, where $\vec{m} = m_1, \ldots, m_k$, or simply $(\nu)\langle M\rangle P$ if $k = 0$. Finally, an *agent* is an abstraction, a process, or a concretion. We use the metavariables A and B to stand for arbitrary agents, and let $fv(A)$ and $fn(A)$ be the sets of free variables and free names of an agent A, respectively.

A *barb* is a name m (representing input) or a co-name $\overline{m}$ (representing output). An *action* is a barb or the distinguished *silent action* τ. The *commitment relation* is written $P \xrightarrow{\alpha} A$, where P is a closed process, α is an action, and A is a closed agent. The exact definition of commitment appears in earlier papers on the spi calculus [AG97b,AG97c]; informally, the definition says:

- $P \xrightarrow{\tau} Q$ means that P becomes Q in one silent step (a τ step).
- $P \xrightarrow{m} (x)Q$ means that, in one step, P is ready to receive an input x on m and then to become Q.
- $P \xrightarrow{\overline{m}} (\nu m_1, \ldots, m_k)\langle M\rangle Q$ means that, in one step, P is ready to create the new names $m_1, \ldots, m_k$, to send M on m, and then to become Q.

2.3   Testing Equivalence

We say that two closed processes P and Q are testing equivalent, and write $P \simeq Q$, when for every closed process R and every barb β, if

$$P \mid R \xrightarrow{\tau}^{*} P' \xrightarrow{\beta} A$$

for some P' and A, then

$$Q \mid R \xrightarrow{\tau}^{*} Q' \xrightarrow{\beta} B$$

for some Q' and B, and vice versa.

For example, the processes $(\nu K)\overline{m}\langle\{0\}_K\rangle$ and $(\nu K)\overline{m}\langle\{1\}_K\rangle$ are testing equivalent. We may interpret this equivalence as a security property, namely that the process $(\nu K)\overline{m}\langle\{x\}_K\rangle$ does not reveal to its environment whether x is 0 or 1. In the examples contained in Section 4 and in earlier papers, various other properties (including, in particular, secrecy properties) are formulated in terms of testing equivalence.

In this paper we develop a sound technique for proving testing equivalence: we introduce a definition of bisimulation and show that if two closed processes are in one of our bisimulation relations then they are testing equivalent.

3   Framed Bisimulation

This section defines our notion of bisimulation, which we call *framed bisimulation*.

3.1   Frames and Theories

Our definition of bisimulation is based on the notions of a *frame* and of a *theory*. A bisimulation does not simply relate two processes P and Q, but instead relates two processes P and Q in the context of a frame and a theory. The frame and the theory represent the knowledge of the environment of P and Q.

- A frame is a finite set of names. Intuitively, a frame is a set of names available to the environment of the processes P and Q. We use fr to range over frames.
- A theory is a finite set of pairs of terms. Intuitively, a theory that includes a pair (M, N) indicates that the environment cannot distinguish the data M coming from process P and the data N coming from process Q. We use th to range over theories.

Next we define the predicate $(fr, th) \vdash M \leftrightarrow N$ inductively, by a set of rules. Intuitively, this predicate means that the environment cannot distinguish M coming from P and N coming from Q, and that the environment has (or can construct) M in interaction with P and N in interaction with Q.

(Eq Frame)	(Eq Theory)	(Eq Variable)
$n \in fr$	$(M, N) \in th$	
$\overline{\qquad\qquad}$	$\overline{\qquad\qquad}$	$\overline{\qquad\qquad}$
$(fr, th) \vdash n \leftrightarrow n$	$(fr, th) \vdash M \leftrightarrow N$	$(fr, th) \vdash x \leftrightarrow x$

(Eq Pair)   (Eq Zero)

$$\frac{(fr, th) \vdash M \leftrightarrow M' \quad (fr, th) \vdash N \leftrightarrow N'}{(fr, th) \vdash (M, N) \leftrightarrow (M', N')} \qquad \frac{}{(fr, th) \vdash 0 \leftrightarrow 0}$$

(Eq Suc)   (Eq Encrypt)

$$\frac{(fr, th) \vdash M \leftrightarrow M'}{(fr, th) \vdash suc(M) \leftrightarrow suc(M')} \qquad \frac{(fr, th) \vdash M \leftrightarrow M' \quad (fr, th) \vdash N \leftrightarrow N'}{(fr, th) \vdash \{M\}_N \leftrightarrow \{M'\}_{N'}}$$

For example, if $fr = \{n\}$ and $th = \{(\{0\}_K, \{n\}_K)\}$, where n and K are distinct names, then we have $(fr, th) \vdash n \leftrightarrow n$ and $(fr, th) \vdash \{0\}_K \leftrightarrow \{n\}_K$, and also $(fr, th) \vdash (n, \{0\}_K) \leftrightarrow (n, \{n\}_K)$, but we have neither $(fr, th) \vdash K \leftrightarrow K$ nor $(fr, th) \vdash \{n\}_K \leftrightarrow \{0\}_K$.

We say that the pair (fr, th) is ok, and write $(fr, th) \vdash ok$, if two conditions hold:

(1) whenever $(M, N) \in th$:
  - M is closed and there are terms M_1 and M_2 such that $M = \{M_1\}_{M_2}$ and there is no N_2 such that $(fr, th) \vdash M_2 \leftrightarrow N_2$;
  - N is closed and there are terms N_1 and N_2 such that $N = \{N_1\}_{N_2}$ and there is no M_2 such that $(fr, th) \vdash M_2 \leftrightarrow N_2$;
(2) whenever $(M, N) \in th$ and $(M', N') \in th$, $M = M'$ if and only if $N = N'$.

Intuitively, the first condition requires that each term in a pair (M, N) in a theory be formed by ciphertexts that the environment cannot decrypt. For example, the requirement that there be no N_2 such that $(fr, th) \vdash M_2 \leftrightarrow N_2$ means that the environment cannot construct M_2 for decrypting M. The second condition guarantees that no ciphertext is equated to two other ciphertexts. This condition is essential because the environment can compare ciphertexts even when it cannot decrypt them (see Example 2 of Section 4).

3.2   Ordering Frame-Theory Pairs

We define an ordering between pairs of frames and theories as follows: we let $(fr, th) \leq (fr', th')$ if and only if for all M and N, $(fr, th) \vdash M \leftrightarrow N$ implies $(fr', th') \vdash M \leftrightarrow N$. This relation is reflexive and transitive. It is not the same as the pairwise ordering induced by subset inclusion; $fr \subseteq fr'$ and $th \subseteq th'$ imply $(fr, th) \leq (fr', th')$, but the converse implication does not hold.

Proposition 1. *Suppose* $(fr', th') \vdash ok$. *Then* $(fr, th) \leq (fr', th')$ *if and only if* $fr \subseteq fr'$ *and* $(fr', th') \vdash M \leftrightarrow N$ *for each* $(M, N) \in th$.

As indicated above, we view a pair (fr, th) as a representation for the knowledge of an environment. With this view, and assuming that $(fr', th') \vdash ok$, the relation $(fr, th) \leq (fr', th')$ means that the environment may go from the knowledge represented in (fr, th) to the knowledge represented in (fr', th'). The definition of $(fr, th) \leq (fr', th')$ implies that the set of names and terms that the environment has (or can construct) grows in this transition. It also implies that any indistinguishable pair of terms remains indistinguishable after the transition. So, if ever we assert that (fr, th) characterises an environment, we should take care that (fr, th) does not imply that the environment cannot distinguish two terms M and N if later information would allow the environment to distinguish these terms. For example, if fr' includes the name n, then th should not contain $(\{0\}_n, \{1\}_n)$. Intuitively, the acquisition of the name n would allow the environment to distinguish $\{0\}_n$ and $\{1\}_n$, so $(fr', th') \vdash \{0\}_n \leftrightarrow \{1\}_n$ would not hold. On the other hand, th may contain $(\{0\}_n, \{0\}_n)$; in that case, th' could not contain $(\{0\}_n, \{0\}_n)$, but we would at least have $(fr', th') \vdash \{0\}_n \leftrightarrow \{0\}_n$.

3.3 Framed Relations and Bisimulations

For a theory th, we let $fn(th) = \bigcup\{fn(M) \cup fn(N) \mid (M, N) \in th\}$. We let $\pi_1(th) = \{M \mid (M, N) \in th\}$ and $\pi_2(th) = \{N \mid (M, N) \in th\}$, and write $fn(\pi_1(th))$ and $fn(\pi_2(th))$ for the sets of names $\bigcup\{fn(M) \mid M \in \pi_1(th)\}$ and $\bigcup\{fn(N) \mid N \in \pi_2(th)\}$ respectively.

A *framed process pair* is a quadruple (fr, th, P, Q) such that P and Q are closed processes, fr is a frame, and th is a theory. When $\mathcal{R}$ is a set of framed process pairs, we write $(fr, th) \vdash P \mathcal{R} Q$ to mean $(fr, th, P, Q) \in \mathcal{R}$. A *framed relation* is a set $\mathcal{R}$ of framed process pairs such that $(fr, th) \vdash ok$ whenever $(fr, th) \vdash P \mathcal{R} Q$.

A *framed simulation* is a framed relation $\mathcal{S}$ such that, whenever $(fr, th) \vdash P \mathcal{S} Q$, the following three conditions hold.

- If $P \xrightarrow{\tau} P'$ then there is a process Q' with $Q \xrightarrow{\tau} Q'$ and $(fr, th) \vdash P' \mathcal{S} Q'$.
- If $P \xrightarrow{c} (x)P'$ and $c \in fr$ then there is an abstraction $(x)Q'$ with $Q \xrightarrow{c} (x)Q'$ and, for all sets $\{\vec{n}\}$ disjoint from $fn(P) \cup fn(Q) \cup fr \cup fn(th)$ and all closed M and N, if $(fr \cup \{\vec{n}\}, th) \vdash M \leftrightarrow N$ then $(fr \cup \{\vec{n}\}, th) \vdash P'[M/x] \mathcal{S} Q'[N/x]$.
- If $P \xrightarrow{\bar{c}} (\nu\vec{m})\langle M\rangle P'$, $c \in fr$, and the set $\{\vec{m}\}$ is disjoint from $fn(P) \cup fn(\pi_1(th)) \cup fr$ then there is a concretion $(\nu\vec{n})\langle N\rangle Q'$ with $Q \xrightarrow{\bar{c}} (\nu\vec{n})\langle N\rangle Q'$ and the set $\{\vec{n}\}$ is disjoint from $fn(Q) \cup fn(\pi_2(th)) \cup fr$, and there is a frame-theory pair (fr', th') such that $(fr, th) \leq (fr', th')$, $(fr', th') \vdash M \leftrightarrow N$, and $(fr', th') \vdash P' \mathcal{S} Q'$.

We may explain these conditions as follows.

- The first condition simply requires that if P can take a τ step then Q can match this step.
- The second condition concerns input steps where the channel c on which the input happens is in fr (that is, it is known to the environment). In this case, we must consider the possible inputs M from the environment to $(x)P'$, namely the terms M that the environment can construct according to $(fr \cup \{\vec{n}\}, th)$. The names in $\vec{n}$ are fresh names, intuitively names just generated by the environment. Correspondingly, we consider the possible inputs N

for $(x)Q'$, for an appropriate $(x)Q'$ obtained from Q. We then require that giving these inputs to $(x)P'$ and $(x)Q'$, respectively, yields related processes $P'[M/x]$ and $Q'[N/x]$.

The choice of $(x)Q'$ is independent of the choices of M and N. So, in the technical jargon, we may say that S is a *late* framed simulation.

- The third condition concerns output steps where the channel c on which the output happens is in fr (that is, it is known to the environment). In this case, P outputs the term M while creating the names $\tilde{m}$. The condition requires that Q can output a corresponding term N while creating some names $\tilde{n}$. It also constrains M and N, and the resulting processes P' and Q'. The constraints concern a new frame-theory pair (fr', th'). Intuitively, this pair represents the knowledge of the environment after the output step. The requirement that $(fr', th') \vdash M \leftrightarrow N$ means that the environment obtains M in interaction with P and N in interaction with Q, and that it should not be able to distinguish them from one another.

Because we do not impose a minimality requirement on (fr', th'), this pair may attribute "too much" knowledge to the environment. For example, fr' may contain names that are neither in fr nor in M or N, so intuitively the environment would not be expected to know these names. On the other hand, the omission of a minimality requirement results in simpler definitions, and does not compromise soundness.

A *framed bisimulation* is a framed relation S such that both S and S^{-1} are framed simulations. *Framed bisimilarity* (written $\sim_f$) is the greatest framed bisimulation. By the Knaster-Tarski fixpoint theorem, since the set of framed relations ordered by subset inclusion forms a complete lattice, framed bisimilarity exists, and equals the union of all framed bisimulations.

Our intent is that our definition of framed bisimulation may serve as the basis for an algorithm, at least for finite-state processes. Unfortunately, the definition contains several levels of quantification. The universal quantifiers present a serious obstacle to any algorithm for constructing framed bisimulations. In particular, the condition for input steps concerns all possible inputs M and N; these inputs are of unbounded size, and may contain an arbitrary number of fresh names. However, we conjecture that the inputs can be classified according to a finite number of patterns—intuitively, because the behaviour of any finite-state process can depend on at most a finite portion of its inputs. An algorithm for constructing framed bisimulations might consider all inputs that match the same pattern at once. We leave the invention of such an algorithm for future work.

3.4 Soundness (Summary)

Our main soundness theorem about framed bisimulation is that it is a sufficient condition for testing equivalence.

Theorem 2. *Consider any closed processes P and Q, and any name $n \notin fn(P) \cup fn(Q)$. Suppose that $(fn(P) \cup fn(Q) \cup \{n\}, \emptyset) \vdash P \sim_f Q$. Then $P \simeq Q$.*

This theorem implies that if we want to prove that two processes are testing equivalent, then we may construct a framed bisimulation S such that $(fn(P) \cup fn(Q) \cup \{n\}, \emptyset) \vdash P\ S\ Q$ where n is a single, arbitrary new name. (The addition of the name n is technically convenient, but may not be necessary.) The next section illustrates this approach through several examples.

The proof of this theorem requires a number of auxiliary notations, definitions, and lemmas. We omit the details of the proof, and only indicate its main idea. In the course of the proof, we extend the relation $\leftrightarrow$ to processes: we define the predicate $(fr, th) \vdash P \leftrightarrow Q$ by the following rules.

(Eq Out)
$$\frac{(fr, th) \vdash M \leftrightarrow M' \quad (fr, th) \vdash N \leftrightarrow N' \quad (fr, th) \vdash P \leftrightarrow P'}{(fr, th) \vdash \overline{M}\langle N \rangle.P \leftrightarrow \overline{M'}\langle N' \rangle.P'}$$

(Eq In)
$$\frac{(fr, th) \vdash M \leftrightarrow M' \quad (fr, th) \vdash P \leftrightarrow P'}{(fr, th) \vdash M(x).P \leftrightarrow M'(x).P'}$$

(Eq Repl)
$$\frac{(fr, th) \vdash P \leftrightarrow P'}{(fr, th) \vdash\ !P \leftrightarrow\ !P'}$$

(Eq Par)
$$\frac{(fr, th) \vdash P \leftrightarrow P' \quad (fr, th) \vdash Q \leftrightarrow Q'}{(fr, th) \vdash P \mid Q \leftrightarrow P' \mid Q'}$$

(Eq Res) (where $n \notin fr \cup fn(th)$)
$$\frac{(fr \cup \{n\}, th) \vdash P \leftrightarrow P'}{(fr, th) \vdash (\nu n)P \leftrightarrow (\nu n)P'}$$

(Eq Match)
$$\frac{(fr, th) \vdash M \leftrightarrow M' \quad (fr, th) \vdash N \leftrightarrow N' \quad (fr, th) \vdash P \leftrightarrow P'}{(fr, th) \vdash [M \text{ is } N]\, P \leftrightarrow [M' \text{ is } N']\, P'}$$

(Eq Nil)
$$\frac{}{(fr, th) \vdash 0 \leftrightarrow 0}$$

(Eq Let)
$$\frac{(fr, th) \vdash M \leftrightarrow M' \quad (fr, th) \vdash P \leftrightarrow P'}{(fr, th) \vdash \text{let } (x, y) = M \text{ in } P \leftrightarrow \text{let } (x, y) = M' \text{ in } P'}$$

(Eq IntCase)
$$\frac{(fr, th) \vdash M \leftrightarrow M' \quad (fr, th) \vdash P \leftrightarrow P' \quad (fr, th) \vdash Q \leftrightarrow Q'}{(fr, th) \vdash \text{case } M \text{ of } 0 : P \ suc(x) : Q \leftrightarrow \text{case } M' \text{ of } 0 : P' \ suc(x) : Q'}$$

(Eq Decrypt)
$$\frac{(fr, th) \vdash M \leftrightarrow M' \quad (fr, th) \vdash N \leftrightarrow N' \quad (fr, th) \vdash P \leftrightarrow P'}{(fr, th) \vdash \text{case } M \text{ of } \{x\}_N \text{ in } P \leftrightarrow \text{case } M' \text{ of } \{x\}_{N'} \text{ in } P'}$$

The core of the proof depends on a relation, S, defined so that $P\ S\ Q$ if and only if there is a frame fr, a theory th, and processes P_1, P_2, Q_1, Q_2, such that

$$P = (\nu \vec{p})(P_1 \mid P_2) \qquad Q = (\nu \vec{q})(Q_1 \mid Q_2)$$

and $(fr, th) \vdash ok$, $(fr, th) \vdash P_1 \sim_f Q_1$, and $(fr, th) \vdash P_2 \leftrightarrow Q_2$, where $\{\vec{p}\} = (fn(P_1) \cup fn(\pi_1(th))) - fr$ and $\{\vec{q}\} = (fn(Q_1) \cup fn(\pi_2(th))) - fr$. By a detailed case analysis, we may show that S satisfies the definition of a standard notion of bisimulation—a barbed bisimulation up to restriction and barbed equivalence. Given some auxiliary lemmas about testing equivalence, the theorem then follows easily. The construction of S also yields that framed bisimilarity is a sufficient condition for a strong equivalence called barbed congruence.

The converse of soundness—completeness—does not hold. The failure of completeness follows from the fact that framed bisimilarity is a sufficient condition for barbed congruence. (Barbed congruence and a fortiori framed bisimilarity are sensitive to τ steps and to branching structure, while testing equivalence is not.) Incompleteness may be somewhat unfortunate but, in our experience, it seems to be compatible with usefulness.

4 Examples

This section shows how bisimulations can be exploited in proofs through some small examples. These examples could not be handled by standard notions of bisimulation (like that of our earlier work [AG97b,AG97c]). We have worked through further examples, including some examples with more steps. In all cases, the proofs are rather straightforward.

Throughout this section, c, K, K_1, and K_2 are distinct names, and n is any name different from c. Moreover, M, M', M'', M_1, M_2, N_1, and N_2 are closed terms; it is convenient to assume that no name occurs in them.

Example 1 As a first example, we show that the processes $(\nu K)\bar{c}\langle\{M\}_K\rangle$ and $(\nu K)\bar{c}\langle\{M'\}_K\rangle$ are in a framed bisimulation, so they are testing equivalent. Intuitively, this means that these processes do not reveal M and M', respectively.

For this example, we let S be the least relation such that:

- $(\{c,n\},\emptyset) \vdash (\nu K)\bar{c}\langle\{M\}_K\rangle \; S \; (\nu K)\bar{c}\langle\{M'\}_K\rangle$
- $(\{c,n\},\{(\{M\}_k,\{M'\}_k)\}) \vdash 0 \; S \; 0$
  for all names $k \notin \{c,n\}$

Since $(\{c,n\},\emptyset) \vdash ok$ and $(\{c,n\},\{(\{M\}_k,\{M'\}_k)\}) \vdash ok$, S is a framed relation. Next we show that S is a framed simulation; symmetric reasoning establishes that S^{-1} is one too. Assuming that $(fr,th) \vdash P \; S \; Q$, we need to examine the commitments of P and Q. We consider two cases, which correspond to the two clauses of the definition of S.

- Suppose that $P = (\nu K)\bar{c}\langle\{M\}_K\rangle$ and $Q = (\nu K)\bar{c}\langle\{M'\}_K\rangle$. In this case, we have $fr = \{c,n\}$ and $th = \emptyset$. Up to renaming of the bound name K, the only commitment of P is $P \xrightarrow{\bar{c}} (\nu K)\langle\{M\}_K\rangle 0$. To establish that S is a framed simulation, we need only consider the case where K is renamed to some $k \notin fn(P) \cup fn(\pi_1(\emptyset)) \cup \{c,n\}$, that is, $k \notin \{c,n\}$. By renaming, we have $Q \xrightarrow{\bar{c}} (\nu k)\langle\{M'\}_k\rangle 0$. We let $th' = \{(\{M\}_k,\{M'\}_k)\}$. We have $(fr,th) \le (fr,th')$, $(fr,th') \vdash \{M\}_k \leftrightarrow \{M'\}_k$, and $(fr,th') \vdash 0 \leftrightarrow 0$. Thus, Q can match P's commitment.

– Suppose that $P = 0$ and $Q = 0$. This case is trivial, since 0 has no commitments.

In short, $(\{c, n\}, \emptyset) \vdash (\nu K)\bar{c}\langle\{M\}_K\rangle \; S \; (\nu K)\bar{c}\langle\{M'\}_K\rangle$, and S is a framed bisimulation, as desired.

Example 2 As a small variant of the first example, we consider the processes $(\nu K)\bar{c}\langle(\{M\}_K, \{M\}_K)\rangle$ and $(\nu K)\bar{c}\langle(\{M'\}_K, \{M''\}_K)\rangle$.

When $M' = M''$, the argument of the first example works for this example too, with only trivial modifications. We define S as the least relation such that:

– $(\{c, n\}, \emptyset) \vdash (\nu K)\bar{c}\langle(\{M\}_K, \{M\}_K)\rangle \; S \; (\nu K)\bar{c}\langle(\{M'\}_K, \{M''\}_K)\rangle$
– $(\{c, n\}, \{(\{M\}_k, \{M'\}_k), (\{M\}_k, \{M''\}_k)\}) \vdash 0 \; S \; 0$
  for all names $k \notin \{c, n\}$

This relation is a framed bisimulation when $M' = M''$. On the other hand, it is not a framed bisimulation when $M' \neq M''$. In fact, in that case it is not even a framed relation, because $(\{c, n\}, \{(\{M\}_k, \{M'\}_k), (\{M\}_k, \{M''\}_k)\}) \vdash ok$ does not hold (because condition (2) of the definition of ok is not satisfied).

The fact that S is not a framed bisimulation in this case should not be a concern. It is actually necessary: the processes $(\nu K)\bar{c}\langle(\{M\}_K, \{M\}_K)\rangle$ and $(\nu K)\bar{c}\langle(\{M'\}_K, \{M''\}_K)\rangle$ are not testing equivalent when $M' \neq M''$. The environment $c(z).let\ (x, y) = z\ in\ [x\ is\ y]\ \bar{c}\langle 0\rangle$ distinguishes them. Thus, this example illustrates that two ciphertexts that cannot be decrypted can still be compared, and justifies part of the definition of framed bisimulation.

Example 3 As a further variant, we study an example with nested encryption. We consider the processes $(\nu K_1)(\nu K_2)\bar{c}\langle\{M_1, \{M_2\}_{K_2}\}_{K_1}\rangle.\bar{c}\langle K_1\rangle$ and $(\nu K_1)(\nu K_2)$ $\bar{c}\langle\{N_1, \{N_2\}_{K_2}\}_{K_1}\rangle.\bar{c}\langle K_1\rangle$. Each of these processes creates two keys K_1 and K_2, sends a ciphertext, and then reveals K_1. Anyone who receives K_1 can partially decrypt the ciphertext.

In order to analyse these processes, we let S be the least relation such that:

– $(\{c, n\}, \emptyset) \vdash (\nu K_1)(\nu K_2)\bar{c}\langle\{M_1, \{M_2\}_{K_2}\}_{K_1}\rangle.\bar{c}\langle K_1\rangle \; S$
    $(\nu K_1)(\nu K_2)\bar{c}\langle\{N_1, \{N_2\}_{K_2}\}_{K_1}\rangle.\bar{c}\langle K_1\rangle$
– $(\{c, n, k_1\}, \{(\{M_2\}_{k_2}, \{N_2\}_{k_2})\}) \vdash \bar{c}\langle k_1\rangle \; S \; \bar{c}\langle k_1\rangle$
    for all names k_1, k_2 with $k_1 \neq k_2$ and $\{k_1, k_2\} \cap \{c, n\} = \emptyset$
– $(\{c, n, k_1\}, \{(\{M_2\}_{k_2}, \{N_2\}_{k_2})\}) \vdash 0 \; S \; 0$
    for all names k_1, k_2 with $k_1 \neq k_2$ and $\{k_1, k_2\} \cap \{c, n\} = \emptyset$

Note how, between the first and the second clauses, the frame has been enlarged with k_1, although the processes considered in the second clause have not yet sent k_1; this simplifies the construction of S and is permitted by the definitions of Section 3. The assumptions guarantee that $(\{c, n, k_1\}, \{(\{M_2\}_{k_2}, \{N_2\}_{k_2})\}) \vdash ok$ and hence that S is a framed relation. Moreover, S is a framed bisimulation if and only if the following condition holds:

$$(\{c, n, k_1\}, \{(\{M_2\}_{k_2}, \{N_2\}_{k_2})\}) \vdash \{M_1, \{M_2\}_{k_2}\}_{k_1} \leftrightarrow \{N_1, \{N_2\}_{k_2}\}_{k_1}$$

In turn, this condition holds if and only if $M_1 = N_1$. Intuitively, the equality $M_1 = N_1$ becomes necessary only when the two processes send the key k_1, since M_1 and N_1 are not visible in the first message. Our definition of $\leq$ guarantees that the necessity of $M_1 = N_1$ is propagated correctly.

Example 4 While all the examples above concern the secrecy of certain outputs, this one concerns the impossibility of certain inputs. We consider the processes $(\nu K)\bar{c}\langle\{0\}_K\rangle.c(x).[x \text{ is } K]\,\bar{c}\langle\{0\}_K\rangle$ and $(\nu K)\bar{c}\langle\{0\}_K\rangle.c(x).\mathbf{0}$. The former process creates a key K, sends $\{0\}_K$, listens for an input, and if it receives K then it sends $\{0\}_K$ again. However, we would expect that K will never arrive as an input to this process, since the process never discloses K (but only $\{0\}_K$, from which K itself cannot be deduced). Therefore, we would expect this process to be equivalent to the latter process, which simply stops upon receipt of a message.

For this example, we let S be the least relation such that:

- $(\{c,n\},\emptyset) \vdash ((\nu K)\bar{c}\langle\{0\}_K\rangle.c(x).[x \text{ is } K]\,\bar{c}\langle\{0\}_K\rangle)\ S\ ((\nu K)\bar{c}\langle\{0\}_K\rangle.c(x).\mathbf{0})$
- $(\{c,n\},\{(\{0\}_k,\{0\}_k)\}) \vdash (c(x).[x \text{ is } k]\,\bar{c}\langle\{0\}_k\rangle)\ S\ (c(x).\mathbf{0})$
  for all names k with $k \notin \{c,n\}$
- $(\{c,n,\vec{m}\},\{(\{0\}_k,\{0\}_k)\}) \vdash ([N \text{ is } k]\,\bar{c}\langle\{0\}_k\rangle)\ S\ \mathbf{0}$
  for all names k with $k \notin \{c,n\}$, for all sets $\{\vec{m}\}$ disjoint from $\{c,n,k\}$,
  and all closed terms N and N' with $(\{c,n,\vec{m}\},\{(\{0\}_k,\{0\}_k)\}) \vdash N \leftrightarrow N'$
  (We are not assuming that no names occur in the closed terms N and N'.)

Since $(\{c,n,\vec{m}\},\{(\{0\}_k,\{0\}_k)\}) \vdash N \leftrightarrow N'$ and $k \notin \{c,n,\vec{m}\}$, the term N is not k, so $[N \text{ is } k]\,\bar{c}\langle\{0\}_k\rangle \xrightarrow{\alpha} A$ is not true for any α and A. In other words, the process $[N \text{ is } k]\,\bar{c}\langle\{0\}_k\rangle$ is stuck. It follows easily that S is a framed bisimulation.

Example 5 In cryptographic protocols, some keys are generated by consulting sources of randomness, but it is also common to generate keys by applying one-way functions to other keys. (Whereas many one-way functions are quite efficient, randomness and key agreement can be relatively expensive [Sch96b].) As a final example, we consider a simple protocol transformation inspired by a common method for generating keys. We compare the process $(\nu K_1)(\nu K_2)$ $\bar{c}\langle\{M_1\}_{K_1}\rangle.\bar{c}\langle\{M_2\}_{K_2}\rangle$, which generates and uses two keys, with the process (νK) $\bar{c}\langle\{N_1\}_{\{0\}_K}\rangle.\bar{c}\langle\{N_2\}_{\{1\}_K}\rangle$, which generates the master key K and then uses the derived keys $\{0\}_K$ and $\{1\}_K$.

In order to show that these processes are testing equivalent, we construct once more a framed bisimulation. We let S be the least relation such that:

- $(\{c,n\},\emptyset) \vdash (\nu K_1)(\nu K_2)\bar{c}\langle\{M_1\}_{K_1}\rangle.\bar{c}\langle\{M_2\}_{K_2}\rangle\ S$
  $\qquad (\nu K)\bar{c}\langle\{N_1\}_{\{0\}_K}\rangle.\bar{c}\langle\{N_2\}_{\{1\}_K}\rangle$
- $(\{c,n\},\{(\{M_1\}_{k_1},\{N_1\}_{\{0\}_k})\}) \vdash (\nu K_2)\bar{c}\langle\{M_2\}_{K_2}\rangle\ S\ \bar{c}\langle\{N_2\}_{\{1\}_k}\rangle$
  for all names k and k_1 with $\{k,k_1\} \cap \{c,n\} = \emptyset$
- $(\{c,n\},\{(\{M_1\}_{k_1},\{N_1\}_{\{0\}_k}),(\{M_2\}_{k_2},\{N_2\}_{\{1\}_k})\}) \vdash \mathbf{0}\ S\ \mathbf{0}$
  for all names k and k_1 with $\{k,k_1\} \cap \{c,n\} = \emptyset$
  and all names k_2 with $k_2 \notin \{c,n,k_1\}$

It is somewhat laborious but not difficult to check that S is a framed bisimulation, much as in the examples above.

5 Related Work

Park [Par81] first suggested the bisimulation proof technique, in the context of Milner's CCS. After Park's work, bisimulation became a cornerstone of the theory of CCS [Mil89]. Milner, Parrow, and Walker [MPW92] extensively studied a variety of forms of bisimulation for the pi calculus, their generalisation of CCS with name-passing and mobile restrictions. Our definition of framed bisimulation generalises (and relaxes) the definition of strong bisimulation from earlier work on the spi calculus [AG97b,AG97c]. We can show that if processes P and Q are strongly bisimilar, then, for all frames fr, $(fr, \emptyset) \vdash P \sim_f Q$. The converse implication fails.

According to most other definitions, a bisimulation is a set of pairs of processes. According to our definition, a framed bisimulation is a set of quadruples consisting of a pair of processes grouped with a frame and a theory. According to a definition of Pierce and Sangiorgi [PS96] for a typed pi calculus, a bisimulation is a set of pairs of processes indexed by a type assumption that binds types to channel names. Our use of a frame is a little like their use of typing assumptions, in that both a frame and a typing assumption delimit the channels on which the environment may observe the processes in the bisimulation. On the other hand, the spi calculus is untyped, and our use of a theory to represent compound terms possessed but not decomposable by the environment seems to be new.

There are also parallels with the work of Pitts and Stark [PS93] on the ν-calculus, a simply-typed λ-calculus enriched with dynamic allocation of names. Pitts and Stark define a logical relation on programs, parameterised by a partial bijection on the names free in related programs. Their logical relation is sound for proving observational equivalence; it is incomplete but more generous than the usual notion of applicative bisimilarity for the ν-calculus. A logical relation is one in which two abstractions are related if and only if they send related arguments to related results. Given the clause for inputs in the definition of framed bisimulation, which requires the bodies of two abstractions $(x)P'$ and $(x)Q'$ to be related on all related terms M and N, we may say that the relations $(fr, th) \vdash M \leftrightarrow N$ and $(fr, th) \vdash P \sim_f Q$ form a parametric logical relation on the terms and processes of the spi calculus. Like Pitts and Stark's logical relation, our logical relation is sound for proving testing equivalence. Further, it is incomplete but more generous than the usual notion of strong bisimilarity; it has parameters (the frame and the theory) that serve to identify certain processes that are distinguished by the usual relation of strong bisimilarity. However, the analogy with Pitts and Stark's work is not perfect; in particular, their use of partial bijections on names is different from our use of frames and theories.

In the last few years, several methods for analysing cryptographic protocols have been developed within action-based or state-based models (see for example [MCF87,Mil95,Kem89,Mea92,GM95,Low96,Sch96a,Bol96,Pau97]). Some of these models are presented as process algebras, others in logical forms. Often, the analysis of a protocol requires defining a particular attacker (an environment) for the protocol; recently, there has been promising progress towards automating the construction of this attacker. Bisimulation techniques do appear in the security literature (as in the work of Focardi and Gorrieri [FG95]), but rarely, and without special tailoring to cryptographic applications.

6 Conclusions

When reasoning about a cryptographic protocol, we must take into account the knowledge of the environment with which the protocol interacts. In our definition of bisimulation, this knowledge is represented precisely as a set of names that the environment has obtained, and as a set of pairs of ciphertexts that the environment has received but cannot distinguish. This precise representation of the knowledge of the environment is the basis for an effective and sound proof technique. Using this technique, we can construct proofs for small but subtle cryptographic protocols. The proofs are fairly concise and do not require much creativity. Therefore, although we have not yet attempted to mechanise our proofs, we believe that such a mechanisation is possible, and that it may enable the automatic verification of substantial examples.

Acknowledgements

Discussions with Davide Sangiorgi were helpful at the start of this work. Andy Pitts made useful comments.

Gordon held a Royal Society University Research Fellowship at the University of Cambridge Computer Laboratory for most of the time we worked on this paper. He now holds a position at Microsoft Research.

References

[Aba97] M. Abadi. Secrecy by typing in security protocols. In *Theoretical Aspects of Computer Software*, volume 1281 of *Lecture Notes in Computer Science*, pages 611–638. Springer-Verlag, 1997.

[AG97a] M. Abadi and A. D. Gordon. A calculus for cryptographic protocols: The spi calculus. In *Proceedings of the Fourth ACM Conference on Computer and Communications Security*, pages 36–47, 1997.

[AG97b] M. Abadi and A. D. Gordon. A calculus for cryptographic protocols: The spi calculus. Technical Report 414, University of Cambridge Computer Laboratory, January 1997.

[AG97c] M. Abadi and A. D. Gordon. Reasoning about cryptographic protocols in the spi calculus. In *CONCUR'97: Concurrency Theory*, volume 1243 of *Lecture Notes in Computer Science*, pages 59–73. Springer-Verlag, 1997.

[Bol96] D. Bolignano. An approach to the formal verification of cryptographic protocols. In *3rd ACM Conference on Computer and Communications Security*, pages 106–118, March 1996.

[DES77] Data encryption standard. Fed. Inform. Processing Standards Pub. 46, National Bureau of Standards, Washington DC, January 1977.

[FG95] R. Focardi and R. Gorrieri. A classification of security properties. *Journal of Computer Security*, 3(1), 1995.

[GM95] J. Gray and J. McLean. Using temporal logic to specify and verify cryptographic protocols (progress report). In *Proceedings of the 8th IEEE Computer Security Foundations Workshop*, pages 108–116, 1995.

[Kem89] R. A. Kemmerer. Analyzing encryption protocols using formal verification techniques. *IEEE Journal on Selected Areas in Communications*, 7, 1989.

[Low96] G. Lowe. Breaking and fixing the Needham-Schroeder public-key protocol using FDR. In *Tools and Algorithms for the Construction and Analysis of Systems*, volume 1055 of *Lecture Notes in Computer Science*, pages 147–166. Springer-Verlag, 1996.

[MCF87] J. K. Millen, S. C. Clark, and S. B. Freedman. The Interrogator: Protocol security analysis. *IEEE Transactions on Software Engineering*, SE-13(2):274–288, February 1987.

[Mea92] C. Meadows. Applying formal methods to the analysis of a key management protocol. *Journal of Computer Security*, 1(1):5–36, 1992.

[Mil89] R. Milner. *Communication and Concurrency*. Prentice-Hall International, 1989.

[Mil95] J. K. Millen. The Interrogator model. In *IEEE Symposium on Security and Privacy*, pages 251–260, 1995.

[MPW92] R. Milner, J. Parrow, and D. Walker. A calculus of mobile processes, parts I and II. *Information and Computation*, pages 1–40 and 41–77, September 1992.

[Par81] D. Park. Concurrency and automata on infinite sequences. In P. Deussen, editor, *Theoretical Computer Science: 5th GI-Conference, Karlsruhe*, volume 104 of *Lecture Notes in Computer Science*, pages 167–183. Springer-Verlag, March 1981.

[Pau97] L. Paulson. Proving properties of security protocols by induction. In *Proceedings of the 10th IEEE Computer Security Foundations Workshop*, pages 70–83, 1997.

[PS93] A. M. Pitts and I. D. B. Stark. Observable properties of higher order functions that dynamically create local names, or: What's new? In *Mathematical Foundations of Computer Science, Proc. 18th Int. Symp., Gdańsk, 1993*, volume 711 of *Lecture Notes in Computer Science*, pages 122–141. Springer-Verlag, 1993.

[PS96] B. Pierce and D. Sangiorgi. Typing and subtyping for mobile processes. *Mathematical Structures in Computer Science*, 6(5):409–453, October 1996.

[Sch96a] S. Schneider. Security properties and CSP. In *IEEE Symposium on Security and Privacy*, pages 174–187, 1996.

[Sch96b] B. Schneier. *Applied Cryptography: Protocols, Algorithms, and Source Code in C*. John Wiley & Sons, Inc., second edition, 1996.

A Polyvariant Binding-Time Analysis for Off-line Partial Deduction

Maurice Bruynooghe, Michael Leuschel, and Konstantinos Sagonas

Katholieke Universiteit Leuven, Department of Computer Science
Celestijnenlaan 200A, B-3001 Heverlee, Belgium
e-mail: {maurice,michael,kostis}@cs.kuleuven.ac.be

Abstract. We study the notion of binding-time analysis for logic programs. We formalise the unfolding aspect of an on-line partial deduction system as a Prolog program. Using abstract interpretation, we collect information about the run-time behaviour of the program. We use this information to make the control decisions about the unfolding at analysis time and to turn the on-line system into an off-line system. We report on some initial experiments.

1 Introduction

Partial evaluation and partial deduction are well-known techniques for specialising respectively functional and logic programs. While both depart from the same basic concept, there is quite a divergence between their application and overall approach. In functional programming, the most widespread approach is to use *off-line specialisers*. These are typically very simple and fast specialisers which take (almost) no control decisions concerning the degree of specialisation. In this context, the specialisation is performed as follows: First, a *binding-time analysis* (BTA) is performed on the program which annotates all its statements as either "reducible" or "non-reducible". The annotated program is then passed to the off-line specialiser, which executes the statements marked reducible and produces residual code for the statements marked non-reducible. In logic programming, the *on-line* approach is almost the only one used. All work is done by a complex on-line specialiser which monitors the whole specialisation process and decides on the degree of specialisation while specialising the program. A few researchers have explored off-line specialisation, but lacking an appropriate notion of BTA, they worked with hand-annotated programs, something which is far from being practical. Until now, it was unclear how to perform BTA for logic programs.

The current paper remedies this situation. It develops a BTA for logic programs, not by translating the corresponding notions from functional programming to logic programming, but by departing from first principles. Given a logic program to be specialised, we develop a logic program which performs its on-line specialisation. The behaviour of this program is analysed and the results are used to take all decisions w.r.t. the degree of specialisation off-line. This turns the on-line specialiser into an off-line specialiser. A prototype has been built and the quality and speed of the off-line specialisation has been evaluated.

2 Background

2.1 Partial Deduction

In contrast to ordinary (full) evaluation, a *partial evaluator* receives a program P along with only *part* of its input, called the *static input*. The remaining part of the input, called the *dynamic input*, will only be known at some later point in time. Given the static input S, the partial evaluator then produces a *specialised* version P_S of P which, when given the dynamic input D, produces the same output as the original program P. The goal is to exploit the static input in order to derive a more efficient program.

In the context of logic programming, full input to a program P consists of a goal G and evaluation corresponds to constructing a complete SLDNF-tree for $P \cup \{G\}$. The static input is given in the form of a *partially instantiated* goal G' (and the specialised program should be correct for all instances of G').

A technique which produces specialised programs is known under the name of *partial deduction* [18]. Its general idea is to construct a finite set of atoms $\mathcal{A}$ and a finite set of finite, but possibly *incomplete* SLDNF-trees (one for every[1] atom in $\mathcal{A}$) which "cover" the possibly infinite SLDNF-tree for $P \cup \{G'\}$. The derivation steps in these SLDNF-trees correspond to the computation steps which have been performed beforehand and the specialised program is then extracted from these trees by constructing one specialised clause per non-failing branch.

In partial deduction one usually distinguishes two levels of control: the *global control*, determining the set $\mathcal{A}$, thus deciding *which* atoms are to be partially deduced, and the *local control*, guiding construction of the finite SLDNF-trees for each individual atom in $\mathcal{A}$ and thus determining *what* the definitions for the partially deduced atoms look like.

2.2 Off-line vs. On-line Control

The (global and local) control problems of partial evaluation and deduction in general have been tackled from two different angles: the so-called *on-line* versus *off-line* approaches. The *on-line* approach performs all the control decisions *during* the actual specialisation phase. The *off-line* approach on the other hand performs a (binding-time) analysis phase *prior* to the actual specialisation phase. This analysis starts from a description of which parts of the inputs will be *"static"* (i.e. sufficiently known) and provides *binding-time annotations* which encode the control decisions to be made by the specialiser, so that the specialiser becomes much more simple and efficient.

Partial evaluation of functional programs [8, 15] has mainly stressed off-line approaches, while supercompilation of functional [32, 31] and partial deduction of logic programs [13, 3, 1, 30, 25, 20] have concentrated on on-line control.

On-line methods, usually obtain better specialisation, because no control decisions have to be taken beforehand, i.e. at a point where the full specialisation

---

[1] Formally, an SLDNF-tree is obtained from an atom or goal by what is called an *unfolding rule*.

information is not yet available. The main reasons for using the off-line approach are to make specialisation itself more efficient and, due to a simpler specialiser algorithm, enable effective self-application (specialisation of the specialiser) [16].

Few authors discuss off-line specialisation in the context of logic programming [27,17], mainly because so far no automated binding-time analysers have been developed. This paper aims to remedy this problem.

3 Towards BTA for partial deduction

3.1 An on-line specialiser

The basic idea of BTA in functional programming is to model the flow of static input: the arguments of a function call flow to the function body, the result of a function flows back to the call expression. The expressions are annotated *reducible* when enough of their parameters are static, i.e. will be known at specialisation time, to allow the (partial) computation of the expression. Modelling the dataflow gives a system of inequalities over variables in a domain {*static, dynamic*} whose least solution yields the best annotation.

This approach does not immediately translate to logic programs. Problems are that the dataflow in unification is bidirectional and that the degree of instantiation of a variable can change over its lifetime (see also [17]).

We follow a different approach and reconstruct binding-time analysis from first principles. We start with a Prolog program which performs the unfolding decisions of an on-line specialiser. However, whereas real on-line specialisers base their unfolding decisions on the history of the specialisation phase, ours bases its decisions solely on the actual arguments of the call (which can be more easily approximated off-line). This is in agreement with the off-line specialisers for functional languages which base their decision to evaluate or residualise an expression on the availability of the parameters of that expression. The next step will be to analyse the behaviour of this program (the binding-time analysis) and to use the results to make the unfolding decisions at compile time.

First we develop the on-line specialiser. Assuming that for each predicate p/m a *test* predicate $unfold\_p/m$ exists which decides whether to unfold a call or not, we obtain an on-line specialiser by replacing each call $p(\bar{t})$ by

$$(unfold\_p(\bar{t}) \rightarrow p(\bar{t}); memoise\_p(\bar{t}))$$

A call to $memoise\_p(\bar{t})$ informs the specialiser that the call $p(\bar{t})$ has to be residualised. The specialiser has to check whether (a generalisation of) $p(\bar{t})$ has already been specialised —if not it has to initiate the specialisation of (a generalisation of) $p(\bar{t})$— and has to perform appropriate renaming of predicates to ensure that residual code calls the proper specialised version of the predicate it calls.

Example 1 (Funny append). Consider the following on-line specialiser for a variant, *funnyapp/3* of the *append/3* predicate in which the first two arguments of the recursive call have been swapped:

```
funnyapp([],X,X).
funnyapp([X|U],V,[X|W]) :-
    ( unfold_funnyapp(V,U,W) -> funnyapp(V,U,W)
                              ; memoise_funnyapp(V,U,W) ).
unfold_funnyapp(X,Y,Z) :- ground(X).
```

Specialising this program for a query funnyapp([a,b],L,R) results in the specialised clause (the residual call is renamed as funnyapp_1)

    funnyapp([a,b],L,[a|R1]) :- funnyapp_1(L,[b],R1).

Specialising the funnyapp program for the residual call funnyapp(L,[b],R1) gives (after renaming) the clauses

    funnyapp_1([],[b],[b]).
    funnyapp_1([X|U],[b],[X,b|R]) :- funnyapp_2(U,[],R).

Once more specialising, now for the residual call funnyapp(U,[],R), gives

    funnyapp_2([],[],[]).
    funnyapp_2([X|U],[],[X|U]).

This completes the specialisation. Note that the sequence of residual calls is terminating in this example. In general, infinite sequences are possible. They can be avoided by generalising some arguments of the residual calls before specialising.

In the above example, instead of using ground(X) as condition of unfolding, one could also use the test nilterminated(X).This would allow to obtain the same level of specialisation for a query funnyappend([X,Y],L,R). This test is another example of a so called *rigid* or *downward closed* property: if it holds for a certain term, it holds also for all its instances. Such properties are well suited for analysis by means of abstract interpretation.

3.2   From on-line to off-line

Turning the on-line specialiser into an off-line one requires to determine the *unfold_p/n* predicates during a preceding analysis and to decide on whether to replace the $(unfold\_p(\bar{t}) \rightarrow p(\bar{t}); memoise(p(\bar{t})))$ construct either by $p(\bar{t})$ or by *memoise*$(p(\bar{t}))$. The decision has to be based on a safe estimate of the calls *unfold_p*$(\bar{t})$ which will occur during the specialisation. Computing such safe approximations is exactly the purpose of *abstract interpretation* [9].

```
:- {grnd(L1)} fap1(L1,L2,R) {grnd(L1)}.
fap1([],X,X).
fap1([X|U],V,[X|W]) :- {grnd(X,U)}
    ( unf_fap1(V,U,W) {grnd(X,U,V)} ->
            {grnd(X,U,V)} fap2(V,U,W) {grnd(X,U,V,W)}
          ; {grnd(X,U)} memo_fap3(V,U,W) {grnd(X,U)}
    ) {grnd(X,U)}.
unf_fap1(X,Y,Z) :- {grnd(Y)} ground(X) {grnd(X,Y)}.
memo_fap3(X,Y,Z).
```

By adding to the code of Example 1 the fact memoise_funnyapp(X,Y,Z)., and an appropriate handling of the Prolog built-in ground/1, one can run a goal-dependent *polyvariant* groundness analysis (using e.g. PLAI coupled with the set-sharing domain) for a query where the first argument is ground and obtain the above annotated program. The annotated code for the version fap2 is omitted because it is irrelevant for us. Indeed, inspecting the annotations for unf_fap1 we see that the analysis cannot infer the groundness of its first argument. So we decide off-line not to unfold, we cancel the test and the *then* branch and simplify the code into:

```
:- {grnd(L1)} fap1(L1,L2,R) {grnd(L1)}.
fap1([],X,X).
fap1([X|U],V,[X|W]) :- {grnd(X,U)} memo_fap3(V,U,W) {grnd(X,U)}.
```

The residual call to funnyappend has a different call pattern than the original call: its second argument is now ground. Thus we perform a second analysis and obtain (the annotated code for fap4 is omitted):

```
:- {grnd(L2)} fap3(L1,L2,R) {grnd(L2)}.
fap3([],X,X).
fap3([X|U],V,[X|W]) :- {grnd(V)}
     ( unf_fap2(V,U,W) {grnd(V)} ->
               {grnd(V)} fap4(V,U,W) {grnd(V)}
          ; {grnd(V)} memo_fap5(V,U,W) {grnd(V)}
     ) {grnd(V)}.
unf_fap2(X,Y,Z) :- {grnd(X)} ground(X) {grnd(X)}.
memo_fap5(X,Y,Z).
```

This time, the annotations for unf_fap2 show that the groundness test will definitely succeed. So we decide off-line always to unfold and only keep the *then* branch. Moreover, the fap4 call has the same call pattern as the original call to funnyapp, so we also rename it as fap1. This yields the second code fragment:

```
:- {grnd(L2)} fap3(L1,L2,R) {grnd(L2)}.
fap3([],X,X).
fap3([X|U],V,[X|W]) :- {grnd(V)} fap1(V,U,W) {grnd(V)}
```

Applying the specialiser on these two code fragments for a query fap1([a,b],L,R) gives the same specialised code as in Example 1. However, this time, no calls to unfold_funnyapp have to be evaluated during specialisation.

3.3 Automation

To weave the step by step analysis sketched above in a single analysis, a special purpose tool has to be built. We implemented a system based on the abstract domain POS, also called PROP [24]. It describes the state of the program variables by means of *positive* boolean formulas, i.e., formulas built from ↔, ∧ and ∨. Its most popular use is for groundness analysis. In that case, the formula X expresses that the program variable X is (definitely) bound to a ground term, $X \leftrightarrow Y$ expresses that X is bound to a ground term iff Y is, so an eventual binding of X to a ground term will be propagated to Y. This domain is extended with *false* as bottom element and is ordered by boolean implication. Groundness analysis corresponds to checking the rigidity[2] of program variables w.r.t. the *termsize norm*[3] and abstracts a unification such as $X = [Y|Z]$ by the boolean formula $X \leftrightarrow Y \wedge Z$. However POS can also be used with other semi-linear norms [4]. In e.g. normalised programs, it only requires to redefine the abstraction of the unifications. For example, with the *listlength norm*[4], unification of $X = [Y|Z]$ is abstracted as $X \leftrightarrow Z$, and a formula X means that the program variable X is bound to a term with a bounded listlength, i.e. either the term is a nil-terminated list, or has a main functor which is not a list constructor.

The analyser has to decide the outcome of the *unfold_p* test and has to decide which branch to take for further analysis while doing the analysis. Also it has to launch the analysis of the generalisations of the memoised calls. The generalisation we employ is to replace an argument which is not rigid under the norm used in the analysis by the abstraction of a fresh variable. These requirements exclude the direct use of the abstract compilation technique in the way advocated by e.g. [5]. One problem of the scheme of [5] is that it handles constructs $(ground(X) \rightarrow p(\bar{t}); memoise(p(\bar{t})))$ too inaccurately. The boolean formula is represented as a truth table, i.e. a set of tuples, and the analyser processes the truth table a tuple at a time. Therefore it cannot infer in a program point that X is true, i.e. that X is definitely ground, so it can never conclude that the *else* branch cannot be taken. The other problem is that the analyses launched for the *memoised* calls should not interfere (i.e. output should not flow back) with the analysis of the clauses containing the memoised calls. Note that defining *memoise* as $memoise\_p(X_1, \ldots, X_n) :- copy(X_1, Y_1), \ldots, copy(X_n, Y_n)$, and abstracting $copy(X, Y)$ as $X \leftrightarrow Y$ does not work: The abstract success state of executing $p(Y_1, \ldots, Y_n)$ will update the abstractions of $X_1, \ldots, X_n$.

Our prototype binding-time analyser currently consists of ≈ 800 lines of Prolog code and uses XSB [29] as a generic tool for semantic-based program analysis [6]. The boolean formulas from the POS domain are represented by their truth tables. This representation enables abstract operations to have straightforward implementations based on the projection and equi-join operations of the relational algebra. The disadvantage is that the size of truth tables quickly increases with the number of variables in a clause. The use of dedicated data structures like BDDs to represent the boolean formulas as in [33] often results in better performance but at the expense of substantial programming efforts.

The main part of the analyser can be seen as a source-to-source transformation (i.e. abstract compilation) that given the program P to be analysed,

---

[2] A term is rigid w.r.t. a norm if all its instances have the same size w.r.t. the norm.
[3] The termsize norm [11] includes all subterms in the *measure* of the term.
[4] The listlength norm [11] includes only the tail of the list in the measure of the list (and measures other terms as 0); nil-terminated lists are rigid under this norm.

produces an abstract program P^α with suitable annotations. The abstract program can be directly run under XSB (using tabling to ensure termination). The execution leaves the results of the analysis in the XSB *tables*. Each predicate p/n of P is abstracted to a predicate $p^\alpha/2$ whose arguments carry input and output *sets* of tuples. The core part of setting up the analysis is then to define the code for the abstract interpretation of each call (at a program point PP$_\#$ of interest):

$$(unfold\_p(\overline{X}) \rightarrow p(\overline{X}); memoise\_p(\overline{X})). \tag{1}$$

is abstracted by the following code fragment:

```
project(Args,TPPin,TC),
( unfold_p(TC) ->
        unfold(TC,PP#), pα(TC,TR)
    ; TR=TC, generalise(TC,TCG), memo(TCG,PP#), pα(TCG,_) ),
equi_join(Args,TPPin,TR,TPPout),
```

Predicates *unfold*/2 and *memo*/2 which abstract the behaviour of each call in the form of (1) above are *tabled* predicates which have no effect on the computation, but only record information containing the results of the analysis. Their arguments are the current abstraction and the current program point. This information is then dumped from the XSB tables and is fed to the off-line specialiser. The variable TPP$_{in}$ holds the truth table which represents the abstraction of the program state in the point prior to the call. The call to *project*/3 projects the truth table on the positions Args of the variables $\overline{X}$ participating in the call. The result is TC (Tuples of the Call). The predicate *unfold_p*/1 (currently supplied by the user for each predicate p/n to be analysed) inspects TC to decide whether there is sufficient information to unfold the call. If it succeeds the *then* branch is taken which analyses the effects of unfolding p/n. This is done by executing $p^\alpha/2$ with TC as abstraction of the call state. The analysis returns TR as abstraction of the program state reached after unfolding p/n. If the call to *unfold_p*/1 fails, the call is memoised, and the program state remains unchanged, so TR = TC. The generalisation of the memoised call also needs to be analysed; therefore the *else* branch first generalises the current state TC into TCG by erasing all dependencies for non-rigid arguments[5] and then calls $p^\alpha/2$ with TCG as initial state, but takes care not to use the returned abstract state as the bindings resulting from specialising memoised calls do not flow back. These actions effectively realise the intended functionality of *memoise_p*/1. Finally, the new program state TR over the variables $\overline{X}$ has to be propagated to the other program variables described by the initial state TPP$_{in}$. This is achieved simply by taking the equi-join over the Args of TPP$_{in}$ and TR. The new program state is described by TPP$_{out}$.

One of our examples (see Section 4.2) uses two different norms in the *unfold* tests: the term norm which tests for groundness, and the listlength norm which tests for the boundedness of lists (whether lists are nil-terminated). This does not pose a problem for our framework, we simply use a truth table which encodes two boolean formulas, one for the term norm and one for the listlength norm.

---

[5] A position is rigid if it has an "s" in each tuple e.g. *generalise*([p(s,s,s), p(s,d,d)],TCG) yields TCG = [p(s,s,s), p(s,s,d), p(s,d,s), p(s,d,d)].

4 Some Experiments and Benchmarks

We first discuss the `parser` and `liftsolve` examples from [17].

4.1 The `parser` example

A small generic parser for languages defined by grammars of the form $S ::= aS|X$ (X is a placeholder for a terminal symbol as well as the first argument to nont/3; arguments 2 and 3 represent the string to be parsed as a difference list):

```
nont(X,T,R) :- t(a,T,V),nont(X,V,R).
nont(X,T,R) :- t(X,T,R).
t(X,[X|Es],Es).
```

A termination analysis can easily determine that calls to t/3 always terminate and that calls to nont/3 terminate if their second argument is ground. One can therefore derive the following unfold predicates:

```
unfold_t(X,S1,S2).
unfold_nont(X,T,R) :- ground(T).
```

Performing our analysis for the entry point :- $\{grnd(X)\}$ nont(X,_,_) we obtain the following annotated program (dynamic arguments [i.e. non-ground ones] and non-reducible predicates [i.e. memoised ones] are underlined):

```
nont(X,T,R) :- t(a,T,V), nont(X,V,R).
nont(X,T,R) :- t(X,T,R).
t(X,[X|Es],Es).
```

Feeding this information into the off-line system LOGEN [17] and specialising nont(c,T,R), we obtain:

```
nont__0([a|B],C) :- nont__0(B,C).
nont__0([c|D],D).
```

Analysing the same specialiser for :- $\{grnd(T)\}$ nont(_,T,_) yields:

```
nont(X,T,R) :- t(a,T,V), nont(X,V,R).
nont(X,T,R) :- t(X,T,R).
t(X,[X|Es],Es).
```

Feeding this information into LOGEN and specialising nont(X,[a,a,c],R) yields:

```
nont__0(c,[]).
nont__0(a,[c]).
nont__0(a,[a,c]).
```

4.2 The `liftsolve` example

The following program is a meta-interpreter for the ground representation, in which the goals are "lifted" to the non-ground representation for resolution. To perform the lifting, an accumulating parameter is used to keep track of the variables that have already been encountered and generated. The predicate mng and l_mng transform (a list of) ground terms (the first argument) into (a list of) non-ground terms (the second argument; the third and fourth arguments represent the incoming and outgoing accumulator respectively). The predicate `solve` uses these predicates to "lift" clauses of a program in ground representation (its first argument) and then use them for resolution with a non-ground goal (its second argument) to be solved.

```
solve(GrP,[]).
solve(GrP,[NgH|NgT]) :-
        non_ground_member(term(clause,[NgH|NgBdy]),GrP),
        solve(GrP,NgBdy), solve(GrP,NgT).
non_ground_member(NgX,[GrH|_GrT]) :- make_non_ground(GrH,NgX).
non_ground_member(NgX,[_GrH|GrT]) :- non_ground_member(NgX,GrT).
make_non_ground(G,NG) :- mng(G,NG,[],_Sub).
mng(var(N),X,[],[sub(N,X)]).
mng(var(N),X,[sub(N,X)|T],[sub(N,X)|T]).
mng(var(N),X,[sub(M,Y)|T],[sub(M,Y)|T1]) :- N \== M, mng(var(N),X,T,T1).
mng(term(F,Args),term(F,IArgs),InS,OutS) :- lmng(Args,IArgs,InS,OutS).
lmng([],[],Sub,Sub).
lmng([H|T],[IH|IT],InS,OutS) :-
        mng(H,IH,InS,InS1), lmng(T,IT,InS1,OutS).
```

The following unfold predicates can be derived by a termination analysis:

```
unfold_lmng(Gs,NGs,InSub,OutSub) :- ground(Gs), bounded_list(InSub).
unfold_mng(G,NG,InSub,OutSub) :- ground(G), bounded_list(InSub).
unfold_make_non_ground(G,NG) :- ground(G).
unfold_non_ground_member(NgX,L) :- ground(L).
unfold_solve(GrP,Query) :- ground(GrP).
```

Analysing the specialiser for the entry point `solve(ground,_)` we obtain:

```
solve(GrP,[]).
solve(GrP,[NgH|NgT]) :-
        non_ground_member(term(clause,[NgH|NgBdy]), GrP),
        solve(GrP,NgBdy), solve(GrP,NgT).
non_ground_member(NgX,[GrH|_GrT]) :- make_non_ground(GrH,NgX).
non_ground_member(NgX,[_GrH|GrT]) :- non_ground_member(NgX,GrT).
make_non_ground(G,NG) :- mng(G,NG, [],_Sub).
mng(var(N),X,[],[sub(N,X)]).
mng(var(N),X,[sub(N,X)|T], [sub(N,X)|T]).
mng(var(N),X,[sub(M,Y)|T], [sub(M,Y)|T1]) :- N \== M, mng(var(N),X,T,T1).
mng(term(F,Args),term(F,IArgs), InS,OutS) :- lmng(Args,IArgs, InS,OutS).
lmng([],[],Sub,Sub).

lmng([H|T],[IH|IT], InS,OutS) :- mng(H,IH,InS,InS1), ⟨ lmng1(T,IT, InS1,OutS) ⟩.
lmng1([],[],Sub,Sub).
lmng1([H|T],[IH|IT], InS,OutS) :- mng1(H,IH,InS,InS1), lmng1(T,IT,InS1,OutS).
mng1(var(N),X,[],[sub(N,X)]).
mng1(var(N),X, [sub(N,X)|T],[sub(N,X)|T]).
mng1(var(N),X, [sub(M,Y)|T],[sub(M,Y)|T1]) :- N \== M, mng1(var(N),X,T,T1).
mng1(term(F,Args),term(F,IArgs), InS,OutS) :- lmng1(Args,IArgs, InS,OutS).
```

One can observe that the call `lmng1(T,IT, InS1,OutS)` has not been unfolded. Indeed, the third argument `InS1` is considered to be dynamic (non-ground) and the call to `unfold_lmng` will thus not always succeed. However, based on the termination analysis, it is actually sufficient for termination if the third arguments to mng and lmng are bounded lists (as the listlength norm can be used in the termination proof). If we use our prototype to also keep track of bounded lists we obtain the desired result: the call `lmng1(T,IT,InS1,OutS)` can be unfolded as the first argument is ground and third argument can be inferred to be a bounded list. By feeding the so obtained annotations into LOGEN [17] we obtain a specialiser which removes (most of) the meta-interpretation overhead. E.g. specialising

```
solve([term(clause,[term(q,[var(1)]), term(p,[var(1)])]),
      term(clause,[term(p,[term(a,[])])])],G)
```

yields the following residual program:

```
solve_0([]).
solve_0([term(q,[B])|C]) :- solve_0([term(p,[B])]),solve_0(C).
solve_0([term(p,[term(a,[])])|D]) :- solve_0([]),solve_0(D).
```

4.3   Some Benchmarks

We now study the efficiency and quality of our approach on a set of benchmarks. Except for the parser benchmark all benchmarks come from the DPPD benchmark library [19]. We ran our prototype analyser, BTA, that performs binding-time analysis and fed the result into the off-line compiler generator LOGEN [17] in order to derive a specialiser for the task at hand. The ECCE on-line partial deduction system [19] has been used for comparison (settings are the same as for ECCE-X in [20], i.e. a mixtus like unfolding, a global control based upon characteristic trees but no use of conjunctive partial deduction). The interested reader can consult [20] to see how ECCE compares with other systems.

All experiments were conducted on a Sun Ultra-1 running SunOS 5.5.1. ECCE and LOGEN were run using Prolog by BIM 4.1.0. BTA was run on XSB 1.7.2.

Benchmark	ECCE - PD	BTA	LOGEN	PD	Ratio
depth.lam	0.34 s	0.05 + 0.579 s	0.05 s	0.003 s	113
liftsolve.app	1.00 s	0.079* + 1.841 s	0.05 s	0.006 s	167
liftsolve.app4	12.32 s	"	"	0.014 s	880
match.kmp	0.18 s	0.06 + 0.031 s	0.01 s	0.006 s	30
parser	0.06 s	0.03 + 0.01 s	0.02 s	0.001 s	60
regexp.r1	0.17 s	0.039 + 0.031 s	0.06 s	0.006 s	28

Table 1. Analysis and Specialisation Times

In Table 1 one can see a summary of the transformation times. The columns under BTA contain: the time to abstract and compile the program + the time for execution of the abstracted program (both under XSB). The column under LOGEN contains the time to generate the specialiser with LOGEN using the so obtained annotations. Observe, that for any given initial annotation, this has only to be performed *once*: the so obtained specialiser can then be used over and over again for different specialisation tasks. E.g. the same specialiser was used for the liftsolve.app and liftsolve.app4 benchmark. The '*' for liftsolve.app indicates the time for the abstract compilation only producing code for the groundness analysis. The extra arguments and instructions for the bounded list analysis were added by hand (but will be generated automatically in the next version of the prototype). The column under PD gives the time for the off-line specialisation. The last column of the table contains the ratio of running ECCE over running the specialisers generated by BTA + LOGEN. As can be seen, the specialisers produced by BTA + LOGEN run 28 – 880 times faster than ECCE. We conjecture that for larger programs (e.g liftsolve with a very big object program) this difference can get even bigger. Also, for 3 benchmarks the combined time of running BTA + LOGEN and then the so obtained specialiser was less than running ECCE, i.e. our off-line approach fares well even in "one-shot" situations. Of course, to arrive at a fully automatic (terminating) system one will still have to add the time for the termination analysis, needed to derive the "unfold" predicates.

Benchmark	Original	ECCE	BTA + LOGEN
depth.lam	0.08 s	0.00 s	0.06 s
	1	≈ 32	1.33
liftsolve.app	0.13 s	0.01 s	0.01 s
	1	13	13
liftsolve.app4	0.17 s	0.00 s	0.02 s
	1	> 34	8.5
match.kmp	0.58 s	0.34 s	0.51 s
	1	1.71	1.14
parser	0.20 s	0.12 s	0.12 s
	1	1.74	1.74
regexp.r1	0.29 s	0.10 s	0.20 s
	1	2.9	1.5

Table 2. Absolute Runtimes and Speedups

Table 2 compares the efficiency of the specialised programs (for the run time queries see [19]; for the parser example we ran $nont(c, [a^{17}, c, b], [b])$ 100 times). As was to be expected, the programs generated by the on-line specialiser ECCE outperform those generated by our off-line system. E.g. for the match.kmp benchmark ECCE is able to derive a Knuth-Morris-Pratt style searcher, while off-line systems (so far) are unable to achieve such a feat. However, one can see that the specialised programs generated by BTA + LOGEN are still very satisfactory. The most satisfactory application is liftsolve.app (as well as liftsolve.app4), where the specialiser generated by BTA + LOGEN runs 167 (resp. 880) times faster than ECCE while producing residual code of equal (resp. almost equal) efficiency. In fact, the specialiser compiled the append object program from the ground representation into the non-ground one in just 0.006 s (to be compared with e.g. the compilers generated by SAGE [14] which run in the order of minutes). Furthermore, the time to produce the residual program and then running it is less than the time needed to run the original program for the given set of runtime queries. This nicely illustrates the potential of our approach for applications such as runtime code generation, where the specialisation time is (also) of prime importance.

5 Discussion

We have formulated a binding-time analysis for logic programs, and have reported on a prototype implementation and on an evaluation of its effectiveness. To develop the binding-time analysis, we have followed an original approach: Given a program P to be analysed we transform it into an on-line specialiser program P', in which the unfolding decision are explicitly coded as calls to predicates unfold_p. The on-line specialiser is different from usual ones in the sense that it — like off-line specialisers — uses the availability of arguments to decide on the unfolding of calls. Next, we apply abstract interpretation —a binding-time analysis— to gather information about the run-time behaviour of P'. The information in the program points related to unfold_p allows to decide whether the test will definitely succeed —in which case the unfolding branch is retained— or will possibly fail —in which case the branch yielding residual code is retained. The resulting program now behaves as an off-line specialiser as all unfolding decisions have been taken at analysis time.

An issue to be discussed in more detail is the termination of the specialisation. First, a specialiser has a global control component. It must ensure that only a finite number of atoms are specialised. In our prototype, we generalise the residual calls before generating a specialised version: arguments which are not rigid[6] w.r.t. the norm used in the unfolding condition are replaced by fresh variables. This works well in practice but is not a sufficient condition for termination. In principle one could define the memoise_p predicates as:

$$\text{memoise\_p}(\overline{X}) \text{ :- copy\_term}(\overline{X}, \overline{Y}), \text{ generalise}(\overline{Y}, \overline{Z}), \text{ p}(\overline{Z}).$$

and then generalise such that quasi-termination [21] of the program, where calls to p are tabulated, can be proven. In practice, the built-in copy_term/2 and the built-ins needed to implement generalise/2 will make this a non-trivial task. Secondly, there is the local control component. It must ensure that the unfolding of a particular atom terminates. This is decided by the code of the transformed program. Defining the unfold_p predicates by hand is error-prone and consequently not entirely reliable. In principle, one could replace the calls memoise_p by true and apply off-the-shelf tools for proving termination of logic programs [22, 7]. Whether these will do well depends on how well they handle the $if - then - else$ construct used in deciding on the unfolding and the built-ins used in the rigidity test (e.g. the analysis has to infer that X is bounded and rigid w.r.t. the norm in the program point following a test ground(X)). It is likely that small extensions to these tools will suffice to apply them successfully in proving termination of the unfolding[7], at least when the unfolding conditions are based on rigidity tests with respect to the norms used by those termination analysis tools.

A more interesting approach for the local control problem is to automatically generate unfolding conditions by program analysis. Actually, one could apply a

---

[6] I.e., "*static*" from functional programming becomes "*rigid* w.r.t. a given norm."

[7] After a small extension by its author, the system of [22] could handle small examples. However, so far we have not done exhaustive testing.

more general scheme for handling the unfolding than the one used so far. Having for each predicate p/n the original clauses with head p/n and transformed clauses with head pt/n, the transformed clauses could be derived from the original by replacing each call q/m by:

(terminates_q($\bar{t}$) -> q($\bar{t}$)
   ; (unfold_q($\bar{t}$) -> qt($\bar{t}$) ; memoise_q($\bar{t}$)))

In [10], Decorte and De Schreye describe how the constraint-based termination analysis of [11] can be adapted to generate a finite set of "most general" termination conditions (e.g. for append/3 they would generate rigidity w.r.t. the listlength norm of the first argument and rigidity w.r.t. the listlength norm of the third argument as the two most general termination conditions; for our funnyapp/3 they would generate rigidity of the first and second argument w.r.t. the listlength norm as the most general termination condition.). These conditions can be used to define the terminates_q predicates. If they succeed, the call q($\bar{t}$) can be executed with the original code and is guaranteed to terminate. Moreover, as they are based on rigidity, they are very well suited to be approximated by our binding-time analysis. Actually, in all our benchmarks programs, we were using termination conditions for controlling the unfolding, so in fact we could have further improved the speed of the specialiser by not checking the condition on each iteration but using the above scheme.

Generating unfold_q definitions is a harder problem. It is related to the generation of "safe" (i.e. termination ensuring) delay declarations in languages such as MU-Prolog and Gödel. This is a subtle problem as discussed in [28, 23]. For example, the condition (nonvar(X); nonvar(Z)) is not safe for a call append(X,Y,Z); execution, and in our case unfolding, could go on infinitely for some non-linear calls (e.g. append([a|L],Y,L)). Also the condition nonvar/1 is not rigid. (For funnyapp/3 we had rigid conditions, however this is rather the exception than the rule.) A safe unfolding condition for append(X,Y,Z) is linear(append(X,Y,Z)), (nonvar(X); nonvar(Z)). Linearity is well suited for analysis (e.g. [2]), but a test nonvar(X) is not. Moreover, unless X is ground, the test is typically not invariant over the different iterations of a recursive predicate. A solution could be to switch to a hybrid specialiser: deciding the linearity test at analysis-time and the simple nonvar tests at run-time. But as said above, perhaps due to lack of a good application (for languages with delay, speed is more important than safety), there seems to be no work on generating such conditions.

Another hybrid approach is taken in a recent work independent of ours [26]. This work also starts from the termination condition. When it is violated, the size of the term w.r.t. the norm used in the termination condition and the maximal reduction of the size in a single iteration is used to compute the number of unfolding steps. The program is transformed and calls to be unfolded are given an extra argument initialised with the allowed number of unfolding steps. An on-line test checks the value of the counter and the call is residualised when the counter reaches zero.

Acknowledgements

M. Bruynooghe and M. Leuschel are supported by the Fund for Scientific Research - Flanders Belgium (FWO). K. Sagonas is supported by the Research Council of the K.U. Leuven. Some of the present ideas originated from discussions and joint work with Jesper Jørgensen, and from the PhD. work of Dirk Dussart [12], to both of whom we are very grateful. We thank Bart Demoen, Stefaan Decorte, Bern Martens, Danny De Schreye and Sandro Etalle for interesting discussions, ideas and comments.

References

1. R. Bol. Loop Checking in Partial Deduction. *The Journal of Logic Programming*, 16(1&2):25–46, May 1993.
2. M. Bruynooghe, M. Codish, and A. Mulkers. Abstracting unification: a key step in the design of logic program analyses. In *Computer Science Today*, pages 406–442. Springer-Verlag, LNCS Vol. 1000, 1995.
3. M. Bruynooghe, D. De Schreye, and B. Martens. A General Criterion for Avoiding Infinite Unfolding During Partial Deduction. *New Generation Computing*, 11(1):47–79, 1992.
4. M. Codish and B. Demoen. Deriving Polymorphic Type Dependencies for Logic Programs Using Multiple Incarnations of Prop. In B. Le Charlier, editor, *Proceedings of the First International Symposium on Static Analysis*, number 864 in LNCS, pages 281–297, Namur, Belgium, September 1994. Springer-Verlag.
5. M. Codish and B. Demoen. Analysing Logic Programs using "Prop"-ositional Logic Programs and a Magic Wand. *Journal of Logic Programming*, 25(3):249–274, December 1995.
6. M. Codish, B. Demoen, and K. Sagonas. Semantic-Based Program Analysis for Logic-Based Languages using XSB. K.U. Leuven TR CW 245. December 1996.
7. M. Codish and C. Taboch. A Semantic Basis for Termination Analysis of Logic Programs and its Realization using Symbolic Norm Constraints. In *Proceedings of the Sixth International Conference on Algebraic and Logic Programming*, number 1298 in LNCS, pages 31–45. Springer-Verlag, September 1997.
8. C. Consel and O. Danvy. Tutorial Notes on Partial Evaluation. In *Proceedings of the ACM Conference on Principles of Programming Languages*, pages 493–501, Charleston, South Carolina, January 1993. ACM Press.
9. P. Cousot and R. Cousot. Abstract Interpretation: A Unified Lattice Model for Static Analysis of Programs by Construction or Approximation of Fixpoints. In *Conference Record of the Fourth ACM Symposium on Principles of Programming Languages*, pages 238–252, Los Angeles, California, January 1977. ACM.
10. S. Decorte and D. De Schreye. Termination Analysis: Some Practical Properties of the Norm and Level Mapping Space. TR, Dept. Comp. Science, K.U. Leuven.
11. S. Decorte and D. De Schreye. Demand-driven and Constraint-based Automatic Termination Analysis for Logic Programs. In L. Naish, editor, *Proceedings of the Fourteenth International Conference on Logic Programming*, pages 78–92, Leuven, Belgium, July 1997. The MIT Press.
12. D. Dussart. *Topics in Program Specialisation and Analysis for Statically Typed Functional Languages*. PhD thesis, Katholieke Universiteit Leuven, May 1997.
13. J. Gallagher and M. Bruynooghe. The Derivation of an Algorithm for Program Specialisation. *New Generation Computing*, 9(3,4):305–333, 1991.
14. C. A. Gurr. *A Self-Applicable Partial Evaluator for the Logic Programming Language Gödel*. PhD thesis, Department of Computer Science, University of Bristol.

15. N. D. Jones, C. K. Gomard, and P. Sestoft. *Partial Evaluation and Automatic Program Generation.* Prentice Hall International Series in Computer Science, 1993.

16. N. D. Jones, P. Sestoft, and H. Søndergaard. MIX: a Self-applicable Partial Evaluator for experiments in Compiler Generation. *LISP and Symbolic Computation*, 2(1):9–50, 1989.

17. J. Jørgensen and M. Leuschel. Efficiently Generating Efficient Generating Extensions in Prolog. In O. Danvy, R. Glück, and P. Thiemann, editors, *Proceedings of the 1996 Dagstuhl Seminar on Partial Evaluation*, number 1110 in LNCS, pages 238–262, Schloß Dagstuhl, February 1996. Springer-Verlag.

18. J. Komorowski. Partial Evaluation as a means for inferencing data structures in an Applicative Language: A Theory and Implementation in the case of Prolog. In *Proceedings of the ACM Conference on Principles of Programming Languages*, pages 255–267, Albuquerque, New Mexico, January 1982. ACM.

19. M. Leuschel. The ECCE partial deduction system and the DPPD library of benchmarks. Obtainable via http://www.cs.kuleuven.ac.be/~lpai, 1996.

20. M. Leuschel, B. Martens, and D. De Schreye. Controlling Generalisation and Polyvariance in Partial Deduction of Normal Logic Programs. *ACM Trans. Prog. Lang. Syst.*, 20, 1998. To Appear.

21. M. Leuschel, B. Martens, and K. Sagonas. Preserving Termination of Tabled Logic Programs While Unfolding. In N. Fuchs, editor, *Proceedings of LOPSTR'97: Logic Program Synthesis and Transformation*, LNCS, Leuven, Belgium, July 1997.

22. N. Lindenstrauss and Y. Sagiv. Automatic Termination Analysis of Logic Programs. In L. Naish, editor, *Proceedings of the Fourteenth International Conference on Logic Programming*, pages 63–77, Leuven, Belgium, July 1997. The MIT Press.

23. E. Marchiori and F. Teusink. Proving Termination of Logic Programs with Delay Declarations. In J. W. Lloyd, editor, *Proceedings of the 1995 International Logic Programming Symposium*, pages 447–461, Portland, Oregon, December 1995.

24. K. Marriott and H. Søndergaard. Precise and Efficient Groundness Analysis for Logic Programs. *ACM Letters on Progr. Lang. and Syst.*, 2(1–4):181–196, 1993.

25. B. Martens and D. De Schreye. Automatic Finite Unfolding Using Well-Founded Measures. *The Journal of Logic Programming*, 28(2):89–146, August 1996.

26. J. Martin. Sonic Partial Deduction. Technical Report, Dept. Elec. and Comp. Sc., University of Southampton, January 1998.

27. T. Mogensen and A. Bondorf. Logimix: A self-applicable partial evaluator for Prolog. In K.-K. Lau and T. Clement, editors, Logic Program Synthesis and Transformation. *Proceedings of LOPSTR'92*, pages 214–227. Springer-Verlag, 1992.

28. L. Naish. Coroutining and the Construction of Terminating Logic Programs. Technical Report TR 92/5, Dept. Computer Science, University of Melbourne, 1992.

29. K. Sagonas, T. Swift, and D. S. Warren. XSB as an Efficient Deductive Database Engine. In *Proceedings of the ACM SIGMOD International Conference on the Management of Data*, pages 442–453, Minneapolis, Minnesota, May 1994. ACM.

30. D. Sahlin. Mixtus: An Automatic Partial Evaluator for Full Prolog. *New Generation Computing*, 12(1):7–51, 1993.

31. M. H. Sørensen and R. Glück. An Algorithm of Generalization in Positive Supercompilation. In J. W. Lloyd, editor, *Proceedings of the 1995 International Logic Programming Symposium*, pages 465–479, Portland, Oregon, December 1995.

32. V. F. Turchin. The Concept of a Supercompiler. *ACM Trans. Prog. Lang. Syst.*, 8(3):292–325, July 1986.

33. P. Van Hentenryck, A. Cortesi, and B. Le Charlier. Evaluation of the Domain Prop. *Journal of Logic Programming*, 23(3):237–278, June 1995.

Verifiable and Executable Logic Specifications of Concurrent Objects in $\mathcal{L}_\pi$

Luís Caires and Luís Monteiro
{lcaires,lm}@di.fct.unl.pt
Departamento de Informática - Universidade Nova de Lisboa

Abstract. We present the core-$\mathcal{L}_\pi$ fragment of $\mathcal{L}_\pi$ and its program logic. We illustrate the adequacy of $\mathcal{L}_\pi$ as a meta-language for jointly defining operational semantics and program logics of languages with concurrent and logic features, considering the case of a specification logic for concurrent objects addressing mobile features like creation of objects and channels in a simple way. Specifications are executable by a translation that assigns to every specification a model in the form of a core-$\mathcal{L}_\pi$ program. We also illustrate the usefulness of this framework in reasoning about systems and their components.

1 Introduction

The "proof-search as computation" paradigm has inspired the design of several programming and specification languages [6]. In [1] we presented $\mathcal{L}_\pi$, a simple language that supports the reduction and state-oriented style of specification of mobile process calculi without compromising the relational style of specification typical of logic programming. In particular, we have shown that both the π-calculus [10] and a version of the logic of hereditary Harrop formulas [7] can be adequately encoded into $\mathcal{L}_\pi$. On the other hand, $\mathcal{L}_\pi$ can itself be encoded in classical linear logic, in such a way that successful computations correspond to proofs [3]. As illustrated in [2], $\mathcal{L}_\pi$ suits itself well as a specification language of the operational semantics of programming languages with concurrent and logic features; we also proposed $\mathcal{L}_\pi$ as a meta-language for the compositional definition of operational semantics and program verification logics of languages of such a kind. Herein, we pursue this general directions, picking the case of declarative object-oriented specification of concurrent systems.

MOTIVATION. Several embeddings of object-oriented constructs into variants of π-calculus have been presented in the literature [12, 16, 14]. However [11], the π-calculus, while supporting the basic features of concurrency, mobility, abstraction and creation of processes and names, is a low level calculus, so the question arises about what kind of idioms are more suitable to model *and* reason about object systems and their components. In this setting, most of the current approaches focus on operational semantics or types, and the object languages have a definite operational character. In this paper, we develop a contribution in this general theme, stressing the instrumental use of the $\mathcal{L}_\pi$ framework in the spirit stated above. More specifically, we consider the case of a declarative specification language and program logic for concurrent objects that provides a unified scenario for specifying and reasoning about systems. This is achieved in the context of a well-defined operational semantics that renders specifications executable and makes essential use of the reductive and deductive features of $\mathcal{L}_\pi$.

OVERVIEW. First, we define core-$\mathcal{L}_\pi$, a small yet expressive fragment of $\mathcal{L}_\pi$, and its program logic $\mu\mathcal{L}_\pi$. The logic $\mu\mathcal{L}_\pi$ is based on a many-sorted first-order version of the μ-calculus enriched with connectives enabling the implicit expression of component location and a hiding quantifier. For instance, a property $\varphi \otimes \psi$ holds of a system with two components that satisfy respectively φ and ψ, and $\Sigma_n \varphi$ holds of a system that satisfies φ in a context where a name n is private. Then, we present a specification logic for concurrent objects that actually reduces to an idiom of $\mu\mathcal{L}_\pi$. From the viewpoint of logical specification, our proposal extends existing ones (for instance, [15]) by addressing mobile features like dynamically changing number of components and creation of private channels in an intrinsic way, while supporting both local and global reasoning by relying on the monoidal structure induced by $\otimes$. Moreover, specifications are executable by means of a syntax-directed encoding that assigns to each specification a model in the form of a core-$\mathcal{L}_\pi$ program. This translation relies on a combination of techniques from process calculi and proof-theoretic approaches to logic programming. We also illustrate the usefulness of this framework in reasoning about systems and their components by giving some examples.

OBJECT MODEL. We consider a standard asynchronous model of concurrent objects as closed entities that exhibit computational behaviour by performing mutually exclusive actions over a private state. Actions are triggered by serving request messages from the environment, but are only allowed to ocurr under certain enabling conditions. Actions can change the object's internal state, cause the sending of action requests to other objects or even the creation of new objects or channels, and display internal non-determinism. Thus, any specification of the behaviour of an object must define conditions under which actions can occur, and also what are their effects.

SPECIFICATION LANGUAGE. Since [13], many authors adopted subsets of some temporal logic (TL) as a specification language for concurrent systems. But unrestricted use of TL often leads to unimplementable specifications, and typical approaches pick some restricted class of formulas as dynamic axioms. For instance in [4], one finds safety formulas like $\varphi \wedge A^* \Rightarrow X\psi$ and liveness formulas like $\varphi \Rightarrow FA^*$ - where A^* denotes the occurrence of action A, and X and F are respectively the *next* and *eventually* operators of (linear) TL. Concerning liveness properties, in our asynchronous model we will not be able to assert such a strong assertion, but just something like the weaker $\varphi \Rightarrow XmA^*$ where mA^* asserts the existence of a pending request for action A. Then, whether mA^* implies FA^* depends on fairness assumptions and on the actual enabling conditions of action A. In summary, we adopt the (branching time) logic inherited from $\mu\mathcal{L}_\pi$ and consider specifications of object classes that enumerate instance attributes, and include dynamic axioms of the form $\varphi \Rightarrow \langle[A]\rangle\,\psi$ and static axioms defining the meaning of non-logical symbols.

STRUCTURE OF THE PAPER. In Sections 2-3 we introduce core-$\mathcal{L}_\pi$ and its program logic. In Section 4, we introduce the object specification language and present its interpretation in $\mathcal{L}_\pi$ in Section 5. After discussing some properties of this interpretation in Section 6, we present in Section 7 an example of reasoning about a system.

2 The core-$\mathcal{L}_\pi$ Language

Here we introduce core-$\mathcal{L}_\pi$, a small yet expressive fragment of $\mathcal{L}_\pi$ [1, 2].

SYNTAX. Given a set $\mathcal{V}$ of variables, the set $\mathcal{T}(\mathcal{V})$ of untyped terms over $\mathcal{V}$ is defined inductively as follows: variables are terms, if x is a variable and $t_1, \cdots, t_n$ are terms then $x(t_1, \cdots, t_n)$ is also a term t (s.t. $head(t) = x$). In general, we will use x, y, z, i, j for variables, a, b, c, t, u, v for terms, $\tilde{x}$ for a list of distinct variables and $\tilde{t}$ for a sequence $(t_1, \cdots, t_n)$ or a multiset $\{t_1, \ldots, t_n\}$ of terms, depending on context. Sometimes, we will write $x.t$ for $x(t)$ and call *names* to variables. Untyped agents of core-$\mathcal{L}_\pi$ are defined by

$$\mathcal{P} ::= \mathbf{0} \mid a \mid \mathcal{P}|\mathcal{P} \mid \nu x \mathcal{P} \mid \tilde{x} \triangleright \tilde{a}[\mathcal{P}]\mathcal{P} \mid !\tilde{x} \triangleright \tilde{a}[\mathcal{P}]\mathcal{P}$$

Inaction $\mathbf{0}$ denotes the well-terminated process. An atom a can be seen either as an elementary message to be sent asynchronously or as a data element in the shared state. $p|q$ stands for the parallel composition of p and q; we sometimes write $\tilde{m}$ for $m_1|\cdots|m_k$ when the m are atoms. Restriction νx induces generation of private names; $\nu x p$ binds x in p. To explain the behaviour of the input prefix $\tilde{x} \triangleright \tilde{a}[g]p$ we start by considering the particular case where the test g is $\mathbf{0}$, which we abbreviate by $\tilde{x} \triangleright \tilde{a}[]p$. The agent $\tilde{x} \triangleright \tilde{a}[]p$ waits for a message $\tilde{b}$ (a multiset of terms) and then behaves like $\sigma(p)$, if there is a substitution σ with domain $\tilde{x}$ such that $\sigma(\tilde{a}) \equiv \tilde{b}$. In general, in addition to receiving the message, $\tilde{x} \triangleright \tilde{a}[g]p$ must also perform successfully the test $\sigma(g)$. Roughly, a test g succeeds if there is an atomically encapsulated computation sequence starting with g and reaching a success state (defined below). The replicable agent $!\tilde{x} \triangleright \tilde{a}[g]p$ behaves just like it's non-replicable version, except that it does not consume itself upon reduction. In input prefix agents, the input variables $\tilde{x}$ must have free occurrences in either $\tilde{a}$ or g, although not in the head of some a. Note however that in non-replicable input prefix, $\tilde{a}$ may be empty, this corresponds to the testing agent of [1]. In both forms, $\tilde{x}$ may be empty, in which case the prefix $\tilde{x} \triangleright$ may be ommited. For agents, we will use normally p, q, r, g.

TYPING. Here we introduce a simple type system for core-$\mathcal{L}_\pi$. Assume given a set Ω of primitive sorts, containing at least o, and a set Δ of primitive basic types containing say nat, bool. Basic types δ and types τ are given by

$$\delta ::= \Delta \mid (\delta_1, \cdots, \delta_k)\delta \qquad \tau ::= \Omega \mid \delta \mid (\tau_1, \cdots, \tau_k)\tau$$

A type that is not basic is called a sort. The definition of types and sorts is stratified in such a way that no term of basic type δ can contain a subterm of some sort. The motivation for this stratification is to limit scope extrusion to terms of sort kind. Signatures are partial maps from variables to types. We use Σ, Ξ, Γ for signatures, and assume that $x \notin \Sigma$ when writing $\Sigma, x{:}\tau$. Terms and

$$\frac{\Sigma \vdash h : (\tau_1, \cdots, \tau_k)\beta \quad \Sigma \vdash t_i : \tau_i}{\Sigma \vdash h(t_1, \cdots, t_k) : \beta}$$

$$\Sigma \vdash \mathbf{0} \qquad \frac{\Sigma \vdash h(t_1, \cdots, t_k) : o}{\Sigma \vdash h(t_1, \cdots, t_k)} \qquad \frac{\Sigma \vdash p \quad \Sigma \vdash q}{\Sigma \vdash p|q}$$

$$\frac{\Sigma, x : \tau \vdash p}{\Sigma \vdash \nu x : \tau p} \qquad \frac{\Sigma, \tilde{x} : \tilde{\tau} \vdash g \quad \Sigma, \tilde{x} : \tilde{\tau} \vdash p \quad \Sigma, \tilde{x} : \tilde{\tau} \vdash a_i : o}{\Sigma \vdash \tilde{x} : \tilde{\tau} \triangleright \tilde{a}[g]p \quad | \quad \Sigma \vdash !\tilde{x} : \tilde{\tau} \triangleright \tilde{a}[g]p}$$

Fig. 1. Typing of terms and agents.

agents are typed by the rules in Figure 1. We will refer by $\mathcal{T}_\tau(\Sigma)$ the set of terms t such that $\Sigma \vdash t : \tau$ is valid. Note that binding occurrences of variables in νx and $\tilde{x}\triangleright$ are now explicitly assigned a type. In the rule for restriction, τ must be a sort and, in the rules for input prefix agents, any variable x not occurring free in $\tilde{a}$ must be assigned a basic type. If $\Sigma \vdash p$ is valid, we will say that $\Sigma; p$ is a well-typed agent, bringing explicit the typing context. For well-typed agents we will use P, Q, R, and write $\mathcal{P}$ for the set of all well-typed agents.

REDUCTION. The operational semantics of $\mathcal{L}_\pi$ is defined by a relation of reduction between agents. Following [8], we first define a structural congruence relation $\cong$ that abstracts away from irrelevant notational distinctions. $\cong$ is the smallest congruence relation over agents containing α-conversion and closed under equations (i) $p|q \cong q|p$, (ii) $(p|q)|r \cong q|(p|r)$, (iii) $p|\mathbf{0} \cong p$, (iv) $\nu x(p|q) \cong \nu x p|q$ if x is not free in q, (v) $\nu x \mathbf{0} \cong \mathbf{0}$, (vi) $!r \cong !r|!r$ and (vii) $!r|\tilde{x} \triangleright \tilde{a}[q]r \cong !r|\tilde{x} \triangleright \tilde{a}[q|!r]r$ if $\tilde{x}$ are not free in p and $!r$ stands for some replicable input prefix agent. Reduction is the least relation $P \to Q$ between well-typed agents P and Q such that

$$\Sigma; \nu x : \tau p \to \Sigma; \nu x : \tau q \qquad \text{if } \Sigma, x : \tau; p \to \Sigma, x : \tau; q$$
$$\Sigma; \tilde{x} \triangleright [g]p|q \to \Sigma; \sigma(p)|q \qquad \text{if } \Sigma; \sigma(g) \xrightarrow{*} \sqrt{}$$
$$\left.\begin{array}{l} \Sigma; \tilde{m}| \, \tilde{x} : \tilde{\tau} \triangleright \tilde{a}[g]p|q \to \Sigma; \sigma(p)|q \\ \Sigma; \tilde{m}|!\tilde{x} : \tilde{\tau} \triangleright \tilde{a}[g]p|q \to \Sigma; \sigma(p)|!\tilde{x} : \tilde{\tau} \triangleright \tilde{a}[g]p|q \end{array}\right\} \text{if } \Sigma; \sigma(g) \xrightarrow{*} \sqrt{} \wedge \tilde{m} \equiv \sigma(\tilde{a})$$

Here σ assigns to each $x : \tau$ a term $t \in \mathcal{T}_\tau(\Sigma)$ and $\sqrt{}$ (a success state) is any agent of the form $\Xi; \nu \tilde{y} : \tilde{\tau}(!p)$, where $!p$ is a composition of a (possibly null) number of replicating agents. As usual, we will refer by $\xrightarrow{*}$ the transitive-reflexive closure of $\to$. Subject reduction holds: if $P \in \mathcal{P}$ and $P \to Q$ then also $Q \in \mathcal{P}$.

LABELLED TRANSITION SYSTEM. To capture the compositional behaviour of agents, an "open" version of the reduction relation must be defined that captures not only the behaviour of agents in isolation but also the behaviour they can exhibit with adequate cooperation of the environment. As usual, this is formalised by means of an action-labelled transition system (LTS), where actions may be output ($\uparrow a$), input ($\downarrow a$) or silent (τ). Several possibilities arise at this point, we must require at least soundness, that is, agreement of $\xrightarrow{\tau}$ with reduction. Additionally, we can also impose a notion of relevance for $\mathcal{P}$, more precisely, that whenever $P \xrightarrow{\downarrow a} Q$ there is $P' \in \mathcal{P}$ such that $P' \xrightarrow{\uparrow a} Q'$, $P|P' \in \mathcal{P}$ and $P|P' \to Q|Q'$, and likewise when $P \xrightarrow{\uparrow a} Q$.

$$\Sigma; a \xrightarrow{\uparrow a} \Sigma; \mathbf{0} \text{ if } head(a) \notin Def \qquad \Sigma; a \xrightarrow{\downarrow! \tilde{z}: \tilde{\tau} \triangleright b[]p} \Sigma; \rho(p) \text{ if } \rho(b) \equiv a \wedge head(a) \in Def$$

$$\Sigma; !p \xrightarrow{\uparrow!p} \Sigma; !p \qquad \dfrac{\Sigma, \tilde{y}: \tilde{\gamma}; !\mathbf{q} | \sigma(g) \xrightarrow{\tau} \checkmark}{\Sigma; \tilde{x}: \tilde{\tau} \triangleright \tilde{a}[g]p \xrightarrow{\downarrow(\tilde{y}:\tilde{\gamma})\sigma(\tilde{a})!\mathbf{q}} \Sigma, \tilde{y}: \tilde{\gamma}; \sigma(p)}$$

$$\dfrac{\Sigma, x: \tau; p \xrightarrow{a} \Sigma', x: \tau; q}{\Sigma; \nu x: \tau p \xrightarrow{a} \Sigma'; \nu x: \tau q} \text{ if } x \notin a \qquad \dfrac{\Sigma, x: \tau; p \xrightarrow{\uparrow a} \Sigma'; q}{\Sigma; \nu x: \tau p \xrightarrow{\uparrow(x:\tau)a} \Sigma'; q} \text{ if } x \in a \wedge x \notin head(a)$$

$$\dfrac{\Sigma; p \xrightarrow{\uparrow(\tilde{x}:\tilde{\tau})a} \Sigma, \tilde{x}: \tilde{\tau}; p' \quad \Sigma; q \xrightarrow{\downarrow(\tilde{x}:\tilde{\tau})a \oplus \downarrow c} \Sigma, \Gamma, \tilde{x}: \tilde{\tau}; q'}{\Sigma; p|q \xrightarrow{\downarrow c} \Sigma, \Gamma; \nu\tilde{x}: \tilde{\tau}(p'|q')}$$

$$[s] \dfrac{\Sigma; p \xrightarrow{a} \Sigma'; p'}{\Sigma'; p|q \xrightarrow{a} \Sigma'; p'|q} \qquad \dfrac{\Sigma; p \xrightarrow{\uparrow a} \Sigma, \Gamma; p' \quad \Sigma; q \xrightarrow{\uparrow c} \Sigma, \Theta; q'}{\Sigma; p|q \xrightarrow{\uparrow a \oplus \uparrow c} \Sigma, \Gamma, \Theta; p'|q'}$$

Fig. 2. LTS specification for core-$\mathcal{L}_\pi$.

ACTIONS. Σ-actions are objects of the forms $\uparrow(\tilde{x}: \tilde{\tau})\tilde{a}!\mathbf{p}$ (output action) or $\downarrow(\tilde{x}: \tilde{\tau})\tilde{a}!\mathbf{p}$ (input action) where $\tilde{x}: \tilde{\tau}$ is a possibly empty signature, each a_i is an atom and each $!p$ a replication such that $\Sigma, \tilde{x}: \tilde{\tau} \vdash a_1| \cdots |a_n|!p_1| \cdots |!p_m$ is valid. To grasp the meaning of the binding signature, just consider it a generalisation of π-calculus bound input and bound output actions, in our notation, $\overline{x(y)}$ would be rendered by $\uparrow(y)x(y)$ and $x(y)$ by $\downarrow(y)x(y)$. When all components $\tilde{x}$, $\tilde{a}$ and $!\mathbf{p}$ of an action are void, both $\uparrow$ and $\downarrow$ will be noted τ (the silent action). To highlight the typing context we may write $\Sigma; a$ for Σ-actions a. The set of all actions will be noted Act, and individual actions by a, b, c. We will also define $head((x: \tau)\tilde{a}!\mathbf{h.p})$ as the set of heads of all $\tilde{a}$ and all $\tilde{h}$. Actions a and b of the same polarity compose into another action $a \circledast b$; composition of $(\tilde{x}: \tilde{\tau})\tilde{a}!\mathbf{p}$ with $(\tilde{y}: \tilde{\gamma})\tilde{c}!\mathbf{q}$ is defined as $(\tilde{x}: \tilde{\tau}, \tilde{y}: \tilde{\gamma})\tilde{a}\tilde{c}!\mathbf{pq}$. Intuitively, $a \circledast b$ is the concurrent execution of a and b; $\circledast$ is commutative, associative and has τ for unit.

LTS SPECIFICATION. In Figure 2, we present a LTS specification for core-$\mathcal{L}_\pi$. Most rules have the form one expects. Substitution σ assigns each $x: \tau$ a term in $\mathcal{T}_\tau(\Sigma, \tilde{y}: \tilde{\gamma})$, and ρ a term in $\mathcal{T}_\tau(\Sigma)$. When we are interested in computations starting from agents $\Gamma; p$ with Γ a given global signature, we let $Def \subset \Gamma$ and define two transitions for an agent $\Sigma; a$, to distinguish the case where a is to be substituted in place by it's definition (when $head(a) \in Def$), from the case where a is to be sent to the environment. This specification defines a sound and relevant transition relation $\xrightarrow{a}$ for all of $\mathcal{P}$, and should be taken as the reference transition relation. Note however that when developing applications of core-$\mathcal{L}_\pi$ (for instance, when studying certain restricted idioms as in this paper) we might be interested just in some subset of $\mathcal{P}$. Since $\xrightarrow{a}$ might not be relevant for that subset, additional provisos may be placed occasionally in some of the rules above, in order to obtain relevance for the fragment under consideration.

$$\Sigma; p \models_{\mathbf{I},v} P(\tilde{t}) \qquad \text{if } \tilde{t} \in \mathbf{I}_\Sigma(P)$$

$$\Sigma; p \models_{\mathbf{I},v} t \doteq t$$

$$\Sigma; p \models_{\mathbf{I},v} \neg\varphi \qquad \text{if not } \Sigma; p \models_{\mathbf{I},v} \varphi$$

$$\Sigma; p \models_{\mathbf{I},v} \varphi \wedge \psi \qquad \text{if } \Sigma; p \models_{\mathbf{I},v} \varphi \text{ and } \Sigma; p \models_{\mathbf{I},v} \psi$$

$$\Sigma; p \models_{\mathbf{I},v} \forall x : \tau\varphi \qquad \text{if } \Sigma; p \models_{\mathbf{I},v} \varphi\{{}^x/t\} \text{ for all } t \in \mathcal{T}_\tau(\Sigma)$$

$$\Sigma; p \models_{\mathbf{I},v} \langle S \rangle\, \varphi \qquad \text{if } \exists (\Sigma; a) \in S \exists (\Sigma'; q) \in \mathcal{P}(\Sigma; p \xrightarrow{a} \Sigma'; q \text{ and } \Sigma'; q \models_{\mathbf{I},v} \varphi)$$

$$\Sigma; p \models_{\mathbf{I},v} X \qquad \text{if } \Sigma; p \in v(X)$$

$$\Sigma; p \models_{\mathbf{I},v} \mu X.\varphi \qquad \text{if } \forall S \subseteq \mathcal{P}(clos(S) \Rightarrow \Sigma; p \in S) \text{ where}$$
$$clos(S) \text{ is } \forall (\Gamma; q) \in \mathcal{P}(\Gamma; q \models_{\mathbf{I},v[X \mapsto S]} \varphi \Rightarrow (\Gamma; q) \in S)$$

$$\Sigma; p \models_{\mathbf{I},v} [a] \qquad \text{if } p \cong a|\sqrt{}$$

$$\Sigma; \nu x : \tau p \models_{\mathbf{I},v} \Sigma_x \varphi \qquad \text{if } \Sigma, x : \tau; p \models_{\mathbf{I},v} \varphi$$

$$\Sigma; p \models_{\mathbf{I},v} \varphi \otimes \psi \qquad \text{if } p \cong q|r \text{ and } \Sigma; q \models_{\mathbf{I},v} \varphi \text{ and } \Sigma; r \models_{\mathbf{I},v} \psi$$

$$\Sigma; 0 \models_{\mathbf{I},v} \mathbf{1}$$

Fig. 3. Satisfaction of $\mu\mathcal{L}_\pi$ formulas.

3 A program logic for core-$\mathcal{L}_\pi$

The program logic $\mu\mathcal{L}_\pi$ is basically a many sorted first-order version of the propositional μ-calculus (see [5]) extended with operators for handling private names and spatial distribution. Formulas of $\mu\mathcal{L}_\pi$ are

$$\varphi ::= P(\tilde{t}) \mid t \doteq u \mid \neg\varphi \mid \varphi \wedge \varphi \mid \forall x : \tau\varphi \mid \langle S \rangle\, \varphi \mid X \mid \mu X.\varphi \mid \Sigma_{x:\tau}\varphi \mid \varphi \otimes \varphi \mid [t] \mid \mathbf{1}$$

The formulas expressing conjunction ($\varphi \wedge \psi$), properties $P(\tilde{t})$, equality ($t \doteq u$), possibility ($\langle S \rangle\, \varphi$), universal quantification ($\forall x : \tau\varphi$), negation ($\neg\varphi$) and least fixed point ($\mu X.\varphi$) are to be understood in the usual way. In a fixed point formula $\mu X.\varphi$, any occurrence of X must be under an even number of negations and under no $\otimes$. The remaining forms are particular to $\mu\mathcal{L}_\pi$ and deserve further comments. $\Sigma_x\varphi$ asserts a property of a state embedded into a context where the name x is private. The formula $\varphi \otimes \psi$ holds in every state that can be partitioned into a component satisfying φ and a component satisfying ψ. $\mathbf{1}$ is the unit for $\otimes$. Finally, $[t]$ is true of those states that essentially contain just the message t. Formulas are expected to be well-typed w.r.t. a signature Σ; for $\mu\mathcal{L}_\pi$ formulas φ, we assume a corresponding judgement form $\Sigma \vdash \varphi$ defined as expected. If such a judgement is valid, φ will be called a Σ-formula.

SEMANTICS. Truth of formulas of $\mu\mathcal{L}_\pi$ is taken with respect to a structure that consists in a labelled transition system for core-$\mathcal{L}_\pi$[1] together with a map $\mathbf{I}$ assigning to each signature Σ an interpretation $\mathbf{I}_\Sigma$. Such interpretations assign to each predicate symbol of type $(\tau_1, \ldots, \tau_n)$ a subset of $\mathcal{T}_{\tau_1}(\Sigma) \times \cdots \times \mathcal{T}_{\tau_n}(\Sigma)$. $\mathbf{I}$ is required to be monotonic, that is $\Sigma \subseteq \Sigma'$ implies that, for every predicate

---

[1] In general, the reference LTS; sometimes a suitable restriction may be required, cf. previous remarks on relevance.

symbol P, $\mathbf{I}_\Sigma(P) \subseteq \mathbf{I}_{\Sigma'}(P)$. In Figure 3 we present the relation $- \models_{\mathbf{I},v} -$ of satisfaction between Σ-terms and well-typed Σ-formulas of $\mu\mathcal{L}_\pi$. The definition is parametric on the interpretation map $\mathbf{I}$ and also on a valuation v. This valuation assigns sets of well-typed terms to propositional variables X, and is needed to interpret the fixed point operator. When interpreting formulas without free propositional variables, the valuation is irrelevant and could be omitted.

Some specific comments about this definition are in order. First, core-$\mathcal{L}_\pi$ terms are taken modulo structural congruence $\cong$. In the clause for $\langle S \rangle \varphi$, S is a set of $\mathcal{L}_\pi$ actions. To follow usual notations we will write $\langle \cdot \rangle \varphi$ for $\langle S \rangle \varphi$ when S is the set of all actions. In the clause of $\mu X.\varphi$, the property $clos(S)$ holds of prefixed points of the mapping that sends sets of terms satisfying a property ψ to the set of terms satisfying the property $\varphi\{^X/_\psi\}$. The syntactic restriction on the occurrences of X in $\mu X.\varphi$ causes this mapping to be monotonic, therefore the clause for $\mu X.\varphi$ defines the least fixed point as the intersection of all prefixed points, cf. Knaster-Tarsky theorem. Other logical connectives (say, $\vee$, $\exists$, $\Rightarrow$) are defined in the usual way according to standard tarskian semantics. The following usual abbreviations will also be used: $[S]\varphi$ for $\neg \langle S \rangle \neg\varphi$ (necessity), $\nu X.\varphi$ for $\neg\mu X.\neg\varphi\{^X/_{\neg X}\}$ (greatest fixed point), $\perp$ for $\mu X.X$ (false) and $\top$ for $\neg\perp$ (true). We will also write $\{\varphi\}$ for $\Sigma_{\tilde{x}}\varphi$ when no x occurs free in φ, and introduce the following derived operators: $\langle [S] \rangle \varphi$ standing for $\langle S \rangle \top \wedge [S]\varphi$, $\mathbf{inv}_{[S]}\varphi$ standing for $\nu X.\varphi \wedge [S]X$ (φ holds along any S-path) and $\mathbf{ev}_{[S]}\varphi$ standing for $\mu X.\varphi \vee \langle S \rangle X$ (φ will eventually hold along some S-path) and $\mathbf{evs}_{[S]}\varphi$ for $\mu X.\varphi \vee (\langle S \rangle \top \wedge [S]X)$ (φ will eventually hold along any S-path); $\mathbf{inv}_{[\cdot]}\varphi$ will be abbreviated by $\mathbf{inv}\varphi$ and likewise for $\mathbf{ev}\varphi$ and $\mathbf{evs}$.

The use of an explicit signature is essential in the definition of satisfaction. For instance, note that $\Sigma_x \top \Rightarrow \forall_y \Sigma_x(\neg x \doteq y)$ is true in any interpretation. This formula asserts intuitively that if a state has some private name, then this name is distinct from every term in the current environment. The scoping behaviour of private names induces the need to consider the brackets $\{\varphi\}$ even when the private names do not ocurr in φ. For instance, $a : o; \nu b : o\, b[]a \models \{\langle \cdot \rangle \langle \uparrow a \rangle \top\}$ but $a : o; \nu b : o\, b[]a \not\models \langle \cdot \rangle \langle \uparrow a \rangle \top$.

4 A specification language for concurrent objects

The specification language we present here is an idiom of the program logic of Section 3. Essentially, we consider specifications of classes of objects that indicate besides the instance state variables, for each possible action A a set of dynamic axioms of the form $\varphi \Rightarrow \langle [A] \rangle \psi$, where φ (the pre-state formula) is a proposition over the object's state and ψ (the pos-state formula) is a proposition defining the new state of the object and other side effects induced by the execution of A. Possible side effects are the posting of action requests $i.m$ (for other objects) and of creation requests $\nu i : c(\tilde{a})$ (for a new object i of class $c(\tilde{a})$). Besides this components, a specification also comprises a post-state formula defining the initial state of objects of the class and a static theory (called so because it does not involve any dynamic modalities) defining the meaning of the non-logical constants (predicate symbols) occurring elsewhere in the specification. At this stage, the reader may want to give a look at the sample specification in Fig. 4.

We assume given a set of basic types and a set of basic sorts (containing, at least o and act). The type $(act)o$ will be abbreviated by obj. A *system specification* is triple $(\Sigma, \mathcal{C}, \mathcal{S})$ where Σ is a signature, the set of class names $\mathcal{C}$ is a subset of Σ, and $\mathcal{S}$ is a mapping assigning to each $c \in \mathcal{C}$ a class specification $\mathcal{S}_c$ of type $\Sigma(c) = \tau_c$. A *parametric Σ-class specification* of type $(\tau_1, \dots, \tau_n)o$ is then a five-tuple $(\mathcal{A}, \mathcal{L}, \mathcal{I}, \mathcal{R}, \mathcal{T})$ such that (1) $\mathcal{A}$ and $\mathcal{L}$ and Σ are pairwise disjoint signatures, (2) $\mathcal{A}$ is of the form $a_1 : \tau_1, \dots, a_n : \tau_n$ (3) $\mathcal{I}$ is a post-state formula, $\mathcal{R}$ is a finite set of dynamic axioms and $\mathcal{T}$ is a finite sets of static axioms. Post-state formulas and dynamic and static axioms will be defined shortly.

PARAMETERS. Signature $\mathcal{A}$ lists the parameters of the class specification. If $\mathcal{A}$ is empty, the specification is non-parametric and therefore fully determined. Given a Σ-class specification $(\mathcal{A}, \mathcal{L}, \mathcal{I}, \mathcal{R}, \mathcal{T})$ of type $(\tau_1, \dots, \tau_n)o$ and terms $t_i \in \mathcal{T}_{\tau_i}(\Sigma)$ we obtain some non-parametric concrete instance $(\emptyset, \mathcal{I}\{\bar{a}/\bar{t}\}, \mathcal{R}\{\bar{a}/\bar{t}\}, \mathcal{T}\{\bar{a}/\bar{t}\})$.

LOCAL SYMBOLS. Signature $\mathcal{L}$ splits in two components: $\mathcal{L}_{\text{attrs}}$, containing the declarations of the class instance's attributes and $\mathcal{L}_{\text{preds}}$, which assigns to each predicate symbol defined by the local static theory $\mathcal{T}$ a predicate type $(\bar{\gamma})o$.

DYNAMIC THEORY. Dynamic axioms have the form $\forall \tilde{x} : \bar{\tau}(S \wedge \varphi \Rightarrow \langle [A] \rangle \psi)$ where the action A is a term of type act, S is a state formula, φ is a static formula, ψ is a post-state formula and $\tilde{x}$ are some variables with free occurrences at least in S, φ or A - those that occur just in φ and ψ should have basic type. A formula of the form $S \wedge \varphi$ will be called a pre-state formula. These kinds of formulas are defined by

$$
\begin{aligned}
\text{(state formulas)} \quad & S ::= \top \mid a = t \mid S \wedge S \\
\text{(static formulas)} \quad & \varphi ::= P(\bar{t}) \mid \top \mid \varphi \wedge \varphi \mid \varphi \vee \varphi \\
\text{(post-state formulas)} \quad & \psi ::= S \mid \nu i : c(\bar{t})\psi \mid i.m \otimes \psi
\end{aligned}
$$

where $a \in \mathcal{L}_{\text{attrs}}$, $P \in \mathcal{L}_{\text{preds}}$ and $c \in \mathcal{C}$. In the definition of post-state formulas, i is assumed of type obj and m is assumed of type act.

INITIAL. $\mathcal{I}$ is a post-state formula specifying the object's state at birth time.

STATIC THEORY. $\mathcal{T}$ is a set of static axioms of the form $\forall \tilde{x} : \bar{\tau}(\varphi \Rightarrow P(\bar{t}))$ where φ is a static formula.

COMMENTS. All formulas in the class specification are well-typed w.r.t. the signature $\Sigma \mathcal{A} \mathcal{L}$, self:obj, except that self cannot occur in $\mathcal{T}$. To avoid useless inconsistencies, no more than a single occurrence of a particular attribute symbol is allowed in pre- and post-state formulas, and the state formulas in the antecedent of dynamic axiom should be pairwise exclusive.

SEMANTICS. Semantics of class specifications is given by translation into a $\mu \mathcal{L}_\pi$ formulas. To perform this, we must understand formulas in a specification as asserting properties of a prototypical object of the given class and bring this arbitrary object explicit. More precisely, if i is a variable of type obj and φ a formula in a class specification, the formula $i.\varphi$ asserts the property φ relativized to the object i. This relativization is essential also to enable global reasoning about systems composed of multiple interacting objects. Now, $i.\varphi$ is obtained from φ as follows: replace self by i, rename predicate symbols P as $c.P$ [2] is the class name, replace actions A in dynamic axioms by $\downarrow i(A)$ and replace equations $a = t$ by $i.a = t$. Moreover, understand $\nu i : c(\tilde{t})\psi$ as $\Sigma_{i:\text{obj}}([c(i, \tilde{t})] \otimes \psi)$ and $j.m$ as $[j(m)]$. Every expression of the form $i.a = t$ must also be translated to some formula of $\mu\mathcal{L}_\pi$. This translation depends on the actual representation of objects as agents of core-$\mathcal{L}_\pi$. Several possibilities arise in this point, we just require invariant validity of the following principles

$P1$ $\forall t : \tau(i.a = t \Rightarrow [\cdot](\exists y : \tau i.a = y))$ (Persistence of Attributes)
$P2$ $\forall t : \tau_t v : \tau_v(i.a = t \wedge i.a = v \Rightarrow v \doteq t)$ (Attribute values are functional)
$P3$ $\neg(\exists z : \tau(i.a = z) \otimes \exists z : \tau(i.a = z) \otimes \top)$ (Unicity)

SPECIFICATION FORMULAS AND MODELS. Let Σ° be obtained from Σ by changing the types assigned to class names in C from $(\tilde{\tau})o$ to $(\text{obj}, \tilde{\tau})o$ and $\mathcal{L}^\circ$ be obtained from $\mathcal{L}$ by renaming each predicate symbol in $\mathcal{L}_{preds}$ from P to $c.P$. Then, every Σ-class specification $C = (\mathcal{A}, \mathcal{L}, \mathcal{I}, \mathcal{R}, \mathcal{T})$ yields the $\Sigma^\circ \mathcal{AL}^\circ_{preds}$-formula

$$C^*(i, \tilde{a}) = \exists \tilde{v}(\bigwedge_{a_l \in \mathcal{L}_{attrs}} i.a_l = v_l) \wedge (\bigwedge_{D_j \in \mathcal{R}} i.D_j) \wedge (\bigwedge_{P_k \in \mathcal{T}} c.P_k)$$

This formula expresses the full content of the specification and can be used to define a notion of model for a system specification.

Definition 1 *A model for a system specification $\Psi = (\Sigma, \mathcal{C}, \mathcal{S})$ is an interpretation map $\mathbf{I}$ and an assignment of a Σ°-agent $!d_c$ to each $c \in \mathcal{C}$ such that*

$$\text{for all } c \in \mathcal{C} \ P_c \models_{\mathbf{I}} \langle !d_c \rangle \, (i.\mathcal{I} \wedge \mathbf{inv}\{\mathcal{S}^*_c(i, \tilde{v}) \otimes \top\})$$

where $P_c \equiv \Sigma^\circ \mathcal{L}^{C\circ}_{preds}, i : obj; c(i, \tilde{v})$ for some $\tilde{v}$, and satisfaction is taken w.r.t. some sound restriction of the reference LTS relevant to $\{Q|P_c \xrightarrow{*} Q \text{ for } c \in \mathcal{C}\}$.

5 From Specifications to Agents

In this section, we show how models for class specifications can be systematically constructed in a rather simple way. Basically, an object "located at" name i will be represented by an agent of the form $\nu s : \sigma(s(i, \tilde{v})|\nu c.p(R\langle\mathcal{R}\rangle^i_s|\top\langle c.\mathcal{T}\rangle))$ where $R\langle\mathcal{R}\rangle^i_s$ and $\top\langle c.\mathcal{T}\rangle$ are encodings of respectively the dynamic and static theory, and $s(i, \tilde{v})$ is a "record" of the attribute values. We first introduce a canonic form for dynamic axioms in which all of the object's attributes occur both in pre- and post -state formulas. The motivation is that this simplifies the description of the translation and renders explicit the intended frame condition.

CANONIC FORM. Let $\forall x(S_1 \wedge \varphi \Rightarrow \langle[a]\rangle \psi_{(S_2)})$ be a dynamic axiom where S_2 is the maximal state formula embedded into the post-state formula ψ. Then, its canonic form is $\forall \tilde{x}\tilde{y}_k(S_1 \wedge S'_1 \wedge \varphi \Rightarrow \langle[a]\rangle \psi_{(S_2 \wedge S'_2)})$ where S'_1 is $a_1 = y_1 \wedge \cdots \wedge a_k = y_k$

---

[2] When φ is a static axiom, we also write $c.\varphi$ for $i.\varphi$

for those attributes a_i not occurring in S_1 and S_2' is $b_1 = v_1 \wedge \cdots \wedge b_l = v_l$ where $b_i = v_i$ is the (unique) equation in $S \wedge S_1'$ for an attribute b_i not occurring in S_2.

From now on, we fix a Σ-class specification $S = (\mathcal{A}, \mathcal{L}, \mathcal{I}, \mathcal{R}, \mathcal{T})$ associated to $c : (\tau_1, \ldots , \tau_\ell)o$ in some system specification $(\Sigma, \mathcal{C}, \mathcal{S})$, and consider its associated specification formula $S^*(i, \tilde{a}_\ell)$ for some i of type obj. W.l.o.g. we will take the canonic form of every axiom in $\mathcal{R}$.

STATIC FORMULAS AND AXIOMS. Are encoded by the mapping $\mathsf{T}\langle - \rangle$

$$
\begin{aligned}
\mathsf{T}\langle \mathsf{T} \rangle &\mapsto \mathbf{0} \\
\mathsf{T}\langle \varphi_1 \wedge \varphi_2 \rangle &\mapsto [\mathsf{T}\langle \varphi_1 \rangle]\mathsf{T}\langle \varphi_2 \rangle \\
\mathsf{T}\langle \varphi_1 \vee \varphi_2 \rangle &\mapsto [\nu n : o(n|!n[\mathsf{T}\langle \varphi_1 \rangle]\mathbf{0}|!n[\mathsf{T}\langle \varphi_2 \rangle])]\mathbf{0} \\
\mathsf{T}\langle P(\tilde{t}) \rangle &\mapsto c.P(\tilde{t}) \\
\mathsf{T}\langle \forall \tilde{x} : \tilde{\tau}(\varphi \Rightarrow c.P(\tilde{t})) \rangle &\mapsto !\tilde{x} : \tilde{\tau} \triangleright P(\tilde{t})[\mathsf{T}\langle \varphi \rangle]\mathbf{0}
\end{aligned}
$$

This translation assigns to the theory $\mathcal{T}$ a well-typed core-$\mathcal{L}_\pi$ Γ-term $\mathsf{T}\langle c.\mathcal{T} \rangle$ defined as $\mathsf{T}\langle c.d_1 \rangle | \cdots | \mathsf{T}\langle c.d_n \rangle$ where $\tilde{d}_n$ are the formulas in $\mathcal{T}$. We have

Proposition 1 *Let Ξ be a signature, $\mathcal{T}$ be a static theory and $i.\varphi$ a goal formula over Ξ. Then $\Xi; \mathcal{T} \vdash \varphi$ is provable in classical logic iff $\Xi; \mathsf{T}\langle \mathcal{T} \rangle | \mathsf{T}\langle i.\varphi \rangle \xrightarrow{*} \sqrt{}$.*

STATE AND POST-STATE FORMULAS. We consider now the encoding of post-state formulas; state formulas are but a special case of these. We first sequentialise in an arbitrary way $a_1, a_2, \ldots , a_m$ the attribute names defined in $\mathcal{L}_{attrs}$ and define the type σ_S as $(\text{obj}, o, \mathcal{L}(a_1), \cdots , \mathcal{L}(a_m))o$. Let $\mathsf{P}\langle - \rangle_s^o$ be the translation map

$$
\begin{aligned}
\mathsf{P}\langle a_1 = t_1 \wedge \cdots \wedge a_m = t_m \rangle_s^i &\mapsto s(i, t_1, \ldots , t_m) \\
\mathsf{P}\langle \nu j : C(\tilde{t})\psi \rangle_s^i &\mapsto \nu_{j:\text{obj}}(C(j, \tilde{t})|\mathsf{P}\langle \psi \rangle_s^i) \\
\mathsf{P}\langle j.a \otimes \psi \rangle_s^i &\mapsto j(a)|\mathsf{P}\langle \psi \rangle_s^i
\end{aligned}
$$

$\mathsf{P}\langle - \rangle_s^i$ is parametric on two variables i and s, respectively of type obj and σ_C. This encoding represents the state of an object as a term $s(i, \tilde{v})$, where i is the object name and $\tilde{v}$ are the current values of it's attributes. We now can interpret in $\mu\mathcal{L}_\pi$ attribute valuation formulas $i.a_k = t$ (where a_k is the k-th attribute in sequence defined above) by the formula $\exists \tilde{x} : \tilde{\tau}\Sigma_s[s(i, x_1, \ldots , x_{k_1}, t, x_{k+2}, \ldots , x_{m-1})]$ where the $\tilde{\tau}$ are the appropriate types and t occurs in the k-th argument position of s. We will see shortly that this interpretation fully satisfies principles P1-3.

Proposition 2 *Let φ be a post-state formula in a class specification and $\Xi \vdash i.\varphi$. Then $\Xi; \nu s : \sigma_S(\mathsf{P}\langle \psi \rangle_s^i | \sqrt{}) \models_\mathbf{I} i.\psi$ is valid for every $\mathbf{I}$.*

DYNAMIC AXIOMS. Of the form $\phi = \forall \tilde{x} : \tilde{\tau}(S \wedge \varphi \Rightarrow \langle [a] \rangle \psi)$ are translated by the map $\mathsf{R}\langle - \rangle_s^i$ given by $\mathsf{R}\langle \phi \rangle_s^i = !\tilde{x} : \tilde{\tau} \triangleright \mathsf{P}\langle S \rangle_s^i : i(a)[\mathsf{T}\langle i.\varphi \rangle]\mathsf{P}\langle \psi \rangle_s^i$

CLASSES AND SYSTEMS. A Σ-class specification S is encoded into the Σ^o agent

$$
\mathsf{C}\langle S \rangle = !i : \text{obj}, \tilde{a}_\ell : \tilde{\tau}_\ell \triangleright c(i, \tilde{a})[]Ob_S(i, \tilde{a}_\ell)
$$

where $Ob_S(i, \tilde{a}) \equiv \nu s : \sigma_S(\mathsf{P}\langle \mathcal{I} \rangle_s^i | \nu c^- p : \mathcal{L}_{preds}(\mathsf{R}\langle \mathcal{R} \rangle_s^i | \mathsf{T}\langle c.\mathcal{T} \rangle))$ is the representation of an object i of class C in a state satisfying $\mathcal{I}$. In general, an agent of the form $\nu s : \sigma_S(s(i,\tilde{v})|\nu c.\tilde{p} : \mathcal{L}_{preds}(\mathsf{R}\langle\mathcal{R}\rangle_s^i|\mathsf{T}\langle c.\mathcal{T}\rangle))$ will represent an object "located at" i. Finally, a system $\Psi = (\Sigma, \mathcal{C}, \mathcal{S})$ is encoded into the Σ° agent $\mathsf{S}\langle\Psi\rangle = |_{c\in\mathcal{C}}\mathsf{C}\langle\mathcal{S}_c\rangle$ and we will take $Def = \mathcal{C}$ when defining the open operational semantic of a system of objects using the LTS of Section 2. Some remarks are needed before stating and proving the correctness of above defined encoding.

COMPUTATIONS AND CONFIGURATIONS. A computation in system $\Psi = (\Sigma, \mathcal{C}, \mathcal{S})$ is a reduction sequence $I \to S_1 \to S_2 \cdots$ with I of the form $\Sigma^\circ; \mathsf{S}\langle\Psi\rangle\,|p$ and $I \models [c(i,\tilde{v})]$ for some class $c \in \mathcal{C}$. Every S_i must have the form $\Sigma'; \mathsf{S}\langle\Psi\rangle\,|\nu\tilde{x} : \bar{\tau}(Ob_1|\cdots|Ob_n|m_1|\cdots|m_k)$ where the Ob_j are objects and the m_j are either creation requests or messages $i(a)$. Since the agent $\mathsf{S}\langle\Psi\rangle$ encoding Ψ is fixed once for all, we can abstract of its presence and consider just agents like $\Sigma'; \nu\tilde{x} : \bar{\tau}(Ob_1|\cdots|Ob_n|m_1|\cdots|m_k)$, assuming that for transitions $\xrightarrow{!!d.C}$ the action $!d.C$ is always the encoding of some class specification in $\mathsf{S}\langle\Psi\rangle$. Moreover, any component of a system also has this particular structure, so we can focus our concern just on well-typed agents of this form, to be called *configurations*. The following characterises the kind of actions configurations can perform with and without cooperation of the environment in a system reduction.

Proposition 3 *Let C be a configuration of a system Ψ. If $C \xrightarrow{c} C'$ is a transition occurring inside the derivation of a reduction between system configurations, then c is of the forms $\tau, \uparrow i.m, \downarrow i.m$ or $\Downarrow p$ for some definition $p = C\langle\mathcal{S}\rangle$.*

Hence, for instance when proving a (safety) property like $I \Rightarrow \mathbf{inv}\varphi$ from $I \Rightarrow \varphi$ and $\varphi \Rightarrow [\cdot]\varphi$ we can soundly restrict the universe of actions. Now, note that if $\Sigma; p \xrightarrow{\uparrow i.a} Q$ and $\Sigma; p \xrightarrow{\downarrow i.b} Q'$ then there is no configuration r such that $\Sigma; r \xrightarrow{\downarrow i.a} r'$ and $\Sigma; p|r$ is also configuration, because an object i cannot be located both in p and r. Hence, the reference LTS can be refined to approximate relevance, by adding to rule $[s]$ the proviso: "if not ($a \equiv\uparrow i(a)$ and $q \xrightarrow{\downarrow i.b}$ for some b)". The transition relation obtained thus is easily seen to be a subset of the reference transition relation and can be proven (still) sound w.r.t. the fragment of system configurations. Therefore, in the sequel, we will always refer to this restricted transition relation. We can now state correctness of the translation.

Lemma 1 *Let $\mathcal{S} = (\mathcal{A}, \mathcal{L}, \mathcal{I}, \mathcal{R}, \mathcal{T})$ be a Σ-class specification of a class c. Let $\mathbf{I}$ be any interpretation such that $\mathbf{I}_\Xi(c.P) = \{(t_1, \ldots, t_n) \mid \Xi; c.\mathcal{T} \vdash c.P(\tilde{t})\}$. Then*

$$\Gamma, i : obj; Ob_\mathcal{S}(i,\tilde{v}) \models_\mathbf{I} i.\mathcal{I} \wedge \mathbf{inv}\{\mathcal{S}_c^*(i,\tilde{v}) \otimes \top\}$$

where Γ is of the form $\Sigma^\circ\mathcal{L}^\circ\Sigma'$ for any Σ'.

An immediate consequence of Lemma 1 is that the translation just presented provides a model for system specifications.

Theorem 1 *Let $\Psi = (\Sigma, \mathcal{C}, \mathcal{S})$ be a system specification. Then*

$$\Sigma^\circ\mathcal{L}_{preds}^{C\circ}, i : obj; c(i,\tilde{v}) \models_\mathbf{I} \langle C\langle\mathcal{S}_c\rangle\rangle\,(i.\mathcal{I} \wedge \mathbf{inv}\{\mathcal{S}_c^*(i,\tilde{v}) \otimes \top\})$$

for every $c \in \mathcal{C}$ and $\tilde{v}$ of the appropriate types, $\mathbf{I}$ assigns to each signature Σ the interpretation $\mathbf{I}_\Xi(c.P) = \{(v_1, \ldots, v_{k_P}) \mid \Xi; c.\mathcal{T} \vdash c.P(\tilde{v})\}$ and satisfaction is taken w.r.t. the relevant LTS for system configurations.

6   Some General Properties of Systems

In this section, we state several properties found useful to reason about systems and that can be proven valid in any configuration. We start by stating correctness of the interpretation of attribute valuations w.r.t. principles P1-3.

Proposition 4 *For every configuration P of a system $\Psi = (\Sigma, \mathcal{C}, \mathcal{S})$, and every class $c \in \mathcal{C}$ such that $a \in \mathcal{L}_{attrs}^C$ we have $P \models P1 \wedge P2 \wedge P3$.*

We now introduce the following properties R1 and R2 that are true of all of $\mathcal{P}$.

R1. PRIVACY. $\Sigma_{x:\tau}\varphi \Rightarrow \forall_{y:\tau}\Sigma_{x:\tau}(\varphi \wedge \neg x \doteq y)$. If a state has some private name, then this name is distinct from every term in the current environment.

R2. TELESCOPING. $\Sigma_{\tilde{v}:\tilde{\tau}}(\mathbf{ev}_{[S]}\varphi \wedge \mathbf{inv}[U]\bot) \Rightarrow \mathbf{ev}\Sigma_{\tilde{v}:\tilde{\tau}}\varphi$ where S is the set of actions without free occurrences of $v \in \tilde{v}$ and U is the set of actions extruding some v. Thus, we can move a restriction "forward" in a computation if the internal context does not extrude any of the restricted names.

The remaining properties are specific to object system configurations. We assume that i, j are generic object names.

R3. LOCALITY. $(\neg i \doteq j) \wedge i.\varphi \otimes \top \Rightarrow [j.m](i.\varphi \otimes \top)$ for every pre-state formula φ. Attribute values of an object can only be changed by the object's own actions.

R4. GROUPING. $(\neg i \doteq j) \wedge (i.\varphi \otimes \top) \wedge (j.\psi \otimes \top) \Rightarrow (i.\varphi \otimes j.\psi \otimes \top)$ allows the concatenation of assertions about disjoint components of a configuration.

R5. MERGING. $(i.\varphi \otimes \top) \wedge (i.\psi \otimes \top) \Rightarrow ((i.\varphi \wedge i.\psi) \otimes \top)$ allows the merging of assertions about the same component of a configuration.

R6. RELEVANCE I. $\langle \downarrow i.a \rangle \top \Rightarrow [\uparrow i.m]\bot$ expresses that if some object is located in the system then no messages directed to it could be sent to the environment.

R7. RELEVANCE II. $S_c^*(i, \tilde{a}) \otimes \varphi \Rightarrow S_c^*(i, \tilde{a}) \otimes (\varphi \wedge [\downarrow i.m]\bot)$ Messages directed to an object i cannot be received by the internal context surrounding i.

R8. SUPPORT. $\forall \tilde{x} : \tilde{\tau}(\langle i.a \rangle \top \Rightarrow i.\varphi)$ given that $\forall \tilde{x} : \tilde{\tau}(i.\varphi \Rightarrow \langle [i.a] \rangle i.\psi)$ is the single dynamic axiom for the action a in $S_c^*(\tilde{i}, \tilde{a})$.

R9. ACT. $([a] \otimes \mathbf{inv}(\top \otimes (\mathbf{evs}\varphi) \wedge (\varphi \Rightarrow \langle \downarrow a \rangle \psi))) \Rightarrow \mathbf{ev}_{[S]}\{\psi \otimes \top\}$ where S is any action set containing τ. Together with a fairness assumption, this ensures that every request for a message that is never forever disabled will be attended.

R10. CREATION. For each class c of type $(\tau_1, \ldots, \tau_n)o$, the principle $c(i, \tilde{a}) \otimes [i.m_1] \otimes \cdots \otimes [i.m_k] \otimes \top) \Rightarrow \mathbf{ev}_{[S]}(\mathcal{I} \wedge S_c^*(i, \mathbf{a}) \otimes [i.m_1] \otimes \cdots \otimes [i.m_k] \otimes \top$ where S can be anything not excluding $\downarrow d$ with d is $\mathsf{C}\langle \mathcal{S}_c \rangle$ for some $c \in \mathcal{C}$. Every request for a new object is fulfilled. We now bring explicit a fairness assumption.

Definition 2 *A computation $P_1 \overset{a_1}{\to} P_2 \overset{a_2}{\to} \cdots$ is fair if whenever $P_i \cong \nu \tilde{x} : \tilde{\tau}(b|Q)$ and $Q \models \mathbf{inv} \, \mathbf{evs} \langle \downarrow b \rangle \top$ then for some $n \geq i$, $P_n \cong \nu \tilde{y} : \tilde{\gamma}(b|Q')$, $Q' \overset{\downarrow b}{\to} Q''$, $P_{n+1} \cong \nu \tilde{y} : \tilde{\gamma} \, Q''$ and $P_n \overset{\tau}{\to} P_{n+1}$.*

In a fair computation, a message request for an action that is only sometimes disabled will necessarily result in its execution. The important remark to make is that the weak eventualities asserted in the creation and synchronisation axioms above express in fact *strong eventualities*, if we restrict our concern just to fair computations. For instance, we can prove that if $P \models_I ([a] \otimes \mathbf{inv}(\top \otimes (\mathbf{evs}\varphi) \wedge$

Ser() is
attrs
$req : li$
$ch : \textbf{obj}$
initial
$\nu n : N(req = nil \wedge ch = n)$
dynamic
$\forall r, a : \textbf{obj}\ ch = r \Rightarrow \langle[open(a)]\rangle$
$\quad \nu t : Thr(r,s)a.ans(t)$
$\forall s : li\ r : \textbf{obj}, l : li\ ch = r \wedge req = s$
$\quad \Rightarrow \langle[done(r,l)]\rangle\ req = l \bullet s$
$\forall l : lli\ a : \textbf{obj}\ req = l \Rightarrow \langle[dump(a)]\rangle$
$\quad req = nil \otimes a.sl(l)$
end

N() is
end

Thr(s:obj,r:obj) is
attrs
$up : \textbf{bool}$
$sl : li$
initial
$up = \textbf{T} \wedge sl = nil$
dynamic
$\forall l : li, x : i\ up = \textbf{T} \wedge sl = l \Rightarrow$
$\quad \langle[ins(x)]\rangle\ sl = x \bullet l$
$\forall l u : li, x : i\ up = \textbf{T} \wedge sl = l$
$\quad \wedge rem(l,x,u) \Rightarrow$
$\quad \langle[del(x)]\rangle\ sl = u$
$\forall l : li\ up = \textbf{T} \wedge sl = l \Rightarrow$
$\quad \langle[quit]\rangle\ up = \textbf{F} \otimes s.done(r,l)$
static
$\forall x : i, l : li\ rem(x, x \bullet l, l)$
$\forall xy : i, lr : li\ rem(x, y \bullet l, x \bullet r)$
$\quad \Leftarrow rem(x, l, r)$
end

Fig. 4. A sample specification

$(\varphi \Rightarrow \langle a\rangle\,\psi))$ then for all fair reduction paths $P \equiv P_1 \overset{a_1}{\rightarrow} P_2 \overset{a_2}{\rightarrow} \cdots$ there is P_i such that $P_i \models \{\psi \otimes \top\}$.

7 Reasoning about Systems

We now present a toy specification of a commercial server usable for instance at a bookseller network site, and prove a couple of very simple properties about it with the program logic. Servers can perform three types of actions: $open(a)$, that creates a new thread whose identity is returned to the user a by means of a message $a.ans(t)$, $dump(a)$ that returns to a the current list of orders, clearing it afterwards, and $done(r,l)$, explained shortly. Each thread can execute insertions $ins(i)$ and deletions $del(i)$ of items i in the current shopping list at the user command, until $quit$ is invoked. After this happens, the thread yields the collected shopping list (the order) to the server via a $done(r,l)$ request, committing itself to no further action. Obviously, only $s.done(r,l)$ requests originated by threads should be served by the server. This is achieved in the proposed specification by the use of a private communication channel kept in the ch attribute of servers. The specification is presented in Figure 4, in a sugared syntax not hard to relate to the definitions in Section 4.

So, let $I = \Sigma_{n:\textbf{obj}}(s.req = nil \wedge s.ch = n) \wedge \textbf{inv}\{Ser^*(s) \otimes \top\}$ characterise the initial state of a system. We now prove that $I \Rightarrow \textbf{inv}\ \forall r : obj, l : li[s.done(r,l)]\bot$ that is, the privacy assumption just mentioned. To that end, we first show the safety property $I \Rightarrow \textbf{inv}P$ where $P = \Sigma_{n:\textbf{obj}}(s.ch = n \otimes \top) \wedge \textbf{inv}\{Ser^*(s) \otimes \top\}$. Since $I \Rightarrow P$, we first argue informally that $P \Rightarrow [a]P$ for every action a. Since attribute $s.ch$ is never mentioned in s post-formulas, its value n never changes by the frame condition. So we must just prove that such private value is never extruded. The only possibility is in an action $\uparrow (n : \text{obj})s.done(n, l)$. But since say $P \Rightarrow \langle\downarrow(u : \text{obj})s.open(u)\rangle \top$ then $P \Rightarrow [\uparrow (n : \text{obj})s.done(n, l)]\bot$ by R6, and therefore $P \Rightarrow [\uparrow(n)s.done(n, l)]P$. Thus $I \Rightarrow \text{inv}P$. We now prove in detail that $P \Rightarrow \forall RL[s.done(R, L)]\bot$.

1. $\Sigma_n((Ser^*(s) \wedge s.ch = n) \otimes \top)$, hypothesis and R5. By def of $Ser^*(s)$ and R8
2. $\Sigma_n(((\forall s'r'l's.ch = r' \wedge s.req = s' \Leftarrow \langle s.done(r', l')\rangle \top) \wedge s.ch = n) \otimes \top)$
4. $\Sigma_n(((\forall r'l'\neg s.ch = r' \Rightarrow [s.done(r', l')]\bot) \wedge s.ch = n) \otimes \top)$, by pure logic.
5. $\Sigma_n((\forall r'l'\neg n \doteq r' \Rightarrow [s.done(r', l')]\bot) \otimes \top)$, by P2.
6. $\exists RL \langle s.done(R, L)\rangle \top$, hypothesis.
7. $\exists RL(\langle s.done(R, L)\rangle \top \wedge \Sigma_n((\forall r'l'\neg n \doteq r' \Rightarrow [s.done(r', l')]\bot) \otimes \top)$, by 5,6.
8. $\exists RL(\Sigma_n((\forall r'l'\neg n \doteq r' \Rightarrow [s.done(r', l')]\bot \wedge \langle s.done(R, L)\rangle \top \wedge \neg R \doteq n) \otimes \top)$, by R1 and noting that n is not free in $s.done(R, L)$.
9. $\exists RL(\Sigma_n(([s.done(R, L)]\bot \wedge \langle s.done(R, L)\rangle \top) \otimes \top)$, by pure logic.
10. $\forall RL[s.done(R, L)]\bot$, by 9,6 contradiction.
11. $P \Rightarrow \forall RL[s.done(R, L)]\bot$, by 1 discharge, and we are done.

We now consider the following system-wide property φ stating that, in certain conditions, after a thread executes a *quit* action, it should disable further actions and it's parent server must eventually acquire the shopping list produced by it. Then φ is

$$\Sigma_n(Ser^*(s) \otimes (t.sl = l \wedge Thr^*(t, s, n)) \otimes \top) \Rightarrow [t.quit](\text{ev}\{\exists u(s.reqs = l \bullet u) \otimes \top\} \wedge \text{inv}[S]\bot)$$

where S is the set of all actions by t. We now sketch the proof of φ, highlighting just the main steps. Assume $\Sigma_n(Ser^*(s) \otimes (t.sl = l \wedge Thr^*(t, s, n)) \otimes \top)$. This implies $\Sigma_n(Ser^*(s) \otimes (t.sl = l \wedge Thr^*(t, s, n) \wedge t.T_3(s, n)) \otimes \top)$, where $T_3(s, n)$ is the dynamic axiom for *quit* in the specification for threads. Now, $[t.quit]B$ where $B \equiv \Sigma_n(Ser^*(s) \otimes (t.up = F \wedge Thr^*(t, s, n) \otimes s.done(n, l))$, using $t.T_3(s, n)$, and noting that n is not free in $t.quit$. Note that $B \Rightarrow \text{inv}[S]\bot$, because $B \Rightarrow \text{inv}(t.up = F \otimes \top)$. On the other hand, $B \Rightarrow \Sigma_n(s.done(n, l) \otimes \text{inv}\{Ser^*(s) \otimes \top\})$. Now, $s.done(n, l) \otimes \text{inv}\{Ser^*(s) \otimes \top\}$ implies $s.done(n, l) \otimes \text{inv}(\text{ev}\exists r(s.ch = n \wedge s.reqs = r) \wedge \exists r(s.ch = n \wedge s.reqs = r) \Rightarrow \langle [s.done(n, l)]\rangle \exists r(s.reqs = l \bullet r) \otimes \top)$, and this last formula implies $\text{ev}_{[U_n]}\{(\exists r(s.reqs = l \bullet r) \otimes \top)\}$ by R9, where U_n is the set of actions without free occurrences of n. Since $\Sigma_n\text{ev}_{[U_n]}\phi \Rightarrow \text{ev}\Sigma_n\phi$, by R2, we conclude φ.

8 Conclusions and Further Work

We presented a declarative executable specification language and program logic for concurrent objects providing a unified framework for specifying and reasoning about systems, thus demonstrating the usefulness of the $\mathcal{L}_\pi$ language as a meta-language for structuring the definition of operational semantics and program verification logics of languages with concurrent and logic features. An aspect not covered in the present paper was object types, we expect also types to be accommodated in this framework. The proposed model can be extended in several directions (for instance, modelling and reasoning about inheritance, transactions, or mobile code). An interesting observation about $\mu\mathcal{L}_\pi$ is that the monoidal structure induced by $\otimes, \mathbf{1}$ together with $\Rightarrow$ and $\Sigma_{x:\tau}$ induces an Action Structure [9]. This fact may be explored in the definition of a more abstract characterisation of a verification logic for global/local properties of modular systems in the presence of private names.

Acknowledgements To the anonymous referees for their useful comments and Project ESCOLA PRAXIS/2/2.1/MAT/46/94 for partially supporting this work.

References

1. L. Caires. A language for the logical specification of processes and relations. In Michael Hanus, editor, *Proceedings of the Algebraic and Logic Programming International Conference*, number 1139 in LNCS, pages 150–164, 1996.
2. L. Caires. A language for the logical specification of processes and relations. Technical Report 6.96, Universidade Nova de Lisboa, DI/FCT, 1996. http://www-ctp.di.fct.unl.pt/~lcaires/writings/lpi6.96.ps.gz.
3. L. Caires and L. Monteiro. Proof net semantics of proof search computation. In K. Meinke and M. Hanus, editors, *Proceedings of the Algebraic and Logic Programming International Conference*, number 1298 in LNCS, pages 194–208, 1997.
4. J. Fiadeiro and T. Maibaum. Temporal theories as modularisation units for concurrent system specification. *Formal Aspects of Computing*, 4(3):239–272, 1992.
5. D. Kozen. Results on the propositional μ-calculus. *TCS*, 27(3):333–354, 1983.
6. D. Miller. A survey of linear logic programming. *Computational Logic*, 2(2), 1995.
7. D. Miller, G. Nadathur, F. Pfenning, and A. Scedrov. Uniform proof as a foundation for logic programming. *Ann. of Pure and App. Logic*, (51):125–157, 1991.
8. R. Milner. Functions as processes. *Math. Struc. in Computer Sciences*, 2(2):119–141, 1992.
9. R. Milner. Calculi for interaction. *Acta Informatica*, 33(8):707–737, 1996.
10. R. Milner, J. Parrow, and D. Walker. A calculus of mobile processes, Part I + II. *Information and Computation*, 100(1):1–77, 1992.
11. O. Nierstrasz, J-G. Schneider, and M. Lumpe. Formalizing composable software systems – A research agenda. In *Proceedings 1st IFIP Workshop on Formal Methods for Open Object-based Distributed Systems FMOODS'96*, pages 271–282. Chapmann and Hall, 1996.
12. B. Pierce and D. Turner. Concurrent objects in a process calculus. In Takayasu Ito and Akinori Yonezawa, editors, *Theory and Practice of Parallel Programming (TPPP), Sendai, Japan (Nov. 1994)*, number 907 in Lecture Notes in Computer Science, pages 187–215. Springer-Verlag, April 1995.
13. A. Pnueli. The temporal semantics of concurrent programs. In G. Kahn, editor, *Semantics of Concurrent Computations*, volume 70 of *LNCS*, pages 1–20, Evian, France, July 1979. Springer-Verlag , Berlin, Germany.
14. D. Sangiorgi. An interpretation of typed objects into the typed π-calculus. Technical report, INRIA Technical Report RR-3000, 1996.
15. A. Sernadas, C. Sernadas, and J. Costa. Object specification logic. *Journal of Logic and Computation*, 5(5):603–630, October 1995.
16. D. Walker. Objects in the π-calculus. *Journal of Information and Computation*, 116(2):253–271, 1995.

Complexity of Concrete Type-Inference in the Presence of Exceptions[*]

Ramkrishna Chatterjee[1] Barbara G. Ryder[1] William A. Landi[2]

[1] Department of Computer Science, Rutgers University, Piscataway, NJ 08855 USA,
Fax: 732 445 0537, {ramkrish,ryder}@cs.rutgers.edu
[2] Siemens Corporate Research Inc, 755 College Rd. East, Princeton, NJ 08540 USA,
wlandi@scr.siemens.com

Abstract. Concrete type-inference for statically typed object-oriented programming languages (e.g., Java, C^{++}) determines at each program point, those objects to which a reference may refer or a pointer may point during execution. A *precise* compile-time solution for this problem requires a flow-sensitive analysis. Our new complexity results for concrete type-inference distinguish the difficulty of the intraprocedural and interprocedural problem for languages with combinations of single-level types[3], exceptions with or without subtyping, and dynamic dispatch. Our results include:

- The first polynomial-time algorithm for concrete type-inference in the presence of exceptions, which handles Java without threads, and C^{++};
- Proofs that the above algorithm is always safe and provably precise on programs with single-level types, exceptions without subtyping, and without dynamic dispatch;
- Proof that intraprocedural concrete type-inference problem with single-level types and exceptions with subtyping is **PSPACE-complete**, while the interprocedural problem without dynamic dispatch is **PSPACE-hard**.

Other complexity characterizations of concrete type-inference for programs without exceptions are also presented.

1 Introduction

Concrete type-inference (*CTI* from now on) for statically typed object-oriented programming languages (e.g., Java, C^{++}) determines at each program point, those objects to which a reference may refer or a pointer may point during execution. This information is crucial for static resolution of dynamically dispatched calls, side-effect analysis, testing, program slicing and aggressive compiler optimization.

---

[*] The research reported here was supported, in part, by NSF grant GER-9023628 and the Hewlett-Packard Corporation.
[3] These are types with data members only of primitive types.

The problem of *CTI* is both intraprocedurally and interprocedurally flow-sensitive. However, there are approaches with varying degrees of flow-sensitivity for this problem. Although some of these have been used for pointer analysis of C, they can be adapted for *CTI* of Java without exceptions and threads, or C++ without exceptions. At the one end of the spectrum are intraprocedurally and interprocedurally flow-insensitive approaches [Ste96, SH97, ZRL96, And94], which are the least expensive, but also the most imprecise. While at the other end are intraprocedurally and interprocedurally flow-sensitive approaches [LR92, EGH94, WL95, CBC93, MLR+93, Ruf95], which are the most precise, but also the most expensive. Approaches like [PS91, PC94, Age95] are in between the above two extremes.

An intraprocedurally flow-insensitive algorithm does not distinguish between program points within a method; hence it reports the same solution for all program points within each method. In contrast, an intraprocedurally flow-sensitive algorithm tries to compute different solutions for distinct program points.

An interprocedurally flow-sensitive (i.e. context-sensitive) algorithm considers (sometimes approximately) only interprocedurally *realizable paths* [RHS95, LR91]: paths along which calls and returns are properly matched, while an interprocedurally flow-insensitive (i.e. context-insensitive) algorithm does not make this distinction. For the rest of this paper, we will use the term *flow-sensitive* to refer to an intra- and interprocedurally flow-sensitive analysis.

In this paper, we are interested in a flow-sensitive algorithm for *CTI* of a robust subset of Java with exceptions, but without threads (this subset is described in Section 2). The complexity of flow-sensitive *CTI* in the presence of exceptions has not been studied previously. None of the previous flow-sensitive pointer analysis algorithms [LR92, WL95, EGH94, PR96, Ruf95, CBC93, MLR+93] for C/C++ handle exceptions. However, unlike in C++, exceptions are *frequently* used in Java programs, making it an *important* problem for Java.

The main contributions of this paper are:

- The first polynomial-time algorithm for *CTI* in the presence of exceptions that handles a robust subset of Java without threads, and C++[4],
- Proofs that the above algorithm is always safe and provably precise on programs with single-level types, exceptions without subtyping, and without dynamic dispatch; thus this case is in **P**,
- Proof that intraprocedural *CTI* for programs with single-level types and exceptions with subtyping is **PSPACE-complete**, while the interprocedural problem (even) without dynamic dispatch is **PSPACE-hard**.
- New complexity characterizations of *CTI* in the absence of exceptions.

These results are summarized in table 1, which also gives the sections of the paper containing these results.

The rest of this paper is organized as follows. First, we present a flow-sensitive algorithm, called the *basic* algorithm, for *CTI* in the absence of exceptions, and discuss our results about complexity of *CTI* in the absence of exceptions. Next,

---

[4] In this paper, we present our algorithm only for Java.

results	paper section	single-level types	exceptions without subtypes	exceptions with subtypes	dynamic dispatch
interprocedural CTI in $\mathbf{P}$, $O(n^7)$	sec 4	x	x		
intraprocedural CTI $\mathbf{PSPACE}$-complete	sec 4	x		x	
interprocedural CTI $\mathbf{PSPACE}$-hard	sec 4	x		x	
interprocedural CTI $\mathbf{PSPACE}$-hard	sec 3	x			x
interprocedural CTI in $\mathbf{P}$, $O(n^5)$	sec 3	x			
intraprocedural CTI in $\mathbf{NC}$	sec 3	x			

Table 1. Complexity results for *CTI* summarized

we extend the *basic* algorithm for *CTI* in the presence of exceptions, and discuss the complexity and correctness of the extended algorithm. Finally, we present **PSPACE**-hardness results about *CTI* in the presence of exceptions. Due to lack of space, we have omitted all proofs. These proofs and further details about the results in this paper are given in [CRL97][5].

2 Basic definitions

Program representation. Our algorithm operates on an interprocedural control flow graph or ICFG [LR91]. An ICFG contains a control flow graph (CFG) for each method in the program. Each statement in a method is represented by a node in the method's CFG. Each call site is represented using a pair of nodes: a call-node and a return-node. Information flows from a call-node to the entry-node of a target method and comes back from the exit-node of the target method to the return-node of the call-node. Due to dynamic dispatch, interprocedural edges are constructed iteratively during data-flow analysis as in [EGH94]. Details of this construction are shown in Figure 3. We will denote the entry-node of *main* by *start-node* in the rest of this paper.

Representation of dynamically created objects. All run-time objects (or arrays) created at a program point n are represented symbolically by *object_n*. No distinction is made between different elements of an array. Thus, if an array is created at n, *object_n* represents all elements of the array.

Precise solution for *CTI*. A *reference variable* is one of the following:

- a static variable (class variable) of reference[6] type;

---

[5] available at http://www.prolangs.rutgers.edu/refs/docs/tr341.ps.

[6] may refer to an instance of a class or an array.

- a local variable of reference type;
- Av, where Av is $V[t_1]...[t_d]$, and
  - V is a static/local variable or V is an array $object_n$ allocated at program point n, such that V is either a d-dimensional array of reference type or an array of any type having more than d dimensions and
  - each t_i is a non-negative integer; or
- $V.s_1...s_k$, where
  - V is either a static/local variable of reference type or V is Av or V is object $object_n$ created at program point n,
  - for $1 \leq i \leq k$, each $V.s_1...s_{i-1}$ (V for $i = 1$) has the type of a reference to a class T_i and each s_i is a field of reference type of T_i or $s_i = f_i[t_{i_1}]...[t_{i_{r_i}}]$ and f_i is a field of T_i and f_i is an array having at least r_i dimensions and each t_{i_j} is a non-negative integer, and
  - $V.s_1...s_k$ is of reference type.

Using these definitions, the precise solution for CTI can be defined as follows: given a *reference variable* RV and an object $object\_n$, $\langle RV, object\_n \rangle$ belongs to the precise solution at a program point n if and only if RV is visible at n and there exists an execution path from the *start-node* of the program to n such that if this path is followed, RV points to $object\_n$ at n (i.e., at the top of n). Unfortunately, all paths in a program are not necessarily executable and determining which are executable is undecidable. Barth[Bar78] defined *precise up to symbolic execution* to be the precise solution under the assumption that all program paths are executable (i.e., the result of a test is independent of previous tests and all the branches are possible). In the rest of this paper we use *precise* to mean *precise up to symbolic execution*.

Points-to. A points-to has the form $\langle var, obj \rangle$; where *var* is one of the following: (1) a static variable of reference type, (2) a local variable of reference type, (3) $object\_m$ - an array object created at program point m or (4) $object\_n.f$ - field f, of reference type, of an object created at a program point n; and *obj* is $object\_s$ - an object created at a program point s.

Single-level type. A single-level type is one of the following: (1) a primitive type defined in [GJS96] (e.g., int, float etc.), (2) a class that has all non-static data-members of primitive types (e.g., class A { int i,j; }) or (3) an array of a primitive type.

Subtype. We use Java's definition of subtyping: a class A is a subtype of another class B if A *extends* B, either directly or indirectly through inheritance.

Safe solution. An algorithm is said to compute a *safe* solution for CTI if and only if at each program point, the solution computed by the algorithm is a superset of the precise solution.

Subset of Java considered. We essentially consider a subset that excludes threads, but in some cases we may need to exclude three other features: finalize methods, static initializations and dynamically defined classes. Since finalize methods are called (non-deterministically) during garbage collection or unloading of classes, if a *finalize* method modifies a variable of reference type (extremely rare), it cannot be handled by our algorithm. Static initializations complicate analysis due to dynamic loading of classes. If static initializations can be done in program order, our algorithm can handle them. Otherwise, if they depend upon dynamic loading (extremely rare), our algorithm cannot handle them. Similarly, our algorithm cannot handle classes that are constructed on the fly and not known statically. We will refer to this subset as *JavaWoThreads*.

Also, we have considered only exceptions generated by *throw* statements. Since run-time exceptions can be generated by almost any statement, we have ignored them. Our algorithm can handle run-time exceptions if the set of statements that can generate these exceptions is given as an input. If all statements that can potentially generate run-time exceptions are considered, we will get a safe solution; however, this may generate far more information than what is useful.

3 *CTI* in the absence of exceptions

Our *basic* algorithm for *CTI* is an iterative worklist algorithm [KU76]. It operates on an ICFG and is similar to the Landi-Ryder algorithm [LR92] for alias analysis, but instead of aliases, it computes points-tos. In Section 4, we will extend this algorithm to handle exceptions.

Lattice for data-flow analysis. In order to restrict data-flow only to realizable paths, points-tos are computed conditioned on *assumed-points-tos* (akin to reaching alias in [LR92] [PR96]), which represent points-tos reaching the entry of a method, and approximate the calling context in which the method has been called (see the example in Appendix A). A points-to along with its *assumed-points-to* is called a *conditional-points-to*. A conditional-points-to has the form ⟨*condition, points-to*⟩, where *condition* is an assumed-points-to or *empty* (meaning this points-to is applicable to all contexts). For simplicity, we will write ⟨*empty,points-to*⟩ as *points-to*. Also a special data-flow element *reachable* is used to check whether a node is reachable from the start-node through a realizable path. This ensures that only such reachable nodes are considered during data-flow analysis and only points-tos generated by them are put on the worklist for propagation. The lattice for data-flow analysis (associated with a program point) is a subset lattice consisting of sets of such conditional-points-tos and the data-flow element *reachable*.

Query. Using these conditional-points-tos, a query for *CTI* is answered as follows. Given a *reference variable V* and a program point *l*, the conditional-points-tos with *compatible* assumed-points-tos computed at *l* are combined to determine the possible values of V. Assumed-points-tos are *compatible* if and only if they do not imply different values for the same user defined variable. For example, if V is *p.f1*, and the solution computed at l contains $\langle empty, \langle p, obj1\rangle\rangle$, $\langle z, \langle obj1.f1, obj2\rangle\rangle$ and $\langle u, \langle obj1.f1, obj3\rangle\rangle$, then the possible values of V are *obj2* and *obj3*.

Algorithm description. Figure 1 contains a high-level description of the main loop of the *basic* algorithm. *apply* computes the effect of a statement on an incoming conditional-points-to. For example, suppose l labels the statement *p.f1* $= q$, *ndf_elm* (i.e. the points-to reaching the top of l) is $\langle z, \langle p, object\_s\rangle\rangle$ and $\langle u, \langle q, object\_n\rangle\rangle$ is present in the solution computed at l so far. Assuming z and u are compatible, *apply* generates $\langle object\_s.f1, object\_n\rangle$ under the condition that both z and u hold at the entry-node of the method containing l. Then either z or u is chosen as the condition for the generated data-flow element. For example, if u is chosen then $\langle u, \langle object\_s.f1, object\_n\rangle\rangle$ will be generated. When a conjunction of conditions is associated with a points-to, any fixed-size subset of these conditions may be stored without affecting safety. At a program point where this data-flow element is used, if all the conjuncts are true then any subset of the conjuncts is also true. This may cause overestimation of solution at program points where only a proper subset of the conjuncts is true. At present, we store only the first member of the list of conditions. *apply* is defined in Appendix B.

add_to_solution_and_worklist_if_needed checks whether a data-flow element is present in the solution set (computed so far) of a node. If not, it adds the data-flow element to the solution set, and puts the node along with this data-flow element on the worklist.

process_exit_node propagates data-flow elements from the exit-node of a method to the return-node of a call site of this method. Suppose $\langle z, u\rangle$ holds at the exit-node of a method M. Consider a return-node R of a call site C of M. For each assumed-points-to x such that $\langle x, t\rangle$ is in the solution set at C and t implies z at the entry-node of M, $\langle x, u\rangle$ is propagated by *process_exit_node* to R. *process_exit_node* is defined in Figure 2.

process_call_node propagates data-flow elements from a call site to the entry-node of a method called from this site. Due to dynamic dispatch, the set of methods invoked from a call site is iteratively computed during the data-flow analysis as in [EGH94]. Suppose $\langle x, t\rangle$ holds at a call site C which has a method M in its set of invocable methods computed so far. If t implies a points-to z at the entry-node of M (e.g., through an actual to formal binding), $\langle z, z\rangle$ is forwarded to the entry-node of M. *process_call_node* also remembers the association between x and z at C because this is used by *process_exit_node* as described above. *process_call_node* is defined in Figures 3 and 4.

Other functions used by the above routines are defined in Appendix B. Appendix A contains an example which illustrates the *basic* algorithm.

Precision of the *basic* algorithm. By induction on the number of iterations needed to compute a data-flow element and the length of a path associated with a data-flow element, in [CRL97], we prove that the *basic* algorithm computes the

```
// initialize worklist. Each worklist node contains a data-flow element, which
// is a conditional-points-to or reachable, and an ICFG node.
create a worklist node containing the entry-node of main
and reachable, and add it to the worklist;

while ( worklist is not empty ) {
  WLnode = remove a node from the worklist;
  ndf_elm = WLnode.data-flow-element;
  node = WLnode.node;

  if ( node ≠ a call_node and node ≠ exit_node of a method ) {
    // compute the effect of the statement associated with node on ndf_elm.
    generated_data_flow_elements = apply( node, ndf_elm );

    for ( each successor succ of node ) {
      for ( each df_elm in generated_data_flow_elements )
        add_to_solution_and_worklist_if_needed( df_elm, succ );
    }
  } // end of if

  if ( node is an exit_node of a method )
    process_exit_node( node, ndf_elm );
  if ( node is a call_node )
    process_call_node( node, ndf_elm );
} // end of while
```

Fig. 1. High-level description of the *basic* algorithm

precise solution for programs with only single-level types and without dynamic dispatch, exceptions or threads. For programs of this form, *CTI* is distributive and a conditional-points-to at a program point can never require the simultaneous occurrence of multiple conditional-points-tos at (any of) its predecessors. Intuitively this is why the above proof works. The presence of general types, dynamically dispatched calls or exceptions with subtyping violate this condition and hence *CTI* is not polynomial-time solvable in the presence of these constructs. We also prove that the *basic* algorithm computes a safe solution for programs written in *JavaWoThreads*, but without exceptions.

Complexity of the *basic* algorithm. The complexity of the *basic* algorithm for programs with only single-level types and without dynamic dispatch, exceptions or threads is $O(n^5)$, where n is approximately the number of statements in the input program. This an improvement over the $O(n^7)$ worst-case bound achievable by applying previous approaches of [RHS95] and [LR91] to this case. Note that $O(n^3)$ is a trivial worst-case lower bound for obtaining a precise solution for this case. For programs written in *JavaWoThreads*, but without exceptions, the *basic* algorithm is polynomial-time.

Other results on the complexity of *CTI* in the absence of exceptions. In [CRL97], we prove the following two theorems:

Theorem 1 *Intraprocedural CTI for programs with only single-level types is in non-deterministic log-space and hence* **NC.**

```
void process_exit_node( exit_node, ndf_elm ) {
    // Let M be the method containing the exit_node.
    if ( ndf_elm represents the value of a local variable )
        // it need not be forwarded to the successors (return-nodes of call sites for
        // this method) because the local variable is not visible outside this method.
        return;

    if ( ndf_elm is reachable ) {
        for ( each call site C in the current set of call sites of M ){
            if ( solution at C contains reachable ) {
                add_to_solution_and_worklist_if_needed( ndf_elm, R );
                // R is the return-node for C.
                for ( each s in C.waiting_local_points_to_table ) {
                    // conditional-points-tos representing values of local variables reaching
                    // C are not forwarded to R until it is found reachable.
                    // C.waiting_local_points_to_table contains such conditional-points-tos.

                    // Since R has been found to be reachable
                    delete s from C.waiting_local_poinst_to_table;
                    add_to_solution_and_worklist_if_needed( s, R );
                }
            }
        }
        return;
    }

    add_to_table_of_conditions( ndf_elm, exit_node );
    // This table is accessed from the call sites of M for expanding assumed-points-tos.

    for ( each call site C in the current set of call sites of M ) {
        S = get_assumed_points_tos( C, ndf_elm.assumed_points_to, M );
        for ( each assumed_points_to Apt in S ) {
            CPT = new conditional-points-to( Apt, ndf_elm.points_to );
            add_to_solution_and_worklist_if_needed( CPT, R );
            // R is the return-node for C.
        }
    }
} // end of process_exit_node
```

Fig. 2. Code for processing an exit-node

Recall that non-deterministic log-space is the set of languages accepted by non-deterministic Turing machines using logarithmic space[Pap94] and **NC** is the class of efficiently parallelizable problems which contains non-deterministic log-space.

Theorem 2
CTI for programs with only single-level types and dynamic dispatch is **PSPACE**-*hard.*

4 Algorithm for *CTI* in the presence of exceptions

In this section we extend the *basic* algorithm for *CTI* of *JavaWoThreads*, and discuss the complexity and precision of this extended algorithm.

Data-flow Elements: The data-flow elements propagated by this extended algorithm have one of the following forms:

```
void process_call_node( C, ndf_elm ){
// R is the return-node for call_node C.
  if ( ndf_elm implies an increase in the set CM of methods invoked
       from this site ) {
     // Recall that due to dynamic dispatch, the interprocedural
     // edges are constructed on the fly, as in [EGH94].
     add this new method nM to CM;
     for ( each dfelm in the solution set of C )
        interprocedurally_propagate( dfelm, C, nM );  // defined in Figure 4
  }

  if ( ndf_elm represents value of a local variable ) {
     if ( solution set for R contains reachable )
        // Forward ndf_elm to the return-node because (unlike C++ )
        // a local variable cannot be modified by a call in Java.
        add_to_solution_and_worklist_if_needed( ndf_elm, R );
     else
        // Cannot forward till R is found to be reachable.
        add ndf_elm to waiting_local_points_to_table;
  }

  for ( each method M in CM )
     interprocedurally_propagate( ndf_elm, C, M );
}
```

Fig. 3. Code for processing a call-node

1. $\langle reachable \rangle$,
2. $\langle label, reachable \rangle$,
3. $\langle excp\text{-}type, reachable \rangle$,
4. $\langle z, u \rangle$,
5. $\langle label, z, u \rangle$,
6. $\langle excp\text{-}type, z, u \rangle$,
7. $\langle excp, z, obj \rangle$.

Here z and u are points-tos. The lattice for data-flow analysis associated with a program point is a subset lattice consisting of sets of these data-flow elements. In the rest of this section, we present definitions of these data-flow elements and a brief description of how they are propagated. Further details are given in [CRL97]. First we describe how a *throw* statement is handled. Next, we describe propagation at a method *exit-node*. Finally, we describe how a *finally* statement is handled.

throw statement: In addition to the conditional-points-tos described previously, this algorithm uses another kind of conditional-points-tos, called *exceptional-conditional-points-tos*, which capture propagation due to exceptions. The conditional part of these points-tos consists of an exception type and an assumed points-to (as before). Consider a *throw* statement l in a method *Proc*, which throws an object of type T (run-time type and not the declared type). Moreover let $\langle \langle q, obj1 \rangle, \langle p, obj2 \rangle \rangle$ be a conditional-points-to reaching the top of l. At the *throw* statement, this points-to is transformed to $\langle T, \langle q, obj1 \rangle, \langle p, obj2 \rangle \rangle$ and

```
interprocedurally_propagate( ndf_elm, C, M) {
    // C is a call_node, R is the return-node of C and M is a method called from C.
    if ( ndf_elm == reachable ) {
        add_to_solution_and_worklist_if_needed(ndf_elm, M.entry_node);
        if ( M.exit_node has reachable ) {
            add_to_solution_and_worklist_if_needed(ndf_elm, R);
            for ( each s in C.waiting_local_points_to_table ) {
                // Since R has been found to be reachable
                delete s from C.waiting_local_poinst_to_table;
                add_to_solution_and_worklist_if_needed( s, R );
            }
        }
        propagate_conditional_points_tos_with_empty_condition(C,M);
        return;
    }

    // get the points-tos implied by ndf_elm at the entry-node of M
    S = get_implied_conditional_points_tos(ndf_elm,M,C);

    for ( each s in S ) {
        add_to_solution_and_worklist_if_needed( s, M.entry_node );
        add_to_table_of_assumed_points_tos( s.assumed_points_to,
            ndf_elm.assumed_points_to, C );
        // This table is accessed from exit-nodes of methods called from C
        // for expanding assumed points-tos.

        if ( ndf_elem.apt is a new apt for s.apt ) {
            // apt stands for assumed-points-to
            Pts = lookup_table_of_conditions( s.assumed_points_to, M.exit_node );
            // ndf_elm.assumed_points_to is an assumed-points-to for each element of Pts

            for ( each pts in Pts ) {
                cpt = new conditional_points_to( ndf_elm.assumed_points_to, pts );
                add_to_solution_and_worklist_if_needed( cpt, R );
            }
        }
    } // end of each s in S
}
```

Fig. 4. Code for interprocedurally_propagate

propagated to the exit-node of the corresponding *try* statement, if there is one. A precalculated *catch-table* at this node is checked to see if this exception (identified by its type T) can be caught by any of the corresponding *catch* statements. If so, this exceptional-conditional-points-to is forwarded to the entry-node of this *catch* statement, where it is changed back into an ordinary conditional-points-to $\langle\langle q, obj1\rangle, \langle p, obj2\rangle\rangle$. If not, this exceptional-conditional-points-to is forwarded to the entry-node of a *finally* statement (if any), or the exit-node of the innermost enclosing *try*, *catch*, *finally* or the method body.

A *throw* statement also generates a data-flow element for the exception itself. Suppose the thrown object is *obj* and it is the thrown object under the assumed points-to $\langle p, obj1\rangle$. Then $\langle excp, \langle p, obj1\rangle, obj\rangle$ representing the exception is generated. Such data-flow elements are handled like exceptional-conditional-points-tos, described above. If such a data-flow element reaches the entry of a *catch* statement, it is used to instantiate the parameter of the *catch* statement.

In addition to propagating *reachable* (defined in section 3), this algorithm also propagates data-flow elements of the form ⟨*excp-type, reachable*⟩. When ⟨*reachable*⟩ reaches a *throw* statement, it is transformed into ⟨*excp-type, reachable*⟩, where *excp-type* is a run-time type of the exception thrown, which is then propagated like other exceptional-conditional-points-tos.

If the *throw* is not directly contained in a *try* statement, then the data-flow elements generated by it are propagated to the exit-node of the innermost enclosing *catch, finally* or method body.

exit-node of a method: At the exit-node of a method, a data-flow element of type 4,6 or 7 is forwarded (after replacing the assumed points-to as described in section 3) to the return-node of a call site of this method if and only if the assumed points-to of the data-flow element holds at the call site. At a return-node, ordinary conditional-points-tos (type 4) are handled as before. However, a data-flow element of type 6 or 7 is handled as if it were generated by a *throw* at this return-node.

finally statement: The semantics of exception handling in Java is more complicated than other languages like C++ because of the *finally* statement. A *try* statement can optionally have a *finally* statement associated with it. It is executed no matter how the *try* statement terminates: normally or due to an exception. A *finally* statement is always entered with a reason, which could be an exception thrown in the corresponding *try* statement or one of the corresponding *catch* statements, or leaving the *try* statement or one of its *catch* clauses by a *return*, (labelled) *break* or (labelled) *continue*, or by falling through. This reason is remembered on entering a *finally*, and unless the *finally* statement itself creates its own reason to exit the *finally*, at the exit-node of the *finally* this reason is used to decide control flow. If the *finally* itself creates its own reason to exit itself (e.g., due to an exception), then this new reason **overrides** any previous reason for entering the *finally*. Also, nested *finally* statements cause reasons for entering them to stack up. In order to correctly handle this involved semantics, for all data-flow elements entering a *finally*, the algorithm remembers the reason for entering it. For data-flow elements of type 3, 6 or 7 (enumerated above), the associated exception already represents this reason. A *label* is associated with data-flow elements of type 1 or 4, which represents the statement number to which control should go after exit from the *finally*. Thus the data-flow elements in a *finally* have one of the following forms:

1. ⟨*label, reachable*⟩,
2. ⟨*excp-type, reachable*⟩,
3. ⟨*label, z, u*⟩,
4. ⟨*excp-type, z, u*⟩,
5. ⟨*excp, z, obj*⟩.

When a labelled data-flow element reaches the labelled statement, the label is dropped and it is transformed into the corresponding unlabelled data-flow element.

Inside a *finally*, due to labels and exception types associated with data-flow elements, *apply* uses a different criterion for combining data-flow elements (at an assignment node) than the one given in section 3. Two data-flow elements $\langle x1,y1,z1 \rangle$ and $\langle x2,y2,z2 \rangle$ can be combined if and only if both $x1$ and $x2$ represent the same exception type or the same label, and $y1$ and $y2$ are compatible (as defined in section 3).

At a call statement (inside a *finally*), if a data-flow element has a *label* or an exception type associated with it, it is treated as part of the context (assumed points-to) and not forwarded to the target node. It is put back when assumed points-tos are expanded at an exit-node of a method. For exceptional-conditional-points-tos or data-flow elements representing exceptions, the exceptions associated with them at the exit-node **override** any *label* or exception type associated with their assumed points-tos at a corresponding call site. Data-flow elements of the form $\langle label,reachable \rangle$ or $\langle excp\text{-}type,reachable \rangle$ are propagated across a call if and only if $\langle reachable \rangle$ reaches the exit-node of one of the called methods. A mechanism similar to the one used for handling a call is used for handling a *try* statement nested inside a *finally* because it can cause labels and exceptions to stack up. Details of this are given in [CRL97].

If the *finally* generates a reason of its own for exiting itself, the previous *label/exception-type* associated with a data-flow element is discarded, and the new *label/exception-type* representing this reason for leaving the *finally* is associated with the data-flow element.

Example. The example in Figure 5 illustrates the above algorithm.

Precision of the extended algorithm. In [CRL97], we prove that the extended algorithm described in Section 4 computes the precise solution for programs with only single-level types, exceptions without subtyping, and without dynamic dispatch. We also prove that this algorithm computes a safe solution for programs written in *JavaWoThreads*.

Complexity of the extended algorithm. The the worst-case complexity of the extended algorithm for programs with only single-level types, exceptions without subtyping, and without dynamic dispatch is $O(n^7)$. Since we have proved that the algorithm is precise for this case, this shows that this case is in P. If we disallow *trys* nested inside a *finally*, the worst-case complexity is $O(n^6)$. For general programs written in *JavaWoThreads*, the extended algorithm is polynomial-time.

Complexity due to exceptions with subtyping. In [CRL97], we prove the following theorem:

Theorem 3 *Intraprocedural CTI for programs with only single-level types and exceptions with subtyping is* **PSPACE**-*complete; while the interprocedural case (even) without dynamic dispatch is* **PSPACE**-*hard.*

```
// Note: for simplicity only a part of the solution is shown
class A {}; class excp_t extends Exception {};
class base {
  public static A a;
  public static void method( A param ) throws excp_t {
    excp_t unexp;

    a = param;
    l1: unexp = new excp_t;

    // ⟨empty, ⟨unexp, object_l1 ⟩ ⟩,
    // ⟨⟨param, object_l2 ⟩, ⟨a, object_l2 ⟩ ⟩
    throw unexp;

    // ⟨excp, empty, object_l1 ⟩,
    // ⟨excp_t, ⟨param, object_l2 ⟩, ⟨a, object_l2 ⟩ ⟩
  }
};

class test {
  public static void test_method( ) {
    A local;

    l2: local = new A;

    try {
      base.method( local );

      // ⟨excp, empty, object_l1 ⟩, ⟨excp_t, empty, ⟨a, object_l2 ⟩ ⟩
    }
    catch( excp_t param ) {
      // ⟨empty, ⟨param, object_l1 ⟩ ⟩, ⟨empty, ⟨a, object_l2 ⟩ ⟩
      l3:
    }
    finally {
      // ⟨l4, empty, ⟨a, object_l2 ⟩ ⟩
    }
    // ⟨empty, ⟨a, object_l2 ⟩ ⟩
    l4:
  }
};
```

Fig. 5. *CTI* in the presence of exceptions

Theorems 2 and 3 show that in the presence of exceptions, among all the reasonable special cases that we have considered, programs with only single-level types, exceptions without subtyping, and without dynamic dispatch comprise the only natural special case that is in **P**. Note that just adding subtyping for exception types and allowing overloaded *catch* clauses increase complexity from P to **PSPACE**-hard.

5   Related work

As mentioned in the introduction, no previous algorithm for pointer analysis or *CTI* handles exceptions. This work takes state-of-the-art in pointer analysis one step further by handling exceptions. Our algorithm differs from other pointer analysis and *CTI* algorithms [EGH94, WL95, Ruf95, PC94, PS91, CBC93,

MLR$^+$93] in the way it maintains context-sensitivity by associating assumed-points-tos with each data-flow element, rather than using some approximation of the call stack. This way of handling context-sensitivity enables us to obtain precise solution for polynomial-time solvable cases, and handle exceptions. This way of maintaining context is similar to Landi-Ryder's[LR92] method of storing context using reaching aliases, except that our algorithm uses points-tos rather than aliases. Our algorithm also differs from approaches like [PS91, Age95] in being intraprocedurally flow-sensitive.

6 Conclusion

In this paper, we have studied the complexity *CTI* for a subset of Java, which includes exceptions. To the best of our knowledge, the complexity of *CTI* in the presence of exceptions has not been studied before. The following are the main contributions of this work (proofs are not presented in this paper, but appear in [CRL97]):

1. The first polynomial-time algorithm for *CTI* in the presence of exceptions which handles a robust subset of Java without threads, and C^{++}.
2. A proof that *CTI* for programs with only single-level types, exceptions without subtyping, and without dynamic dispatch is in **P** and can be solved in $O(n^7)$ time.
3. A proof that intraprocedural *CTI* for programs with only single-level types, exceptions with subtyping, and without dynamic dispatch is **PSPACE**-complete, and the interprocedural case is **PSPACE**-hard.

Additional contributions are:

1. A proof that *CTI* for programs with only single-level types, dynamic dispatch, and without exceptions is **PSPACE**-hard.
2. A proof that *CTI* for programs with only single-level types can be done in $O(n^5)$ time. This is an improvement over the $O(n^7)$ worst-case bound achievable by applying previous approaches of [RHS95] and [LR91] to this case.
3. A proof that intraprocedural *CTI* for programs with only single-level types is in non-deterministic log-space and hence *NC*.

References

[Age95] Ole Agesen. The cartesian product algorithm: Simple and precise type inference of parametric polymorphism. In *Proceedings of European Conference on Object-oriented Programming (ECOOP '95)*, 1995.

[And94] L. O. Andersen. *Program Analysis and Specialization for the C Programming Language*. PhD thesis, DIKU, University of Copenhagen, 1994. Also available as DIKU report 94/19.

[Bar78]   J. M. Barth. A practical interprocedural data flow analysis algorithm. *Communications of the ACM*, 21(9):724–736, 1978.

[CBC93]   Jong-Deok Choi, Michael Burke, and Paul Carini. Efficient flow-sensitive interprocedural computation of pointer-induced aliases and side effects. In *Proceedings of the ACM SIGPLAN/SIGACT Symposium on Principles of Programming Languages*, pages 232–245, January 1993.

[CRL97]   Ramkrishna Chatterjee, Barbara Ryder, and William Landi. Complexity of concrete type-inference in the presence of exceptions. Technical Report DCS-TR-341, Dept of CS, Rutgers University, September 1997.

[EGH94]   Maryam Emami, Rakesh Ghiya, and Laurie J. Hendren. Context-sensitive interprocedural points-to analysis in the presence of function pointers. In *Proceedings of the ACM SIGPLAN Conference on Programming language design and implementation*, pages 242–256, 1994.

[GJS96]   James Gosling, Bill Joy, and Guy Steele. *The Java Language Specification*. Addison-Wesley, 1996.

[KU76]   J.B. Kam and J.D. Ullman. Global data flow analysis and iterative algorithms. *Journal of ACM*, 23(1):158–171, 1976.

[LR91]   W.A. Landi and Barbara G. Ryder. Pointer-induced aliasing: A problem classification. In *Proceedings of the ACM SIGPLAN/SIGACT Symposium on Principles of Programming Languages*, pages 93–103, January 1991.

[LR92]   W.A. Landi and Barbara G. Ryder. A safe approximation algorithm for interprocedural pointer aliasing. In *Proceedings of the ACM SIGPLAN Conference on Programming Language Design and Implementation*, pages 235–248, June 1992.

[MLR+93] T. J. Marlowe, W. A. Landi, B. G. Ryder, J. Choi, M. Burke, and P. Carini. Pointer-induced aliasing: A clarification. *ACM SIGPLAN Notices*, 28(9):67–70, September 1993.

[Pap94]   C. H. Papadimitriou. *Computational Complexity*. Addison–Wesley, 1994.

[PC94]   J. Plevyak and A. Chien. Precise concrete type inference for object oriented languages. In *Proceeding of Conference on Object-Oriented Programming Systems, Languages and Applications (OOPSLA '94)*, pages 324–340, October 1994.

[PR96]   Hemant Pande and Barbara G. Ryder. Data-flow-based virtual function resolution. In *LNCS 1145, Proceedings of the Third International Symposium on Static Analysis*, 1996.

[PS91]   J. Palsberg and M. Schwartzbach. Object-oriented type inference. In *Proceedings of Conference on Object-Oriented Programming Systems, Languages, and Applications (OOPSLA '91)*, pages 146–161, October 1991.

[RHS95]   T. Reps, S. Horwitz, and M. Sagiv. Precise interprocedural dataflow analysis via graph reachability. In *Proceedings of the ACM SIGPLAN/SIGACT Symposium on Principles of Programming Languages*, pages 49–61, 1995.

[Ruf95]   E. Ruf. Context-insensitive alias analysis reconsidered. In *Proceedings of the ACM SIGPLAN Conference on Programming language design and implementation*, pages 13–22, June 1995.

[SH97]   M. Shapiro and S. Horwitz. Fast and accurate flow-insensitive points-to analysis. In *Proceedings of the ACM SIGPLAN/SIGACT Symposium on Principles of Programming Languages*, pages 1–14, 1997.

[Ste96]   Bjarne Steensgaard. Points-to analysis in almost linear time. In *Proceedings of the ACM SIGPLAN/SIGACT Symposium on Principles of Programming Languages*, pages 32–41, 1996.

[WL95]   Robert P. Wilson and Monica S. Lam. Efficient context-sensitive pointer analysis for c programs. In *Proceedings of the ACM SIGPLAN Conference on Programming language design and implementation*, pages 1–12, 1995.

[ZRL96] S. Zhang, B. G. Ryder, and W. Landi. Program decomposition for pointer aliasing: A step towards practical analyses. In *Proceedings of the 4th Symposium on the Foundations of Software Engineering*, October 1996.

A   Example for the *basic* algorithm

// *Note: due to lack of space only a part of the solution is shown*

```
class A {};   class B {              class C {
                 public B field1;       public B field1;
              };                      };
```

```
class base {                         class derived extends base {
 public static A a;                    public void method( ) {
 public void method( ){                  // overrides base::method
   l1: a = new A;                       l2: a = new A;

   // ⟨empty, ⟨a, object_l1 ⟩ ⟩        // ⟨empty, ⟨a, object_l2 ⟩ ⟩
   exit_node:                            exit_node:
 };                                   };
};                                   };
```

```
class caller {
  public static void call( base param ) {
    // ⟨⟨param, object_l4 ⟩, ⟨param, object_l4 ⟩ ⟩,
    // ⟨⟨param, object_l5 ⟩, ⟨param, object_l5 ⟩ ⟩,

    l3: param.method();

    // ⟨param, object_l4 ⟩ => base::method is called.
    // ⟨param, object_l5 ⟩ => derived::method is called.
    //⟨empty, ⟨a, object_l1 ⟩ ⟩ is changed to
    // ⟨⟨param, object_l4 ⟩, ⟨a, object_l1 ⟩ ⟩ because base::method is
    // called only when ⟨param, object_l4 ⟩.
    // ⟨empty, ⟨a, object_l2 ⟩ ⟩ is changed to
    // ⟨⟨param, object_l5 ⟩, ⟨a, object_l2 ⟩ ⟩ because derived::method is
    // is called only when ⟨param, object_l5 ⟩.
  };
}; // end of class caller
```

```
class potpourri {
  public static void example( C param ) {
    // Let S = { ⟨⟨param, object_l6 ⟩, ⟨param, object_l6 ⟩ ⟩,
    // ⟨⟨param, object_l7 ⟩, ⟨param, object_l7 ⟩ ⟩,
    // ⟨⟨object_l6.field1, null ⟩, ⟨object_l6.field1, null ⟩ ⟩,
    // ⟨⟨object_l7.field1, null ⟩, ⟨object_l7.field1, null ⟩ ⟩}
    // solution at this point is S
    local = param;

    // Let S1 = S U {⟨⟨param, object_l6 ⟩, ⟨local, object_l6 ⟩ ⟩,
    //                ⟨⟨param, object_l7 ⟩, ⟨local, object_l7 ⟩ ⟩ }
    // solution at this point is S1
    l8: local.field1 = new B;

    // solution =
    // S1 U { ⟨⟨param, object_l6 ⟩, ⟨object_l6.field1, object_l8 ⟩ ⟩,
    //        ⟨⟨param, object_l7 ⟩, ⟨object_l7.field1, object_l8 ⟩ ⟩,
    //        ⟨empty, ⟨object_l8.field1, null ⟩ ⟩ }
```

```
    exit_node:
  };
};

class test {
  public void test1( ) {              public void test2( ) {
    base p;                             derived p;
    l4: p = new base;                   l5: p = new derived;

    // ⟨empty, ⟨p, object_l4 ⟩ ⟩       l10: caller.call(p);
    l9: caller.call(p);

    // ⟨empty, ⟨p, object_l4 ⟩ ⟩ .     // ⟨empty, ⟨p, object_l5 ⟩ ⟩ .
    // At l9 ⟨p, object_l4 ⟩           // At l10 ⟨p, object_l5 ⟩ =>
    // => ⟨empty, ⟨a, object_l1 ⟩ ⟩.   // ⟨empty, ⟨a, object_l2 ⟩ ⟩.
    exit_node:                          exit_node:
  };                                  };

  public void test3( ) {              public void test4( ) {
    C q;                                C q;
    l6: q = new C;                      l7: q = new C;
    potpouri.example( q );              potpouri.example( q );
  };                                  };
};
```

B Auxiliary functions

// CPT stands for a conditional-points-to. DFE stands for a
// data-flow-element which could be a CPT or 'reachable'.

```
set of data-flow-elements apply( node, rDFE ) {
// this function computes the effect of the statement (if any) associated
// with node on rDFE, i.e. the resulting data-flow-elements at the bottom
// of node.
  set of data-flow-elements retVal = empty set;
  if ( node is a not an assignment node ) {
    add rDFE to retVal;
    return retVal;
  }

  if ( rDFE == reachable ) {
    add rDFE to retVal;
    if (node unconditionally generates a conditional-points-to) {
      // e.g. l: p = new A; unconditionally generates
      // ⟨empty, ⟨p, object_l⟩ ⟩.
      add this conditional-points-to to retVal;
    }
  }
  else {
    // rDFE is a conditional-points-to
    lhs_set = combine compatible CPTs in the solution set computed
      so far (including rDFE) to generate the set of locations
      represented by the left-hand-side.
    // Note: each element in lhs_set has a set of assumed
    // points-tos associated with it

    similarly compute rhs_set for the right-hand-side.

    retVal = combine compatible elements from lhs_set and rhs_set.
    // only one of the assumed points-tos associated with a
    // resulting points-to is chosen as its assumed points-to.

    if ( rDFE is not killed by this node )
      add rDFE to retVal;
  }
```

```
    return retVal;
} // end of apply
```

```
void add_to_table_of_conditions( rCPT, exit-node ) {
    // each exit-node has a table condTable associated with it,
    // which stores for each assumed points-to, the points-tos
    // which hold at the exit-node with this assumed points-to.
    // This function stores rCPT in this table. }
```

```
void add_to_table_of_assumed_points_tos(s, condition, C) {
// C is a call-node, condition is an assumed-points-to and s is a
// points-to passed to the entry-node of a method invoked from C.
// Each call-node has a table asPtTtable associated with it, which
// stores for each points-to that is passed to the entry-node of a
// method invoked from this site, the assumed-points-tos which
// imply this point-to at the call site. This function stores
// condition with s in this table. }
```

```
set of points-tos get_assumed_points_tos( C, s, M ) {
    if ( s is empty ) {
        if ( the solution set at C does not contain reachable )
            return empty set;
        else {
            if (C is a dynamically-dispatched-call site)
                return the set of assumed-points-tos for the values
                of receiver, which result in a call to method M;
            else
                return a set containing empty;
        }
    }
    else {
        return the assumed-points-tos stored with s in C.asPtTtable;
        // asPtTtable is defined in add_to_table_of_assumed_points_tos.
    }
}
```

```
set of points-tos lookup_table_of_conditions( condition, exit-node ) {
    // It returns the points-tos stored with condition in
    // exit-node.condTable, which is defined in add_to_table_of_conditions.
}
```

```
set of conditional-points-tos get_implied_conditional_points_tos( rCPT, M, C ) {
    // It returns conditional-points-tos implied by rCPT.points-to
    // at the entry-node of method M at call-node C. This means it also
    // performs actual to formal binding. Note that it may return
    // an empty set. }
```

```
void propagate_conditional_points_tos_with_empty_condition( C, M ) {
    if ( C is not a dynamically_dispatched_call site )
        S = { empty };
    else
        S = set of assumed-points-tos for the values
            of receiver, which result in a call to method M;

    Pts = lookup_table_of_conditions( empty, M.exit_node );
    for ( each s in S ) {
        for ( each pts in Pts ) {
            cpt = new conditional_points_to( s, pts );
            add_to_solution_and_worklist_if_needed( cpt, R );
            // R is the return-node of C
        }
    }
}
```

Synchronisation Analysis to Stop Tupling[*]

Wei-Ngan Chin[1], Siau-Cheng Khoo[1], and Tat-Wee Lee[2]

[1] National University of Singapore
[2] Singapore Police Academy

Abstract. Tupling transformation strategy can be used to merge loops together by combining recursive calls and also to eliminate redundant calls for a class of programs. In the latter case, this transformation can produce super-linear speedup. Existing works in deriving a safe and automatic tupling only apply to a very limited class of programs. In this paper, we present a novel parameter analysis, called *synchronisation analysis*, to solve the termination problem for tupling. With it, we can perform tupling on functions with multiple recursion *and* accumulative arguments without the risk of non-termination. This significantly widens the scope for tupling, and potentially enhances its usefulness. The analysis is shown to be of polynomial complexity; this makes tupling suitable as a compiler optimisation.

1 Introduction

Source-to-source transformation can achieve global optimisation through specialisation for recursive functions. Two well-known techniques are *partial evaluation* [9] and *deforestation* [20]. Both techniques have been extensively investigated [18,8] to discover automatic algorithms and supporting analyses that can ensure correct and terminating program optimisations.

Tupling is a lesser known but equally powerful transformation technique. The basic technique works by grouping calls with common arguments together, so that their multiple results can be computed simultaneously. When successfully applied, redundant calls can be eliminated, and multiple traversals of data structures combined.

As an example, consider the Tower of Hanoi function.

$$hanoi(0,a,b,c) = [];$$
$$hanoi(1+n,a,b,c) = hanoi(n,a,c,b) +\!\!+ [(a,b)] +\!\!+ hanoi(n,c,b,a);$$

Note that $+\!\!+$ denotes list catenation. The call $hanoi(n,a,b,c)$ returns a list of moves to transfer n discs from pole a to b, using c as a spare pole. The first parameter is a *recursion* parameter which strictly decreases, while the other three parameters are *permuting* parameters which are *bounded* in values. (A formal classification of parameters will be given later in Sec 2.) This definition contains *redundant calls*, which can be eliminated. By gathering each set of overlapping calls, which share common recursion arguments into a tupled function, the tupling method introduces:

[*] This work was done while Lee was a recipient of a NUS Graduate Scholarship.

$ht2(n,a,c,b)$ $= (hanoi(n,a,c,b), hanoi(n,c,b,a))$;
$ht3(n,a,b,c)$ $= (hanoi(n,a,b,c), hanoi(n,b,c,a), hanoi(n,c,a,b))$;

and transforms *hanoi* to the following :

$hanoi(1+n,a,b,c)$ $= let\ (u,v)=ht2(n,a,c,b)\ in\ u+\!\!+[(a,b)]+\!\!+v;$
$ht2(0,a,c,b)$ $= ([],[]);$
$ht2(1+n,a,c,b)$ $= let\ (u,v,w)=ht3(n,a,b,c)\ in\ (u+\!\!+[(a,c)]+\!\!+v,w+\!\!+[(c,b)]+\!\!+u)$;
$ht3(0,a,b,c)$ $= ([],[],[]);$
$ht3(1+n,a,b,c)$ $= let\ (u,v,w)=ht3(n,a,c,b)$
                    $in\ (u+\!\!+[(a,b)]+\!\!+v,w+\!\!+[(b,c)]+\!\!+u,\ v+\!\!+[(c,a)]+\!\!+w);$

Despite a significant loss in modularity and clarity, the resulting tupled function is *desirable* as their better performance can be mission critical. Sadly, manual and error-prone coding of such tupled functions are frequently practised by functional programmers. Though the benefits of tupling are clear, its wider adoption is presently hampered by the difficulties of ensuring that its transformation always terminates. This problem is crucial since it is possible for tupling to meet infinitely many different tuples of calls, which can cause infinite number of tuple functions to be introduced. Consider the knapsack definition below, where $W(i)$ and $V(i)$ return the weight and value of some i-th item.

$knap(0,w)$ $= 0$;
$knap(1+n,w)$ $= if\ w < W(1+n)\ then\ knap(n,w)$
                 $else\ max(knap(n,w),knap(n,w\text{-}W(1+n))+V(1+n))$;

Redundant calls exist but tupling fails to stop when it is performed on the above function. Specifically, tupling encounters the following growing tuples of calls.

1. $(knap(n,w),knap(n,w\text{-}W(1+n)))$
2. $(knap(n_1,w),knap(n_1,w\text{-}W(1+n_1)),knap(n_1,w\text{-}W(2+n_1)),$
   $knap(n_1,w\text{-}W(2+n_1)\text{-}W(1+n_1)))$
3. $(knap(n_2,w),knap(n_2,w\text{-}W(1+n_2)),knap(n_2,w\text{-}W(2+n_2)\text{-}W(1+n_2)),$
   $knap(n_2,w\text{-}W(2+n_2)),knap(n_2,w\text{-}W(3+n_2)),knap(n_2,w\text{-}W(3+n_2)\text{-}W(1+n_2)),$
   $knap(n_2,w\text{-}W(3+n_2)\text{-}W(2+n_2)),knap(n_2,w\text{-}W(3+n_2)\text{-}W(2+n_2)\text{-}W(1+n_2)))$
   $\vdots$

Why did tupling failed to stop in this case? It was because the calls of *knap* overlap, but their recursion parameter n did not *synchronise* with an accumulative parameter w.

To avoid the need for parameter synchronisation, previous proposals in [2,7] restrict tupling to only functions with a single recursion parameter, and without any accumulative parameters. However, this blanket restriction also rules out many useful functions with multiple recursion and/or accumulative parameters that could be tupled. Consider:

$repl(Leaf(n),xs)$ $= Leaf(head(xs));$
$repl(Node(l,r),xs)$ $= Node(repl(l,xs),repl(r,sdrop(l,xs)));$
$sdrop(Leaf(n),xs)$ $= tail(xs);$
$sdrop(Node(l,r),xs) = sdrop(r,sdrop(l,xs));$

Functions *repl* and *sdrop* are used to replace the contents of a tree by the items from another list, without any changes to the shape of the tree. Redundant *sdrop* calls exist, causing *repl* to have a time complexity of $O(n^2)$ where n is the size of the input tree. The two functions each has the first parameter being recursion and the second being accumulative. For the calls which overlap, the two parameters synchronise with each other (see Sec. 6 later). Hence, we can gather $repl(l,xs)$ and $sdrop(l,xs)$ to form the following function:

$$rstup(l,xs) \qquad = (repl(l,xs),sdrop(l,xs))$$

Applying tupling to $rstup$ yields the following $O(n)$ definition:

$$rstup(Leaf(n),xs) \quad = (Leaf(head(xs)),tail(xs)) ;$$
$$rstup(Node(l,r),xs) = let \{(u,v)=rstup(l,xs); (a,b)=rstup(r,v)\} in (Node(u,a),b) ;$$

This paper proposes a novel parameter analysis, called *synchronisation analysis*, to solve the termination problem for tupling. With it, we can considerably widen the scope of tupling by selectively handling functions with multiple recursion (and/or accumulative) parameters. If our analysis shows that the multiple parameters synchronises for a given function, we guarantee that tupling will stop when it is applied to the function. However, if our analysis shows possible non-synchronisation, we must skip tupling. (This failure may be used to suggest more advanced but expensive techniques, such as *vector-based* [3] or *list-based* [14] memoisations. These other techniques are complimentary to tupling since they may be more widely applicable but yield more expensive codes.) Lastly, we provide a costing for our analysis, and show that it can be practically implemented.

In Sec. 2, we lay the foundation for the discussion of tupling transformation and synchronisation analysis. Sec. 3 gives an overview of the tupling algorithm and the two obstacles towards terminating transformation. Sec. 4 provides a formal treatment of segments, which are used to determine synchronisation. In Sec. 5, we formulate prevention of indefinite unfolding via investigation of the behaviour of segment concatenation. In Sec. 6, we formally introduce synchronisation analysis, and state the conditions that ensure termination of tupling transformation. Sec. 7 describes related work, before a short conclusion in Sec. 8. Due to space constraint, we refer the reader to [4] for more in-depth discussion of related issues.

2 Language and Notations

We consider a strict first-order functional language.

Definition 1 (A Simple Language). A program in our simple language consists of sets of mutual-recursive functions:

P	$::= [M_i]_{i=0}^n$	(Program)
M	$::= [F_i]_{i=0}^n$	(Set of Mut. Rec. Fns)
F	$::= \{f(p_{i1},\ldots,p_{in}) = t_i\}_{i=0}^m$	(Set of Equations)
t	$::= v \mid C(t_1,\ldots,t_n) \mid f(t_1,\ldots,t_n)$	(Expression)
	$\mid if\ t_1\ then\ t_2\ else\ t_3 \mid let\ \{p_i = t_i\}_{i=0}^n\ in\ t$	
p	$::= v \mid C(p_1,\ldots,p_n)$	(Pattern)

We allow use of infix binary data construction in this paper. Moreover, we shall construct any Peano integer as a data constructed from 0 and $1+n$. Applying the constructor, $(1+)$, k times to a variable m will be abbreviated as $k+m$.

For clarity, we adopt the following multi-holes context notation :

Definition 2 (Multi-holes Context Notation). The RHS of an equation of a function f can be expressed as $E_f[t_1,\ldots,t_n]$ where $t_1, \ldots, t_n$ are sub-expressions occurring in the RHS. □

Safety of tupling transformation relies on the ability to determine systematic change in the arguments of successive function calls. Such systematic change can be described with appropriate operators, as defined below:

Definition 3 (Argument Operators).

1. Each data constructor C of arity n in the language is associated with n *descend operators*, which are data destructors. Notation-wise, let $C(t_1,\ldots,t_n)$ be a data structure, then any of its corresponding data destructors is denoted by C^{-i}, and defined as $C^{-i} C(t_1,\ldots,t_n) = t_i$.
2. For each constant (i.e. variable-free constructor subterm), denoted by c in our program, a *constant operator* $\underline{c}$ always return that constant upon application.
3. An *identity*, id, is the unit under function composition.
4. For any n-tuple argument $(a_1,\ldots,a_n)$, the ith *selector*, $\sharp_i$, is defined as $\sharp_i$ $(a_1,\ldots, a_n) = a_i$.
5. An *accumulative operator* is any operator that is not defined above. For instance, a data constructor, such as C described in item 1 above, is an accumulative operator; and so is the tuple constructor $(op_1,\ldots,op_n)$. □

Composition of operators is defined by $(f \circ g)\, x = f\, (g\, x)$. A composition of argument operators forms an *operation path*, denoted by op. It describes how an argument is changed from a caller to a callee through call unfolding. This can be determined by examining the relationship between the parameters and the call arguments appearing in the RHS of the equation. For instance, consider the equation $g(x) = E_g[g(C(x,2))]$. $C(x,2)$ in the RHS can be constructed from parameter x via the operation path : $C \circ (id, \underline{2})$.

Changes in an n-tuple argument can be described by an n-tuple of operation paths, called a *segment*, and denoted by $(op_1,\ldots,op_n)$. For convenience, we overload the notion id to represent an identity operation as well as a segment containing tuple of identity operation paths.

Segments can be used in a function graph to show how the function arguments are transformed:

Definition 4 (Labelled Call Graph). The *labelled call graph* of a set of mutual-recursive functions F, denoted as (N_F, E_F), is a graph whereby each function name from F is a node in N_F; and each caller-callee transition is represented by an arrow in E_F, labelled with the segment information. □

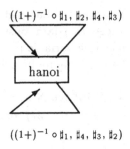

$$((1+)^{-1} \circ \natural_1, \natural_2, \natural_4, \natural_3)$$

hanoi

$$((1+)^{-1} \circ \natural_1, \natural_4, \natural_3, \natural_2)$$

Fig. 1. Labelled Call Graph of *Hanoi* defined in Sec. 1.

We use segments to characterise function parameters. The characterisation stems from the way the parameters are changed across labelled call graph of mutually recursive functions.

Definition 5 (Characterising Parameters/Arguments). Given an equation of the form $f(p_1,\ldots,p_n) = t$,

1. A group of f's parameters are said to be *bounded parameters* if their corresponding arguments in each recursive call in t are derived via either constants, identity, or application of selectors to this group of parameters.
2. The ith parameter of f is said to be a *recursion parameter* if it is not bounded and the ith argument of each recursive call in t is derived by applying a series of either descend operators or identity to the ith parameter.
3. Otherwise, the f's parameter is said to be an *accumulative parameter*. □

Correspondingly, an argument to a function call is called a *recursion/accumulative argument* if it is located at the position of a recursion/accumulative parameter.

We can partition a segment according to the kinds of parameters it has:

Definition 6 (Projections of Segments). Given a segment, s, characterising the parameters of an equation, we write $\pi_R(s)/\pi_A(s)/\pi_B(s)$ to denote the (sub-)tuple of s, including only those operation paths which characterise the recursion/accumulative/bounded parameters. The sub-tuple preserves the original ordering of the operation paths in the segment.

Furthermore, we write $\overline{\pi_B}(s)$ to denote the sub-tuple of s excluding $\pi_B(s)$. □

As examples, the first parameter of function *hanoi* is a recursion parameter, whereas its other parameters are bounded. In the case of functions *repl* and *sdrop* (defined in Sec. 1 too), both their first parameters are recursion parameters, and their second parameters are accumulative.

Our analysis of segments requires us to place certain restrictions on the parameters and its relationship with the arguments. This is described as follows:

Definition 7 (Restrictions on Parameters).

1. Each set of mutual-recursive functions (incl. recursive auxiliary functions), M, has the same number of recursion/accumulative parameters but can have an arbitrary number of bounded parameters.
2. Given an equation from M, the ith recursion/accumulative argument of any recursive call in the RHS is constructed from the ith parameter of the equation. □

The second restriction above enables us to omit the selector operation from the operation paths derived for recursion/accumulative parameters. Though restrictive, these requirements can be selectively lifted by pre-processing transformation and/or improved analysis. Due to space constraint, the details are described in a companion technical report [4].

3 Tupling Algorithm

Redundant calls may arise during executing of a function f when two (or more) calls in f's RHS have overlapping recursion arguments. We define the notion of overlapping below:

Definition 8 (Call Overlapping).

1. Two recursion arguments are said to *overlap* each other if they share some common variables.
2. Two accumulative arguments are said to *overlap* each other if one is a substructure of the other.
3. Two calls *overlap* if all its corresponding recursion and accumulative arguments overlap. Otherwise, they are *disjoint*. □

For example, if two functions $f1$ and $f2$ have only recursion arguments, then $f1(C_1(x_1,x_2), C_2(x_4,C_1(x_5,x_6)))$ and $f2(C_2(x_2,x_3), C_2(x_5,x_7))$ have overlapping recursion arguments, whereas $f1(C_1(x_1,x_2), C_2(x_4,C_1(x_5,x_6)))$ and $f2(x_2,x_7)$ are disjoint.

If two calls overlap, the call graphs initiated from them may overlap, and thus contain redundancy. Hence, it is useful, during tupling transformation, to gather the overlapping calls into a common function body with the hope that redundant calls (if any) will eventually be detected and eliminated (via abstraction). Once these redundant calls have been eliminated, what's left behind in the RHS will be disjoint calls.

Applying tupling on a function thus attempts to transform the function into one in which every pair of calls in the new RHS are disjoint. Fig. 2 gives an operational description of the tupling algorithm.[1]

There are two types of unfolds in the tupling algorithm: In Step 4.2, calls are *unfolded without instantiation*; ie., a call is unfolded only when all its arguments matches the LHS of an equation. On the other hand, in Step 4.4.2.2, a call is selected and forced to unfold. This henceforth requires instantiation. Among the

---

[1] Please refer to [10] for detail presentation.

1. Decide a set of recursive function calls to tuple, C.
2. Let E contains a set of equations (with C calls in their RHS) to transform.
3. Let D be empty. (D will be the set of tuple definitions.)
4. While E is not empty,
4.1. Remove an equation, say $f(p_1, \ldots, p_n) = t$, from E.
4.2. Modify $t \Rightarrow t_1$ by repeatedly *unfolding without instantiation* each function call to C in t.
4.3. Gather each subset of overlapping C calls, s_i, and perform the following *tuples abstraction steps*:
4.3.1.   For each tuple s_i, abstract the common substructure, $t_{i,j}$, occurring in the accumulative arguments of all calls in s_i, and modify
$$s_i \Rightarrow let \ \{v_{i,j} = t_{i,j}\}_{j=1}^{k_i} \ in \ s_i'.$$
4.3.2.   Modify $t_1 \Rightarrow let \ \bigcup_{i=1}^{m} \{v_{i,j} = t_{i,j}\}_{j=1}^{k_i} \ in \ let \ \{(v_{i,1}, \ldots, v_{i,n_i}) = s_i'\}_{i=1}^{m} \ in \ t_2.$
4.4. For each tuple s_i' from $\{s_i'\}_{i=1}^{m}$, we transform to s_i'' as follows :
Let $\{v_1, \ldots, v_n\} = Vars(s_i')$ where $Vars(e)$ returns free variables of e
4.4.1.   If s_i' has ≤ 1 function call, then $s_i'' = s_i'$. (No action taken.)
4.4.2.   If there is no tuple definition for s_i' in D, then
4.4.2.1.   Add a new definition, $g(v_1, \ldots, v_n) = s_i'$ to D.
4.4.2.2.   Instantiate g by *unfolding (with instantiation)* a call in s_i' that has maximal recursion argument. This introduces several new equations for g, which are then added to E.
4.4.2.3.   Set $s_i'' = g(v_1, \ldots, v_n)$.
4.4.3.   Otherwise, a tuple definition, of name say h, matching s_i' is found in D.
4.4.3.1.   *Fold* s_i' against definition of h to yield a call to h, by setting
$$s_i'' = h(v_1, \ldots, v_n).$$
4.5. Output a transformed equation
$$f(p_1, \ldots, p_n) = let \ \bigcup_{i=1}^{m} \{v_{i,j} = t_{i,j}\}_{j=1}^{k_i} \ in \ let \ \{(v_{i,1}, \ldots, v_{i,n_i}) = s_i''\}_{i=1}^{m} \ in \ t_2.$$
5. Halt.

Fig. 2. Tupling Algorithm, $\mathcal{T}$

calls available, we choose to unfold a call having *maximal recursion* arguments; that is, the recursion arguments, treated as a tree-like data structure, is deepest in depth among the calls.

Although effective in eliminating redundant calls, execution of algorithm $\mathcal{T}$ may not terminate in general due to one of the following reasons: (1) Step 4.2 may unfold calls indefinitely; (2) Step 4.4.2 may introduce infinitely many new tuple definitions as tupling encounters infinitely many different tuples.

We address these two termination issues in Sec. 5 and Sec. 6 respectively. But first, we give a formal treatment of algebra of segments.

4   Algebra of Segments

A set of segments forms an algebra under concatenation operation.

Definition 9 (Concatenation of Operation Paths). Concatenation of two operation paths *op1* and *op2*, denoted by *op1 ; op2*, is defined as *op2 ∘ op1*. □

Definition 10 (Concatenation of Segments). Concatenation of two segments *s1* and *s2*, denoted by *s1;s2*, is defined componentwise as follows:

$$s1 = (op_1,...,op_n) \ \& \ s2 = (op'_1,...,op'_n) \Rightarrow s1 ; s2 = (op_1;op'_1,...,op_n;op'_n). \quad □$$

A concatenated segment can be expressed more compactly by applying the following reduction rules:

1. For any operator *O*, *id ∘ O* reduces to *O*, and *O ∘ id* reduces to *O*.
2. ∀ *O1, ..., On* and *O*, *(O1 ∘ O, ..., On ∘ O)* reduces to *(O1,..., On) ∘ O*.

Applying the above reduction rules to a segment yields a *compacted segment*. Henceforth, we deal with compacted segments, unless we state otherwise.

Lastly, concatenating a segment, *s*, *n* times is expressed as s^n. Such repetition of segment leads to the notion of factors of a segment, as described below:

Definition 11 (Factorisation of Segments). Given segments *s* and *f*. *f* is said to be a *factor* of *s* if (1) *f* is a substring of *s*, and (2) $\exists n > 0. \ s = f^n$. We call *n* the *power* of *s* wrt *f*. □

For example, (C^{-2}, id) is a factor of $(C^{-2} \circ C^{-2} \circ C^{-2}, id)$, since $(C^{-2}, id)^3 = (C^{-2} \circ C^{-2} \circ C^{-2}, id)$. It is trivial to see that every segment has at least one factor – itself. However, when a segment has *exactly one* factor, it is called a *prime segment*. An example of prime segment is $(C_1^{-1} \circ C_2^{-1}, id)$.

Lemma 12 (Uniqueness of Prime Factorisation[10]). *Let s be a compacted segment, there exists a* unique *prime segment f such that* $s = f^k$ *for some k>0.*
□

5 Preventing Indefinite Unfolding

We now provide a simple condition that prevents tupling transformation from admitting indefinite unfolding at Step 4.2. This condition has been presented in [2]. Here we rephrase it using segment notation, and extend it to cover multiple recursion arguments.

We first define a *simple cycle* as a simple loop (with no repeating node, except the first one) in a labelled call graph. The set of segments corresponding to the simple cycles in a labelled call graph *(N,E)* is denoted as *SCycle(N,E)*. This can be computed in time of complexity $O(|N||E|^2)$ [10].

Theorem 13 (Preventing Indefinite Unfolding). *Let F be a set of mutual-recursive functions, each of which has non-zero number of recursion parameters. If* ∀ *s* ∈ *SCycle(N_F,E_F), $\pi_R(s) \neq (id,...,id)$, then given a call to f* ∈ *F with arguments of finite size, there exists a number N>0 such that the call can be successively unfolded (without instantiation) not more than N times.* □

6 Synchronisation Analysis

We now present analysis that prevents tupling from generating infinitely many new tuple functions at Step 4.4.2. The idea is to ensure the finiteness of syntactically different (modulo variable renaming) tupled calls. As a group of bounded arguments is obtained from itself by the application of either selectors, identity or constants operators, it can only have finitely many different structures. Consequently, bounded arguments do not cause tupling transformation to loop infinitely. Hence, we focus on determining the structure of recursion and accumulative arguments in this section. Specifically, *we assume non-existence of bounded arguments in our treatment of segments.*

Since syntactic changes to call arguments are captured by series of segments, differences in call arguments can be characterised by the relationship between the corresponding segments. We discuss below a set of relationships between segments.

Definition 14 (Levels of Synchronisation). Two segments s_1 and s_2 are said to be :

1. *level-1 synchronised*, denoted by $s_1 \simeq_1 s_2$, if $\exists s_1', s_2'.(s_1; s_1' = s_2; s_2')$. Otherwise, they are said to be *level-0 synchronised*, or simply, *unsynchronised*.
2. *level-2 synchronised* $(s_1 \simeq_2 s_2)$ if $\exists s_1', s_2'.((s_1; s_1' = s_2; s_2') \wedge (s_1' = id \vee s_2' = id))$.
3. *level-3 synchronised* $(s_1 \simeq_3 s_2)$ if $\exists s.\exists n, m > 0.(s_1 = s^n \wedge s_2 = s^m)$.
4. *level-4 synchronised* $(s_1 \simeq_4 s_2)$ if $s_1 = s_2$.   □

Levels 1 to 4 of synchronisation form a strict hierarchy, with synchronisation at level i implying synchronisation at level j if $i > j$. Together with level-0, these can help identify the termination property of tupling transformation.

Why does synchronisation play an important role in the termination of tupling transformation? Intuitively, if two sequences of segments synchronise, then calls following these two sequences will have finite variants of argument structures. This thus enables folding (in Step 4.4.3) to take effect, and eventually terminates the transformation.

In this section, we provide an informal account of some of the interesting findings pertaining to tupling termination, as implied by the different levels of synchronisation.

Finding 1. *Transforming two calls with identical arguments but following level-0 synchronised segments will end up with disjoint arguments.*[2]

Example 15. Consider the following two equations for functions $g1$ and $g2$ respectively:

---
[2] Sometimes, two apparently level-0 synchronised may turn into synchronisation of other levels when they are prefixed with some initial segment. Initial segments may be introduced by the argument structures of the two initially overlapping calls. Such hidden synchronisation can be detected by extending the current technique to handle "rotate/shift synchronisation" [5].

$$g1(C_1(x_1,x_2),C_2(y_1,y_2)) \quad = E_{g1}[g1(x_1,y_1)] \;;$$
$$g2(C_1(x_1,x_2),C_2(y_1,y_2)) \quad = E_{g2}[g2(x_1,y_2)] \;;$$

The segment leading to call $g1(x_1,y_1)$ is (C_1^{-1},C_2^{-1}), whereas that leading to call $g2(x_1,y_2)$ is (C_1^{-1},C_2^{-2}). These two segments are level-0 synchronised. Suppose that we have an expression containing two calls, to $g1(u,v)$ and $g2(u,v)$ respectively, with identical arguments. Tupling-transform these two calls causes the definition of a tuple function:

$$g\_tup(u,v) = (\; g1(u,v),\; g2(u,v)\;) \;;$$

which will then transform (through instantiation) to the following:

$$g\_tup(C_1(u_1,u_2),C_2(v_1,v_2)) = (E_{g1}[g1(u_1,v_1)],E_{g2}[g2(u_1,v_2)]) \;;$$

As the arguments of the two calls in the RHS above are now disjoint, tupling terminates. However, the effect of tupling is simply an unfolding of the calls. Thus, it is safe[3] but not productive to transform two calls with identical arguments if these calls follow segments that are level-0 synchronised. □

Finding 2. *Applying tupling transformation on calls that follow level-2 synchronised segments may not terminate.*

Example 16. Consider the binomial function, as defined below:

$$bin(0,k) \qquad = 1 \;;$$
$$bin(1+n,0) \qquad = 1 \;;$$
$$bin(1+n,1+k) = if\ k{\geq}n\ then\ 1\ else\ bin(n,k)+bin(n,1+k) \;;$$

Redundant call exists in executing the two overlapping calls $bin(n,k)$ and $bin(n,1+k)$. Notice that the segments leading to these calls $(((1+)^{-1},(1+)^{-1}\ )$ and $((1+)^{-1},id\ ))$ are level-2 synchronised. Performing tupling transformation on $(bin(n,k),bin(n,1+k))$ will keep generating new set of overlapping calls at Step 4.4.2.2, as shown below:

1. $(bin(n,k),bin(n,1+k))$
2. $(bin(1+n_1,k),bin(n_1,k),bin(n_1,1+k))$
3. $(bin(n_1,k_1),bin(n_1,1+k_1),bin(n_1,2+k_1))$
4. $(bin(1+n_2,k_1),bin(n_2,k_1),bin(n_2,1+k_1),bin(n_2,2+k_1))$

$$\vdots$$

Hence, tupling transformation fails to terminate. □

Non-termination of transforming functions such as *bin* can be predicted from the (non-)synchronisability of its two segments — Given two sequences of segments, $s_1 = ((1+)^{-1},\ (1+)^{-1}\ )$ and $s_2 = ((1+)^{-1},\ id\ )$. If these two sequences are constructed using only s_1 and s_2 respectively, then it is impossible for the two sequences to be identical (though they overlap).

However, if two segments are level-3 synchronised, then it is always possible to build from these two segments, two sequences that are identical; thanks to the following Prop. 17(a) about level-3 synchronisation.

---

[3] with respect to termination of tupling transformation.

Property 17 (Properties of Level-3 Synchronisation).

(a) Let f_1, f_2 be prime factors of s_1 and s_2 respectively, then $s_1 \simeq_3 s_2 \Rightarrow f_1 = f_2$.

(b) Level-3 synchronisation is an *equivalence* relation over segments (*ie.*, it is reflexive, symmetric, and transitive). □

This, thus, provides an opportunity for termination of tupling transformation. Indeed, the following theorem highlights such an opportunity.

Theorem 18 (Termination Induced by Level-3 Synchronisation). *Let F be a set of mutual-recursive functions with S being the set of segments corresponding to the edges in (N_F, E_F). Let C be an initial set of overlapping F-calls to be tupled. If*

1. $\forall s \in SCycle(N_F, E_F)$. $\pi_R(s) \neq (id, \ldots, id)$,

2. $\forall s_1, s_2 \in S$. $\overline{\pi_B}(s_1) \simeq_3 \overline{\pi_B}(s_2)$.

then performing tupling transformation on C terminates. □

The notion $\overline{\pi_B}(s)$ was defined in Defn. 6. The first condition in Theorem 18 prevents infinite number of unfolding, whereas the level-3 synchronisation condition ensures that the number of different tuples generated during transformation is finite. The proof is available in [4].

Example 19. Consider the equation of f defined below:

$f(2+n,4+m,y) = E_f[f(1+n,2+m,C(y)),f(n,m,C(C(y)))]$;

Although the recursion arguments in $f(1+n,2+m,C(y))$ and $f(n,m,C(C(y)))$ are consumed at different rate, the argument consumption (and accumulating) patterns for both calls are level-3 synchronised. Subjecting the calls to tupling transformation yields the following result:

$f(2+n,4+m,y)$ $= $ let $\{y1 = C(y)\}$ in let $\{(u,v) = f\_tup(n,m,y1)\}$ in $E_f[u,v]$;

$f_tup(1+n,2+m,y) = $ let $\{y2 = C(y)\}$ in let $\{(u,v) = f\_tup(n,m,y2)\}$ in $(E_f[u,v],u)$; □

Finally, since level-4 synchronisation implies level-3 synchronisation, *Theorem 18 applies to segments of level-4 synchronisation as well.*

In situation where segments are not all level-3 synchronised with one another, we describe here a sufficient condition which guarantees termination of tupling transformation. To begin with, we observe from Prop. 17(b) above that we can partition the set of segments S into disjoint *level-3 sets* of segments. Let $\Pi_S = \{ [s_1], \ldots, [s_k] \}$ be such a partition. By Prop. 17(a), all segments in a level-3 set $[s_i]$ share a unique prime factor, f_i say, such that all segments in $[s_i]$ can be expressed as $\{f_i^{p_1}, \ldots, f_i^{p_{ni}}\}$. We then define $HCF([s_i]) = f_i^{gcd(p_1, \ldots, p_{ni})}$, where *gcd* computes the greatest common divisor. $HCF([s_i])$ is thus the *highest common factor* of the level-3 set $[s_i]$.

Definition 20 (Set of Highest Common Factors). Let S be a set of segment. The *set of highest common factors* of S, $HCFSet(S)$, is defined as

$HCFSet(S) = \{\ HCF([s_i])\ |\ [s_i] \in \Pi_S\ \}.$

The following theorem states a sufficient condition for preventing infinite definition during tupling transformation[4]

Theorem 21 (Preventing Infinite Definition). *Let F be a set of mutual-recursive functions. Let S be the set of segments corresponding to the edges in (N_F, E_F). Let C be a set of overlapping calls occurring in the RHS of an equation in F. If $\forall\ s_1,\ s_2 \in HCFSet(S)\ .\ \overline{\pi_B}(s_1) \simeq_0 \overline{\pi_B}(s_2)$, then performing tupling transformation on C will generate a finite number of different tuples.* □

A proof of the theorem is available in [10, 4].

A note on the complexity of this analysis: We notice from Theorem 21 that the main task of synchronisation analysis is to determine that all segments in $HCFSet(S)$ are level-0 synchronised. This involves expressing each segment in S as its prime factorisation, partitioning S under level-3 synchronisation, computing the highest common factors for each partition, and lastly, determining if $HCFSet(S)$ is level-0 synchronised. Conservatively, the complexity of synchronisation analysis is *polynomial* wrt the number of segments in S and the maximum length of these segments.

Theorem 22 summarises the results of Theorem 13 and Theorem 21.

Theorem 22 (Termination of Tupling Transformation). *Let F be a set of mutual-recursive functions, each of which has non-zero number of recursion parameters. Let S be the set of segments correspond to the edges in (N_F, E_F). Let C a set of overlapping calls occurring in the RHS of an equation in F. If*

1. *$\forall\ s \in SCycle(N_F, E_F)\ .\ \pi_R(s) \neq (id,\ldots,id)$, and*
2. *$\forall\ s_1,\ s_2 \in HCFSet(S)\ .\ \overline{\pi_B}(s_1) \simeq_0 \overline{\pi_B}(s_2)$,*

then performing tupling transformation on C will terminate. □

7 Related Work

One of the earliest mechanisms for avoiding redundant calls is memo-functions [13]. Memo-functions are special functions which remember/store some or all of their previously computed function calls in a memo-table, so that re-occurring calls can have their results retrieved from the memo-table rather than re-computed. Though general (with no analysis required), memo-functions are less practical since they rely on expensive run-time mechanisms.

---

[4] It is possible to extend Theorem 21 further by relaxing its premises. In particular, we can show the prevention of infinite definition in the presence of segments that are level-2 synchronisation, provided such segment can be broken down into two sub-segment, of which one is level-3 synchronised with some of the existing segments, and the other is level-0 synchronised [10].

Other transformation techniques (e.g. tupling and tabulation) may result in more efficient programs but they usually require program analyses and may be restricted to sub-classes of programs. By focusing on a restricted bi-linear self-recursive functions, Cohen [6] identified some algebraic properties, such as *periodic commutative, common generator*, and *explicit* descent relationships, to help predict redundancy patterns and corresponding tabulation schemes. Unfortunately, this approach is rather limited since the functions considered are restricted. In addition, the algebraic properties are difficult to detect, and yet limited in scope. (For example, the Tower-of-Hanoi function does not satisfy any of Cohen's algebraic properties, but can still be tupled by our method.)

Another approach is to perform *direct* search of the DG. Pettorossi [16] gave an informal heuristic to search the DG (dependency graph of calls) for eureka tuples. Later, Proietti & Pettorossi [17] proposed an Elimination Procedure, which combines fusion and tupling, to eliminate unnecessary intermediate variables from logic programs. To ensure termination, they only handled functions with a single recursion parameter, while the accumulative parameters are generalised whenever possible. No attempt is made to analyse the synchronizability of multiple recursion/accumulating parameters.

With the aim of deriving incremental programs, Liu and Teitelbaum [12,11] presented a three-stage method to cache, incrementalize and prune user programs. The *caching* stage gathers all intermediate and auxiliary results which might be needed to *incrementalize*, while *pruning* removes unneeded results. While their method may be quite general, its power depends largely on the incrementalize stage, which often requires heuristics and deep intuitions. No guarantee on *termination*, and the *scope* of this difficult stage is presently offered.

Ensuring termination of transformers has been a central concern for many automatic transformation techniques. Though the problem of determining termination is in general undecidable, a variety of analyses can be applied to give meaningful results. In the case of deforestation, the proposals range from simple *pure treeless* syntactic form [20], to a sophisticated constraint-based analysis [18][5] to stop the transformation. Likewise, earlier tupling work [2,7] were based simply on restricted functions. In [2], the transformable functions can only have a single recursion parameter each, while accumulative parameters are forbidden. Similarly, in the calculational approach of [7], the allowed functions can only have a single recursion parameter each, while the other parameters are lambda abstracted, as per [15]. When lambda abstractions are being tupled, they yield effective elimination of multiple traversals, but *not* effective elimination of redundant function-type calls. For example, if functions *sdrop* and *repl* are lambda-abstracted prior to tupling, then redundant calls will not be properly eliminated.

By engaging a more powerful synchronisation analysis for multiple parameters, we have managed to extend considerably the class of functions which could be tupled safely. Some initial ideas of our synchronisation analysis can be found in [5]. The earlier work is informal and incomplete since it did not cover *accumu-*

---

[5] from which the title of this paper was inspired

lative parameters. The present proposal is believed to be comprehensive enough to be practical.

8 Conclusion

There is little doubt that tupled functions are extremely useful. Apart from the elimination of redundant calls and multiple traversals, tupled function are often *linear* with respect to the common arguments (i.e. each now occurs only once in the RHS of the equation). This linearity property has a number of advantages, including:

- It can help avoid *space leaks* that are due to unsynchronised multiple traversals of large data structures, via a compilation technique described in [19].
- It can facilitate deforestation (and other transformations) that impose a *linearity* restriction [20], often for efficiency and/or termination reasons.
- It can improve opportunity for *uniqueness typing* [1], which is good for storage overwriting and other optimisations.

Because of these nice performance attributes, functional programmers often go out of their way to write such tupled functions, despite them being more awkward, error-prone and harder to write and read.

In this paper, we have shown the effectiveness and safeness of tupling transformation, when coupled with synchronisation analyses. Furthermore, not only do we generalise the analyses from handling of single recursion argument to that of multiple recursion arguments, we also bring together both recursion and accumulative arguments under one framework for analysis. These have considerably widened the scope of functions admissible for safe tupling. Consequently, the tupling algorithm $\mathcal{T}$ and associated synchronisation analysis could now be used to improve run-time performance, whilst preserving the clarity/modularity of programs.

Acknowledgments We thank the annonymous referees for their valuable comments and Peter Thiemann for his contribution to earlier work.

References

1. E. Barendsen and J.E.W. Smetsers. Conventional and uniqueness typing in graph rewrite systems. In *13th Conference on the Foundations of Software Technology & Theoretical Computer Science*, pages 45–51, Bombay, India, December 1993.
2. Wei-Ngan Chin. Towards an automated tupling strategy. In *ACM SIGPLAN Symposium on Partial Evaluation and Semantics-Based Program Manipulation*, pages 119–132, Copenhagen, Denmark, June 1993. ACM Press.
3. Wei-Ngan Chin and Masami Hagiya. A bounds inference method for vector-based memoisation. In *2nd ACM SIGPLAN Intl. Conference on Functional Programming*, pages 176–187, Amsterdam, Holland, June 1997. ACM Press.

4. W.N. Chin, S.C. Khoo, and T.W. Lee. Synchronisation analysis to stop tupling – extended abstract. Technical report, Dept of IS/CS, NUS, Dec 1997. http://www.iscs.nus.sg/~khoosc/paper/synTech.ps.gz.

5. W.N. Chin, S.C. Khoo, and P. Thiemann. Synchronisation analyses for multiple recursion parameters. In *Intl Dagstuhl Seminar on Partial Evaluation (LNCS 1110)*, pages 33–53, Germany, February 1996.

6. Norman H. Cohen. Eliminating redundant recursive calls. *ACM Trans. on Programming Languages and Systems*, 5(3):265–299, July 1983.

7. Z. Hu, H. Iwasaki, M. Takeichi, and A. Takano. Tupling calculation eliminates multiple traversals. In *2nd ACM SIGPLAN International Conference on Functional Programming*, pages 164–175, Amsterdam, Netherlands, June 1997. ACM Press.

8. N.D. Jones, C.K. Gomard, and P. Sestoft. *Partial Evaluation and Automatic Program Generation*. Prentice Hall, 1993.

9. N.D. Jones, P. Sestoft, and H. Sondergaard. An experiment in partial evaluation: the generation of a compiler generator. *Journal of LISP and Symbolic Computation*, 2(1):9–50, 1989.

10. Tat Wee Lee. Synchronisation analysis for tupling. Master's thesis, DISCS, National University of Singapore, 1997. http://www.iscs.nus.sg/~khoosc/paper/ltw_thesis.ps.gz.

11. Y A. Liu, S D. Stoller, and T. Teitelbaum. Discovering auxiliary information for incremental computation. In *23rd ACM Symposium Principles of Programming Languages*, pages 157–170, St. Petersburg, Florida, January 1996. ACM Press.

12. Y A. Liu and T. Teitelbaum. Caching intermediate results for program improvement. In *ACM SIGPLAN Symposium on Partial Evaluation and Semantics-Based Program Manipulation*, pages 190–201, La Jolla, California, June 1995. ACM Press.

13. Donald Michie. Memo functions and machine learning. *Nature*, 218:19–22, April 1968.

14. A. Pettorossi and M. Proietti. Program derivation via list introduction. In *IFIP TC 2 Working Conf. on Algorithmic Languages and Calculi*, Le Bischenberg, France, February 1997. Chapman & Hall.

15. A. Pettorossi and A. Skowron. Higher order generalization in program derivation. In *TAPSOFT 87*, Pisa, Italy, (LNCS, vol 250, pp. 306–325), March 1987.

16. Alberto Pettorossi. A powerful strategy for deriving programs by transformation. In *3rd ACM LISP and Functional Programming Conference*, pages 273–281. ACM Press, 1984.

17. M. Proietti and A. Pettorossi. Unfolding - definition - folding, in this order for avoiding unnecessary variables in logic programs. In *Proceedings of PLILP*, Passau, Germany, (LNCS, vol 528, pp. 347–258) Berlin Heidelberg New York: Springer, 1991.

18. H. Seidl and M.H. Sørensen. Constraints to stop higher-order deforestation. In *24th ACM Symposium on Principles of Programming Languages*, Paris, France, January 1997. ACM Press.

19. Jan Sparud. How to avoid space-leak without a garbage collector. In *ACM Conference on Functional Programming and Computer Architecture*, pages 117–122, Copenhagen, Denmark, June 1993. ACM Press.

20. Phil Wadler. Deforestation: Transforming programs to eliminate trees. In *European Symposium on Programming*, Nancy, France, (LNCS, vol 300, pp. 344–358), March 1988.

Propagating Differences:
An Efficient New Fixpoint Algorithm
for Distributive Constraint Systems

Christian Fecht[1] and Helmut Seidl[2]

[1] Universität des Saarlandes, Postfach 151150, D-66041 Saarbrücken, Germany,
fecht@cs.uni-sb.de
[2] Fachbereich IV – Informatik, Universität Trier, D-54286 Trier, Germany,
seidl@psi.uni-trier.de

Abstract. Integrating *semi-naive* fixpoint iteration from deductive data bases [3, 2, 4] as well as continuations into worklist-based solvers, we derive a new application independent local fixpoint algorithm for distributive constraint systems. Seemingly different efficient algorithms for abstract interpretation like those for linear constant propagation for imperative languages [17] as well as for control-flow analysis for functional languages [13] turn out to be instances of our scheme. Besides this systematizing contribution we also derive a new efficient algorithm for abstract OLDT-resolution as considered in [15, 16, 25] for Prolog.

1 Introduction

Efficient application independent local solvers for general classes of constraint systems have been successfully used in program analyzers like GAIA [9, 6], PLAIA [20] or GENA [10, 11] for Prolog and PAG [1] for imperative languages. The advantages of application independence are obvious: the algorithmic ideas can be pointed out more clearly and are not superseded by application specific aspects. Correctness can therefore be proven more easily. Once proven correct, the solver then can be instantiated to different application domains – thus allowing for reusable implementations. For the overall correctness of every such application it simply remains to check whether or not the constraint system correctly models the problem to be analyzed. Reasoning about the solution process itself can be totally abandoned.

In [12], we considered systems of equations of the form $x = f_x$ (x a variable) and tried to minimize the number of evaluations of right-hand sides f_x during the solution process. Accordingly, we viewed these as (almost) atomic actions. In practical applications, however, like the abstract interpretation of Prolog programs, right-hand sides represent complicated functions. In this paper, we therefore try to minimize not just the number of evaluations but the overall work on right-hand sides. Clearly, improvements in this direction can no longer abstract completely from algorithms implementing right-hand sides. Nonetheless, we aim at optimizations in an as application independent setting as possible.

We start by observing that right-hand sides f_x of defining equations $x = f_x$ often are of the form $f_x \equiv t_1 \sqcup \ldots \sqcup t_k$ where the t_i represent independent contributions to the value of x. We take care of that by considering now systems of *constraints* of the form $x \sqsupseteq t$. Having adapted standard worklist-based equation solvers to such constraint systems, we investigate the impact of two further optimizations. First, we try to avoid identical subcomputations which would contribute nothing new to the next iteration. Thus, whenever a variable y accessed during the last evaluation of right-hand side t has changed it's value, we try to avoid reevaluation of t as a whole. Instead, we resume evaluation just with the access to y.

To do this in a clean way, we adapt the model of (generalized) *computation trees*. We argue that many common expression languages for right-hand sides can easily and automatically be translated into this model. This model has the advantage to make *continuations*, i.e., remaining parts of computations after returns from variable look-ups, explicit. So far, continuations have not been used in connection with worklist-based solver algorithms. Only for *topdown*-solver **TD** of Le Charlier and Van Hentenryck [5, 12] a related technique has been suggested and practically applied to the analysis of Prolog, by Englebert et al. in [9].

In case, however, computation on larger values is much more expensive than on smaller ones, continuation based worklist solvers can be further improved by calling continuations not with the *complete* new value of the modified variable but just its *increment*. This concept clearly is an instance of the very old idea of optimization through *reduction in strength* as considered, e.g., by Paige [22]. A similar idea has been considered for recursive query evaluation in deductive databases to avoid computing the same tuples again and again [3, 4]. *Semi-naive* iteration, therefore, propagates just those tuples to the respective next iteration which have been newly encountered. Originally, this optimization has been considered for rules of the form $x \supseteq f\,y$ where x and y are mutually recursive relations and unary operator f is distributive, i.e., $f\,(s_1 \cup s_2) = f\,s_1 \cup f\,s_2$. An extension to n-ary f is contained in [2]. A general combination, however, of this principle with continuations and local worklist solvers seems to be new. To make the combination work, we need an operator diff which when applied to abstract values d_1 and d_2 determines the necessary part from $d_1 \sqcup d_2$ given d_1 for which reevaluation should take place. We then provide a set of sufficient conditions guaranteeing the correctness of the resulting algorithm.

Propagating differences is orthogonal to the other optimizations of worklist solvers considered in [12]. Thus, we are free to add timestamps or just depth-first priorities to obtain even more competitive fixpoint algorithms (see [12]). We refrained from doing so to keep the exposition as simple as possible. We underline generality as well as usefulness of our new fixpoint algorithm by giving three important applications, namely, distributive framework *IDE* for interprocedural analysis of imperative languages [17], control-flow analysis for higher-order functional languages [13], and abstract OLDT-resolution as considered in [15, 16] for Prolog. In the first two cases, we obtain similar complexity results as for known special purpose algorithms. Completely new algorithms are obtained for abstract OLDT-resolution.

Another effort to exhibit computational similarities at least between control-flow analysis and certain interprocedural analyses has been undertaken by Reps and his coworkers [18, 19]. It is based on the graph-theoretic notion of *context-free language reachability*. This approach, however, is much more limited in its applicability than ours since it does not work for binary operators and lattices which are *not* of the form $D = 2^A$ for some un-ordered base set A.

The paper is organized as follows. In sections 2 through 6 we introduce our basic concepts. Especially, we introduce the notions of computation trees and weak monotonicity of computation trees. In the following three sections, we successively derive differential fixpoint algorithm $\mathbf{WR}_\Delta$. Conventional worklist solver **WR** is introduced in section 7. Continuations are added in section 8 to obtain solver $\mathbf{WR}_C$ from which we obtain algorithm $\mathbf{WR}_\Delta$ in section 9. The results of section 9 are sufficient to derive fast algorithms for framework *IDE* (section 10) as well as control-flow analysis (section 11). Framework *IDE* has been proposed by Horwitz, Reps and Sagiv for interprocedural analysis of imperative programs and applied to interprocedural *linear constant propagation* [17]. A variant of control-flow analysis ("set-based analysis") has been proposed by Heintze for the analysis of ML [13]. Another variant, even more in the spirit of the methods used here, has been applied in [26] to a higher-order functional language with call-by-need semantics to obtain a termination analysis for *deforestation*. In section 12 we extend applicability of algorithm $\mathbf{WR}_\Delta$ further by introducing *generalized computation trees*. This generalization takes into account independence of subcomputations. Especially, it allows to derive new algorithms for abstract OLDT-resolution [15, 16, 25] (section 13). As an example implementation, we integrated an enhanced version of fixpoint algorithm $\mathbf{WR}_\Delta$ into program analyzer generator GENA for Prolog [10, 11] and practically evaluated the generated analyzers on our benchmark suite of large Prolog programs. The results are reported in section 14.

2 Constraint Systems

Assume D is a complete lattice of *values*. A *constraint system* S with set variables V over lattice D consists of a set of constraints $x \sqsupseteq t$ where left-hand side $x \in V$ is a variable and t, the right-hand side, represents a function $[\![t]\!] : (V \to D) \to D$ from variable assignments to values. Le Charlier and Van Hentenryck in [5] and Fecht and Seidl in [12] presented their solvers in a setting which was (almost) independent of the implementation of right-hand sides. In this paper, we insist on a general formulation as well. As in [12] we assume that

1. set V of variables is always finite;
2. complete lattice D has finite height;
3. evaluation of right-hand sides is always terminating.

In contrast to [5, 12], however, our new algorithms take also into account *how* right-hand sides are evaluated.

3 Computation Trees

Operationally, every evaluation of right-hand side t on variable assignment σ can be viewed as a sequence alternating between variable lookups and internal computations which, eventually, terminates to return the result. Formally, this type of evaluation can be represented as a D-branching *computation tree* (ct for short) of finite depth. The set $\mathcal{T}(V, D)$ of all computation trees is the least set $\mathcal{T}$ containing $d \in D$, $x \in V$ together with all pairs $\langle x, C \rangle$ where $x \in V$ and $C : D \to \mathcal{T}$. Given $t \in \mathcal{T}(V, D)$, function $[\![t]\!] : (V \to D) \to D$ *implemented* by t and set $\mathrm{dep}(t, \_)$ of variables *accessed* during evaluation of t are given by:

$$
\begin{array}{llll}
[\![d]\!]\, \sigma & = d & \mathrm{dep}(d, \sigma) & = \emptyset \\
[\![x]\!]\, \sigma & = \sigma\, x & \mathrm{dep}(x, \sigma) & = \{x\} \\
[\![\langle x, C \rangle]\!]\, \sigma & = [\![C\, (\sigma\, x)]\!]\, \sigma & \mathrm{dep}(\langle x, C \rangle, \sigma) & = \{x\} \cup \mathrm{dep}(C\, (\sigma\, x), \sigma)
\end{array}
$$

Clearly, ct x can be viewed as an abbreviation of ct $\langle x, \lambda d.d \rangle$. Representations of equivalent computation trees can be obtained for various expression languages.

Example 1. Assume right-hand sides are given by

$$e \ ::= \ d \mid x \mid f \, x \mid g \, (x_1, x_2)$$

where, d denotes an element in D, and f and g represent monotonic functions $D \to D$ and $D^2 \to D$, respectively. For simplicity, we do not distinguish (notationally) between these symbols and their respective meanings. Standard intra-procedural data-flow analyzes for imperative languages naturally introduce constraint systems of this simple type (mostly even without occurrences of *binary* operators g). The computation tree t for expression e can be chosen as e itself if $e \in D \cup V$. For $e \equiv f \, x$, we set $t = \langle x, f \rangle$ and for $e \equiv g \, (x_1, x_2)$, $t = \langle x_1, C \rangle$ where $C \, d = \langle x_2, C_d \rangle$ and $C_d \, d' = g \, (d, d')$. $\quad \Box$

Further examples of useful expression languages together with their translations into (generalized) computation trees can be found in sections 11, 12, and 13. It should be emphasized that we do not advocate ct's as *specification language* for right-hand sides. In the first place, ct's serve as an abstract notion of algorithm for right-hand sides. In the second place, however, ct's (resp. their generalization as considered in section 12) can be viewed as the *conceptual* intermediate representation for our fixpoint iterators to rely on, meaning, that evaluation of right-hand sides should provide for every access to variable y some representation C of the remaining part of the evaluation. As in example 1, such C typically consists of a tuple of values together with the reached program point.

4 Solutions

Variable assignment $\sigma : V \to D$ is called *solution* for S if $\sigma \, x \sqsupseteq [\![t]\!] \, \sigma$ for all constraints $x \sqsupseteq t$ in S. Every system S has at least one solution, namely the trivial one mapping every variable to $\top$, the top element of D. In general, we are interested in computing a "good" solution, i.e., one which is as small as possible or, at least, non–trivial. With system S we associate function $G_S : (V \to D) \to V \to D$ defined by $G_S \, \sigma \, x = \bigsqcup \{ [\![t]\!] \, \sigma \mid x \sqsupseteq t \in S \}$. If we are lucky, all right-hand sides t represent monotonic functions. Then G_S is monotonic as well, and therefore has a least fixpoint which is also the least solution of S. As observed in [8, 12], the constraint systems for interprocedural analysis of (imperative or logic) languages often are not monotonic but just *weakly* monotonic.

5 Weak Monotonicity of Computation Trees

Assume we are given a partial ordering "$\leq$" on variables. Variable assignment $\sigma : V \to D$ is called *monotonic* if for all $x_1 \leq x_2$, $\sigma \, x_1 \sqsubseteq \sigma \, x_2$. On computation trees we define a relation "$\leq$" by:

- $\bot \leq t$ for every t; and $d_1 \leq d_2$ if $d_1 \sqsubseteq d_2$;
- $x_1 \leq x_2$ as ct's if also $x_1 \leq x_2$ as variables;
- $\langle x_1, C_1 \rangle \leq \langle x_2, C_2 \rangle$ if $x_1 \leq x_2$ and $C_1 \, d_1 \leq C_2 \, d_2$ for all $d_1 \sqsubseteq d_2$.

Constraint system S is called *weakly* monotonic iff for every $x_1 \leq x_2$ and constraint $x_1 \sqsupseteq t_1$ in S, some constraint $x_2 \sqsupseteq t_2 \in S$ exists such that $t_1 \leq t_2$. S is called *monotonic* if it is weakly monotonic for variable ordering "$=$". We have:

Proposition 2. Assume σ_1, σ_2 are variable assignments where $\sigma_1 \sqsubseteq \sigma_2$ and at least one of the σ_i is monotonic. Then $t_1 \leq t_2$ implies:

1. $\mathsf{dep}(t_1, \sigma_1) \le \mathsf{dep}(t_2, \sigma_2)$;   2. $[\![t_1]\!] \, \sigma_1 \sqsubseteq [\![t_2]\!] \, \sigma_2$.   □

Here, $s_1 \le s_2$ for sets $s_1, s_2 \subseteq V$ iff for all $x_1 \in s_1$, $x_1 \le x_2$ for some $x_2 \in s_2$. Semantic property 2 coincides with what was called "weakly monotonic" in [12] – adapted to constraint systems. It is a derived property here since we started out from *syntactic* properties of computation trees (not just their meanings as in [12]). As in [12] we conclude:

Corollary 3. If S is weakly monotonic, then:

1. If σ is monotonic, then $G_S \, \sigma$ is again monotonic;
2. S has a unique least solution μ given by $\mu = \bigsqcup_{j \ge 0} G_S^j \perp$.
   Especially, this least solution μ is monotonic.   □

6   Local Fixpoint Computation

Assume set V of variables is tremendously large while at the same time we are only interested in the values for a rather small subset X of variables. Then we should try to compute the values of a solution only for variables from X and all those variables y that "influence" values for variables in X. This is the idea of *local* fixpoint computation.

Evaluation of computation tree t on argument σ does not necessarily consult *all* values $\sigma \, x, x \in V$. Therefore, evaluation of t may succeed already for *partial* $\sigma : V \rightsquigarrow D$. If evaluation of t on σ succeeds, we can define the set $\mathsf{dep}(t, \sigma)$ accessed during this evaluation in the same way as in section 3 for complete functions. Given partial variable assignment $\sigma : V \rightsquigarrow D$, variable y *directly* influences (relative to σ) variable x if $y \in \mathsf{dep}(t, \sigma)$ for some right-hand side t of x. Let then *"influencing"* denote the reflexive and transitive closure of this relation. Partial variable assignment σ is called X*-stable* iff for every $y \in V$ influencing some $x \in X$ relative to σ, and every constraint $y \sqsupseteq t$ in S for y, $[\![t]\!] \, \sigma$ is defined with $\sigma \, y \sqsupseteq [\![t]\!] \, \sigma$. A *solver*, finally, computes for constraint system S and set X of variables an X-stable partial assignment σ; furthermore, if S is weakly monotonic and μ is its least solution, then $\sigma \, y = \mu \, y$ for all y influencing some variable in X (relative to σ).

7   The Worklist Solver with Recursion

The first solver **WR** we consider is a local worklist algorithm enhanced with recursive descent into new variables (Fig. 1). Solver **WR** is an adaption of a simplification of solver **WRT** in [12] to constraint systems. Opposed to **WRT**, no time stamps are maintained.

For every encountered variable x algorithm **WR** (globally) maintains the current value $\sigma \, x$ together with a set $\mathsf{infl} \, x$ of constraints $z \sqsupseteq t$ such that evaluation of t (on σ) may access value $\sigma \, x$. The set of constraints to be reevaluated is kept in data structure W, called *worklist*. Initially, W is empty. The algorithm starts by initializing all variables from set X by calling procedure Init. Procedure Init when applied to variable x first checks whether x has already been encountered, i.e., is contained in set dom. If this is not the case, x is added to dom, $\sigma \, x$ is initialized to $\perp$ and set $\mathsf{infl} \, x$ of constraints potentially influenced by x is initialized to $\emptyset$. Then a first approximation for x is computed by evaluating all right-hand sides t for x and adding the results to $\sigma \, x$. If a value different from $\perp$ has been obtained, all elements from set $\mathsf{infl} \, x$ have to be added to W. After that, set $\mathsf{infl} \, x$ is emptied.

```
dom = ∅;  W = ∅;
forall (x ∈ X) Init(x);
while (W ≠ ∅) {
    x ⊒ t = Extract(W);
    new = [t] (λy.Eval(x ⊒ t, y));
    if (new ⋢ σ x) {
        σ x = σ x ⊔ new;
        W = W ∪ infl x;
        infl x = ∅;
    }
}
void Init(V x) {
    if (x ∉ dom) {
        dom = dom ∪ {x};
        σ x = ⊥; infl x = ∅;
        forall (x ⊒ t ∈ S)
            σ x = σ x ⊔ [t] (λy.Eval(x ⊒ t, y));
        if (σ x ≠ ⊥) {
            W = W ∪ infl x;
            infl x = ∅;
        }
    }
}
D Eval(Constraint r, V y) {
    Init(y);
    infl y = infl y ∪ {r};
    return σ y;
}
```

Fig. 1. Algorithm **WR**.

As long as W is nonempty, the algorithm now iteratively extracts constraints $x \sqsupseteq t$ from W and evaluates right-hand side t on current partial variable assignment σ. If $[t]\sigma$ is not subsumed by σx, the value of σ for x is updated. Since the value for x has changed, the constraints r in infl x may no longer be satisfied by σ; therefore, they are added to W. Afterwards, infl x is reset to $\emptyset$.

However, right-hand sides t of constraints r are *not* evaluated on σ directly. There are two reasons for this. First, σ may not be defined for all variables y the evaluation of t may access; second, we have to determine all y accessed by the evaluation of t on σ. Therefore, t is applied to auxiliary function $\lambda y.\text{Eval}(r, y)$. When applied to constraint r and variable y, Eval first initializes y by calling Init. Then r is added to infl y, and the value of σ for y (which now is always defined) is returned.

Theorem 4. Algorithm **WR** is a solver.   □

8   The Continuation Solver

Solver **WR** contains inefficiencies. Consider constraint $x \sqsupseteq t$ where, during evaluation of t, value σy has been accessed at subtree $t' = \langle y, C \rangle$ of t. Now assume σy obtains new value *new*. Then reevaluation of *complete* right-hand side t is initiated. Instead of doing so, we would like to initiate reevaluation only of subtree C *new*. Function C in subtree t' can be interpreted as (syntactic representation of) the *continuation* where reevaluation of t has to proceed if the value of σ for y has been returned. We modify solver **WR** therefore as follows:

- Whenever during evaluation of right-hand side of constraint $x \sqsupseteq t$, subtree $t' = \langle y, C \rangle$ is reached, we not just access value $\sigma\, y$ and apply continuation C but additionally add (x, C) to the infl-set of variable y.
- Whenever $\sigma\, y$ has obtained a new value, we add to W all pairs $(x, \langle y, C \rangle)$, $(x, C) \in$ infl y, to initiate their later reevaluations.

The infl-sets of resulting algorithm $\mathbf{WR}_C$ now contain elements from $V \times \mathbf{Cont}$ where $\mathbf{Cont} = D \to \mathcal{T}(V, D)$, whereas worklist W obtains elements from $V \times \mathcal{T}(V, D)$. In order to have continuations explicitly available for insertion into infl-sets, we change the functionality of the argument of [.] (and hence also [.]) by passing down the current continuation into the argument. We define:

$$[d]\,\sigma' = d \qquad [x]\,\sigma' = \sigma'\,(\lambda d.d)\,x \qquad [\langle x, C \rangle]\,\sigma' = [C\,(\sigma'\,C\,x)]\,\sigma'$$

where $\sigma'\,C\,x = \sigma\,x$. Using this modified definition of the semantics of computation trees we finally adapt the functionality of Eval. The new function Eval consumes three arguments, namely variables x and y together with continuation C. Here, variable x represents the left-hand side of the current constraint, y represents the variable whose value is being accessed, and C is the current continuation. Given these three arguments, Eval first calls Init for y to make sure that $\sigma\, y$ as well as infl y have already been initialized. Then it adds (x, C) to set infl y. Finally, it returns $\sigma\, y$. We obtain:

Theorem 5. Algorithm $\mathbf{WR}_C$ is a solver. $\qquad\qquad\qquad\qquad\qquad\qquad\Box$

A similar optimization for topdown solver **TD** [5, 12] in the context of analysis of Prolog programs has been called *clause prefix optimization* [9]. As far we know, an *application independent* exposition for worklist based solvers has not considered before.

9 The Differential Fixpoint Algorithm

Assume variable y has changed its value. Instead of reevaluating all trees $\langle y, C \rangle$ from set infl of y with the new value, we may initiate reevaluation just for the *increment*. This optimization is especially helpful, if computation on "larger" values is much more expensive than computations on "smaller" ones. The increase of values is determined by some function diff : $D \times D \to D$ satisfying

$$d_1 \sqcup \mathrm{diff}(d_1, d_2) = d_1 \sqcup d_2$$

Example 6. If $D = 2^A$, A a set, we may choose for diff set difference.
   If $D = M \to R$, M a set and R a complete lattice, $\mathrm{diff}(f_1, f_2)$ can be defined as $\mathrm{diff}(f_1, f_2)\,v = \bot$ if $f_2\,v \sqsubseteq f_1\,v$ and $\mathrm{diff}(f_1, f_2)\,v = f_2\,v$ otherwise. $\qquad\Box$

To make our idea work, we have to impose further restrictions onto the structure of right-hand sides t. We call S *distributive* if S is weakly monotonic and for every subterm $\langle x, C \rangle$ of right-hand sides of S, d_1, d_2, and d such that $d = d_1 \sqcup d_2$ and arbitrary variable assignment σ:

$$\mathrm{dep}(C\,d_1, \sigma) \cup \mathrm{dep}(C\,d_2, \sigma) \supseteq \mathrm{dep}(C\,d, \sigma) \quad \text{and} \quad [C\,d_1]\,\sigma \sqcup [C\,d_2]\,\sigma \sqsupseteq [C\,d]\,\sigma$$

```
dom = ∅; W = ∅;
forall (x ∈ X) Init(x);
while (W ≠ ∅) {
    (x, C, Δ) = Extract(W);
    new = [C Δ] (λC, y.Eval(x, C, y));
    if (new ⋢ σ x){
        Δ = diff(σ x, new);
        σ x = σ x ⊔ new;
        forall ((x', C') ∈ infl x)
            W = W ∪ {(x', C', Δ)};
    }
}
void Init(V x){
    if (x ∉ dom) {
        dom = dom ∪ {x};
        σ x = ⊥; infl x = ∅;
        forall (x ⊒ t ∈ S))
            σ x = σ x ⊔ [t] (λC, y.Eval(x, C, y));
        if (σ x ≠ ⊥)
            forall ((x', C') ∈ infl x)
                W = W ∪ {(x', C', (σ x))};
    }
}
D Eval(V x, Cont C, V y) {
    Init(y);
    infl y = infl y ∪ {(x, C)};
    return σ y;
}
```

Fig. 2. Algorithm $\mathbf{WR}_\Delta$.

In interesting applications, S is even monotonic and variable dependencies are "static", i.e., independent of σ. Furthermore, equality holds in the second inclusion. This is especially the case if right-hand sides are given through expressions as in Example 1, where all operators f and g are distributive in each of their arguments.

In order to propagate increments, we change solver $\mathbf{WR}_C$ as follows. Assume σy has obtained a new value which differs from the old one by Δ and $(x, C) \in$ infl y.

- Instead of adding $(x, \langle y, C \rangle)$ to W (as for $\mathbf{WR}_C$), we add (x, C, Δ). Thus, now worklist W contains elements from $V \times \mathbf{Cont} \times D$.
- If we extract triple (x, C, Δ) from W, we evaluate ct C Δ to obtain a (possibly) new increment for x.

In contrast, however, to $\mathbf{WR}_C$ and $\mathbf{WR}$, it is no longer safe to empty sets infl y after use. The resulting *differential* worklist algorithm with recursive descent into new variables ($\mathbf{WR}_\Delta$ for short) is given in Figure 2.

Theorem 7. For distributive S, $\mathbf{WR}_\Delta$ computes an X-stable partial least solution.

□

Note that we did not claim algorithm $\mathbf{WR}_\Delta$ to be a solver: and indeed this is not the case. Opposed to solvers $\mathbf{WR}$ and $\mathbf{WR}_C$, algorithm $\mathbf{WR}_\Delta$ may *fail* to compute the least solution for constraint systems which are not distributive.

10 The Distributive Framework *IDE*

As a first application, let us consider the distributive framework *IDE* for interprocedural analysis of imperative languages as suggested by Horwitz et al. [17] and applied, e.g., to *linear constant propagation*. Framework *IDE* assigns to program points elements from lattice $D = M \to L$ of program states, where M is some finite base set (e.g., the set of currently visible program variables), and L is a lattice of abstract values.

The crucial point of program analysis in framework *IDE* consists in determining summary functions from $D \to D$ to describe effects of procedures. The lattice of possible transfer functions for statements as well as for summary functions for procedures in *IDE* is given by $\mathcal{F} = M^2 \to \mathcal{R}$ where $\mathcal{R} \subseteq L \to L$ is assumed to be a lattice of distributive functions of (small) finite height (e.g., 4 for linear constant propagation) which contains $\lambda x.\bot$ and is closed under composition. The transformer in $D \to D$ defined by $f \in \mathcal{F}$ is given as

$$[f]\, \eta\, v' = \bigsqcup_{v \in M} f\,(v,v')\,(\eta\, v)$$

Clearly, $[f]$ is distributive, i.e., $[f]\,(\eta_1 \sqcup \eta_2) = [f]\,\eta_1 \sqcup [f]\,\eta_2$. Computing the summary functions for procedures in this framework boils down to solving a constraint system S over $\mathcal{F}$ where right-hand sides e are of the form:

$$e ::= f \mid x \mid f \circ x \mid x_2 \circ x_1$$

where $f \in \mathcal{F}$. Since all functions in $\mathcal{F}$ are distributive, function composition $\circ : \mathcal{F}^2 \to \mathcal{F}$ is distributive in each argument. Thus, constraint system S is a special case of the constraint systems from example 1. Therefore, we can apply $\mathbf{WR}_\Delta$ to compute the least solution of S efficiently – provided operations "$\circ$" and "$\sqcup$" can be computed efficiently. Using a diff-function similar to the last one of Example 6, we obtain:

Theorem 8. If operations in $\mathcal{R}$ can be executed in time $\mathcal{O}(1)$, then the summary functions for program p according to interprocedural framework *IDE* can be computed by $\mathbf{WR}_\Delta$ in time $\mathcal{O}(|p| \cdot |M|^3)$. $\qquad\qquad\Box$

The complexity bound in Theorem 8 should be compared with $\mathcal{O}(|p| \cdot |M|^5)$ which can be derived for $\mathbf{WR}$. By saving factor $|M|^2$, we find the same complexity as has been obtained in [17] for a special purpose algorithm.

11 Control-Flow Analysis

Control-flow analysis (cfa for short) is an analysis for higher-order functional languages possibly with recursive data types [13]. Cfa on program p tries to compute for every expression t occurring in p a superset of expressions into which t may evolve during program execution, see, e.g., [23, 24, 21, 26]. Let A denote the set of subexpressions of p and $D = 2^A$. Then cfa for a lazy language as in [26] can be formalized through a constraint system S over domain D with set V of in variables $y_t, t \in A$, where right-hand sides of constraints consist of expressions e of one of the following forms:

$$e ::= \{a\} \mid x \mid (a \in x_1); x_2$$

for $a \in A$. Here, we view $(a \in x_1); x_2$ as specification of ct $\langle x_1, C \rangle$ where $C\, d = \emptyset$ if $a \notin d$ and $C\, d = x_2$ otherwise. Let us assume set V of variables is just ordered by equality. Then S is not only monotonic but also distributive. As function diff, we simply choose set diffrence. With these definitions, algorithm $\mathbf{WR}_\Delta$ can be applied.

Let us assume that the maximal cardinality of an occurring set is bounded by $s \leq |p|$. Furthermore, let I denote the complexity of inserting a single element into a set of maximally s elements. In case, for example, we can represent sets as bit vectors, $I = \mathcal{O}(1)$. In case, the program is large but we nevertheless expect sets to be sparse we may use some suitable hashing scheme to achieve approximately the same effect. Otherwise, we may represent sets through balanced ordered trees giving extra cost $I = \mathcal{O}(\log s)$.

Cfa introduces $\mathcal{O}(|p|^2)$ constraints of the form $y \supseteq (a \in x_1); x_2$. Inorder to avoid creation of (a representation of) all these in advance, we introduce the following additional optimization. We start iteration with constraint system S_0 lacking all constraints of this form. Instead, we introduce function $r : V \to D \to 2^{\text{constraints}}$ which, depending on the value of variables, returns the set of constraints to be added to the present constraint system. r is given by:

$$r\, x\, d = \{y \supseteq x_2 \mid a \in d, y \supseteq (a \in x); x_2 \in S\}$$

Thus especially, $r\, x\, (d_1 \cup d_2) = (r\, x\, d_1) \cup (r\, x\, d_2)$. Whenever variable x is incremented by Δ, we add all constraints from $r\, x\, \Delta$ to the current constraint system by inserting them into worklist W. For cfa, each application $r\, x\, \Delta$ can be evaluated in time $\mathcal{O}(|\Delta|)$. Thus, if the cardinalities of all occurring sets is bounded by s, at most $\mathcal{O}(|p| \cdot s)$ constraints of the form $y \supseteq x$ are added to S_0. Each of these introduces an amount $\mathcal{O}(s \cdot I)$ of work. Therefore, we obtain:

Theorem 9. If s is the maximal cardinality of occurring sets, the least solution of constraint system S for cfa on program p can be computed by the optimized $\mathbf{WR}_\Delta$ algorithm in time $\mathcal{O}(|p| \cdot s^2 \cdot I)$. $\square$

The idea of dynamic extension of constraint systems is especially appealing and clearly can also be cast in a more general setting. Here, it results in an efficient algorithm which is comparable to the one proposed by Heintze in [13].

12   Generalized Computation Trees

In practical applications, certain subcomputations for right-hand sides turn out to be independent. For example, the values for a set of variables may be accessed in any order if it is just the least upper bound of returned values which matters. To describe such kinds of phenomena formally, we introduce set $\mathcal{GT}(V, D)$ of *generalized computation trees* (gct's for short). Gct's t are given by:

$$t ::= d \mid x \mid S \mid \langle t, C \rangle$$

where $S \subseteq \mathcal{GT}(V, D)$ is finite and $C : D \to \mathcal{GT}(V, D)$. Thus, we not only allow *sets* of computation trees but also (sets of) computation trees as *selectors* of computation trees. Given $t \in \mathcal{GT}(V, D)$, function $[t] : (V \to D) \to D$ implemented by t as well as set $\text{dep}(t, \_)$ of variables accessed during evaluation are defined by:

$$
\begin{aligned}
[d]\, \sigma &= d & \text{dep}(d, \sigma) &= \emptyset \\
[x]\, \sigma &= \sigma\, x & \text{dep}(x, \sigma) &= \{x\} \\
[S]\, \sigma &= \bigsqcup \{[t]\, \sigma \mid t \in S\} & \text{dep}(S, \sigma) &= \bigcup \{\text{dep}(t, \sigma) \mid t \in S\} \\
[\langle t, C \rangle]\, \sigma &= [C\, ([t]\, \sigma)]\, \sigma & \text{dep}(\langle t, C \rangle, \sigma) &= \text{dep}(t, \sigma) \cup \text{dep}(C\, ([t]\, \sigma), \sigma)
\end{aligned}
$$

While *sets* of trees conveniently allow to make independence of subcomputations explicit (see our example application in section 13), nesting of trees into selectors eases the translation of deeper nesting of operator applications.

Example 10. Assume expressions e are given by the grammar:

$$e ::= d \mid x \mid f\,e \mid g\,(e_1, e_2)$$

where $d \in D$ and f and g denote monotonic functions in $D \to D$ and $D^2 \to D$, respectively. The gct t_e for e can then be constructed by:

- $t_e = e$ if $e \in D \cup V$;
- $t_e = \langle t_{e'}, \lambda d.f\,d \rangle$ if $e \equiv f\,e'$;
- $t_e = \langle t_{e_1}, C \rangle$ with $C\,d_1 = \langle t_{e_2}, \lambda d_2.g\,(d_1, d_2) \rangle$ if $e \equiv g\,(e_1, e_2)$. □

For partial ordering "$\leq$" on set V of variables, we define relation "$\leq$" on gct's by:

- $\perp \leq t$ for every t; and $d_1 \leq d_2$ if $d_1 \sqsubseteq d_2$;
- $x_1 \leq x_2$ as gct's if also $x_1 \leq x_2$ as variables;
- $S_1 \leq S_2$ if for all $t_1 \in S_1$, $t_1 \leq t_2$ for some $t_2 \in S_2$;
- $\langle t_1, C_1 \rangle \leq \langle t_2, C_2 \rangle$ if $t_1 \leq t_2$ and for all $d_1 \sqsubseteq d_2$, $C\,d_1 \leq C\,d_2$.

Now assume the right-hand sides of constraint system S all are given through gct's. Then S is called *weakly monotonic* iff for every $x_1 \leq x_2$ and constraint $x_1 \sqsupseteq t_1$ in S some constraint $x_2 \sqsupseteq t_2$ in S exists such that $t_1 \leq t_2$. With these extended definitions prop. 2, cor. 3 as well as Theorem 4 hold. Therefore, algorithm **WR** is also a solver for constraint systems where right-hand sides are represented by gct's.

Function C in $t = \langle t', C \rangle$ can now only be interpreted as a representation of the continuation where reevaluation of t has to start if the evaluation of subtree t' on σ has terminated. t' again may be of the form $\langle s, C' \rangle$. Consequently, we have to deal with *lists* γ of continuations. Thus, whenever during evaluation of t an access to variable y occurs, we now have to add pairs (x, γ) to the infl-set of variable y. As in section 8, we therefore change the functionality of $[.]$ by defining:

$$\begin{aligned}
&[d]\,\sigma'\,\gamma = d & &[S]\,\sigma'\,\gamma = \bigsqcup\{[t]\,\sigma'\,\gamma \mid t \in S\} \\
&[x]\,\sigma'\,\gamma = \sigma'\,\gamma\,x & &[\langle t, C \rangle]\,\sigma'\,\gamma = [C\,([t]\,\sigma'\,(C{:}\gamma))]\,\sigma'\,\gamma
\end{aligned}$$

where $\sigma'\,\gamma\,x = \sigma\,x$. The goal here is to avoid reevaluation of whole set S just because one of its elements has changed its value. Therefore, we propagate list γ arriving at *set* S of trees immediately down to each of its elements.

Now assume $\sigma\,y$ has changed its value by Δ. Then we add all triples (x, γ, Δ) to W where $(x, \gamma) \in \text{infl}\,y$. Having extracted such a triple from the worklist, the new solver applies list γ to the new value Δ. The iterative application process is implemented by:

$$\mathsf{app}\,[]\,d\,\sigma' = d \qquad \mathsf{app}\,(C{:}\gamma)\,d\,\sigma' = \mathsf{app}\,\gamma\,([C\,d]\,\sigma'\,\gamma)\,\sigma'$$

The resulting value then gives the new contribution to the value of σ for x. As for $\mathbf{WR}_\Delta$ for ordinary evaluation trees, infl-sets cannot be emptied after use. Carrying the definition of distributivity from section 9 over to gct's, we obtain:

Theorem 11. For distributive S with gct's as right-hand sides, algorithm $\mathbf{WR}_\Delta$ computes an X-stable partial least solution. □

As an advanced application of gct's, we consider abstract OLDT-resolution [15, 16, 25].

13   Abstract OLDT-Resolution

Given Prolog program p, abstract OLDT-resolution tries to compute for every program point x the set of (abstract) values arriving at x. Let A denote the set of possible values. Lattice D to compute in is then given by $D = 2^A$. *Coarse-grained* analysis assigns to each predicate an abstract state transformer $A \to D$, whereas *fine-grained* analysis additionally assigns transformers also to every program point [15]. Instead of considering transformers as a whole (as, e.g., in the algorithm for framework *IDE* in section 10), transformer valued variable x is replaced by a *set* of variables, namely $x\,a, a \in A$, where $x\,a$ represents the return value of the transformer for x on input a. Thus, each variable $x\,a$ potentially receives a value from D. The idea is that, in practice, set A may be tremendously large, while at the same time each transformer is called only on a small number of inputs. Thus, in this application we explicitly rely on demand-driven exploration of the variable space.

To every transformer variable x the analysis assigns a finite set of *constraint schemes* $x \bullet \supseteq e$ where $\bullet$ formally represents the argument to the transformer, and e is an expression built up according to the following grammar (see [25]):

$$e ::= \mathbf{s} \bullet \mid \mathcal{E}\, f\, e \qquad f ::= \lambda a.\mathbf{s}\,(g\,a) \mid x \mid \lambda a.(x\,(g\,a)\,\square\,a)$$

Here, $\mathbf{s} : A \to D$ denotes the singleton map defined by $\mathbf{s}\,a = \{a\}$, and $\mathcal{E} : (A \to D) \to D \to D$ denotes the usual extension function defined by $\mathcal{E}\,f\,d = \bigcup\{f\,a \mid a \in d\}$. Thus, expressions e are built up from $\mathbf{s} \bullet = \{\bullet\}$ by successive applications of extensions $\mathcal{E}\,f$ for three possible types of functions $f : A \to D$. Unary functions $g : A \to A$ are used to model basic computation steps, passing of actual parameters into procedures and returning of results, whereas binary operators $\square : D \times A \to D$ conveniently allow to model *local states* of procedures. They are used to combine the set of return values of procedures with the local state before the call [25]. In case of fine-grained analysis, every scheme for right-hand sides contains at most two occurrences of "$\mathcal{E}$", whereas coarse-grained analysis possibly introduces also deeper nesting.

The set of constraints for variable $x\,a, a \in A$, are obtained from the set of constraint schemes for x by instantiating $\bullet$ with actual parameter a. The resulting right-hand sides can be implemented through gct's $t_{\{a\}}$. For $d \in D$, gct t_d is of the form $t_d = d$ or $t_d = \langle S_d, C \rangle$ such that $C\,d'$ returns some tree $t'_{d'}$, and $S_d = \{s_a \mid a \in d\}$. The forms for elements s_a of S_d correspond to the three possible forms for f in expressions $\mathcal{E}\,f\,e$, i.e,

$$s_a ::= \mathbf{s}\,(g\,a) \mid x\,a \mid \langle x\,(g\,a), \lambda d'.d'\,\square\,a \rangle$$

Constraint system S for abstract OLDT-resolution then turns out to be monotonic as well as distributive. As operator diff, we choose: $\mathrm{diff}(d_1, d_2) = d_2 \backslash d_1$. Therefore, we can apply algorithm $\mathbf{WR}_\triangle$. Let us assume that applications $g\,a$ and insertion into sets can be executed in time $\mathcal{O}(1)$, whereas evaluation of $d \square a$ needs time $\mathcal{O}(\#d)$. Then:

Theorem 12. Fine-grained OLDT-resolution for program p with abstract values from A can be executed by $\mathbf{WR}_\triangle$ in time $\mathcal{O}(N \cdot s^2)$ where $N \leq |p| \cdot \#A$ is the number of considered variables, and $s \leq \#A$ is the maximal cardinality of occurring sets. $\square$

$\mathbf{WR}_\triangle$ saves an extra factor $\mathcal{O}(s^2)$ over solver $\mathbf{WR}$. An algorithm with similar savings has been suggested by Horwitz et al. [18]. Their graph-based algorithm, however, is neither able to treat *binary* operators nor deeper nested right-hand sides as ours.

In the usual application for program analysis, A is equipped with some partial abstraction ordering "$\sqsubseteq$", implying that set $d \subseteq A$ contains the same information as its lower closure $d\!\downarrow = \{a \in A \mid \exists a' \in d : a \sqsubseteq a'\}$. In this case, we may decide to compute with *lower* subsets of A right from the beginning [15, 25]. Here, subset $d \subseteq A$ is called lower iff $d = d\downarrow$. If all occurring functions f as well as operators $\square$ are monotonic, then we can represent lower sets d by their maximal elements and do all computations just with such anti-chains. The resulting constraint system then turns out to be no longer monotonic. However, it is still *weakly* monotonic w.r.t. variable ordering "$\leq$" given by $x_1 a_1 \leq x_2 a_2$ iff $x_1 \equiv x_2$ and $a_1 \sqsubseteq a_2$. As function diff for anti-chains, we choose

$$\mathsf{diff}(d_1, d_2) = d_2 \backslash (d_1 \downarrow) = \{a_2 \in d_2 \mid \forall a_1 \in d_1 : a_2 \not\sqsubseteq a_1\}$$

Again, we can apply the differential worklist algorithm. Here, we found no comparable algorithm in the literature. $\mathbf{WR}_\Delta$ beats conventional solvers for this application (see section 14). A simple estimation of the runtime complexity, however, is no longer possible since even large sets may have succinct representations by short anti-chains.

14   Practical Experiments

We have adapted the fastest general-purpose equation solver from [12], namely $\mathbf{WDFS}$ (for a distinction called $\mathbf{WDFS}^{Equ}$ here), to constraint systems giving general-purpose constraint solver $\mathbf{WDFS}^{Con}$. Solver $\mathbf{WDFS}^{Con}$ is similar to solver $\mathbf{WR}$, but additionally maintains priorities on variables and, before return from an update of σ for variable x, evaluates all constraints $y \sqsupseteq t$ from the worklist where y has higher priority as the variable below x (cf. [12]). To solver $\mathbf{WDFS}^{Con}$ we added propagation of differences (the "Δ") in the same way as we added propagation of differences to solver $\mathbf{WR}$ in section 9. All fixpoint algorithms have been integrated into GENA [10, 11]. GENA is a generator for Prolog program analyzers written in SML. We generated analyzers for abstract OLDT-resolution for PS+POS+LIN which is Søndergaard's pair sharing domain enhanced with POS for inferring groundness [27, 7]. Its abstract substitutions are pairs of bdd's and graphs over variables. Thus, we maintain anti-chains of such elements. The generated analyzers were run on large real-world programs. aqua-c (about 560KB) is the source code of an early version of Peter van Roy's Aquarius Prolog compiler. chat (about 170KB) is David H.D. Warren's chat-80 system. The numbers reported in table 1, are the absolute runtimes in seconds (including system time) obtained for SML-NJ, version 109.29, on a Sun 20 with 64 MB main memory.

Comparing the three algorithms for OLDT-resolution, we find that all of these have still quite acceptable runtimes (perhaps with exeption of aqua-c) where algorithm $\mathbf{WDFS}_\Delta^{Con}$ almost always outperforms the others. Compared with equation solver $\mathbf{WDFS}^{Equ}$, algorithm $\mathbf{WDFS}_\Delta^{Con}$ saves approximately 40% of the runtime where usually less than half of the gain is obtained by maintaining constraints. The maximal relative gain of 48% could be observed for program readq where no advantage at all could be drawn out of constraints. Opposed to that, for Stefan Diehl's interpreter for action semantics action, propagation of differences did not give (significantly) better numbers than considering constraints alone – program ann even showed a (moderate) decrease in efficiency (factor 3.32). Also opposed to the general picture, constraints for aqua-c resulted in an improvement of 25% only – of which 9% was lost through propagation of differences! This slowdown is even more surprising, since it could not be confirmed with analyzer runs on aqua-c for other abstract domains. Table 2 reports the runtimes found for aqua-c on domain CompCon. Abstract domain CompCon analyzes whether variables are bound to atoms or are composite. For CompCon, constraints introduced a slowdown of 18% whereas propagation of differences resulted in a gain of efficiency by 38% over $\mathbf{WDFS}^{Equ}$.

program	WDFS^{Equ}	WDFS^{Con}	WDFS$^{Con}_\Delta$
action.pl	32.97	19.37	19.35
ann.pl	1.36	1.62	4.52
aqua-c.pl	1618.00	1209.00	1361.00
b2.pl	2.41	2.14	1.82
chat.pl	77.73	67.94	53.14
chat-parser.pl	29.62	27.72	17.28
chess.pl	0.40	0.38	0.37
flatten.pl	0.36	0.34	0.26
nand.pl	0.47	0.38	0.32
readq.pl	14.96	15.09	7.85
sdda.pl	0.73	0.59	0.50

Table 1. Comparison of **WDFS**^{Equ}, **WDFS**^{Con}, and **WDFS**$^{Con}_\Delta$ with PS+POS+LIN.

program	WDFS^{Equ}	WDFS^{Con}	WDFS$^{Con}_\Delta$
aqua-c.pl	214.67	252.43	133.61

Table 2. Comparison of **WDFS**^{Equ}, **WDFS**^{Con}, and **WDFS**$^{Con}_\Delta$ with CompCon.

15 Conclusion

We succeeded to give an application independent exposition of two further improvements to worklist-based local fixpoint algorithms. This allowed us not only to exhibit a common algorithmic idea in seemingly different fast special purpose algorithms like the one of Horwitz et al. for interprocedural framework *IDE* [17] of Heintze's algorithm for control-flow analysis [13]. Our exposition furthermore explains how such algorithms can be practically *improved* – namely by incorporating recursive descent into variables as well as timestamps [12]. Finally, our approach allowed to develop completely new efficient algorithms for abstract OLDT-resolution.

References

1. M. Alt and F. Martin. Generation of Efficient Interprocedural Analyzers with PAG. In *2nd SAS*, 33–50. LNCS 983, 1995.
2. I. Balbin and K. Ramamohanarao. A Generalization of the Differential Approach to Recursive Query Evaluation. *JLP*, 4(3):259–262, 1987.
3. F. Bancilhon and R. Ramakrishnan. An Amateur's Introduction to Recursive Query Processing Strategies. In *ACM SIGMOD Conference 1986*, 16–52, 1986.
4. F. Bancilhon and R. Ramakrishnan. Performance Evaluation of Data Intensive Logic Programs. In Jack Minker, editor, *Foundations of Deductive Databases and Logic Programming*, chapter 12, 439–517. Morgan Kaufmann Publishers, 1988.
5. B. Le Charlier and P. Van Hentenryck. A Universal Top-Down Fixpoint Algorithm. Technical Report CS-92-25, Brown University, Providence, RI 02912, 1992.
6. B. Le Charlier and P. Van Hentenryck. Experimental Evaluation of a Generic Abstract Interpretation Algorithm for Prolog. *ACM TOPLAS*, 16(1):35–101, 1994.
7. M. Codish, D. Dams, and E. Yardeni. Derivation of an Abstract Unification Algorithm for groundnes and Aliasing Analysis. In *ICLP*, 79–93, 1991.

8. P. Cousot and R. Cousot. Static Determination of Dynamic Properties of Recursive Programs. In E.J. Neuhold, editor, *Formal Descriptions of Programming Concepts*, 237–277. North-Holland Publishing Company, 1977.

9. V. Englebert, B. Le Charlier, D. Roland, and P. Van Hentenryck. Generic Abstract Interpretation Algorithms for Prolog: Two Optimization Techniques and their Experimental Evaluation. *SPE*, 23(4):419–459, 1993.

10. C. Fecht. GENA - A Tool for Generating Prolog Analyzers from Specifications. *2nd SAS*, 418–419. LNCS 983, 1995.

11. C. Fecht. *Abstrakte Interpretation logischer Programme: Theorie, Implementierung, Generierung*. PhD thesis, Universität des Saarlandes, Saarbrücken, 1997.

12. C. Fecht and H. Seidl. An Even Faster Solver for General Systems of Equations. *3rd SAS*, 189–204. LNCS 1145, 1996. Extended version to appear in SCP'99.

13. N. Heintze. Set-Based Analysis of ML Programs. *ACM Conf. LFP*, 306–317, 1994.

14. N. Heintze and D.A. McAllester. On the Cubic Bottleneck in Subtyping and Flow Analysis. *IEEE Symp. LICS*, 342–351, 1997.

15. P. Van Hentenryck, O. Degimbe, B. Le Charlier, and L. Michel. Abstract Interpretation of Prolog Based on OLDT Resolution. Technical Report CS-93-05, Brown University, Providence, RI 02912, 1993.

16. P. Van Hentenryck, O. Degimbe, B. Le Charlier, and L. Michel. The Impact of Granularity in Abstract Interpretation of Prolog. *3rd WSA*, 1–14. LNCS 724, 1993.

17. S. Horwitz, T.W. Reps, and M. Sagiv. Precise Interprocedural Dataflow Analysis with Applications to Constant Propagation. *6th TAPSOFT*, 651–665. LNCS 915, 1995.

18. S. Horwitz, T.W. Reps, and M. Sagiv. Precise Interprocedural Dataflow Analysis via Graph Reachability. *22nd POPL*, 49–61, 1995.

19. D. Melski and T.W. Reps. Interconvertability of Set Constraints and Context-Free Language Reachability. *ACM SIGPLAN Symp. PEPM*, 74–89, 1997.

20. K. Muthukumar and M. V. Hermenegildo. Compile-Time Derivation of Variable Dependency Using Abstract Interpretation. *JLP*, 13(2&3):315–347, 1992.

21. H. Riis Nielson and F. Nielson. Infinitary Control Flow Analysis: A Collecting Semantics for Closure Analysis. *24th POPL*, 332–345, 1997.

22. R. Paige. Symbolic Finite Differencing – Part I. *3rd ESOP*, 36–56. LNCS 432, 1990.

23. J. Palsberg. Closure Analysis in Constraint Form. *ACM TOPLAS*, 17:47–82, 1995.

24. J. Palsberg and P. O'Keefe. A Type System Equivalent to Flow Analysis. *ACM TOPLAS*, 17:576–599, 1995.

25. H. Seidl and C. Fecht. Interprocedural Analysis Based on PDAs. Technical Report 97-06, University Trier, 1997. Extended Abstract in: *Verification, Model Checking and Abstract Interpretation*. A Workshop in Assiciation with ILPS'97.

26. H. Seidl and M.H. Sørensen. Constraints to Stop Higher-Order Deforestation. *24th POPL*, 400–413, 1997.

27. H. Søndergaard. An Application of Abstract Interpretation of Logic Programs: Occur Check Reduction. *1st ESOP*, 327–338. LNCS 213, 1986.

Reasoning about Classes in Object-Oriented Languages: Logical Models and Tools

Ulrich Hensel[1] Marieke Huisman[2] Bart Jacobs[2] Hendrik Tews[1]

[1] Inst. Theor. Informatik, TU Dresden, D-01062 Dresden, Germany.
{hensel,tews}@tcs.inf.tu-dresden.de
[2] Dep. Comp. Sci., Univ. Nijmegen,
P.O. Box 9010, 6500 GL Nijmegen, The Netherlands.
{marieke,bart}@cs.kun.nl

Abstract. A formal language CCSL is introduced for describing specifications of classes in object-oriented languages. We show how class specifications in CCSL can be translated into higher order logic. This allows us to reason about these specifications. In particular, it allows us (1) to describe (various) implementations of a particular class specification, (2) to develop the logical theory of a specific class specification, and (3) to establish refinements between two class specifications.

We use the (dependently typed) higher order logic of the proof-assistant PVS, so that we have extensive tool support for reasoning about class specifications. Moreover, we describe our own front-end tool to PVS, which generates from CCSL class specifications appropriate PVS theories and proofs of some elementary results.

1 Introduction

During the last two decades, object-orientation has established itself in analysis, design and programming. At this moment, c++ and JAVA are probably the most popular object-oriented programming languages. Despite this apparent success, relatively little work has been done on formal (logical) methods for object-oriented programming. One of the reasons, we think, is that there is no generally accepted formal computational model for object-oriented programming. Such a model is needed as domain of reasoning.

One such formal model has recently emerged in the form of "coalgebras" (explicitly *e.g.* in [21]). It should be placed in the tradition of behavioural specification, see also [6, 8, 4]. Coalgebras are the formal duals of algebras, see [14] for background information. They consist of a (hidden) state space—typically written as Self in this context—together with several operations (or methods) acting on Self. These operations may be attributes giving some information about objects (the elements of Self), or they may be procedures for modifying objects. All access to elements of Self should go via the operations of the coalgebra. In contrast, elements of abstract data types represented as algebras can only be built via the "constructor" operations (of the algebra). We consider coalgebras together with initial states as classes, and elements of the carrier Self of a coalgebra as (states of) objects of the class.

For verification purposes involving coalgebraic classes and objects we are interested in the observable behavior and not in the concrete representation of elements of Self. A behavior of an object in this context is the objects reaction pattern, *i.e.* what we can observe via the attributes after performing internal computations triggered by pressing procedure buttons. This naturally leads to notions like bisimilarity (indistinguishability of objects via the available operations) and invariance.

Based on coalgebras, a certain format has been developed for class specifications, see [21, 11, 10]. This format typically consists of three sections, describing the class specifications' methods, assertions, and creation-conditions—which hold for newly created objects. We have developed this format into a formal language CCSL, for *Coalgebraic Class Specification Language*, which will be sketched below. *Ad hoc* representations of these class specifications in the higher order logic of the proof-tool PVS [18, 17] have been used in [12, 13] to reason about such classes—notably for refinement arguments. Further experiments with formal reasoning about classes and objects have led us to a general representation of CCSL class specifications in higher order logic. Below we explain this model (in the logic of PVS), and also a (preliminary version of a) front-end tool that we use for generating such models from class specifications.

The code for this tool (called LOOP for *Logic of Object-Oriented Programming*) is written in OCAML [22]. It basically performs three consecutive steps: it first translates a CCSL class specification into some representation in OCAML; this representation is then internally analysed and finally transformed into PVS theories and proof. The generated PVS file contains several theories describing the representation of the class specification, via appropriate definitions and associated lemmas (*e.g.* stating that bisimilarity is an equivalence relation). Another file that is generated by our tool contains instructions for proofs of the lemmas in the PVS file. The architecture of our tool allows for easy extensions, *e.g.* to accept JAVA [7] or EIFFEL [16] classes, or to generate files for other proof assistants such as ISABELLE [19]. The diagram below describes (via the solid lines) what our tool currently does, see Section 5 for some more details. The dashed lines indicate possible future extensions.

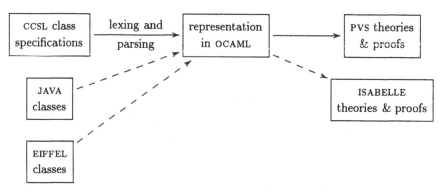

The idea behind the dashed lines on the left is that classes in actual programming languages should lead to executable class specifications, about which one can reason. We have made some progress—which will be reported elsewhere—in reasoning about JAVA classes in this setting. Here we concentrate on the upper solid lines.

The paper is organised as follows. We start in Sections 2 and 3 with an elaborate discussion of two examples, involving a class specification of a register in which one can store data at addresses, and a subclass specification of a bounded register, in which writing is only allowed if the register is not full. This involves overriding of the original write method. Then, in Section 4 we discuss some further aspects of the way that we model class specifications and that we reason about them. Finally, in Section 5, we describe the current stage of the implementation of our front-end tool.

We shall be using the notation of PVS's higher order logic when we describe our models. It is largely self-explanatory, and any non-standard aspects will be explained as we proceed. The LOOP front-end tool that will be described in Section 5 is still under development. Currently, it does the basics of the translation from CCSL class specification to PVS theories and proofs (without any fancy GUI). It may take some time before it reaches a stable form. Instead of elaborating implementation details, this paper focuses on the basic ideas of our models.

2 A simple register: specification and modeling

We start by considering a simple register, which can store data at an address. It contains read, write and erase operations, satisfying some obvious requirements. It is described in our coalgebraic class specification language CCSL in Figure 1. The type constructor $A \mapsto \text{Lift}[A]$ adds a bottom element 'bot' to a type A, and keeps all elements a from A as up(a). A *total* function $B \to \text{Lift}[A]$ may then be identified with a *partial* function $B \to A$. We use square brackets $[A_1, \ldots, A_n]$ for the Cartesian product $A_1 \times \cdots \times A_n$.

```
Begin Register[ Data : Type, Address : Type ] : ClassSpec
   Method       read  : [Self, Address] -> Lift[Data];
                write : [Self, Address, Data] -> Self;
                erase : [Self, Address] -> Self
   Assertion    read_write : PVS FORALL(a,b : Address, d : Data)
                   read(write(x, a, d), b) =
                      IF a = b THEN up(d) ELSE read(x, b) ENDIF ENDPVS
                read_erase : PVS FORALL(a,b : Address) :
                   read(erase(x, a), b) =
                      IF a = b THEN bot ELSE read(x, b) ENDIF ENDPVS
   Constructor new : Self
   Creation     read_new : PVS FORALL(a:Address) : read(new,a) = bot ENDPVS
End Register
```

Fig. 1. A register class specification in CCSL

The types Data and Address are parameters in this specification, which can be suitably instantiated in a particular situation. What is coalgebraic about such specifications is that all methods act on Self, *i.e.* have Self as one of their input types[1]. Usually this type Self is not written explicitly in object-oriented languages, but it is there implicitly as the receiver of method invocations. The constructor section declares **new** as a constructor (without parameters) for creating a new register. Notice that assertions and creation-conditions have names. The PVS and ENDPVS tags are used to delimit strings, which are basically boolean expressions in PVS[2]. It is assumed that **x** is a variable in Self.

In order to reason (with PVS tool support) about such a Register class specification, we first model it in the higher order logic of PVS. This is what our LOOP tool does automatically. It generates several PVS theories to capture this specification. Space restrictions prevent us from discussing all these theories in detail, so we concentrate on the essentials.

The first step is to introduce a (single) type which captures the interface of a class specification, via a labeled product. For Register, this is done in the following PVS theory.

```
RegisterInterface[ Self, Data, Address : TYPE ] : THEORY
BEGIN
  RegisterIFace : TYPE = [# read  : [Address -> Lift[Data]],
                            write : [Address, Data -> Self],
                            erase : [Address -> Self] #]
END RegisterInterface
```

The square brace notation $[A_1, \ldots, A_n \to B]$ is used in PVS for the type of (total) functions with n inputs from $A_1, \ldots, A_n$ and with result in B. Notice that in the types of the operations in this interface the input type Self is omitted[3]. This is intended: a crucial step in our approach is that we use *coalgebras* of the form

```
c : [Self -> RegisterIFace[Self, Data, Address]]
```

as models of the method section of the Register specification, with Self as state space. The individual methods can be extracted from such a coalgebra c via the definitions:

```
read(c) : [Self, Address -> Lift[Data]] =
  LAMBDA(x : Self, a : Address) : read(c(x))(a)
write(c) : [Self, Address, Data -> Self] =
  LAMBDA(x : Self, a : Address, d : Data) : write(c(x))(a,d)
erase(c) : [Self, Address -> Self] =
  LAMBDA(x : Self, a : Address) : erase(c(x))(a)
```

Thus the individual methods of a class can be extracted from such a single coalgebra c.

---

[1] A bit more precisely, the methods can all be written, possibly using currying, of the form Self $\to F_i(\text{Self})$; and they can be combined into a single operation Self $\to F_1(\text{Self}) \times \cdots \times F_n(\text{Self})$.

[2] Our front-end tool simply passes the string in PVS ... ENDPVS on to the PVS tool, where it is parsed and typechecked.

[3] Categorically, the type RegisterIFace captures the functor associated with the signature of operations in the class specification, see [14].

Next, our formalisation deals with invariants and bisimulations. These are special kinds of predicates and relations on Self which are suitably closed under the above operations. For example, an invariant $P \subseteq$ Self with respect to a Register coalgebra c satisfies, by definition:

$$P(x) \Rightarrow \begin{cases} \forall a\colon \text{Address}, d\colon \text{Data. } P(\text{write}(c)(x,a,d)) \\ \forall a\colon \text{Address. } P(\text{erase}(c)(x,a)). \end{cases}$$

A bisimulation $w.r.t.$ c is a relation $R \subseteq$ Self $\times$ Self satisfying:

$$R(x,y) \Rightarrow \begin{cases} \forall a\colon \text{Address. } \text{read}(c)(x,a) = \text{read}(c)(y,a) \\ \forall a\colon \text{Address}, d\colon \text{Data. } R(\text{write}(c)(x,a,d), \text{write}(c)(y,a,d)) \\ \forall a\colon \text{Address. } R(\text{erase}(c)(x,a), \text{erase}(c)(y,a)). \end{cases}$$

Bisimilarity `bisim?` is then the greatest bisimulation relation. Interestingly, these notions of invariant and bisimulation are completely determined by the class interface RegisterIFace. They are generated automatically (by our tool) by induction on the structure of the types in the interface, based on liftings of these types to predicates and relations, as introduced in [9] (see also [13]). These PVS theories about invariants and bisimulations contain several standard lemmas (stating *e.g.* that invariants are closed under finite conjunctions $\wedge$ and universal quantification $\forall$), for which proof instructions are generated automatically (again using induction).

The next theory RegisterSemantics deals with the assertions and creation-conditions. The two assertions in Figure 1 are translated into two predicates on the carrier type Self of a Register coalgebra $c\colon [\text{Self} \to \text{RegisterIFace}[\text{Self}, \text{Data}, \text{Address}]]$. Assuming that x is a variable of type Self, we generate:

```
read_write?(c)(x) : bool =
  FORALL(a,b : Address, d : Data) : read(c)(write(c)(x, a, d), b) =
    IF a = b THEN up(d) ELSE read(c)(x, b) ENDIF
read_erase?(c)(x) : bool =
  FORALL(a,b : Address) : read(c)(erase(c)(x, a), b) =
    IF a = b THEN bot ELSE read(c)(x, b) ENDIF
```

For convenience, these predicates are collected in a single predicate:

```
RegisterAssert?(c) : bool =
  FORALL(x : Self) : read_write?(c)(x) AND read_erase?(c)(x)
```

Similarly, we put the creation-condition in a predicate

```
RegisterCreate?(c) : PRED[Self] =
  {x : Self | FORALL(a : Address) : read(c)(x, a) = bot}
```

At this stage we are able to say what actually constitutes a class implementation that satisfies a class specification as in Figure 1: it is a coalgebra $c\colon [\text{Self} \to \text{RegisterIFace}[\text{Self}, \text{Data}, \text{Address}]]$ satisfying the predicate RegisterAssert?, together with some element new: Self satisfying the predicate RegisterCreate?(c). This is formalised in the following theory using a (dependent!) labeled product.

```
RegisterClassStructure [Self, Data, Address : TYPE] : THEORY
BEGIN
   IMPORTING RegisterSemantics[Self, Data, Address]
   RegisterClass : TYPE = [# clg : (RegisterAssert?),
                            new : (RegisterCreate?(clg)) #]
END RegisterClassStructure
```

The notation (P) for a predicate P:[A -> bool] on A:TYPE is used in PVS as
an abbreviation for the predicate subtype {x:A|P(x)}. A class thus consists of
a state space Self with appropriate operations (combined in a coalgebra clg on
Self) and with an appropriate constructor new. An object of such a class is then
simply an inhabitant of the state space Self. Thus, in the way that we model
classes and objects, the methods are part of the class, and not of the object.
This is called the delegation implementation, in contrast to the embedding implementation, where the operations are part of the object, see [1, Sections 2.1
and 2.2].

Once we have all this settled, we can start reasoning about the class specification. The two things we can do immediately are: (1) describing an implementation of the specification, and (2) developing its theory. Both are user tasks:
the tool only provides theory frames which the user can fill in. We give a sketch
of what can be done.

As to (1), it is a wise strategy to write out an implementation, immediately
after finishing the specification. It is notoriously hard to write "good" specifications which capture the informal description of the matter in question and,
at the same time, are consistent in the logic used. This is sometimes called the
"ground problem". Usually, specialists have a good understanding of a particular implementation. Once this implementation is formally written out it can be
checked against the assertions and creation-conditions.

For example, for the Register class specification, an obvious implementation
describes registers as partial functions from addresses to data. This can be done
via the Lift[-] type constructor, and yields as state space:

```
FunctionSpace : TYPE = [Address -> Lift[Data]]
```

This type can be equipped with a suitable coalgebra structure and a constructor:

```
c : [FunctionSpace -> RegisterIFace[FunctionSpace, Data, Address]] =
  LAMBDA(f : FunctionSpace) :
    (# read := LAMBDA(a : Address) : f(a),
       write := LAMBDA(a : Address, d : Data) : f WITH [(a) := up(d)],
       erase := LAMBDA(a : Address) : f WITH [(a) := bot] #)
new : FunctionSpace = LAMBDA(a : Address) : bot
```

(The notation g WITH [(y) := z] is an abbreviation for LAMBDA x : IF x = y
THEN z ELSE g(x) ENDIF.) This coalgebra structure on the state space Function-
Space clearly captures our intuition, and it is not hard to prove that both propo-
sitions RegisterAssert?(c) and RegisterCreate?(c)(new) hold. Actually, PVS can
prove both of them with a single command, (GRIND).

Of course, we can also define other implementations. For example, one can define an implementation in which the sequence of operations applied to an object is recorded for each address. This can be done by taking as state space:

```
HistorySpace : TYPE = [Address -> list[Lift[Data]]]
```

The implementation of the methods and constructor on this state space is left to the interested reader. Again, (GRIND) in PVS proves that the assertions and creation-conditions hold (for our implementation).

When class specifications are used as components in other classes (*e.g.* via class-valued attributes, see Section 4) we need a model for them. Obvious choices for a model are (1) an arbitrary, so-called "loose" model and (2) a final model. Both are generated. Once we know that our class specification has a non-trivial model (and hence that it is consistent) we can safely postulate the existence of a loose model. A final model enables the use of subclasses for components, but its existence is an open question in presence of binary methods. Due to a lack of space, only the loose model is described here. It has the following form.

```
LooseRegisterClass[Data, Address : TYPE] : THEORY
BEGIN
  LooseRegisterType : TYPE
  IMPORTING RegisterClassStructure[LooseRegisterType, Data, Address]
  loose_Register_existence : AXIOM
    EXISTS(cl : RegisterClass) : TRUE
  LooseRegisterClass : RegisterClass
END LooseRegisterClass
```

In this theory the existence of an arbitrary model of the class specification is guaranteed via an axiom. In principle this can be dangerous, because it may lead to inconsistencies. However, as long as a non-trivial implementation has been given (earlier) by hand, there is no such danger. The type LooseRegisterType in this theory is simply postulated, and we know nothing about its internal structure. This ensures that when this model is used as a component in another class, no internal details can be accessed (simply because there are no such details).

We turn to the second way to reason about a (translated) specification. Our tool generates an almost empty PVS theory frame called RegisterUserTheory. This theory starts by declaring a coalgebra structure c satisfying the predicate RegisterAssert?, together with a constructor satisfying the creation-condition RegisterCreate?(c). Under these assumptions a user can start proving various logical consequences of the assertions in the class specification. For example, a useful proposition that can be proved in RegisterUserTheory is the following characterisation of bisimilarity.

```
bisim_char : LEMMA
  bisim?(c)(x,y) IFF FORALL(a : Address) : read(c)(x,a) = read(c)(y,a)
```

This expresses that two objects (or states) x, y: Self are bisimilar (*i.e.* indistinguishable) *w.r.t.* the assumed (arbitrary) model c if and only if they give the same read output at each address. Intuitively this may be clear: if we cannot see a difference between two objects via reading, then using a write or erase will not create a difference between these objects (because a read after a write or erase is completely determined by the Register assertions).

Using this characterization, it is easy to prove, for example,

```
write_commutation : LEMMA
  FORALL(a,b : Addresses, d,e : Data) : a /= b IMPLIES
    bisim?(c)(write(c)(write(c)(x, a, d), b, e),
             write(c)(write(c)(x, b, e), a, d))
```

This result says that one can exchange write operations at different addresses. Notice that we are careful in only stating that the outcomes are bisimilar, and not necessarily equal. We avoid the use of equality of objects/states, since we regard these as hidden, and we restrict access to (public) methods. In addition, the use of bisimilarity entails that the results that we prove also hold in implementations where bisimilar states need not be (internally) equal, like in the above HistorySpace model. There we can have equal reads at all addresses in two states, even though the histories of these states are quite different. Hence such states are bisimilar, but internally different.

At the end, it may be instructive to compare this coalgebraic way of combining methods, with the approach taken in [1] (explicitly *e.g.* in Section 8.5.2). There the methods of a class are combined in a slightly different manner, namely in a labeled product, called "trait type":

$$\text{RegisterTrait} = [\# \ \text{read: Self} \to [\text{Address} \to \text{Lift[Data]}],$$
$$\text{write: Self} \to [\text{Address, Data} \to \text{Self}],$$
$$\text{erase: Self} \to [\text{Address} \to \text{Self}] \ \#]$$

What we do is basically the same, except that our methods are combined "coalgebraically", with the common input type Self on the outside. What is called a "class type" in [1] is such a "trait type" together with a constructor new, see the RegisterClass type above. Thus, when it comes to interfaces, there is no real difference between our approach and the one in [1]. But we go further in two essential ways: (a) we restrict the methods and constructors so that they satisfy certain requirements (given in the assertions and creation-conditions in the specification), and (b) we (automatically) generate appropriate notions of invariance and bisimilarity for (the interface of) each class specification, and use them systematically in reasoning about these specifications.

3   A bounded register: inheritance and overriding

Having described an implementation for the Register class specification—and developed part of its theory—we now introduce a new class specification BoundedRegister by inheritance. A bounded register is a subclass of a register, which overrides the write operation and defines a new attribute count. A bounded register can only store a limited number of data elements, and the count attribute is

```
Begin BoundedRegister[ Data : Type, Address : Type, n : nat ] : ClassSpec
  Inherit from Register[Data,Address]
  Method      write : [Self,Address,Data] -> Self;
              count : Self -> nat
  Assertion   override_write_def : PVS FORALL(a : Address, d : Data) :
                 bisim?(write(x, a, d), IF count(x) < n OR up?(read(x,a))
                                        THEN super_write(x, a, d)
                                        ELSE x
                                        ENDIF) ENDPVS
              count_super_write : PVS FORALL(a : Address, d : Data) :
                 count(super_write(x, a, d)) = IF bot?(read(x,a))
                                               THEN count(x) + 1
                                               ELSE count(x)
                                               ENDIF ENDPVS
              count_erase : PVS FORALL(a : Address) :
                 count(erase(x, a)) = IF bot?(read(x, a))
                                      THEN count(x)
                                      ELSE max(0, count(x) - 1)
                                      ENDIF ENDPVS
  Constructor new : Self
  Creation    count_new : PVS count(new) = 0 ENDPVS
End BoundedRegister
```

Fig. 2. A bounded register class specification in CCSL

used to keep track of how much data is currently stored. When the bounded register is full (*i.e.* when its count is above a certain number n given as parameter), a write operation does not have any effect; otherwise it acts as the write operation from the superclass Register. Further, the read and erase operations from Register are used without modification. A CCSL class specification of a bounded register is given in Figure 2. The predicates bot? and up? on Lift[Data] tell us whether an element x : Lift[Data] is bot or up(d), for some d : Data.

Again, our tool generates several PVS theories from this specification. This section will discuss the essential consequences the use of inheritance (in combination with overriding) has on the generated theories.

We model inheritance by letting the interface of the BoundedRegister not only contain the operations write and count, but also the superclass as a field (super_Register). This enables access to the methods of the superclass.

```
BoundedRegisterIFace : TYPE =
  [# super_Register : RegisterIFace[Self, Data, Address],
     write : [Address, Data -> Self],
     count : nat #]
```

Now we provide access not only to the individual methods of the Bounded-Register class but also to the methods from the superclass, via the following definitions.

```
c : VAR [Self -> BoundedRegisterIFace[Self, Data, Address]]

super_Register(c) : [Self -> RegisterIFace[Self, Data, Address]] =
  LAMBDA (x:Self) : super_Register(c(x))
read(c) : [[Self, Address] -> Lift[Data]] =
```

```
  LAMBDA (x:Self, a:Address) : read(super_Register(c(x)))(a)
super_write(c) : [[Self, Address, Data] -> Self] =
  LAMBDA (x:Self, a:Address, d:Data) : write(super_Register(c(x)))(a, d)
write(c) : [[Self, Address, Data] -> Self] =
  LAMBDA (x:Self, a:Address, d:Data) : write(c(x))(a, d)
erase(c) : [Self, Address -> Self] =
  LAMBDA(x : Self, a : Address) : erase(super_register(c(x)))(a)
count(c) : [Self -> nat] =
  LAMBDA(x : Self) : count(c(x))
```

Via these explicit definitions, all methods of superclasses can be used in subclasses. The number of such definitions may be considerable when there are high inheritance trees, but our tool generates all of them automatically. In fact, this is one of the reasons for developing such a tool.

The write operation in the subclass specification in Figure 2 also occurs in the superclass. This double occurrence is used to signal overriding. Our tool recognizes it, and generates as a result two write operations. A "direct" one from the current subclass (simply called **write**) and an "indirect" one from the superclass (called **super_write**). Notice that the coalgebra c—used as variable in this theory—combines both the structure of the subclass and the superclass.

The theories about invariants and bisimulations are generated incrementally, *i.e.* they extend the predicates and relations on Register with appropriate clauses for the additional methods of the subclass.

The assertions and creation-conditions of BoundedRegister are translated into PVS predicates, just as in the Register example. The resulting predicate BoundedRegisterAssert? combines these assertions with the assertions in RegisterAssert?. The predicate BoundedRegisterCreate? similarly combines the new creation-conditions with the "super" creation-conditions from Register. This implies that, although we override a method, we can still expect the superclass to behave as specified.

```
BoundedRegisterAssert?(c) : bool =
  RegisterAssert?[Self, Data, Address](super_register(c))
    AND FORALL(x : Self) : override_write_def?(c)(x)
                           AND count_super_write?(c)(x)
                           AND count_erase?(c)(x)
BoundedRegisterCreate?(c) : PRED[Self] =
  {x : Self | count(c)(x) = 0
    AND RegisterCreate?[Self, Data, Address](super_register(c))(x)}
```

The BoundedRegisterStructure theory now contains an additional casting operation from BoundedRegisterClass to RegisterClass.

```
BoundedRegisterClass : TYPE =
  [# clg : (BoundedRegisterAssert?),
     new : (BoundedRegisterCreate?(clg)) #]

cast : [BoundedRegisterClass -> RegisterClass] =
  LAMBDA(cl : BoundedRegisterClass) :
    [# clg := super_Register(clg(cl)),
       new := new(cl) #]
```

(Well-definedness of **cast** involves proving two easy results.) When an implementation for a bounded register is described, definitions for the methods in BoundedRegister (*i.e.* count and write) and for those in the superclass (*i.e.* read, write, erase) have to be given. An obvious implementation of the bounded register specification uses the Cartesian product [nat, FunctionSpace] as state space, where FunctionSpace is the state space of the first Register implementation in the previous section. The first component **nat** describes the value of count. Appropriate operations on this state are easily defined, by re-using the Register implementation on FunctionSpace. The contents of the theory with the loose model is not influenced by inheritance and also the way the theory is generated is not altered.

4 Modeling other object-oriented aspects

This section briefly discusses how—and to what extend—various typically object-oriented features are realised in our formalisation. Not all of the aspects that we touch upon have fully crystalised into stable form, and the further development and use of our tool may lead to certain changes.

Component classes. When specifying a new class one often wishes to use another class as a component. By component we mean an attribute which is an instance of another class. This is also known as an aggregation realising a *has-a* relationship between two classes.

```
Begin Counter [ n: posnat, val_init : nat] : CLASSSPEC
   Method      val : Self -> nat;
               next : Self -> Self;
               clear : Self -> Self
   Assertion   val_next : PVS val(next(x)) =
                               IF val(x) = n-1 THEN 0 ELSE val(x)+1 ENDIF
                           ENDPVS
               val_init : PVS val_init <= n ENDPVS
               val_clear : PVS val(clear(x)) = 0 ENDPVS
   Constructor new : Self
   Creation    val_new : PVS val(new) = val_init ENDPVS
End Counter
```

Fig. 3. A counter (modulo n) class specification in CCSL

To demonstrate the use of components we adopt an example from [12]. Suppose that we have a class Counter, which counts modulo a parameter n, as in Figure 3. This class Counter is used (twice) as a component in the class specification of a DoubleCounter in Figure 4. A DoubleCounter has two counters as components, both counting modulo n. It has operations next, val and clear. The first counter is incremented every time a next operation is executed. The second counter is only incremented when the first counter reaches n.

As we have seen, our tool automatically generates loose and final models (without any internal structure) for every specification, and presents an option for the user. Both these models can be used for components, but a final model enables subclassing for components.

```
Begin DoubleCounter[ n: posnat ] : CLASSSPEC
   Method     val : Self -> nat;
              first : Self -> Counter[n,0];
              second : Self -> Counter[n,0];
              next : Self -> Self;
              clear : Self -> Self
 Assertion val_def : PVS val(x) =
                          n * val(second(x)) +
                             val(first(x)) ENDPVS
           first_next : PVS bisim?(first(next(x)), next(first(x))) ENDPVS
           second_next : PVS bisim?(second(next(x)),
                            IF val(first(x)) = n-1
                            THEN next(second(x))
                            ELSE second(x) ENDIF) ENDPVS
           first_clear : PVS bisim?(first(clear(x)), clear(first(x))
                            ENDPVS
           second_clear : PVS bisim?(second(clear(x)), clear(second(x)))
                            ENDPVS
   Constructor new : Self
   Creation first_new: PVS bisim?(first(new), new)   ENDPVS
           second_new: PVS bisim?(second(new), new)   ENDPVS
End DoubleCounter
```

Fig. 4. A double counter class specification in CCSL

As an example, the interface for DoubleCounter, using a loose model for the components, will be generated as follows.

```
DoubleCounterIFace : TYPE = [# val : nat,
                               first : LooseCounterType[n,0],
                               second : LooseCounterType[n,0],
                               next : Self,
                               clear : Self #]
```

When generating the other theories for DoubleCounter, components are handled just as normal attributes (with bisimilarity as their equality relation).

Refinement. Earlier we mentioned how to implement a class specification and how to develop its theory. A third important activity is proving refinements between class specifications. We say that a "concrete" class refines an "abstract" class when a model (*i.e.* an implementation) of the abstract class can be described in terms of the concrete class. We construct this model as abstract(c): [Self→ AbstractIFace[Self,···]], where c: [Self → ConcreteIFace[Self,···]] is an arbitrary model of the concrete class[4]. Following [13] we do not need the entire state space Self to obtain an "abstract" model, but we can restrict ourselves to the subtype (P) of Self arising from an invariant P on Self (*w.r.t.* the abstract class). Then abstract(c) restricts to an operation of type $[(P) \rightarrow$ AbstractIFace$[(P),···]]$. Of course, it has to be proven that the model satisfies the assertions and creation-conditions of the abstract class, as expressed by the following lemma.

```
Abstract_refine : LEMMA
   AbstractAssert?(abstract(c)) AND AbstractCreate?(abstract(c))(new)
```

---

[4] Such a model abstract(c) should actually incorporate models of all the superclasses of the abstract class. Therefore, in practice, the model abstract(c) is best constructed by first constructing all these "super" models.

As an example, we can prove that DoubleCounter with parameter n refines a counter modulo n^2. The model for this refinement uses the invariant that the values of both component counters are bounded by n.

Overloaded methods. Some object-oriented languages allow overloading of methods: multiple methods with the same name may occur in the same class as long as their types are different. This is also possible in CCSL. PVS does allow overloading of functions, but field names in a labeled product—used as types of interfaces—are not permitted, hence we use ordinary products in interfaces with overloading.

Multiple inheritance. In our formalization we allow multiple inheritance (even though some object-oriented languages do not). This requires coping with name clashes, for instance: (1) if different superclasses define a method with the same name, and (2) if one class is inherited twice via different paths. To solve the first problem, the user can rename the conflicting methods in the INHERIT FROM section in the CCSL specification, like in EIFFEL [16]. As an example, a class can inherit both from Counter and from DoubleCounter in the following manner.

```
INHERIT FROM Counter[n,0] RENAMING val AS val_c AND
                          next AS next_c AND
                          clear AS clear_c,
             DoubleCounter[n] RENAMING val AS val_d AND
                          next AS next_d AND
                          clear AS clear_d
```

This will lead to method definitions like

```
val_c(c) : [Self -> nat] =
  LAMBDA(x : Self) : val(super_Counter(c(x)))
val_d(c) : [Self -> nat] =
  LAMBDA(x : Self) : val(super_DoubleCounter(c(x)))
```

Renaming is also necessary for different instances of the same class. The second problem of multiple paths to the same method is solved essentially by using sets of ancestor methods.

Creation with parameters. So far we have simply used 'new' in CCSL specifications as a constructor which returns a new instance of a class. In object-oriented languages one can usually parametrise such constructors with the initial values of the attributes. Typically, in a point class (specification) with attributes **fst** and **snd** for first and second coordinate, one may wish to have **new** as a (binary) constructor satisfying the following creation-conditions.

```
fst(new(a, b)) = a AND snd(new(a, b)) = b
```

This option also exists in CCSL: one can put constructors as functions with type $[A_1, \cdots, A_n] \rightarrow$ Self in the constructor section. They are handled in PVS via a labeled product containing all these constructors, instead of a single constructor **new**, as in the examples in Sections 2 and 3. Since we have not yet reached agreement on whether or not constructors should be inherited in object-oriented specifications, we included both options.

Subtyping. The usual object-oriented view is that inheritance (subclassing) implies subtyping (see [1, Section 3.2]), namely of the form: in every place where an object from a superclass is expected, an object from a subclass may be used as well. This is because all methods from the superclass also exist in the subclass—possibly in overridden form, but still with the same type. Precisely this aspect of subclassing exists in our formalisation because all methods from superclasses are explicitly (re-)defined in subclasses, see the definitions of **read(c)** *etc.* for bounded registers in Section 3. This "structural" subtyping (see again [1, Section 3.2]) arises because the Register interface is part of the BoundedRegister interface. Also we use explicit casting operations from subclasses to superclasses, as described for bounded registers in Section 3. Such casting operations are generated for components as final models.

Binary methods. Binary methods are a topic of intense debate in the object-oriented community, see [3]. They are allowed in many object-oriented languages, but can lead to various problems (notably type insecurities). A standard example of a binary method is the union (or intersection) operation in a class (specification) of sets (over some parameter type A).

```
...
elem? : [Self, A -> bool];
add, delete : [Self, A -> Self];
union, intersection : [Self, Self -> Self];
...
```

Typically, a binary (or n-ary, for $n > 1$) method takes multiple inputs of type Self. Methods of type $[\text{Self}, A_1, \cdots, A_n] \to F(\text{Self})$ are allowed in CCSL under the following two restrictions: (1) if Self occurs in A_i then $A_i = \text{Self}$, (2) Self occurs only positively in F.

Late binding. Consider a Point class specification with attributes **fst** and **snd** (as above) and with a **move** method satisfying:

```
fst(move(x,da,db)) = fst(x) + da AND snd(move(x,da,db)) = snd(x) + db
```

Suppose now that we often need the **move** operation with parameters da = db = 1, and decide to define it explicitly as **move1(x)** = **move(x,1,1)**. Late binding means that if we later override **move** in a subclass of Point, then the **move1** method will change accordingly: its definition will then use the overridden **move**. At this moment we have an *ad hoc* solution to model late binding, and we are still testing its appropriateness in various examples.

5 The front-end LOOP tool

Thus far we have seen how (CCSL) class specifications can be translated into higher order logic. This translation is done automatically by our tool, which is constructed as a front-end to a proof assistant. In general, front-end tools provide a higher level interface tailored to a specific application domain [2, 20, 23, 15, 5]. They vary in the degree of sophistication and user support. While simple systems feature theory blueprints where the user fills out special slots in combination with specialised high level tactics [2, 5], more advanced approaches define a special language and provide command line compilers [20] or even interactive user interfaces [15].

Our development aims at an environment in which the user can specify classes in several languages and frameworks and can then reason about their properties and relationships in a suitable proof assistant of choice. Ultimately, we desire a tool, called LOOP (for: Logic of Object-Oriented Programming), which provides an interactive (emacs) shell for the proof assistant. Thus far, as a first step, we focus on the compiler, which generates for a given class specification the corresponding theory and proof representations for the target proof assistant. It should be easy to extend the tool to other object-oriented languages and proof assistants. Also, it should come with a suitable graphical user interface. These aims influenced the choice of the implementation language and the architecture of the compiler.

We use the typed functional language Objective Caml (OCAML) [22], the current release of the French ML dialect CAML. Objective Caml provides, above the strict typing and readable syntax of an ML dialect, a typed module system, command line compilers with the capability of generating native machine code, lexer and parser generators, and an extensive library including an X-Window interface.

The architecture of the compiler (see Figure 5) exploits standard compiler construction techniques. It is organised in a number of passes which work on fixed interface data structures. This enables us to easily plug-in modules for other input languages (than CCSL) and other target proof assistants (than PVS).

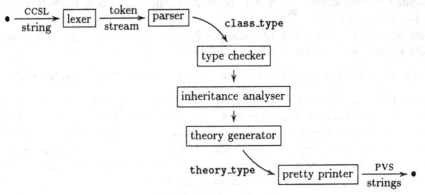

Fig. 5. Tool architecture

The compiler basically consists of the input modules lexer and parser, the internal modules (the vertical part in Figure 5), and the pretty printer. The lexer and parser are generated by the OCAML tools OCAMLLEX and OCAMLYACC which resemble the well-known LEX and YACC from C programming environments. Parsing a (CCSL) string yields an internal symbolic class represented as a value of the complicated, inductively defined OCAML type **class_type**. The parser can be replaced by any other function which generates values of **class_type**. All internal passes have input and output values in this type. The real work is carried out at a symbolic level. Extra steps can easily be inserted. After type checking and performing several semantic checks (for instance to determine the full inheritance tree of a class) the final internal pass produces symbolic theories and proofs as values of the OCAML type **theory_type**. This latter pass is the workhorse of the whole system. Finally, a target specific pretty printer converts the symbolic representation for PVS (or another proof assistant).

Currently, the compiler accepts CCSL class specifications in a file *name*.beh and generates the corresponding theories and proofs as described in the previous sections. For instance, compilation of a file **register.beh** containing the simple specification from Figure 1 will generate the files **register.pvs** and **register.prf**. The file **register.pvs** can then be loaded, parsed, and type checked in PVS. Before filling out the theory frames as described above the user can prove automatically all the standard lemmas with the **proof-file** command.

Conclusions and future work

We have elaborated a way to model object-oriented class specifications in higher order logic in such detail that it is amenable to tool support. Future work, as already mentioned at various points in this paper, involves: elaboration of the formal definition of CCSL (including *e.g.* visibility modifiers and late bindings), completion of the implementation of the LOOP tool, definition of appropriate tactics, stepwise refinement, development of various extensions to the tool and of course: use of the tool in reasoning about various object-oriented systems.

Acknowledgements

We thank David Griffioen for helpful discussions.

References

1. M. Abadi and L. Cardelli. *A Theory of Objects*. Monographs in Comp. Sci. Springer, 1996.
2. M. Archer and C. Heitmeyer. TAME: A specialized specification and verification system for timed automata. In A. Bestavros, editor, *Work In Progress (WIP) Proceedings of the 17th IEEE Real-Time Systems Symposium (RTSS'96)*, pages 3–6, Washington, DC, December 1996. The WIP Proceedings is available at http://www.cs.bu.edu/pub/ieee-rts/rtss96/wip/proceedings.
3. K. Bruce, L. Cardelli, G. Castagna, The Hopkins Objects Group, G. Leavens, and B. Pierce. On binary methods. *Theory & Practice of Object Systems*, 1(3), 1996.
4. C. Cîrstea. Coalgebra Semantics for Hidden Algebra: parametrised objects and inheritance. To appear in: *Workshop on Algebraic Development Techniques* (Springer LNCS), 1998.
5. A. Dold, F.W. von Henke, H. Pfeifer, and H. Rueß. Formal verification of transformations for peephole optimization. In *FME '97: Formal Methods: Their Industrial Application and Strengthened Foundations*, Lecture Notes in Computer Science.
6. J.A. Goguen and G. Malcolm. An extended abstract of a hidden agenda. In J. Meystel, A. Meystel, and R. Quintero, editors, *Proceedings of the Conference on Intelligent Systems: A Semiotic Perspective*, pages 159–167. Nat. Inst. Stand. & Techn., 1996.

7. J. Gosling, B. Jay, and G. Steele. *The Java Language Specification*. Addison-Wesley, 1996.

8. R. Hennicker, M. Wirsing, and M. Bidoit. Proof systems for structured specifications with observability operators. *Theor. Comp. Sci.*, 173(2):393–443, 1997.

9. C. Hermida and B. Jacobs. Structural induction and coinduction in a fibrational setting. *Information & Computation* (to appear).

10. B. Jacobs. Inheritance and cofree constructions. In P. Cointe, editor, *European Conference on Object-Oriented Programming*, number 1098 in Lect. Notes Comp. Sci., pages 210–231. Springer, Berlin, 1996.

11. B. Jacobs. Objects and classes, co-algebraically. In B. Freitag, C.B. Jones, C. Lengauer, and H.-J. Schek, editors, *Object-Orientation with Parallelism and Persistence*, pages 83–103. Kluwer Acad. Publ., 1996.

12. B. Jacobs. Behaviour-refinement of coalgebraic specifications with coinductive correctness proofs. In M. Bidoit and M. Dauchet, editors, *TAPSOFT'97: Theory and Practice of Software Development*, number 1214 in Lect. Notes Comp. Sci., pages 787–802. Springer, Berlin, 1997.

13. B. Jacobs. Invariants, bisimulations and the correctness of coalgebraic refinements. In M. Johnson, editor, *Algebraic Methodology and Software Technology*, number 1349 in Lect. Notes Comp. Sci., pages 276–291, Berlin, 1997.

14. B. Jacobs and J. Rutten. A tutorial on (co)algebras and (co)induction. *EATCS Bulletin*, 62:222–259, 1997.

15. J. Knappman. A PVS based tool for developing programs in the refinement calculus. Master's thesis, Inst. of Comp. Sci. & Appl. Math., Christian-Albrechts-Univ. of Kiel, 1996. http://www.informatik.uni-kiel.de/inf/deRoever/DiplJKm.html

16. B. Meyer. *Object-Oriented Software Construction*. Prentice Hall, 2nd rev. edition, 1997.

17. S. Owre, S. Rajan, J.M. Rushby, N. Shankar, and M. Srivas. PVS: Combining specification, proof checking, and model checking. In R. Alur and T.A. Henzinger, editors, *Computer Aided Verification*, number 1102 in Lect. Notes Comp. Sci., pages 411–414. Springer, Berlin, 1996.

18. S. Owre, J.M. Rushby, N. Shankar, and F. von Henke. Formal verification for fault-tolerant architectures: Prolegomena to the design of PVS. *IEEE Trans. on Softw. Eng.*, 21(2):107–125, 1995.

19. L.C. Paulson. *Isabelle: A Generic Theorem Prover*. Number 828 in Lect. Notes Comp. Sci. Springer, Berlin, 1994.

20. C.H. Pratten. An Introduction to Proving AMN Specifications with PVS and the AMN-Proof Tool. http://www.dsse.ecs.soton.ac.uk/~chp/amn_proof/papers.html.

21. H. Reichel. An approach to object semantics based on terminal co-algebras. *Math. Struct. in Comp. Sci.*, 5:129–152, 1995.

22. D. Rémy and J. Vouillon. Objective ML: A simple object-oriented extension of ML. In *Princ. of Progr. Lang.*, pages 40–53. ACM Press, 1997.

23. J.U. Skakkebæk. *A Verification Assistant for a Real Time Logic*. PhD thesis, Dep. of Computer Science, Techn. Univ. Denmark, 1994.

Language Primitives and Type Discipline for Structured Communication-Based Programming

KOHEI HONDA[*], VASCO T. VASCONCELOS[†], AND MAKOTO KUBO[‡]

ABSTRACT. We introduce basic language constructs and a type discipline as a foundation of structured communication-based concurrent programming. The constructs, which are easily translatable into the summation-less asynchronous π-calculus, allow programmers to organise programs as a combination of multiple flows of (possibly unbounded) reciprocal interactions in a simple and elegant way, subsuming the preceding communication primitives such as method invocation and rendez-vous. The resulting syntactic structure is exploited by a type discipline à la ML, which offers a high-level type abstraction of interactive behaviours of programs as well as guaranteeing the compatibility of interaction patterns between processes in a well-typed program. After presenting the formal semantics, the use of language constructs is illustrated through examples, and the basic syntactic results of the type discipline are established. Implementation concerns are also addressed.

1. Introduction

Recently, significance of programming practice based on communication among processes is rapidly increasing by the development of networked computing. From network protocols over the Internet to server-client systems in local area networks to distributed applications in the world wide web to interaction between mobile robots to a global banking system, the execution of complex, reciprocal communication among multiple processes becomes an important element in the achievement of the goals of applications. Many programming languages and formalisms have been proposed so far for the description of software based on communication. As programming languages, we have CSP [7], Ada [28], languages based on Actors [2], POOL [3], ABCL [33], Concurrent Smalltalk [32], or more recently Pict and other π-calculus-based languages [6, 23, 29]. As formalisms, we have CCS [15], Theoretical CSP [8], π-calculus [18], and other process algebras. In another vein, we have functional programming languages augmented with communication primitives, such as CML [26], dML [21], and Concurrent Haskell [12]. In these languages and formalisms, various communication primitives have been offered (such as synchronous/asynchronous message passing, remote procedure call, method-call and rendez-vous), and the description of communication behaviour is done by combining these primitives. What we observe in these primitives is that, while they do express one-time interaction between processes, there is no construct to structure a series of reciprocal interactions between two parties as such. That is, the only way to represent a series of communications following a certain scenario (think of interactions between a file server and its client) is to describe them as a collection of distinct, unrelated interactions. In applications based on complex interactions among concurrent processes, which are appearing more and more in these days, the lack of structuring methods would result in low readability and careless bugs in final programs, apart from the case when the whole communication behaviour can be simply described as, say, a one-time remote procedure call. The situation may be illustrated in comparison with the design history

[*]Dept. of Computer Science, University of Edinburgh, UK. [†]Dept. of Computer Science, University of Lisbon, Portugal. [‡]Dept. of Computer Science, Chiba University of Commerce, Japan.

of imperative programming languages. In early imperative languages, programs were constructed as a bare sequence of primitives which correspond to machine operations, such as assignment and goto (consider early Fortran). As is well-known, as more programs in large size were constructed, it had become clear that such a method leads to programs without lucidity, readability or verifiability, so that the notion of structured programming was proposed in 1970's. In present days, having the language constructs for structured programming is a norm in imperative languages.

Such a comparison raises the question as to whether we can have a similar structuring method in the context of communication-based concurrent programming. Its objective is to offer a basic means to describe complex interaction behaviours with clarity and discipline at the high-level of abstraction, together with a formal basis for verification. Its key elements would, above all, consist of (1) the basic communication primitives (corresponding to assignment and arithmetic operations in the imperative setting), and (2) the structuring constructs to combine them (corresponding to "if-then-else" and "while"). Verification methodologies on their basis should then be developed.

The present paper proposes structuring primitives and the accompanying type discipline, as a basic structuring method for communication-based concurrent programming. The proposed constructs have a simple operational semantics, and various communication patterns, including those of the conventional primitives as well as those which go beyond them, are representable as their combination with clarity and rigor at the high-level of abstraction. The type discipline plays a fundamental role, guaranteeing compatibility of interaction patterns among processes via a type inference algorithm in the line of ML [19]. Concretely our proposal consists of the following key ideas.

- A basic structuring concept for communication-based programming, called *session*. A session is a chain of dyadic interactions whose collection constitutes a program. A session is designated by a private port called *channel*, through which interactions belonging to that session are performed. Channels form a distinct syntactic domain; its differentiation from the usual port names is a basic design decision we take to make the logical structure of programs explicit. Other than session, the standard structuring constructs for concurrent programming, *parallel composition*, *name hiding*, *conditional* and *recursion* are provided. In particular the combination of recursion and session allows the expression of unbounded thread of interactions as a single abstraction unit.

- Three basic communication primitives, *value passing*, *label branching*, and *delegation*. The first is the standard synchronous message passing as found in e.g. CSP or π-calculus. The second is a purified form of method invocation, deprived of value passing. The third is for passing a channel to another process, thus allowing a programmer to dynamically distribute a single session among multiple processes in a well-structured way. Together with the session structure, the combination of these primitives allows the flexible description of complex communication structures with clarity and discipline.

- A *basic type discipline* for the communication primitives, as an indispensable element of the structuring method. The typability of a program ensures two possibly communicating processes always own compatible communication patterns. For example, a procedural call has a pattern of output-input from the caller's viewpoint; then the callee should have a communication pattern of input-output. Because incompatibility of interaction patterns between processes would be one of the main reasons for bugs in communication-based programming, we believe such a type discipline has important pragmatic significance. The derived type gives high-level abstraction of interactive behaviours of a program.

Because communication between processes over the network can be done between modules written in different programming languages, the proposed communication constructs may as well be used by embedding them in various programming languages; however for simplicity we present them as a self-contained small programming language, which has been stripped to the barest minimum necessary for explanation of its novel features. Using the language, the basic concept of the proposed constructs is illustrated through programming examples. They show how extant communication primitives such as remote procedural-call and method invocation can be concisely expressed as sessions of specific patterns (hence with specific type abstractions). They also show how sessions can represent those communication structures which do not conform to the preceding primitives but which would naturally arise in practice. This suggests that the session-based program organisation may constitute a synthesis of a number of familiar as well as new programming ideas concerning communication. We also show the proposed constructs can be simply translatable into the asynchronous polyadic π-calculus with branching [31]. This suggests the feasibility of implementation in distributed environment. Yet much remains to be studied concerning the proposed structuring method, including the efficient implementation of the constructs and the accompanying reasoning principles. See Section 6 for more discussions.

The technical content of the present paper is developed on the basis of the preceding proposal [27] due to Kaku Takeuchi and the present authors. The main contributions of the present proposal in comparison with [27] are: the generalisation of session structure by delegation and recursive sessions, which definitely enlarges the applicability of the proposed structuring method; the typing system incorporating these novel concepts; representation of conventional communication primitives by the structuring constructs; and basic programming examples which show how the constructs, in particular through the use of the above mentioned novel features, can lucidly represent complex communication structures which would not be amenable to conventional communication primitives.

In the rest of the paper, Section 2 introduces the language primitives and their operational semantics. Section 3 illustrates how the primitives allow clean representation of extant communication primitives. Section 4 shows how the primitives can represent those interaction structures beyond those of the conventional communication primitives through key programming examples. Section 5 presents the typing system and establishes the basic syntactic results. Section 6 concludes with discussions on the implementation concerns, related works and further issues.

2. Syntax and Operational Semantics

2.1. **Basic Concepts.** The central idea in the present structuring method is a *session*. A session is a series of reciprocal interactions between two parties, possibly with branching and recursion, and serves as a unit of abstraction for describing interaction. Communications belonging to a session are done via a port specific to that session, called a *channel*. A fresh channel is generated when initiating each session, for the use in communications in the session. We use the following syntax for the initiation of a session.

request $a(k)$ in P accept $a(k)$ in P initiation of session

The request first requests, via a name a, the initiation of a session as well as the generation of a fresh channel, then P would use the channel for later communications. The accept, on the other hand, receives the request for the initiation of a session via a, generates a new channel k, which would be used for communications in P. In the above grammar, the parenthesis (k) and the key word in shows the binding and its scope.

Thus, in request $a(k)$ in P, the part (k) binds the free occurrences of k in P. This convention is used uniformly throughout the present paper.

Via a channel of a session, three kinds of atomic interactions are performed: *value sending* (including name passing), *branching* and *channel passing* (or *delegation*).

$k![e_1 \cdots e_n]; P$	$k?(x_1 \cdots x_n)$ in P	data sending/receiving
$k \lhd l; P$	$k \rhd \{l_1 : P_1 \| \cdots \| l_n : P_n\}$	label selection/branching
throw $k[k']; P$	catch $k(k')$ in P	channel sending/receiving (delegation)

Data sending/receiving is the standard synchronous message passing. Here e_i denotes an expression such as arithmetic/boolean formulae as well as names. We assume variables $x_1..x_n$ are all distinct. We do not consider program passing for simplicity, cf. [11]. The *branching/selection* is the minimisation of method invocation in object-based programming. $l_1, .., l_n$ are *labels* which are assumed to be pairwise distinct. The *channel sending/receiving*, which we often call *delegation*, passes a channel which is being used in a session to another process, thus radically changing the structure of a session. Delegation is the generalisation of the concept with the same name originally conceived in the concurrent object-oriented programming [34]. See Section 4.3 for detailed discussions. In passing we note that its treatment distinct from the usual value passing is essential for both disciplined programming and a tractable type inference.

Communication primitives, organised by sessions, are further combined by the following standard constructs in concurrent programming.

$P_1 \mid P_2$	concurrent composition
$(\nu a)P \quad (\nu k)P$	name/channel hiding
if e then P else Q	conditional
def $X_1(\tilde{x}_1 \tilde{k}_1) = P_1$ and $\cdots$ and $X_n(\tilde{x}_n \tilde{k}_n) = P_n$ in P	recursion

We do not need sequencing since each communication primitive already accompanies one. We also use inact, the *inaction*, which denotes the lack of action (acting as the unit of "$\mid$"). *Hiding* declares a name/channel to be local in its scope (here P). Channel hiding may not be used for usual programming, but is needed for the operational semantics presented later. In conditional, e should be a boolean expression. In recursion, X, a process variable, would occur in $P_1...P_n$ and P zero or more times. Identifiers in $\tilde{x}_i \tilde{k}_i$ should be pairwise distinct. We can use replication (or a single recursion) to achieve the same effect, but multiple recursion is preferable for well-structured programs.

This finishes the introduction of all language constructs we shall use in this paper. We give a simple example of a program.

accept $a(k)$ in $k![1]; k?(y)$ in $P \quad \mid \quad$ request $a(k)$ in $k?(x)$ in $k![x + 1];$ inact.

The first process receives a request for a new session via a, generates k, sends 1 and receives a return value via k, while the second requests the initiation of a session via a, receives the value via the generated channel, then returns the result of adding 1 to the value. Observe the compatibility of communication patterns between two processes.

2.2. Syntax Summary. We summarise the syntax we have introduced so far. Base sets are: *names*, ranged over by $a, b, \ldots$; *channels*, ranged over by k, k'; *variables*, ranged over by $x, y, \ldots$; *constants* (including names, integers and booleans), ranged over by $c, c', \ldots$; *expressions* (including constants), ranged over by $e, e', \ldots$; *labels*, ranged over by $l, l', \ldots$; and *process variables*, ranged over by $X, Y, \ldots$. $u, u', \ldots$ denote names and channels. Then *processes*, ranged over by $P, Q \ldots$, are given by the following grammar.

P	$::=$	request $a(k)$ in P	session request
	$\mid$	accept $a(k)$ in P	session acceptance
	$\mid$	$k![\tilde{e}]; P$	data sending
	$\mid$	$k?(\tilde{x})$ in P	data reception
	$\mid$	$k \triangleleft l; P$	label selection
	$\mid$	$k \triangleright \{l_1 : P_1 [\!] \cdots [\!] l_n : P_n\}$	label branching
	$\mid$	throw $k[k']; P$	channel sending
	$\mid$	catch $k(k')$ in P	channel reception
	$\mid$	if e then P else Q	conditional branch
	$\mid$	$P \mid Q$	parallel composition
	$\mid$	inact	inaction
	$\mid$	$(\nu u)P$	name/channel hiding
	$\mid$	def D in P	recursion
	$\mid$	$X[\tilde{e}\tilde{k}]$	process variables
D	$::=$	$X_1(\tilde{x}_1\tilde{k}_1) = P_1$ and $\cdots$ and $X_n(\tilde{x}_n\tilde{k}_n) = P_n$	declaration for recursion

The association of "$\mid$" is the weakest, others being the same. Parenthesis $(\cdot)$ denotes binders which bind the corresponding free occurrences. The standard *simultaneous substitution* is used, writing e.g. $P[\tilde{c}/\tilde{x}]$. The sets of free names/channels/variables/process variables of say P, defined in the standard way, are respectively denoted by $\mathrm{fn}(P), \mathrm{fc}(P), \mathrm{fv}(P)$ and $\mathrm{fpv}(P)$. The alpha-equality is written $\equiv_\alpha$. We also set $\mathrm{fu}(P) \stackrel{\text{def}}{=} \mathrm{fc}(P) \cup \mathrm{fn}(P)$. Processes without free variables or free channels are called *programs*.

2.3. Operational Semantics. For the concise definition of the operational semantics of the language constructs, we introduce the *structural equality* $\equiv$ (cf. [4, 16]), which is the smallest congruence relation on processes including the following equations.

1. $P \equiv Q$ if $P \equiv_\alpha Q$.
2. $P \mid \text{inact} \equiv P$, $\quad P \mid Q \equiv Q \mid P$, $\quad (P \mid Q) \mid R \equiv P \mid (Q \mid R)$.
3. $(\nu u)\text{inact} \equiv \text{inact}$, $\quad (\nu uu)P \equiv (\nu u)P$, $\quad (\nu uu')P \equiv (\nu u'u)P$, $\quad (\nu u)P \mid Q \equiv$ $(\nu u)(P \mid Q)$ if $u \notin \mathrm{fu}(Q)$, $\quad (\nu u)\text{def } D \text{ in } P \equiv \text{def } D \text{ in } (\nu u)P$ if $u \notin \mathrm{fu}(D)$.
4. $(\text{def } D \text{ in } P) \mid Q \equiv \text{def } D \text{ in } (P \mid Q)$ if $\mathrm{fpv}(D) \cap \mathrm{fpv}(Q) = \emptyset$.
5. def D in $(\text{def } D' \text{ in } P) \equiv \text{def } D \text{ and } D' \text{ in } P$ if $\mathrm{fpv}(D) \cap \mathrm{fpv}(D') = \emptyset$.

Now the operational semantics is given by the *reduction relation* $\rightarrow$, denoted $P \rightarrow Q$, which is the smallest relation on processes generated by the following rules.

[LINK] $\quad$ (accept $a(k)$ in P_1) $\mid$ (request $a(k)$ in P_2) $\rightarrow (\nu k)(P_1 \mid P_2)$

[COM] $\quad (k![\tilde{e}]; P_1) \mid (k?(\tilde{x})$ in $P_2) \rightarrow P_1 \mid P_2[\tilde{c}/\tilde{x}] \quad (\tilde{e} \downarrow \tilde{c})$

[LABEL] $\quad (k \triangleleft l_i; P) \mid (k \triangleright \{l_1 : P_1[\!] \cdots [\!] l_n : P_n\}) \rightarrow P \mid P_i \quad (1 \le i \le n)$

[PASS] $\quad$ (throw $k[k']; P_1$) $\mid$ (catch $k(k')$ in P_2) $\rightarrow P_1 \mid P_2$

[IF1] $\quad$ if e then P_1 else $P_2 \rightarrow P_1 \quad (e \downarrow \text{true})$

[IF2] $\quad$ if e then P_1 else $P_2 \rightarrow P_2 \quad (e \downarrow \text{false})$

[DEF] $\quad$ def D in $(X[\tilde{e}\tilde{k}] \mid Q) \rightarrow \text{def } D \text{ in } (P[\tilde{c}/\tilde{x}] \mid Q) (\tilde{e} \downarrow \tilde{c}, X(\tilde{x}\tilde{k}) = P \in D)$

[SCOP] $\quad P \rightarrow P' \Rightarrow (\nu u)P \rightarrow (\nu u)P'$

[PAR] $\quad P \rightarrow P' \Rightarrow P \mid Q \rightarrow P' \mid Q$

[STR] $\quad P \equiv P'$ and $P' \rightarrow Q'$ and $Q' \equiv Q \Rightarrow P \rightarrow Q$

Above we assume the standard *evaluation relation* $\downarrow$ on expressions is given. We write $\rightarrow^*$ for the reflexive, transitive closure of $\rightarrow$. Note how a fresh channel is generated in [LINK] rule as the result of interaction (in this way request $a(k)$ in P corresponds to the *bound output* in π-calculus[18]). In the [LABEL] rule, one of the branches is selected, discarding the remaining ones. Note we do not allow reduction under various communication prefixes, as in standard process calculi. As an example, the simple program in 2.1 has the following reduction (below and henceforth we omit trailing inactions).

$$\text{accept } a(k) \text{ in } k![1]; k?(y) \text{ in } P \mid \text{request } a(k) \text{ in } k?(x) \text{ in } k![x+1]$$
$$\rightarrow (\nu k)(k![1]; k?(y) \text{ in } P \mid k?(x) \text{ in } k![x+1])$$
$$\rightarrow (\nu k)(k?(y) \text{ in } P \mid k![x+1]) \quad \rightarrow \quad P[2/y].$$

Observe how interaction proceeds in a lock-step fashion. This is due to the synchronous form of the present communication primitives.

3. Representing Communication (1) Extant Communication Primitives

This section discusses how structuring primitives can represent with ease the communication patterns of conventional communication primitives which have been in use in programming languages. They show how we can understand the extant communication patterns as a fixed way of combining the proposed primitives.

3.1. Call-return. The *call-return* is a widely used communication pattern in which a process calls another process, then the callee would, after some processing, returns some value to the caller. Usually the caller just waits until the reply message arrives. This concept is widely used as a basic primitive in distributed computing under the name of *remote procedure call*. We may use the following pair of notations for call-return.

$$x = \text{call } f[e_1 \cdots e_n] \text{ in } P, \qquad \text{fun } f(x_1 \cdots x_n) \text{ in } P.$$

On the right, the return command return[e] would occur in P. Assume these constructs are added to the syntax in 2.2. A simple programming example follows.

Example 3.1 (Factorial).

$$\text{Fact}(f) = \text{fun } f(x) \text{ in}$$
$$\text{if } x = 1 \text{ then return}[1]$$
$$\text{else } (\nu b)(\text{Fact}[b] \mid y = \text{call } b[x-1] \text{ in return}[x * y])$$

Here and henceforth we write $X(\bar{x}\bar{k}) = P$, or a sequence of such equations, for the declaration part of recursion, leaving the body part implicit. This example implements the standard recursive algorithm for the factorial function. $y = \text{call } f[5]$ in P would give its client process.

The communication patterns based on call-return are easily representable by the combination of request/accept and send/receive. We first show the mapping of the caller. Below [·] denotes the inductive mapping into the structuring primitives.

$$[x = \text{call } a[\tilde{e}] \text{ in } P] \stackrel{\text{def}}{=} \text{request } a(k) \text{ in } k![\tilde{e}]; k?(x) \text{ in } [P].$$

Naturally we assume k is chosen fresh. The basic scenario is that a caller first initiates the session, sends the values, and waits until it receives the answer on the same channel. On the other hand, the callee is translated as follows:

$$[\text{fun } a(\tilde{x}) \text{ in } P] \stackrel{\text{def}}{=} \text{accept } a(k) \text{ in } k?(\tilde{x}) \text{ in } [P][k![e]/\text{return}[e]].$$

Here [$k![e]/\text{return}[e]$] denotes the syntactic substitution of $k![e]$ for each return[e]. Observe that the original "return" operation is expressed by the "send" primitive of the structuring primitives. As one example, let us see how the factorial program in Example 3.1 is translated by the above mapping.

Example 3.2 (Factorial, translation).

$$\text{Fact}(f) \ = \ \texttt{accept}\ f(k)\ \texttt{in}\ k?(x)\ \texttt{in}$$
$$\texttt{if}\ x = 1\ \texttt{then}\ k![1];$$
$$\texttt{else}\ (\nu b)(\text{Fact}[b]\ |\ \texttt{request}\ b(k')\ \texttt{in}\ k'![x-1]; k'?(y)\ \texttt{in}\ k![x*y])$$

Notice how the usage of k' and k differentiates the two contexts of communication. If we compose the translation of factorial with that of its user, we have the reduction:

$$\text{Fact}[f]\ |\ [\![y = \texttt{call}\ f[3]\ \texttt{in}\ P]\!]\ \to^*\ \text{Fact}[f]\ |\ [\![P]\!][6/y].$$

In this way, the semantics of the synchronous call-return is given by that of the structuring primitives via the translation. Some observations follow.

(1) The significance of the specific notations for call-return would lie in the declaration of the assumed fixed communication pattern, which would enhance readability and help verification. At the same time, the translation retains the same level of clarity as the original code, even if it does need a few additional key strokes.

(2) In translation, the caller and the callee in general own complementary communication patterns, i.e. input-output meets output-input. However if, for example, the return commands appear twice in the callee, the complementarity is lost. This relates to the notion of types we discuss later: indeed, non-complementary patterns are rejected by the typing system.

(3) The translation also suggests how structuring primitives would generalise the traditional call-return structure. That is, in addition to the fixed pattern of input-output (or, correspondingly, output-input), we can have a sequence of interactions of indefinite length. For such programming examples, see Section 4.

3.2. Method Invocation. The idea of method invocation originates in object-oriented languages, where a caller calls an object by specifying a method name, while the object waits with a few methods together with the associated codes, so that, when invoked, executes the code corresponding to the method name. The call may or may not result in returning an answer. As a notation, an "object" would be written:

$$\texttt{obj}\ a\colon \{l_1(\tilde{x}_1)\ \texttt{in}\ P_1 [\![\cdots [\![l_n(\tilde{x}_n)\ \texttt{in}\ P_n \},$$

where a gives an object identifier, $l_1, \ldots, l_n$ are labels (all pairwise distinct) with formal parameters $\tilde{x}_i$, and P_i gives the code corresponding to each l_i. The return action, written $\texttt{return}[e]$, may occur in each P_i as necessary. A caller then becomes:

$$x = a.\,l_i[\tilde{e}]\ \texttt{in}\ P \qquad a.\,l_i[\tilde{e}]; P.$$

The left-hand side denotes a process which invokes the object with a method l_i together with arguments $\tilde{e}$, then, receiving the answer, assigns the result to x, and finally executes the continuation P. The right-hand side is a notation for the case when the invocation does not need the return value. As an example, let us program a simple cell.

Example 3.3 (Cell).

$$\text{Cell}(a, c)\ =\ \texttt{obj}\ c\colon \{\texttt{read}()\ \texttt{in}\ (\texttt{return}[c]\ |\ \text{Cell}[a, c])\ [\![\texttt{write}(x)\ \texttt{in}\ \text{Cell}[a, x]\ \}.$$

The cell $\text{Cell}[a, c]$ denotes an object which saves its value in c and has a name a. There are two methods, $\texttt{read}$ and $\texttt{write}$, each with the obvious functionalities. A caller which "reads" this object would be written, for example, $x = a.\,\texttt{read}[\ ]\ \texttt{in}\ P$.

The method invocation can be represented in the structuring constructs by combining label branching and value passing. We show the translations of an object, a caller which expects the return, and a caller which does not expect the return, in this order.

$$[\text{obj } a\colon \{l_1(\tilde{x}_1) \text{ in } P_1 \| \cdots \| l_n(\tilde{x}_n) \text{ in } P_n\}] \stackrel{\text{def}}{=}$$
$$\text{accept } a(k) \text{ in } k \triangleright \{l_1 : k?(\tilde{x}_1) \text{ in } [P_1]\sigma \| \cdots \| l_n : k?(\tilde{x}_n) \text{ in } [P_n]\sigma\}$$
$$[x = a.l_i[\tilde{e}] \text{ in } P] \stackrel{\text{def}}{=} \text{request } a(k) \text{ in } k \triangleleft l_i; k![\tilde{e}]; k?(x) \text{ in } [P]$$
$$[a.l_i[\tilde{e}]; P] \stackrel{\text{def}}{=} \text{request } a(k) \text{ in } k \triangleleft l_i; k![\tilde{e}]; [P]$$

In each translation, k should be fresh. In the first equation, σ denotes the substitution $[k![e]/\text{return}[e]]$, replacing all occurrences of return$[e]$ by $k![e]$. Observe that a method invocation is decomposed into label branching and value passing. Using this mapping, the cell is now translated into:

Example 3.4 (Cell, translation).

$$\text{Cell}(a, c) = \text{accept } a(k) \text{ in } k \triangleright \{\text{read} : k![e]; \text{Cell}[a, c] \| \text{write} : k?(x) \text{ in } \text{Cell}[a, x]\}.$$

Similarly, $x = a.\text{read}[]$ in P is translated as request $c(k)$ in $k \triangleleft \text{read}; k?(x)$ in P, while $a.\text{write}[3]$ becomes request $a(k)$ in $k \triangleleft \text{write}; k![3]$. Some observations follow.

(1) The translation is not much more complex than the original text. The specific notation however has a role of declaring the fixed communication pattern and saves key-strokes.

(2) Here again, the translation of the caller and the callee in general results in complementary patterns. There are however two main cases where the complementarity is lost, one due to the existence/lack of the return statement (e.g. $x = a.\text{write}[3]$ in Q above) and another due to an invocation of an object with a non-existent method. Again such inconsistency is detectable by a typing system introduced later.

(3) The translation suggests how structuring primitives can generalise the standard method invocation. For example, an object may in turn invoke the method of the caller after being invoked. We believe that, in programming practice based on the idea of interacting objects, such reciprocal, continuous interaction would arise naturally and usefully. Such examples are discussed in the next section.

In addition to call-return and method invocation, we can similarly represent other communication patterns in use with ease, for example asynchronous call-return (which includes *rendez-vous* [28] and *future* [2]) and simple message passing. For the space sake we leave their treatment to [11]. Section 6 gives a brief discussion on the significance of specific notations for these fixed communication patterns in language design.

4. Representing Communication (2) Complex Communication Patterns

This section shows how the structuring primitives can cleanly represent various complex communication patterns which go beyond those represented in conventional communication primitives.

4.1. Continuous Interactions. The traditional call-return primitive already encapsulates a sequence of communications, albeit simple, as a single abstraction unit. The key possibility of the session structure lies in that it extends this idea to arbitrarily complex communication patterns, including the case when multiple interaction sequences interleave with each other. The following shows one such example, which describes the behaviour of a banking service to the user (essentially an automatic teller machine).

Example 4.1 (ATM).

$ATM(a, b) =$ accept $a(k)$ in $k![id];$

$\qquad k \triangleright \{$deposit : request $b(h)$ in $k?(amt)$ in

$\qquad\qquad h \triangleleft$ deposit; $h![id, amt];$ ATM$[a, b]$

$\qquad\qquad \|$withdraw : request $b(h)$ in $k?(amt)$ in

$\qquad\qquad h \triangleleft$ withdraw; $h![id, amt];$

$\qquad\qquad h \triangleright \{$success : $k \triangleleft$ dispense; $k![amt];$ ATM$[a, b]$

$\qquad\qquad\qquad \|$failure : $k \triangleleft$ overdraft; ATM$[a, b]\}$

$\qquad\qquad \|$balance : request $b(h)$ in $h \triangleleft$ balance; $h?(amt)$ in

$\qquad\qquad k![amt];$ ATM$[a, b]\}$

The program, after establishing a session with the user via a, first lets the user input the user code (we omit such details as verification of the code etc.), then offers three choices, deposit, withdraw, and balance. When the user selects one of them, the corresponding code is executed. For example, when the withdraw is chosen, the program lets the user enter the amount to be withdrawn, then interacts with the bank via b, asking with the user code and the amount. If the bank answers there is enough amount in the account, the money is given to the user. If not, then the overdraft message results. In either case the system eventually returns to the original waiting mode. Note in particular the program should communicate with the bank in the midst of interaction with the user, so three parties are involved in interaction as a whole. A user may be written as:

$\quad$ request $a(k)$ in $k![myId];$ $k \triangleleft$ withdraw; $k![58];$

$\qquad\qquad\qquad\qquad\qquad k \triangleright \{$dispense : $k?(amt)$ in $P\|$overdraft : $Q\}.$

Here we may consider Q as a code for "exception handling" (invoked when the balance is less than expected). Notice also interactions are now truly reciprocal.

4.2. Unbounded Interactions. The previous example shows how structuring primitives can easily describe the situation which would be difficult to program in a clean way using the conventional primitives. At the same time, the code does have room for amelioration. If a user wants to look at his balance before he withdraws, he should enter his user code twice. The following refinement makes this redundancy unnecessary.

Example 4.2 (Kind ATM).

$ATM'(a, b) =$ accept $a(k)$ in $k![id];$ Actions$[a, b, id, k]$

Actions$(a, b, id, k) = k \triangleright \{$deposit : request $b(h)$ in $k?(amt)$ in

$\qquad\qquad h \triangleleft$ deposit; $h![id, amt];$ Actions$[a, b, id, k]$

$\qquad\qquad \|$withdraw : request $b(h)$ in $k?(amt)$ in

$\qquad\qquad h \triangleleft$ withdraw; $h![id];$ $h![amt];$

$\qquad\qquad h \triangleright \{$success : $k \triangleleft$ dispense; $k![amt];$ Actions$[a, b, id, k]$

$\qquad\qquad\qquad \|$failure : $k \triangleleft$ overdraft; Actions$[a, b, id, k]\}$

$\qquad\qquad \|$balance : request $b(h)$ in $h \triangleleft$ balance; $h?(amt)$ in

$\qquad\qquad k![amt];$ Actions$[a, b, id, k]$

$\qquad\qquad \|$quit : ATM$'[a, b]\}$

As can be seen, the main difference lies in that the process is still within the same session even after recurring to the waiting mode, after processing each request: once a user establishes the session and enters the user code, she can request various services as many times as she likes. To exit from this loop, the branch quit is introduced.

This example shows how recursion within a session allows a flexible description of interactive behaviour which goes beyond the recursion in usual objects (where each session consists of a fixed number of interactions). It is notable that the unbounded session owns a rigorous syntactic structure so as to allow type abstraction, see Section 5. Unbounded interactions with a fixed pattern naturally arise in practice, e.g. interactions between a file server and its client. We believe recursion within a session can be effectively used for varied programming practice.

4.3. Delegation. The original idea of delegation in object-based concurrent programming [34] allows an object to delegate the processing of a request it receives to another object. Its basic purpose is *distribution of processing*, while maintaining the transparency of name space for clients of that service. Practically it can be used to enhance modularity, to express exception handing, and to increase concurrency. The following example shows how we can generalise the original notion to the present setting.

Example 4.3 (Ftp server). Below $\bigotimes_n P$ denotes the n-fold parallel composition.

$$\text{Init}(pid, nis) = (\nu b)(\text{Ftpd}[pid, b] \mid \bigotimes_n \text{FtpThread}[b, nis])$$

$$\text{Ftpd}(pid, b) = \text{accept } pid(s) \text{ in request } b(k) \text{ in throw } k[s]; \text{Ftpd}[pid, b]$$

$$\text{FtpThread}(b, nis) = \text{accept } b(k) \text{ in catch } k(s) \text{ in } s?(userid, passwd) \text{ in}$$
$$\text{request } nis(j) \text{ in } j \lhd \text{checkUser}; j![userid, passwd];$$
$$j \rhd \{\text{invalid} : s \lhd \text{sorry} \| \text{valid} : s \lhd \text{welcome}; \text{Actions}[s, b]\}$$

$$\text{Actions}(s, b) = s \rhd \{\text{get} : \cdots ; s?(file) \text{ in } \cdots ; \text{Actions}[s, b]$$
$$\| \text{put} : \cdots ; s?(file) \text{ in } \cdots ; \text{Actions}[s, b]$$
$$\| \text{bye} : \cdots ; \text{FtpThread}[b, nis]\}.$$

The above code shows an outline of the code of a ftp server, which follows the behaviour of the standard ftp servers with TCP/IP protocol. Initially the program Init generates a server Ftpd and n threads with the identical behaviour (for simplicity we assume all threads share the same name b). Suppose, in this situation, a server receives a request for a service from some client, establishing the session channel s. A server then requests for another session with an idle thread (if it exists) and "throws" a channel s to that thread, while getting ready for the next request from clients itself. It is now the thread FtpThread which actually processes the user's request, receiving the user name, referring to NIS, and executing various operations (note recursion within a session is used). Here the delegation is used to enable the ftp server to process multiple requests concurrently without undue delay in response. The scheme is generally applicable to a server interacting with many clients. Some observations follow.

(1) The example shows how the generalised delegation allows programmers to cleanly describe those interaction patterns which generalise the original form of delegation. Other examples of the usage of delegation abound, for example a file server with geographically distributed sites or a server with multiple services each to be processed by a different sub-server.

(2) A key factor of the above code is that a *client does not have to be conscious of the delegation which takes place on the server's side*: that is, a client program can be

written as if it is interacting with a single entity, for example as follows.

$$\texttt{request } pid(s) \texttt{ in } s![myId]; s \rhd \{\texttt{sorry} : \cdots \| \texttt{welcome} : \cdots \}$$

Observe that, between the initial **request** and the next sending operation, the catch/throw interaction takes place on the server's side: however the client process does not have to be conscious of the event. This shows how delegation enables distribution of computation while maintaining the transparency of the name space.

(3) If we allow each ftp-thread to be dynamically generated, we can use parallel composition to the same effect, just as the use of "fork" to pass process resources in UNIX. While this scheme has a limitation in that we cannot send a channel to an already running process, it offers another programming method to realise flexible, dynamic communication structures. We also observe that the use of throw/catch, or the "fork" mentioned above, would result in complexly woven sequences of interactions, which would become more error-prone than without. In such situations, the type discipline discussed in the next section would become an indispensable tool for programming, where we can algorithmically verify if a program has coherent communication structure and, in particular, if it contains interaction errors.

5. The Type Discipline

5.1. Preliminaries. The present structuring method allows the clear description of complex interaction structures beyond conventional communication primitives. The more complex the interaction becomes, however, the more difficult it would be to capture the whole interactive behaviour and to write correct programs. The type discipline we shall discuss in this section gives a simple solution to these issues at a basic level. We first introduce the basic notions concerning types, including duality on types which represents complementarity of interactions.

Definition 5.1 (Types). Given *type variables* $(t, t', \dots)$ and *sort variables* $(s, s', \dots)$, *sorts* $(S, S', \dots)$ and *types* $(\alpha, \beta, \dots)$ are defined by the following grammar.

$$S ::= \mathbf{nat} \mid \mathbf{bool} \mid \langle \alpha, \overline{\alpha} \rangle \mid s \mid \mu s.S$$

$$\alpha ::= \downarrow[\tilde{S}]; \alpha \mid \downarrow[\alpha]; \beta \mid \&\{l_1 : \alpha_1, \dots, l_n : \alpha_n\} \mid \mathbf{1} \mid \perp$$
$$\mid \uparrow[\tilde{S}]; \alpha \mid \uparrow[\alpha]; \beta \mid \oplus\{l_1 : \alpha_1, \dots, l_n : \alpha_n\} \mid t \mid \mu t.\alpha$$

where, for a type α in which $\perp$ does not occur, we define $\overline{\alpha}$, the *co-type* of α, by:

$$\overline{\uparrow[\tilde{S}]; \alpha} = \downarrow[\tilde{S}]; \overline{\alpha} \quad \overline{\oplus\{l_i : \alpha_i\}} = \&\{l_i : \overline{\alpha_i}\} \quad \overline{\uparrow[\alpha]; \beta} = \downarrow[\alpha]; \overline{\beta} \quad \overline{\mathbf{1}} = \mathbf{1}$$

$$\overline{\downarrow[\tilde{S}]; \alpha} = \uparrow[\tilde{S}]; \overline{\alpha} \quad \overline{\&\{l_i : \alpha_i\}} = \oplus\{l_i : \overline{\alpha_i}\} \quad \overline{\downarrow[\alpha]; \beta} = \uparrow[\alpha]; \overline{\beta} \quad \overline{t} = t \quad \overline{\mu t.\alpha} = \mu t.\overline{\alpha}.$$

A *sorting* (resp. a *typing*, resp. a *basis*) is a finite partial map from names and variables to sorts (resp. from channels to types, resp. from process variables to the sequences of sorts and types). We let $\Gamma, \Gamma', \dots$ (resp. $\Delta, \Delta', \dots$, resp. $\Theta, \Theta', \dots$) range over sortings (resp. typings, resp. bases). We regard types and sorts as representing the corresponding regular trees in the standard way [5], and consider their equality in terms of such representation.

A sort of form $\langle \alpha, \overline{\alpha} \rangle$ represents two complementary structures of interaction which are associated with a name (one denoting the behaviour starting with **accept**, another that which starts with **request**), while a type gives the abstraction of interaction to be done through a channel. Note $\overline{\overline{\alpha}} = \alpha$ holds whenever $\overline{\alpha}$ is defined. $\perp$ is a specific type indicating no further connection is possible at a given name. The following partial algebra on the set of typings, cf. [10], plays a key role in our typing system.

Definition 5.2 (Type algebra). Typings Δ_1 and Δ_2 are *compatible*, written $\Delta_1 \asymp \Delta_2$, if $\Delta_1(k) = \overline{\Delta_2(k)}$ for all $k \in \text{dom}(\Delta_1) \cap \text{dom}(\Delta_2)$. When $\Delta_1 \asymp \Delta_2$, the *composition of Δ_1 and Δ_2*, written $\Delta_1 \circ \Delta_2$, is given as a typing such that $(\Delta_1 \circ \Delta_2)(k)$ is (1) $\perp$, when $k \in \text{dom}(\Delta_1) \cap \text{dom}(\Delta_2)$; (2) $\Delta_i(k)$, if $k \in \text{dom}(\Delta_i) \setminus \text{dom}(\Delta_{i+1 \bmod 2})$ for $i \in \{1,2\}$; and (3) undefined otherwise.

Compatibility means each common channel k is associated with complementary behaviours, thus ensuring the interaction on k to run without errors. When composed, the type for k becomes $\perp$, preventing further connection at k (note $\perp$ has no co-type). One can check the partial operation $\circ$ is partially commutative and associative.

5.2. Typing System. The main sequent of our typing system has a form

$$\Theta; \Gamma \vdash P \triangleright \Delta$$

which reads: "under the environment $\Theta; \Gamma$, a process P has a typing Δ." Sorting Γ specifies protocols at the free names of P, while typing Δ specifies P's behaviour at its free channels. When P is a program, Θ and Δ become both empty.

Given a typing or a sorting, say Φ, write $\Phi \cdot s : p$ for $\Phi \cup \{s : p\}$ together with the condition that $s \notin \text{dom}(\Phi)$; and $\Phi \setminus s$ for the result of taking off $s : \Phi(s)$ from Φ if $\Phi(s)$ is defined (if not we take Φ itself). Also assume given the evident inference rules for arithmetic and boolean expressions, whose sequent has the form $\Gamma \vdash e \triangleright \alpha$, enjoying the standard properties such as $\Gamma \vdash e \triangleright S$ and $e \downarrow c$ imply $\Gamma \vdash c \triangleright S$. The main definition of this section follows.

Definition 5.3 (Basic typing system). The typing system is defined by the axioms and rules in Figure 1, where we assume the range of Δ in [INACT] and [VAR] contains only 1 and $\perp$.

For simplicity, the rule [DEF] is restricted to single recursion, which is easily extendible to multiple recursion. If $\Theta; \Gamma \vdash P \triangleright \Delta$ is derivable in the system, we say *P is typable under $\Theta; \Gamma$ with Δ*, or simply *P is typable*. Some comments on the typing system follow.

(1) In the typing system, the left-hand side of the turnstile is for shared names and variables ("classical realm"), while the right-hand side is for channels sharable only by two complementary parties (a variant of "linear realm"). It differs from various sorting disciplines in that a channel k is in general ill-sorted, e.g. it may carry an integer at one time and a boolean at another. In spite of this, the manipulation of linear realm by typing algebra ensures linearised usage of channels, as well as preventing interaction errors, cf. Theorem 5.4 below.

(2) In [THR], the behaviour represented by α for channel k' is actually performed by the process which "catches" k' (note k' cannot occur free in Δ, hence neither in P, by our convention on "·"). To capture the interactions at k' as a whole, $k' : \alpha$ is added to the linear realm. On the other hand, the rule [CAT] guarantees that the receiving side does use the channel k' as is prescribed. Reading from the conclusions to the antecedents, [THR] and [CAT] together illustrate how k' is "thrown" from the left to the right.

(3) The simplicity of the typing rules is notable, utilising the explicit syntactic structure of session. In particular it is syntax-directed and has a principal type when we use a version of kinding [22]. It is then easy to show there is a typing algorithm à la ML, which extracts the principal type of a given process iff it is typable. It should be noted that simplicity and tractability of typing rules do *not* mean that the obtainable type information is uninteresting: the resulting type abstraction richly represents the interactive behaviour of programs, as later examples exhibit.

$$[\text{Acc}] \frac{\Theta;\Gamma \vdash P \rhd \Delta \cdot k : \alpha}{\Theta;\Gamma, a : \langle \alpha, \overline{\alpha}\rangle \vdash \texttt{accept } a(k) \texttt{ in } P \rhd \Delta} \qquad [\text{Req}] \frac{\Theta;\Gamma \vdash P \rhd \Delta \cdot k : \overline{\alpha}}{\Theta;\Gamma, a : \langle \alpha, \overline{\alpha}\rangle \vdash \texttt{request } a(k) \texttt{ in } P \rhd \Delta}$$

$$[\text{Send}] \frac{\Gamma \vdash \tilde{e} \rhd \tilde{S} \quad \Theta;\Gamma \vdash P \rhd \Delta \cdot k : \alpha}{\Theta;\Gamma \vdash k![\tilde{e}]; P \rhd \Delta \cdot k :\uparrow[\tilde{S}]; \alpha} \qquad [\text{Rcv}] \frac{\Theta;\Gamma \cdot \tilde{x} : \tilde{S} \vdash P \rhd \Delta \cdot k : \alpha}{\Theta;\Gamma \vdash k?(\tilde{x}) \texttt{ in } P \rhd \Delta \cdot k :\downarrow[\tilde{S}]; \alpha}$$

$$[\text{Br}] \frac{\Theta;\Gamma \vdash P_1 \rhd \Delta \cdot k : \alpha_1 \quad \cdots \quad \Theta;\Gamma \vdash P_n \rhd \Delta \cdot k : \alpha_n}{\Theta;\Gamma \vdash k \rhd \{l_1 : P_1 \| \cdots \| l_n : P_n\} \rhd \Delta \cdot k : \&\{l_1 : \alpha_1, \ldots, l_n : \alpha_n\}}$$

$$[\text{Sel}] \frac{\Theta;\Gamma \vdash P \rhd \Delta \cdot k : \alpha_j}{\Theta;\Gamma \vdash k \lhd l_j; P \rhd \Delta \cdot k : \oplus\{l_1 : \alpha_1, \ldots, l_n : \alpha_n\}} \quad (1 \le j \le n)$$

$$[\text{Thr}] \frac{\Theta;\Gamma \vdash P \rhd \Delta \cdot k : \beta}{\Theta;\Gamma \vdash \texttt{throw } k[k']; P \rhd \Delta \cdot k :\uparrow[\alpha]; \beta \cdot k' : \alpha} \qquad [\text{Cat}] \frac{\Theta;\Gamma \vdash P \rhd \Delta \cdot k : \beta \cdot k' : \alpha}{\Theta;\Gamma \vdash \texttt{catch } k(k') \texttt{ in } P \rhd \Delta \cdot k :\downarrow[\alpha]; \beta}$$

$$[\text{Conc}] \frac{\Theta;\Gamma \vdash P \rhd \Delta \quad \Theta;\Gamma \vdash Q \rhd \Delta'}{\Theta;\Gamma \vdash P \mid Q \rhd \Delta \circ \Delta'}(\Delta \asymp \Delta') \quad [\text{If}] \frac{\Gamma \vdash e \rhd \texttt{bool} \quad \Theta;\Gamma \vdash P \rhd \Delta \quad \Theta;\Gamma \vdash Q \rhd \Delta}{\Theta;\Gamma \vdash \texttt{if } e \texttt{ then } P \texttt{ else } Q \rhd \Delta}$$

$$[\text{NRes}] \frac{\Theta;\Gamma \cdot a : S \vdash P \rhd \Delta}{\Theta;\Gamma \vdash (\nu a)P \rhd \Delta} \qquad [\text{CRes}] \frac{\Theta;\Gamma \vdash P \rhd \Delta \cdot k :\perp}{\Theta;\Gamma \vdash (\nu k)P \rhd \Delta} \qquad [\text{Inact}] \; \Theta;\Gamma \vdash \texttt{inact} \rhd \Delta$$

$$[\text{Var}] \frac{\Gamma \vdash \tilde{e} \rhd \tilde{S}}{\Theta, X : \tilde{S}\tilde{\alpha};\Gamma \vdash X[\tilde{e}\tilde{k}] \rhd \Delta \cdot \tilde{k} : \tilde{\alpha}} \qquad [\text{Def}] \frac{\Theta;\Gamma \cdot \tilde{x} : \tilde{S} \vdash P \rhd \tilde{k} : \tilde{\alpha} \quad \Theta;\Gamma \vdash Q \rhd \Delta}{\Theta \backslash X;\Gamma \vdash \texttt{def } X(\tilde{x}\tilde{k}) = P \texttt{ in } Q \rhd \Delta}(\Theta(X) = \tilde{S}\tilde{\alpha})$$

FIGURE 1. The typing system

Below we briefly summarise the fundamental syntactic properties of the typing system. We need the following notion: a *k-process* is a prefixed process with subject k (such as $k![\tilde{e}]; P$ and catch $k(k')$ in P). Next, a *k-redex* is a pair of dual k-processes composed by $|$, i.e. either of forms $(k![\tilde{e}]; P \mid k?(x) \texttt{ in } Q)$, $(k \lhd l; P \mid k \rhd \{l_1 : Q_1 \| \cdots \| l_n : Q_n\})$, or $(\texttt{throw } k[k']; P \mid \texttt{catch } k(k'') \texttt{ in } Q)$. Then P is an *error* if $P \equiv \texttt{def } D \texttt{ in } (\nu \tilde{u})(P'|R)$ where P' is, for some k, the $|$-composition of *either* two k-processes that do not form a k-redex, *or* three or more k-processes. We then have:

Theorem 5.4.

1. (Invariance under $\equiv$) $\Theta;\Gamma \vdash P \rhd \Delta$ and $P \equiv Q$ imply $\Theta;\Gamma \vdash Q \rhd \Delta$.
2. (Subject reduction) $\Theta;\Gamma \vdash P \rhd \Delta$ and $P \rightarrow^* Q$ imply $\Theta;\Gamma \vdash Q \rhd \Delta$.
3. (Lack of run-time errors) *A typable program never reduces into an error.*

We omit the proofs, which are straightforward due to the syntax-directed nature of the typing rules. See [11] for details. We note that we can easily extend the typing system with ML-like polymorphism for recursion, which is useful for e.g. template processes (such as def $Cell(cv) = \cdots$ in $Cell[a \; 42] \mid Cell[b \; true])$, with which all the properties in Theorem 5.4 are preserved. This and other basic extensions are discussed in [11].

5.3. Examples. We give a few examples of typing, taking programs in the preceding sections. We omit the final **1** from the type, e.g. we write $\downarrow[\alpha]$ for $\downarrow[\alpha]; \mathbf{1}$. First, the factorial in Example 3.2 is assigned, at its free name, a type $\downarrow[\texttt{nat}];\uparrow[\texttt{nat}]$ (for factorial) and its dual $\uparrow[\texttt{nat}];\downarrow[\texttt{nat}]$ (for its user). Next, the cell in Example 3.3 is given a type

&{read :↑[α], write :↓[α]} (for the cell) and its dual ⊕{read :↓[α], write :↑[α]} (for its user). The type of a cell says a cell waits with two options, and, when "read" is selected, it would send an integer and the session ends, and when "write" is selected, it would receive an integer and again the session ends: its dual says a user may do either "read" or "write", and, according to which of them it selects, it behaves as prescribed.

As a more interesting example, take the "kind ATM" in Example 4.2. Consider ATM′[ab] under the declaration in the example. Then a typing $a : \langle \alpha, \overline{\alpha} \rangle$, $b : \langle \beta, \overline{\beta} \rangle$ is given to the process, where we set α, which abstracts the interaction with a user, as:

$$\alpha \stackrel{\text{def}}{=} \downarrow[\text{nat}]; \mu t.\&\{\text{deposit} :\downarrow[\text{nat}]; t,$$
$$\text{withdraw} :\downarrow[\text{nat}]; \oplus\{\text{dispense} :\uparrow[\text{nat}]; t, \text{ overdraft} : t\},$$
$$\text{balance} :\uparrow[\text{nat}]; t,$$
$$\text{quit} :\uparrow[\text{nat}]\},$$

while $\overline{\beta}$, which abstracts the interaction with the banking system, is given as:

$$\overline{\beta} \stackrel{\text{def}}{=} \oplus\{\text{deposit} :\uparrow[\text{nat nat}],$$
$$\text{withdraw} :\uparrow[\text{nat nat}]; \&\{\text{success} : 1, \text{failure} : 1\},$$
$$\text{balance} :\uparrow[\text{nat}]; \downarrow[\text{nat}]\}.$$

Notice the type abstraction is given separately for the user (at a) and the bank (at b), describing the behaviour of ATM′ for each of its interacting parties.

As a final example, the ftp server of Example 4.3 is given the following type at its principal name:

$$\downarrow[\text{nat nat}]; \oplus\{\text{sorry} : 1, \text{ welcome} : \mu t. \&\{\text{get} : \cdots ; t, \text{ put} : \cdots ; t, \text{ bye} : \cdots\}\}.$$

This example shows that the throw/catch action is abstracted away in the type with respect to the user (but not in the type with respect to the thread, which we omit) so that the user can interact without concerning himself with the delegation occurring on the other's side. In these ways, not only the type discipline offers the correctness verification of programs at a basic level, but also it gives a clean abstraction of interactive behaviours of programs, which would assist programming activities.

6. Discussions

6.1. **Implementation Concerns.** In the previous sections, we have seen how the session structure enables clean description of complex communication behaviours, employing the synchronous form of interactions as its essential element. For implementation of the primitives, however, the use of asynchronous communication is essential, since the real distributed computing environments are inherently asynchronous. To study such implementation in a formal setting, which should then be applied to the realistic implementation, we consider a translation of the present language primitives into TyCO[14], a sorted summation-less polyadic asynchronous π-calculus with branching structure (which is ultimately translatable into its monadic, branch-less version). The existence of the branching structure makes TyCO an ideal intermediate language. For the space sake we cannot discuss the technical details of the translation, for which the reader may refer to [11]. We only list essential points.

(1) The translation converts both channels and names into names. Each synchronous interaction (including the branching-selection) is translated into two asynchronous interactions, the second one acting as acknowledgement. This suggests the primitives are amenable for distributed implementation, at least at the rudimentary level.

(2) In spite of (1) above, the resulting code is far from optimal: as a simple example, if a value is sent immediately after the request operation, clearly the value can be "piggy-backed" to the request message. A related example is the translation of the factorial in Section 3 in comparison with its standard "direct" encoding in Pict or TyCO in a continuation-passing style, cf. [24]. To find the effective, well-founded optimisation methods in this line would be a fruitful subject of study (see 6.2 below).

(3) The encoding translates the typable programs into well-sorted TyCO codes. It is an intriguing question how we can capture, in a precise way, the well-typedness of the original code at the level of TyCO (this question was originally posed by Simon Gay for a slightly different kind of translation).

6.2. Related Works and Further Issues. In the following, comparisons with a few related works are given along with some of the significant further issues.

First, in the context of conventional concurrent programming languages, the key departure of the proposed framework lies in that the session structure allows us to form an arbitrary complex interaction pattern as a unit of abstraction, rather than being restricted to a fixed repertoire. Examples in Section 4 show how this feature results in clean description of complex communication behaviours which may not be easy to express in conventional languages. For example, if we use, for describing those examples, so-called *concurrent object-oriented languages* [34], whose programming concept based on objects and their interaction is proximate to the present one, we need to divide each series of interactions into multiple chunks of independent communications, which, together with the nesting of method invocations, would make the resulting programs hard to understand. The explicit treatment of session also enables the type-based verification of compatibility of communication patterns, which would facilitate the writing of correct communication-based programs at an elementary level.

In spite of these observations, we believe that various communication primitives in existing programming languages, such as object-invocation and RPC, would not diminish their significance even when the present primitives are incorporated. We already discussed how they would be useful for declaring fixed communication patterns, as well as for saving key strokes (in particular the primitives for simple message passing would better be given among language constructs since their description in the structuring primitives is, if easy, roundabout). Notice we can still maintain the same type discipline by regarding these constructs as standing for combination of structuring primitives, as we did in Section 3. In another vein, the communication structures which we can extract from such declaration would give useful information for performing optimisation.

Secondly, the field of research which is closely related to the present work is the study of various typed programming languages based on π-calculi [6, 23, 29], and, more broadly, the study of types for π-calculi (see for example [17, 24, 25, 13, 30, 35]). In 6.1, we already noted that the proposed primitives are easily translatable into TyCO, hence into π-calculus. Indeed, the encoding of various interaction structures in π-calculus is the starting point of the present series of study (cf. Section 2 of [27]). Comparisons with these works may be done from two distinct viewpoints.

(1) From the viewpoint of language design, Pict and other π-calculus-based languages use the primitives of (polyadic) asynchronous π-calculus or its variants as the basic language constructs, and build further layers of abstraction on their basis. The present proposal differs in that it incorporates the session-based structure as a fundamental stratum for programming, rather than relying on chains of direct name passing for describing communication behaviour. While the former is operationally translatable into the latter as discussed in 6.1, the very translation of, say,

the programming examples in the preceding sections would reveal the significance of the session structure for abstraction concerns. In particular, any such translation should use multiple names for actions belonging to a single session, which damages the clarity and readability of the program. We note that we are far from claiming that the proposed framework would form the sole stratum for high-level communication-based programming: abstraction concerns for distributed computing are so diverse that any single framework cannot meet all purposes. However we do believe that the proposed constructs (with possible variations) would offer a basic and useful building block for communication-based programming, especially when concerned communication behaviours tend to become complex.

(2) From the viewpoint of type disciplines, one notable point would be that well-typed programs in the present typing system are in general ill-sorted (in the sense of [17]) when they are regarded as π-terms, since the same channel k may be used for carrying values of different sorts at different occasions. This is in a sharp contrast with most type disciplines for π-calculus in literature. An exception is the typing system for monadic π-calculus presented in [35], where, as in the present setting, the incorporation of sequencing information in types allows certain ill-sorted processes to be well-typed. Apart from a notable difference in motivation, a main technical difference is that the rules in [35] are not syntax-directed; at the same time, the type discipline in [35] guarantees a much stronger behavioural property. Another notable feature of the present typing system is the linear usage of channels it imposes on programs. In this context, the preceding study on linearity in π-calculus such as [10, 13] offers the clarification of the deterministic character of interaction at channels (notice interaction at names is still non-deterministic in general). Also [THR] and [CAT] rules have some resemblance to the rules for linear name communication presented in [10, 13]. Regarding these and other works on types for π-calculus, we note that various cases of redundant codes in translation mentioned in 6.1 above often concern certain fixed ways of using names in processes, which would be amenable to type-based analysis.

Finally one of the most important topics which we could not touch in the present paper is the development of reasoning principles based on the proposed structuring method. Notice the type discipline in Section 5 already gives one simple, though useful, example. However it is yet to be studied whether reasoning methods on deeper properties of programs (cf. [1, 3, 20]) which are both mathematically well-founded and are applicable to conspicuous practical situations, can be developed or not. We wish to touch on this topic in our future study.

Acknowledgements. We sincerely thank three reviewers for their constructive comments. Discussions with Simon Gay, Luís Lopes, Benjamin Pierce, Kaku Takeuchi and Nobuko Yoshida have been beneficial, for which we are grateful. We also thank the last two for offering criticisms on an earlier version of the paper. Vasco Vasconcelos is partially supported by Project PRAXIS/2/2.1/MAT/46/94.

References

[1] S. Abramsky, S. Gay, and R. Nagarajan, Interaction Categories and Foundations of Typed Concurrent Computing. *Deductive Program Design*, Springer-Verlag, 1995.

[2] G. Agha. *Actors: A Model of Concurrent Computation in Distributed Systems*. MIT Press, 1986.

[3] P. America and F. de Boer. Reasoning about Dynamically Evolving Process Structures. *Formal Aspects of Computing*, 94:269–316, 1994.

[4] G. Berry and G. Boudol. The chemical abstract machine. *TCS*, 96:217–248, 1992.

[5] B. Courcelle. Fundamental properties of infinite trees. *TCS*, 25:95–169, 1983.

[6] C. Fournet and G. Gonthier. The reflexive chemical abstract machine and the join-calculus. In *POPL'96*, pp. 372–385, ACM Press, 1996.

[7] C.A.R. Hoare. Communicating sequential processes. *CACM*, 21(8):667–677, 1978.

[8] C.A.R. Hoare. *Communicating Sequential Processes*. Prentice Hall, 1995.

[9] Jones, C.B., *Process-Algebraic Foundations for an Object-Based Design Notation*. UMCS-93-10-1, Computer Science Department, Manchester University, 1993.

[10] K. Honda. Composing processes. In *POPL'96*, pp. 344–357, ACM Press, 1996.

[11] K. Honda, V. Vasconcelos, and M. Kubo. Language primitives and type disciplines for structured communication-based programming. Full version of this paper, in preparation.

[12] S. Peyton Jones, A. Gordon, and S. Finne. Concurrent Haskell. In *POPL'96*, pp. 295–308, ACM Press, 1996.

[13] N. Kobayashi, B. Pierce, and D. Turner. Linearity and the pi-calculus. In *POPL'96*, pp. 358–371, ACM Press, 1996.

[14] L. Lopes, F. Silva, and V. Vasconcelos. *A framework for compiling object calculi*. In preparation.

[15] R. Milner. *Communication and Concurrency*. C.A.R. Hoare Series Editor. Prentice Hall, 1989.

[16] R. Milner. Functions as processes. *MSCS*, 2(2):119–141, 1992.

[17] R. Milner, Polyadic π-Calculus: a tutorial. *Logic and Algebra of Specification*, Springer-Verlag, 1992.

[18] R. Milner, J. Parrow, and D. Walker. A calculus of mobile processes, Parts I and II. *Journal of Information and Computation*, 100:1–77, September 1992.

[19] R. Milner and M. Tofte. *The Definition of Standard ML*. MIT Press, 1991.

[20] H. R. Nielson and F. Nielson. Higher-order concurrent programs with finite communication topology. In *POPL '94*. ACM Press, 1994.

[21] A. Ohori and K. Kato. Semantics for communication primitives in a polymorphic language. In *POPL 93*. ACM Press, 1993.

[22] A. Ohori. A compilation method for ML-style polymorphic record calculi. In *POPL 92*, pp. 154–165. ACM Press, 1992.

[23] B. Pierce and D. Turner. Pict: A programming language based on the pi-calculus. CSCI Technical Report 476, Indiana University, March 1997.

[24] B. Pierce, and D. Sangiorgi, Typing and subtyping for mobile processes. In *LICS'93*, pp. 187–215, 1993.

[25] B. Pierce and D. Sangiorgi, Behavioral Equivalence in the Polymorphic Pi-Calculus. *POPL 97*, ACM Press, 1997.

[26] J-H. Reppy. CML: A higher-order concurrent language. In *PLDI 91*, pp. 293–305. ACM Press, 1991.

[27] K. Takeuchi, K. Honda, and M. Kubo. An interaction-based programming language and its typing system. In *PARLE'94*, volume 817 of *LNCS*, pp. 398–413. Springer-Verlag, July 1994.

[28] US Government Printing Office, Washington DC. *The Ada Programming Language*, 1983.

[29] V. Vasconcelos. Typed concurrent objects. In *ECOOP'94*, volume 821 of *LNCS*, pp. 100–117. Springer-Verlag, 1994.

[30] V. Vasconcelos and K. Honda, Principal Typing Scheme for Polyadic π-Calculus. *CONCUR'93*, Volume 715 of *LNCS*, pp.524-538, Springer-Verlag, 1993.

[31] V. Vasconcelos and M. Tokoro. A typing system for a calculus of objects. In *1st ISOTAS*, volume 742 of *LNCS*, pp. 460–474. Springer-Verlag, November 1993.

[32] Y. Yokote and M. Tokoro. Concurrent programming in ConcurrentSmalltalk. In Yonezawa and Tokoro [34].

[33] A. Yonezawa, editor. *ABCL, an Object-Oriented Concurrent System*. MIT Press, 1990.

[34] A. Yonezawa and M. Tokoro, editors. *Object-Oriented Concurrent Programming*. MIT Press, 1987.

[35] N. Yoshida, Graph Types for Monadic Mobile Processes. In *FST/TCS'16*, volume 1180 of *LNCS*, pp. 371–386, Springer-Verlag, 1996. The full version as LFCS Technical Report, ECS-LFCS-96-350, 1996.

The Functional Imperative: Shape!

C.B. Jay   P.A. Steckler

School of Computing Sciences,
University of Technology, Sydney,
P.O. Box 123, Broadway NSW 2007, Australia;
email: {cbj,steck}@socs.uts.edu.au
fax: 61 (02) 9514 1807

1   Introduction

FISH is a new programming language for array computation that compiles higher-order polymorphic programs into simple imperative programs expressed in a sub-language TURBOT, which can then be translated into, say, C. Initial tests show that the resulting code is extremely fast: two orders of magnitude faster than HASKELL, and two to four times faster than OBJECTIVE CAML, one of the fastest ML variants for array programming.

Every functional program must ultimately be converted into imperative code, but the mechanism for this is often hidden. FISH achieves this transparently, using the "equation" from which it is named:

$$\text{Functional} = \text{Imperative} + \text{Shape}$$

Shape here refers to the structure of data, e.g. the length of a vector, or the number of rows and columns of a matrix. The FISH compiler reads the equation from left to right: it converts functions into procedures by using *shape analysis* to determine the shapes of all array expressions, and then allocating appropriate amounts of storage on which the procedures can act.

We can also read the equation from right to left, constructing functions from shape functions and procedures. Let us consider some examples.

```
>-|> let v = [| 0;1;2;3 |] ;;
```

declares v to be a vector whose entries are $0, 1, 2$ and 3. The compiler responds with both the the type and shape of v, that is,

```
v : vec[int]
#v = (~4,int_shape)
```

This declares v has the type of an expression for a vector of integers whose shape #v is given by the pair (~4,int_shape) which determines the length of v, ~4, and the common shape int_shape of its entries. The tilde in ~4 indicates that the value is a *size* used to describe array lengths, which is evaluated statically. By contrast, integers may be used as array entries, and are typically computed dynamically. Arrays can be arbitrarily nested. For example

```
>-|> let x = [| [| 0; 1 |] ; [| 2; 3 |] |] ;;
x : vec[vec[int]]
#x = (~2,(~2,int_shape))
```

is a vector of vectors (or 2×2 matrix). Here too, the entries of the outer vector all have the same shape, namely (~2,int_shape).

FISH primitives can be used to construct higher-order functions. For example, sum_int adds up a vector of integers. Also, we can map functions across arrays. For example, to sum the rows of x above we have

```
>-|> let y = map sum_int x ;;
y : vec[int]
#y = (~2,int_shape)
>-|> %run y ;;
Shape = (~2,int_shape)
Value = [| 1; 5 |]
```

Notice that the compiler was able to compute the shape of y before computing any of the array entries. This shape analysis lies at the heart of the FISH compilation strategy. Let us consider how mapping is achieved in more detail.

Consider the mapping map f x of a function f across a vector x. The resulting vector has the same length as x but what is the common shape of its entries? In FISH, each function f has a shape #f which maps the shape of its argument to the shape of its result. Letting fsh represent #f and xsh represent #x we can describe the shape of map f by the following function

```
>-|> let map_sh fsh xsh = (fst xsh, fsh (snd xsh)) ;;
map_sh : (q -> r) -> s * q -> s * r
```

This function will be used to determine the storage required for y. The procedure for assigning values to its entries is given by the following for-loop

```
>-|> let map_pr f y x =
             for (i< @(len_var x))
             {
               y[i] := f !x[i]
             } ;;
map_pr : (a -> b) -> var[vec[b]] -> var[vec[a]] -> comm
```

Here x:var[vec[a]] is a *phrase variable*, i.e. an assignable location for a vector whose entries are of data type a. Similarly, y:var[vec[b]]. Now len_var x is the length of x, while @ converts from a size to an integer. Also, ! extracts the expression associated to a phrase variable, i.e. de-references it. Note that both x and x[i] are phrase variables.

Finally, the shape function for mapping and its procedure are combined using the function

```
proc2fun : (#[a] -> #[b]) ->
               (var[b] -> var[a] -> comm) -> a -> b
```

It is not a primitive constant of FISH, but itself is defined using simpler constructions, that act directly on shapes and commands. In particular, it is designed to avoid unnecessary copying of its vector argument. Thus, we have the higher-order, polymorphic function

```
>-|> let map f = proc2fun (map_sh #f) (map_pr f)  ;;
map : (a -> b) -> vec[a] -> vec[b]
```

This same strategy is also used to define other polymorphic array functions for reduction, folding, and so on.

Partial evaluation converts arbitrary FISH programs into imperative programs in a sub-language called TURBOT, which can then be translated to the imperative language of choice, currently ANSI C. For example, the TURBOT for map sum_int x is given in Figure 1. The variables B and A store x and y, respectively.

```
new #A = (~2,int_shape) in
  new #B = (~2,(~2,int_shape)) in
    B[0][0] := 0;
    B[0][1] := 1;
    B[1][0] := 2;
    B[1][1] := 3;

    for (0 <= i < 2) {
      new #C = int_shape in
        C := 0;
        A[i] := !C;
        for (0 <= j < 2) {
          A[i] := !A[i] + !B[i][j]
        }
      end
    }
  end
return A
```

Fig. 1. TURBOT program for mapping summation.

It might be objected that this approach is not about functional programming at all, since map is "just" a disguised procedure. In response, we point out that our map is still a higher-order polymorphic function. All functional programs are ultimately compiled into imperative machine code. The difference is that FISH performs the compilation simply, efficiently and transparently, by making clear the role of shapes. Also, note that FISH, like Forsythe [Rey96], supports "call-by-name" evaluation. That is, beta-reduction is always legitimate, despite the presence of commands, and side-effects.

Indeed, there is no obligation to program with the imperative features of FISH directly; we are constructing a library of FISH functions, called GOLDFISH, that includes the usual combinators of the Bird-Meertens Formalism [BW88], such as map, reduce, and many of the standard array operations, such as linear algebra operations and array-based sorting algorithms.

The chief goal of partial evaluation is to compute the shapes of all intermediate expressions. Such static shape analysis has a number of additional benefits over a comparable dynamic analysis. First, many program errors, such as attempting to multiply matrices whose sizes do not match, show up as compile-time *shape errors*. The basic techniques of static shape analysis were developed in the purely functional language Vec [JS97a]. Its shape analyser is able to detect *all* array bound errors statically, at the cost of unrolling all loops. FISH takes a more pragmatic approach: array indices are treated as integers, not sizes, and so some array bound errors escape detection. However, combinations of functions which are free of array-bound errors, such as those in GOLDFISH, produce programs without bound errors.

Second, knowledge of shapes supports compile-time strategies for data layout. On the small scale, this means not having to box array entries, a significant efficiency gain. On a large scale, FISH satisfies many of the pre-requisites for being a portable parallel programming language. Array combinators have been advocated as a powerful mechanism for structuring parallel programs [Ski94], but the inability to determine the appropriate data distributions has proved a major barrier in the quest for efficiency. Shape-based cost analysis offers a solution to this problem [JCSS97]. Also, FISH is a natural candidate for a co-ordination language for parallel programming (see [DGHY95], for example) since it supports both the second-order combinators useful for data distribution, and the imperative code used on individual processors.

Static shape analysis requires significant amounts of function in-lining, so we have adopted the strategy of in-lining all function calls. This might be expected to lead to code explosion, but has not been a problem to date. The ability to analyse shapes means that array arguments can be stored, with only references being passed to functions (as in Figure 1) rather than copying of array expressions. Also, many of the standard functions, such as map, generate for-loops which only require one copy of the function body. Thus we have eliminated the costs associated with closures with little cost in copying of either code or data. This is a major source of the speed gains in our benchmarks.

As FISH evaluation is "call-by-name" the most natural comparison is with another pure language HASKELL[HPJW92] (which is call-by-need). Our tests show FISH to be over 100 times faster than HASKELL on simple mapping and reducing problems. Of course, it is more common to use a "call-by-value" language with reference types for array computation, such as ML. Different implementations of ML vary significantly in their speed on array programs. O'CAML [Obj] is one of the fastest on arrays. But FISH is two to four times faster than O'CAML on a range of typical problems (see Section 3 for details).

Of course, programs built by combining functions will often be slower than hand-built procedures due to the copying inherent in the algorithm, but initial results suggest that the additonal overhead is not so large. We have implemented three matrix multiplication algorithms, using a triple for-loop (pure imperative code), a double for-loop plus inner product (mixed mode) and a purely combinatory algorithm. The combinatory algorithm takes approximately five times longer than the imperative algorithm. If these results scale up for more complex combinations of functions, then the performance penalty for using the functional style will be tolerable for a much larger range of applications than at present.

Finally, observe that FISH supports a smooth transition from prototype to final program. Prototypes written in GOLDFISH can be refined by successively replacing critical parts of the program until the desired efficiency is reached. Hence, there is no need to abandon the prototype when moving to production. Also, because TURBOT is so simple, it can be easily translated to the imperative language of choice, and native code can be embedded in FISH programs.

Thus, FISH is a novel combination of expressive programming style (supporting higher-order, polymorphically typed, functions) and efficient execution that can be integrated with existing imperative languages.

A slightly expanded version of this paper is available [JS97b].

2   The FISH Language

FISH is essentially an Algol-like language [Rey81, OT97]. In particular, it supports a sub-language TURBOT that is a simple imperative language equipped with local variables that obey a stack discipline. Commands act on a store, and function application is call-by-name. To this base, we add the structure of a typed functional language, which can also be used to model procedures.

As in all Algol-like languages, the *data types* (meta-variable τ) are distinguished from the *phrase types* (meta-variable θ). Data types represent storable values, while phrase types represent meaningful program fragments. All of the fundamental types are at play in the rule for typing an assignment

$$\frac{\Gamma \vdash A : \mathsf{var}[\alpha] \quad \Gamma \vdash e : \mathsf{exp}[\alpha]}{\Gamma \vdash A := e : \mathsf{comm}}$$

A is a *phrase variable* for an array of data type α and e is an *expression* for such an array. Phrase variables can be coerced to expressions, e.g. $!A : \mathsf{exp}[\alpha]$. The assignment itself is a *command*.

In most treatments of Algol-like languages the data types are limited to a fixed set of primitives or *datum types* (meta-variable δ), such as integers and booleans (though see Tennent [Ten89] for another approach). Arrays are treated as processes of phrase type, in which a suitable number of local variables are constructed to store the entries. This contradicts our usual notion of arrays, as storable quantities. However, allowing for array data types introduces an additional complexity. If $\alpha = \mathsf{vec}[\mathsf{int}]$ above then the lengths of A and e may differ, and the assignment generate an array bound error. FISH is able to handle this situation since the compiler is able to determine the shapes of all arrays statically, and check for shape equality for assignments.

This is achieved by dividing the data types into data structures, here just *array types* (meta-variable α) and *shape types* (meta-variable σ). Values of shape type are determined by the compiler. The structured types also support structured phrase variables, as shown by the rule

$$\frac{\Gamma \vdash A : \mathsf{var}[\mathsf{vec}[\alpha]] \quad \Gamma \vdash i : \mathsf{exp}[\mathsf{int}]}{\Gamma \vdash A[i] : \mathsf{var}[\alpha]}$$

Thus, FISH supports assignment to whole arrays, and to their sub-arrays. More generally, the array data types support a generous class of polymorphic operations, such as mapping and reducing.

FISH v 0.3 is available at `ftp.socs.uts.edu.au/Users/cbj/Fish` by anonymous ftp. It is implemented in OBJECTIVE CAML and currently runs on Sun SparcStations under Solaris, or using the O'CAML byte-code interpreter.

2.1 Types

Types and their Shapes

$$
\begin{array}{ll}
& \#\delta = \#[\delta] \\
\delta ::= \mathsf{int} \mid \mathsf{bool} \mid \mathsf{float} \mid \ldots & \#X = \#[X] \\
\alpha ::= X_\alpha \mid \delta \mid \mathsf{vec}[\alpha] & \#\#[X] = \#[X] \\
\beta ::= \mathsf{size} \mid \mathsf{fact} & \#\mathsf{vec}[\alpha] = \mathsf{size} \times \#\alpha \\
\sigma ::= X_\sigma \mid \#[X_\alpha] \mid \#[\delta] \mid \beta \mid \sigma \times \sigma & \#\sigma = \sigma \\
\tau ::= \alpha \mid \sigma & \#\mathsf{var}[\tau] = \mathsf{exp}[\#\tau] \\
\theta ::= X_\theta \mid \#[X_\theta] \mid \mathsf{var}[\alpha] \mid \mathsf{exp}[\tau] & \#\mathsf{exp}[\tau] = \mathsf{exp}[\#\tau] \\
\quad \mid \mathsf{comm} \mid \#[\mathsf{comm}] \mid \theta \to \theta & \#\mathsf{comm} = \#[\mathsf{comm}] \\
\phi ::= \theta \mid \forall X_\alpha.\phi \mid \forall X_\sigma.\phi \mid \forall X_\theta.\phi & \#\#[\mathsf{comm}] = \#[\mathsf{comm}] \\
& \#(\theta \to \theta') = \#\theta \to \#\theta'
\end{array}
$$

Fig. 2. FISH types.

The FISH types are given in Figure 2. Most of the constructions have been introduced above. Note that phrase variables are always of array type α, never of shape type. This is because shapes, once declared, cannot be changed by an assignment. There are *type variables* for arrays, shapes or phrases whose kind is indicated by subscripting. Subscripts will often be elided when the kind is clear from the context. *Type schemes* are constructed from phrase types by quantification of type variables. The shape type constructor $\#[-]$ may be applied to array and phrase variables, datum types and the command type. It is then extended to an idempotent function $\#$ that acts on all types. Such types are used to represent the shapes of terms. Only two cases of its definition deserve comment. The shape of a variable is an expression, not a variable, since it cannot be assigned. The shape of a vector is a pair, consisting of its length, and the common shape of its entries. Since all array entries have the same shape, the regularity of arrays is enforced. For example, #vec[vec[int]] = size × (size × #[int]). In other words, the entries in a vector of vectors must all have the same length, so that any vector of vectors is a matrix.

The types of the purely imperative sub-language TURBOT are those FISH types that can be constructed without the function arrow constructor, type variables, and the shape of type variables.

In the displays provided by the FISH implementation, type quantifiers are elided, array type variables are constructed using the letters a,b,c,d, shape type variables using q,r,s,t and phrase type variables using x,y,z. Also, exp[a] is displayed as a. For example, compare the type of map given in the introduction with its type according to the language definition:

$$\forall X_\alpha, Y_\alpha.(\exp[X] \to \exp[Y]) \to \exp[\text{vec}[X]] \to \exp[\text{vec}[Y]].$$

2.2 Terms

The TURBOT terms are given in Figure 3. The FISH terms extend those of TURBOT by the additional rules in Figure 4. Many of the introduction rules for terms are standard, so we will only address the novelties here.

Shape constants and operations are distinguished from their datum counterparts by pre-fixing a tilde (˜). For example, ˜3 : exp[size] is a size numeral, distinct from the integer 3 and ˜true:fact is a fact, distinct from the boolean true. One may think of terms of fact type as "shape booleans"; alternatively, fact terms are compile-time assertions about shape. For example, comparing the shapes of two vectors yields a fact:

```
>-|> let v1 = [| 1;2 |];;
v1 : vec[int]
#v1 = (~2,int_shape)
>-|> let v2 = [| 3;4 |];;
v2 : vec[int]
#v2 = (~2,int_shape)
>-|> let w = #v1 == #v2;;
w : fact
#w = ~true
```

Each phrase variable $A : \text{var}[\alpha]$ has an associated expression $!A : \exp[\alpha]$ which represents its value. There are also coercions from sizes to integers, and facts to booleans (but not the reverse!). In practice, such coercions will often be inferred during parsing or type inference, but the presence of type variables means that they cannot be abandoned altogether.

FISH supports three forms of conditional expression, with key words if, ife and ifsh which express conditional commands and expressions, and shape-based

Term and Phrase Variables

$$\frac{\Gamma(x) \succ \theta}{\Gamma \vdash x : \theta} \qquad \frac{\Gamma \vdash A : \mathsf{var}[\mathsf{vec}[\alpha]] \quad \Gamma \vdash i : \exp[\mathsf{int}]}{\Gamma \vdash A[i] : \mathsf{var}[\alpha]}$$

Expressions

$$\frac{}{\Gamma \vdash d : \exp[\delta]} \qquad \frac{\Gamma \vdash e_1 : \exp[\delta_1] \quad \Gamma \vdash e_2 : \exp[\delta_2]}{\Gamma \vdash e_1 \oplus e_2 : \exp[\delta_3]}$$

$$\frac{}{\Gamma \vdash sh : \exp[\beta]} \qquad \frac{\Gamma \vdash sh_1 : \exp[\beta_1] \quad \Gamma \vdash sh_2 : \exp[\beta_2]}{\Gamma \vdash sh_1 \oplus sh_2 : \exp[\beta_3]}$$

$$\frac{\Gamma \vdash i : \exp[\mathsf{size}]}{\Gamma \vdash @i : \exp[\mathsf{int}]} \qquad \frac{\Gamma \vdash sh : \exp[\mathsf{fact}]}{\Gamma \vdash \mathsf{fact2bool}(sh) : \exp[\mathsf{bool}]}$$

$$\frac{\Gamma \vdash A : \mathsf{var}[\alpha]}{\Gamma \vdash !A : \exp[\alpha]} \qquad \frac{\Gamma \vdash b : \exp[\mathsf{bool}] \quad \Gamma \vdash e_1 : \exp[\alpha] \quad \Gamma \vdash e_2 : \exp[\alpha]}{\Gamma \vdash \mathsf{ife}\ b\ \mathsf{then}\ e_1\ \mathsf{else}\ e_2 : \exp[\alpha]}$$

$$\frac{}{\Gamma \vdash \delta\_\mathsf{shape} : \exp[\#[\delta]]} \qquad \frac{\Gamma \vdash e_1 : \exp[\sigma_1] \quad \Gamma \vdash e_2 : \exp[\sigma_2]}{\Gamma \vdash \langle e_1, e_2 \rangle : \exp[\sigma_1 \times \sigma_2]}$$

Commands

$$\frac{}{\Gamma \vdash \mathsf{skip} : \mathsf{comm}} \qquad \frac{\Gamma \vdash C_1 : \mathsf{comm} \quad \Gamma \vdash C_2 : \mathsf{comm}}{\Gamma \vdash C_1; C_2 : \mathsf{comm}}$$

$$\frac{\Gamma \vdash A : \mathsf{var}[\alpha] \quad \Gamma \vdash e : \exp[\alpha]}{\Gamma \vdash A := e : \mathsf{comm}} \qquad \frac{}{\Gamma \vdash \mathsf{abort} : \mathsf{comm}}$$

$$\frac{\Gamma \vdash b : \exp[\mathsf{bool}] \quad \Gamma \vdash C_1 : \mathsf{comm} \quad \Gamma \vdash C_2 : \mathsf{comm}}{\Gamma \vdash \mathsf{if}\ b\ \mathsf{then}\ C_1\ \mathsf{else}\ C_2 : \mathsf{comm}}$$

$$\frac{\Gamma \vdash m : \exp[\mathsf{int}] \quad \Gamma \vdash n : \exp[\mathsf{int}] \quad \Gamma, i : \exp[\mathsf{int}] \vdash C : \mathsf{comm}}{\Gamma \vdash \mathsf{for}\ (m \leq i < n)\ C : \mathsf{comm}}$$

$$\frac{\Gamma \vdash b : \exp[\mathsf{bool}] \quad \Gamma \vdash C : \mathsf{comm}}{\Gamma \vdash \mathsf{while}\ b\ \mathsf{do}\ C : \mathsf{comm}}$$

$$\frac{\Gamma \vdash e : \exp[\#\alpha] \quad \Gamma, x : \mathsf{var}[\alpha] \vdash C : \mathsf{comm}}{\Gamma \vdash \mathsf{new}\ \#x = e\ \mathsf{in}\ C\ \mathsf{end} : \mathsf{comm}} \qquad \frac{\Gamma \vdash e : \exp[\alpha]}{\Gamma \vdash \mathsf{output}(e) : \mathsf{comm}}$$

Fig. 3. TURBOT terms.

conditionals, respectively. The command form is standard. Expression conditionals ife b then e_1 else e_2 have a special status. Both e_1 and e_2 must have the same shape, which is then the shape of the whole conditional. This is necessary

---

Functions

$$\frac{\Gamma, x : \theta_1 \vdash t : \theta_2}{\Gamma \vdash \lambda x.\, t : \theta_1 \to \theta_2} \qquad\qquad \frac{\Gamma \vdash t : \theta_1 \to \theta_2 \quad \Gamma \vdash t_1 : \theta_1}{\Gamma \vdash t\, t_1 : \theta_2}$$

$$\frac{\Gamma \vdash t_2 : \theta_2 \quad \Gamma,\ x : \mathrm{Clos}_\Gamma(\theta_2) \vdash t_1 : \theta_1}{\Gamma \vdash t_1 \text{ where } x = t_2 : \theta_1} \qquad\qquad \frac{c_\phi \succ \theta}{\Gamma \vdash c : \theta}$$

Combinators

$$
\begin{aligned}
\mathsf{error} &: \forall X_\theta.\ X \\
\mathsf{condsh} &: \forall X_\theta.\ \mathsf{exp}[\mathsf{fact}] \to X \to X \to X \\
\# &: \forall X_\theta.\ X \to \#[X] \\
\mathsf{null} &: \forall X_\theta.\#X \to X \\
\mathsf{prim\_rec} &: \forall X_\theta.\ (\mathsf{exp}[\mathsf{size}] \to X \to X) \to X \to \mathsf{exp}[\mathsf{size}] \to X \\
\mathsf{equal} &: \forall X_\alpha.\ \#X \to \#X \to \mathsf{exp}[\mathsf{fact}] \\
\mathsf{fst} &: \forall X_\sigma, Y_\sigma.\ \mathsf{exp}[X \times Y] \to \mathsf{exp}[X] \\
\mathsf{snd} &: \forall X_\sigma, Y_\sigma.\ \mathsf{exp}[X \times Y] \to \mathsf{exp}[Y] \\
\mathsf{entry} &: \forall X_\alpha.\ \mathsf{exp}[\mathsf{size}] \to \mathsf{exp}[\mathsf{vec}[X]] \to \mathsf{exp}[X] \\
\mathsf{newexp} &: \forall X_\alpha.\ \mathsf{exp}[\#[X]] \to (\mathsf{var}[X] \to \mathsf{comm}) \to \mathsf{exp}[X] \\
\mathsf{hold} &: \#[\mathsf{comm}] \\
\mathsf{heq} &: \#[\mathsf{comm}] \to \#[\mathsf{comm}] \to \mathsf{exp}[\mathsf{fact}] \\
\mathsf{ap2e} &: \forall X_\alpha.\ (\mathsf{var}[X] \to \mathsf{comm}) \to (\mathsf{exp}[X] \to \mathsf{comm})
\end{aligned}
$$

Fig. 4. Additional FISH terms.

for static shape analysis. If the branches are to have different shapes, then the condition must be resolved statically, i.e. must be a fact f. This is done using a *shape conditional* ifsh f then e_1 else e_2 which is sugar for condsh $f\ e_1\ e_2$.

Each (well-shaped) datum of type δ has the same shape δ_shape which may be thought of as describing the storage requirements for such a datum, e.g. the number of bits required for a floating point real number. Similarly, every (well-shaped) command has the same shape hold. This reflects the principle that commands must leave the store in the same shape as they found it.

The command block new $\#x = e$ in C end introduces a local phrase variable x whose shape is e. The combinator newexp is applied to create a local block which returns an expression. The user syntax for newexp's is the same as for command blocks, but with end replaced by return x.

The output construction converts an expression to a command which has no effect on the store, but outputs the value of its argument.

Now let us consider the additional FISH terms in Figure 4. Polymorphic terms are constructed by where-clauses. Although we have not proved it, we believe that polymorphism need not be restricted to syntactic values, as in [MHTM97]. The error combinator arises when shape analysis detects a shape error. The shape combinator # returns the shape of its argument. Its one-sided inverse is null which returns an array expression of the same shape as its argument, but whose entries are undefined. This is mainly for internal use by the compiler. prim_rec is a primitive recursion combinator (see below). hold is the shape of a command without shape errors, while heq compares the shapes of two commands. ap2e allows a procedure to be applied to an expression. Its effect can be modelled using newexp but at the cost of some unnecessary copying.

The FISH primitives can be used to construct a large variety of higher-order polymorphic functions, such as the typical BMF combinators, fundamental linear algebra operations, e.g. matrix multiplication, and other fundamental array operations, e.g. quicksort. A suite of these is being assembled as a purely functional sub-language of FISH, called GOLDFISH.

General recursion introduces some delicate issues for shape analysis. In the most common cases the shapes produced are independent of the number of iterations involved. This is the case for while loops, since commands are not allowed to change any shapes. These are quite adequate for datum-level recursion. Recursion on arrays is more problematic, since the iterated function may produce a new array of different shape to the original, so that the shape of the result depends on the number of iterations. This is not a problem in the most common cases, e.g. mapping and reducing, which are handled directly in GOLDFISH. The prim_rec combinator handles the general, shape-changing operation by requiring that the number of iterations be a size, and using this to unfold the recursion during compilation. The general case, iterating a shape-changing function for an unbounded number of iterations, is not currently handled.

Type unification and inference proceeds by a variant of the usual Algorithm W [Mil78]. The only difficulty is that the idempotence of the shape function # on types means that most general unifiers, and hence principal types, do not always exist. For example, taken alone, the FISH function

```
fun x -> #x == (~2,int_shape)
```

has ambiguous type, since x could have either type size * #[int] or vec[int]. But when applied to a term with known kind, the function's type becomes unambiguous:

```
>-|> (fun x -> #x == (~2,int_shape)) (~3,int_shape) ;;
J : fact
#J = ~false
>-|> (fun x -> #x == (~2,int_shape)) [| 1;2 |] ;;
J : fact
#J = ~true
```

The ambiguities vanish once the kinds are known, so that the ambiguities do not present great practical difficulties. We plan to allow programmer annotations to resolve those that do arise.

2.3 Evaluation

The evaluation rules are not presented, for lack of space. Most are standard, the only novelties being those for applying the shape combinator #. For example, evaluation of #(entry i v) proceeds by evaluating snd #v. Efficiency of the resulting code is greatly enhanced by partial evaluation.

Partial evaluation is used to inline all function calls, apply any constant folding, and evaluate all shapes. It is guaranteed to terminate. This is done without knowledge of the store, other than its shape. Inlining succeeds because we do not support a general fixpoint operator (see above). Shape evaluation succeeds because we have maintained a careful separation of shapes from datum values. The key result is that every FISH term of type comm partially evaluates to a TURBOT command, i.e. a simple imperative program without any function calls or procedures.

The FISH implementation takes the resulting TURBOT and performs a syntax-directed translation of TURBOT to C, which is compiled and executed in the usual way. The C code produced is quite readable. The translation uses the known shapes of TURBOT arrays in their C declarations. If there is sufficient space they will be allocated to the run-time stack. Otherwise they are allocated to the heap using a checked form of C's malloc() called xmalloc().

3 Benchmarks

We have compared the run-time speed of FISH with a number of other polymorphic languages for several array-based problems. All tests were run on a Sun SparcStation 4 running Solaris 2.5. C code for FISH was generated using GNU C 2.7.2 with the lowest optimization level using the -O flag and all floating-point variables of type double (64 bits).

As FISH is a call-by-name language, the most natural comparison is with HASKELL. Preliminary tests using ghc 0.29, the Glasgow HASKELL compiler showed it to be many times slower than FISH. For example, reducing a 100,000-element array in ghc 0.29 took over 16 seconds of user time, compared to 0.04 seconds for FISH. We attribute such lethargy to the fact that Haskell builds its arrays from lists, and may well be boxing its data. Bigloo 1.6, which like FISH compiles a functional language to C, is much slower than FISH.

Now let us consider eager functional languages with mutable arrays, such as ML. O'CAML is one of the faster implementations of ML-related languages, especially for arrays, setting a high standard of performance against which to test our claims about FISH. [1] Hence, we confine further comparisons to O'CAML.

For O'CAML code, we used ocamlopt, the native-code compiler, from the 1.05 distribution, using the flag -unsafe (eliminating arrays bounds checks), and also -inline 100, to enable any inlining opportunities. O'CAML also uses 64 bit floats. Also, O'CAML requires all arrays to be initialised, which will impose a small penalty, especially in the first two examples. None of the benchmarks includes I/O, in order to focus comparison on array computation.

We timed seven kinds of floating point array computations: mapping of constant division over a vector, reduction of addition over a vector, multiplication

---

[1] While there is a good deal of contention about which ML implementation is fastest overall, O'CAML appears to be superior at array processing. See the thread in the USENET newsgroup comp.lang.ml, beginning with the posting by C. Fecht on October 14, 1996.

	Map	Reduce	MM loops	MM semi	MM combr
FISH	1.02	0.37	0.41	0.70	1.11
O'CAML	3.67	2.18	0.71	5.38	3.45

	Leroy FFT	Quicksort mono	Quicksort poly
FISH	3.17	8.41	8.41
O'CAML	4.07	12.10	57.27

Fig. 5. Benchmarks: FISH vs. O'CAML.

of matrices (three ways), the Fast Fourier Transform, and quicksort. The three matrix multiplication algorithms use a triply-nested for-loop; a doubly-nested loop of inner-products; and a fully combinatory algorithm using explicit copying, transposition, mapping and zipping. Its FISH form is

```
let mat_mult_float x y =
    zipop (zipop inner_prod_float))
      (map (copy (cols y)) x)
      (copy (rows x) (transpose y)) ;;
```

For the mapping and reduction tests, we tried vectors containing from 100,000 to 1,000,000 elements. For the matrix multiplications, we tried matrices with dimensions from 10×10 to 100×100. Our FFT test is based on Leroy's benchmark suite for O'CAML, which we translated mechanically to FISH. For quicksort, we implemented two variants of a non-recursive version of the algorithm, one where the comparison operation was fixed (mono), and another where the operation was passed as an argument (poly). We sorted vectors with 10,000 elements.

For each benchmark, the times for FISH were at least 25% faster than for O'CAML. Where function parameters are being passed, FISH is from 3 to 7 times faster. The results for the largest input sizes we tried are summarised in Figure 5. The times indicated are user time as reported by Solaris `/usr/bin/time`.

In the O'CAML code, one of the costs is the application of the function passed to map, or reduce, which the FISH compiler inlines. To isolate this effect, we also in-lined the function calls in O'CAML code by hand. This reduced the slow-down for mapping to a factor of two, and for reducing to a factor of three.

4   Relations to other work

As mentioned, the FISH language borrows many features from ALGOL-like languages. [OT97] is a collection of much of the historically significant work in this area. Non-strict evaluation and type polymorphism are also features of HASKELL [HPJW92]. While HASKELL does feature arrays, speed of array operations is not a particular concern. Key features of FISH are its collection of polymorphic combinators for array programming, and the ability to define new polymorphic array operations. OBJECTIVE CAML also offers some polymorphic operations in its `Array` module, though no compile-time checking of shape and array bound errors is provided [Obj]. APL is a programming language specialized for array operations, though it does not offer higher-order functions [Ive62]. ZPL is a recent language and system for array programming on parallel machines [ZPL].

Turning to compilation techniques, general results on partial evaluation can be found in [NN92, JGS93]. Inlining is still a subject of active research, e.g. using flow analysis to detect inlining opportunities, [JW96, Ash97]. Inlining in FISH is complete, so that there are no functions left in the generated code. Thus, FISH code is specialised for the shapes of its arguments, providing a more refined specialisation than one based just on the type [HM95]. In contrast to the approximations provided by program analyses based on abstract interpretation [CC77], FISH obtains exact shapes of data.

Similarly, unboxing of polymorphic function parameters (e.g. [Ler97]) becomes moot, so our system gives a kind of "radical unboxing". Also, FISH's stack discipline obviates the need for garbage collection. Tofte and Talpin's *regions* inference is an attempt to gain the benefits of stack discipline in ML, while still allowing a global store [TT94]. An implementation of this approach based on the ML Kit has recently become available [TBE+97]. In the regions approach, the best sizes of the regions needed are not easily determined. The ML Kit with Regions has tools for allowing programmers to tune their region allocations. In the FISH system, shape analysis assures that allocations are always of exactly the right size.

5 Future Work

Future work will proceed in several directions. Here are two major goals. First, to extend the language to support more data types, e.g. trees, whose shapes are more complex. We have already begun work on supporting *higher-order arrays*, which have an arbitrary finite number of dimensions, and may contain arrays as elements. Such extensions bring the possibility of combining shape analysis with the other major application of shape, shape polymorphism [BJM96], or polytypism [JJ97]. Second, we are implementing support for general recursion for first-order procedures. Third, FISH is ideally suited to play the role of a co-ordination language for parallel programming, since the GOLDFISH combinators are ideal for distribution and co-ordination, while the imperative code runs smoothly on the individual processors.

6 Conclusions

FISH combines the best features of the functional and imperative programming styles in a powerful and flexible fashion. This leads to significant efficiency gains when executing functional code, and to significant gains in expressiveness for imperative programs. The key to the smooth integration of these two paradigms is shape analysis, which allows polymorphic functional programs to be constructed from imperative procedures and, conversely, functional programs to be compiled into imperative code.

Static shape analysis determines the shapes of all intermediate data structures (i.e. arrays) from those of the arguments, and the shape properties of the program itself. In conventional functional languages this is impossible, since array shapes are given by integers whose value may not be known until execution. FISH avoids this problem by keeping shape types separate from datum types.

Acknowledgements We would like to thank Chris Hankin, Bob Tennent and Milan Sekanina for many productive discussions.

References

[Ash97]   J.M. Ashley. The effectiveness of flow analysis for inlining. In *Proc. 1997 ACM SIGPLAN International Conf. on Functional Programming (ICFP '97)*, pages 99–111, June 1997.

[BJM96]   G. Bellé, C. B. Jay, and E. Moggi. Functorial ML. In *PLILP '96*, volume 1140 of *LNCS*, pages 32–46. Springer Verlag, 1996. TR SOCS-96.08.

[BW88]   R. Bird and P. Wadler. *Introduction to Functional Programming*. International Series in Computer Science. Prentice Hall, 1988.

[CC77]   P. Cousot and R. Cousot. Abstract interpretation: A unified lattice model for static analysis of programs by construction of approximation of fixpoints. In *Conf. Record of the 4th ACM Symposium on Principles of Programming Languages*, pages 238–252, 1977.

[DGHY95]   J. Darlington, Y.K Guo, To H.W., and Jing Y. Functional skeletons for parallel coordination. In *Proceedings of Europar 95*, 1995.

[HM95]   R. Harper and G. Morrisett. Compiling polymorphism using intensional type analysis. In *Conference Record of POPL '95: 22nd ACM SIGPLAN-SIGACT Symposium on Principles of Programming Languages*, pages 130–141, San Francisco, California, January 1995.

[HPJW92]   P. Hudak, S. Peyton-Jones, and P. Wadler. Report on the programming language Haskell: a non-strict, purely functional language. *SIGPLAN Notices*, 1992.

[Ive62]   K.E. Iverson. *A Programming Language*. Wiley, 1962.

[JCSS97]   C.B. Jay, M.I. Cole, M. Sekanina, and P. Steckler. A monadic calculus for parallel costing of a functional language of arrays. In C. Lengauer, M. Griebl, and S. Gorlatch, editors, *Euro-Par'97 Parallel Processing*, volume 1300 of *Lecture Notes in Computer Science*, pages 650–661. Springer, August 1997.

[JGS93]   N.D. Jones, C.K. Gomard, and P. Sestoft. *Partial Evaluation and Automatic Program Generation*. International Series in Computer Science. Prentice Hall, 1993.

[JJ97]   P. Jansson and J. Jeuring. PolyP - a polytypic programming language extension. In *POPL '97: The 24th ACM SIGPLAN-SIGACT Symposium on Principles of Programming Languages*, pages 470–482. ACM Press, 1997.

[JS97a]   C.B. Jay and M. Sekanina. Shape checking of array programs. In *Computing: the Australasian Theory Seminar, Proceedings, 1997*, volume 19 of *Australian Computer Science Communications*, pages 113–121, 1997.

[JS97b]   C.B. Jay and P.A. Steckler. The functional imperative: shape! Technical
            Report 06, University of Technology, Sydney, 1997. 20 pp.

[JW96]   S. Jagannathan and A. Wright. Flow-directed inlining. In *Proc. ACM SIG-
            PLAN 1996 Conf. on Programming Language Design and Implementation*,
            pages 193–205, 1996.

[Ler97]   X. Leroy. The effectiveness of type-based unboxing. In *Abstracts from the
            1997 Workshop on Types in Compilation (TIC97)*. Boston College Com-
            puter Science Department, June 1997.

[MHTM97] R. Milner, R. Harper, M. Tofte, and D. MacQueen. *The Definition of
            Standard ML (Revised)*. MIT Press, 1997.

[Mil78]   R. Milner. A theory of type polymorphism in programming. *JCSS*, 17,
            1978.

[NN92]   F. Nielson and H.R. Nielson. *Two-level functional languages*. Cambridge
            University Press, 1992.

[Obj]   OBJECTIVE CAML home page on the World-Wide Web.
            http://pauillac.inria.fr/ocaml.

[OT97]   P.W. O'Hearn and R.D. Tennent, editors. *Algol-like Languages, Vols I and
            II*. Progress in Theoretical Computer Science. Birkhauser, 1997.

[Rey81]   J.C. Reynolds. The essence of ALGOL. In J.W. de Bakker and J.C. van
            Vliet, editors, *Algorithmic Languages*, pages 345–372. IFIP, North-Holland
            Publishing Company, 1981.

[Rey96]   John C. Reynolds. Design of the programming language Forsythe. Report
            CMU–CS–96–146, Carnegie Mellon University, June 1996.

[Ski94]   D.B. Skillicorn. *Foundations of Parallel Programming*. Number 6 in Cam-
            bridge Series in Parallel Computation. Cambridge University Press, 1994.

[TBE+97] M. Tofte, L. Birkedal, M. Elsman, N. Hallenberg, T.H. Olesen, P. Sestoft,
            and P. Bertelsen. Programming with regions in the ML kit. Technical
            Report 97/12, Univ. of Copenhagen, 1997.

[Ten89]   R.D. Tennent. Elementary data structures in Algol-like languages. *Science
            of Computer Programming*, 13:73–110, 1989.

[TT94]   M. Tofte and J.-P. Talpin. Implementation of the typed call-by-value λ-
            calculus using a stack of regions. In *Conf. Record of POPL '94: 21st ACM
            SIGPLAN-SIGACT Symposium on Principles of Programming Languages*,
            pages 188–201, January 1994.

[ZPL]   ZPL home page. http://www.cs.washington.edu/research/zpl.

Code Motion and Code Placement: Just Synonyms?*

Jens Knoop[1][**], Oliver Rüthing[2], and Bernhard Steffen[2]

[1] Universität Passau, D-94030 Passau, Germany
e-mail: knoop@fmi.uni-passau.de
[2] Universität Dortmund, D-44221 Dortmund, Germany
e-mail: {ruething,steffen}@ls5.cs.uni-dortmund.de

Abstract. We prove that there is no difference between *code motion* (*CM*) and *code placement* (*CP*) in the traditional *syntactic* setting, however, a dramatic difference in the *semantic* setting. We demonstrate this by re-investigating *semantic* CM under the perspective of the recent development of *syntactic* CM. Besides clarifying and highlighting the analogies and essential differences between the syntactic and the semantic approach, this leads as a side-effect to a drastical reduction of the conceptual complexity of the value-flow based procedure for semantic CM of [20], as the original bidirectional analysis is decomposed into purely unidirectional components. On the theoretical side, this establishes a natural semantical understanding in terms of the Herbrand interpretation (transparent equivalence), and thus eases the proof of correctness; moreover, it shows the frontier of semantic CM, and gives reason for the lack of algorithms going beyond. On the practical side, it simplifies the implementation and increases the efficiency, which, like for its syntactic counterpart, can be the catalyst for its migration from academia into industrial practice.

Keywords: Program optimization, data-flow analysis, code motion, code placement, partial redundancy elimination, transparent equivalence, Herbrand interpretation.

1 Motivation

Code motion (*CM*) is a classical optimization technique for eliminating *partial redundancies* (*PRE*).[1] Living in an ideal world a PRE-algorithm would yield the program of Figure 1(b) when applied to the program of Figure 1(a). A truly optimal result; free of any redundancies.

---

* An extended version is available as [14].
** The work of the author was funded in part by the Leibniz Programme of the German Research Council (DFG) under grant Ol 98/1-1.

[1] CM and PRE are often identified. To be precise, however, CM is a specific technique for PRE. As we are going to show here, identifying them is inadequate in general, and thus, we are precise on this distinction.

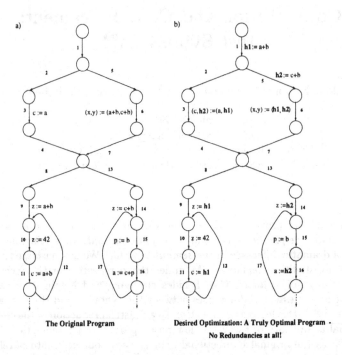

Fig. 1. Living in an Ideal World: The Effect of Partial Redundancy Elimination

Unfortunately, the world is not that ideal. Up to now, there is no algorithm achieving the result of Figure 1(b). In reality, PRE is characterized by two different approaches for CM: a *syntactic* and a *semantic* one. Figure 2 illustrates their effects on the example of Figure 1(a). The point of *syntactic* CM is to treat all term patterns independently and to regard each assignment as destructive to any term pattern containing the left-hand side variable. In the example of Figure 1(a) it succeeds in eliminating the redundancy of $a + b$ in the left loop, but fails on the redundancy of $c + p$ in the right loop, which, because of the assignment to p, is not redundant in the "syntactic" sense inside the loop. In contrast, *semantic* CM fully models the effect of assignments, usually by means of a kind of symbolic execution (value numbering) or by backward substitution: by exploiting the equality of p and b after the assignment $p := b$, it succeeds in eliminating the redundant computation of $c + p$ inside the right loop as well. However, neither syntactic nor semantic CM succeeds in eliminating the partial redundancies at the edges **8** and **13**. This article is concerned with answering why: we will prove that redundancies like in this example are out of the scope of any "motion"-based PRE-technique. Eliminating them requires to switch from motion-based to "placement"-based techniques. This fact, and more generally, the analogies and differences between syntactic and semantic CM and CP as illustrated in Figures 2(a) and (b), and Figure 1(b), respectively, are elucidated for the first time in this article.

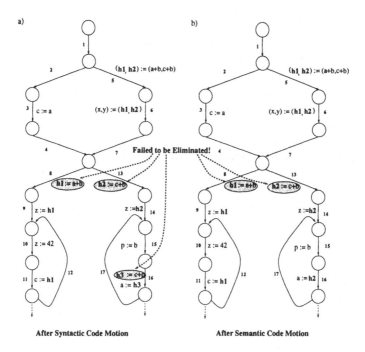

a)

(h1, h2) := (a+b,c+b)

c := a

(x,y) := (h1, h2)

Failed to be Eliminated!

h1 := a+b   h2 := c+b

z := h1

z := 42

c := h1

z :=h2

p := b

h3 := c+b
a := h3

After Syntactic Code Motion

b)

(h1, h2) := (a+b,c+b)

c := a

(x,y) := (h1, h2)

h1 := a+b   h2 := c+b

z := h1

z := 42

c := h1

z :=h2

p := b

a := h2

After Semantic Code Motion

Fig. 2. Back to Reality: Syntactic Code Motion vs. Semantic Code Motion

History and Current Situation: *Syntactic* CM (cf. [2, 5–8, 12, 13, 15, 18]) is well-understood and integrated in many commercial compilers.[2] In contrast, the much more powerful and aggressive *semantic* CM has currently a very limited practical impact. In fact, only the "local" *value numbering* for basic blocks [4] is widely used. Globalizations of this technique can be classified into two categories: limited globalizations, where code can only be moved to dominators [3, 16], and aggressive globalizations, where code can be moved more liberally [17, 20, 21]. The limited approaches are quite efficient, however, at the price of losing significant parts of the optimization power: they even fail in eliminating some of the redundancies covered by syntactic methods. In contrast, the aggressive approaches are rather complex, both conceptually and computationally, and are therefore considered impractical. This judgement is supported by the state-of-the-art here, which is still based on bidirectional analyses and heuristics making the proposed algorithms almost incomprehensible.

In this article we re-investigate (aggressive) semantic CM under the perspective of the very successful recent development of syntactic CM. This investigation highlights the conceptual analogies and differences between the syntactic and the semantic approach. In particular, it allows us to show that:

---

[2] E.g., based on [12, 13] in the Sun SPARCompiler language systems (SPARCompiler is a registered trademark of SPARC International, Inc., and is licensed exclusively to Sun Microsystems, Inc.).

- the decomposition technique into unidirectional analyses developed in [12, 13] can be transferred to the semantic setting. Besides establishing a natural connection between the Herbrand interpretation (transparent equivalence) and the algorithm, which eases the proof of its correctness,[3] this decomposition leads to a more efficient and easier implementation. In fact, due to this simplification, we are optimistic that semantic CM will find its way into industrial practice.
- there is a significant difference between *motion* and *placement* techniques (see Figures 1 and 2), which only shows up in the semantic setting. The point of this example is that the computations of $a + b$ and $c + b$ cannot safely be "moved" to their computation points in Figure 1(b), but they can safely be "placed" there (see Figure 3 for an illustration of the essentials of this example).

The major contributions of this article are thus as follows. On the *conceptual* side: (1) Uncovering that CM and CP are no synomyms in the semantic setting (but in the syntactic one), (2) showing the frontier of semantic CM, and (3) giving theoretical and practical reasons for the lack of algorithms going beyond! On the *technical* side, though almost as a side-effect yet equally important, presenting a new algorithm for computationally optimal semantic CM, which is conceptually and technically much simpler as its predecessor of [20].

Whereas the difference between motion and placement techniques will primarily be discussed on a conceptual level, the other points will be treated in detail.

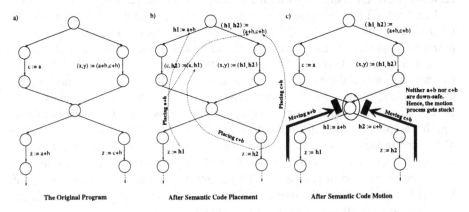

Fig. 3. Illustrating the Difference: Sem. Code Placement vs. Sem. Code Motion

Safety – The Backbone of Code Motion: Key towards the understanding of the conceptual difference between syntactic and semantic CM is the notion of

---

[3] Previously (cf. [20, 21]), this connection, which is essential for the conceptual understanding, had to be established in a very complicated indirect fashion.

safety of a program point for some computation: intuitively, a program point is safe for a given computation, if the execution of the computation at this point results in a value that is guaranteed to be computed by every program execution passing the point. Similarly, *up-safety* (*down-safety*) is defined by requiring that the computation of the value is guaranteed before meeting the program point for the first time (after meeting the program point for the last time).[4]

As properties like these are undecidable in the standard interpretation (cf. [16]), decidable approximations have been considered. Prominent are the abstractions leading to the syntactic and semantic approach considered in this article. Concerning the safety notions established above the following result is responsible for the simplicity and elegance of the syntactic CM-algorithms (cf. [13]):

Theorem 1 (Syntactic Safety). *Safe = Up-safe ∨ Down-safe*

It is the failure of this equality in the semantic setting, which causes most of the problems of semantic CM, because the decomposition of safety in up-safety and down-safety is essential for the elegant syntactic algorithms.

Figure 4 illustrates this failure as follows: placing the computation of $a + b$ at the boldface join-node is (semantically) safe, though it is neither up-safe nor down-safe. As a consequence, simply transferring the algorithmic idea of the syntactic case to the semantic setting without caring about this equivalence results in an algorithm for CM with *second-order effects* (cf. [17]).[5] These can be avoided by defining a *motion-oriented* notion of safety, which allows to reestablish the equality for a hierarchically defined notion of up-safety: the algorithm resulting from the use of these notions captures all the second-order effects of the "straightforwardly transferred" algorithm as well as the results of the original bidirectional version for semantic CM of [20].

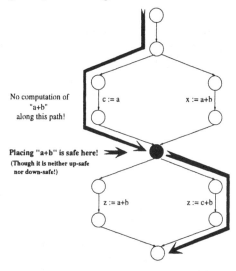

Fig. 4. Safe though neither Up-Safe nor Down-Safe

Motion versus Placement: The step from the motion-oriented notion of safety to "full safety" can be regarded as the step from *motion*-based algorithms to *placement*-based algorithms: in contrast to CM, CP is characterized by allowing arbitrary (safe) placements of computations with subsequent (*total*) *redundancy*

---

[4] Up-safety and down-safety are traditionally called "availability" and "very busyness", which, however, does not reflect the "semantical" essence and the duality of the two properties as precise as up-safety and down-safety.

[5] Intuitively, this means the transformation is not idempotent (cf. [17]).

elimination (*TRE*). As illustrated in Figure 3, not all placements can be realized via motion techniques, which are characterized by allowing the code movement only within areas where the placement would be correct. The power of arbitrary placement leads to a number of theoretic and algorithmic complications and anomalies (cf. Section 5), which we conjecture, can only be solved by changing the graph structure of the argument program, e.g. along the lines of [19].

Retrospectively, the fact that all CM-algorithms arise from notions of safety, which collapse in the syntactic setting, suffices to explain that the syntactic algorithm does not have any second-order effects, and that there is no difference between "motion" and "placement" algorithms in the syntactic setting.

Theorem 2 (Syntactic CM and Syntactic CP).
In the syntactic setting, CM is as powerful as CP (and vice versa).

2 Preliminaries

We consider procedures of imperative programs, which we represent by means of directed edge-labeled *flow graphs* $G = (N, E, \mathbf{s}, \mathbf{e})$ with node set N, edge set E, a unique *start node* $\mathbf{s}$ and *end node* $\mathbf{e}$, which are assumed to have no incoming and outgoing edges, respectively. The edges of G represent both the statements and the nondeterministic control flow of the underlying procedure, while the nodes represent program points only. Statements are *parallel assignments* of the form $(x_1, \ldots, x_r) := (t_1, \ldots, t_r)$, where x_i are pairwise disjoint variables, and t_i terms of the set $\mathbf{T}$, which as usual are inductively composed of variables, constants, and operators. For $r = 0$, we obtain the empty statement "skip". Unlabeled edges are assumed to represent "skip". Without loss of generality we assume that edges starting in nodes with more than one successor are labeled by "skip".[6]

Source and destination node of a flow-graph edge corresponding to a node n of a traditional node-labeled flow graph represent the usual distinction between the *entry* and the *exit* point of n explicitly. This simplifies the formal development of the theory significantly, particularly the definition of the value-flow graph in Section 3.1 because the implicit treatment of this distinction, which, unfortunately is usually necessary for the traditional flow-graph representation, is obsolete here; a point which is intensely discussed in [11].

For a flow graph G, let $pred(n)$ and $succ(n)$ denote the set of all immediate predecessors and successors of a node n, and let $source(e)$ and $dest(e)$ denote the source and the destination node of an edge e. A *finite path* in G is a sequence $\langle e_1, \ldots, e_q \rangle$ of edges such that $dest(e_j) = source(e_{j+1})$ for $j \in \{1, \ldots, q-1\}$. It is a path from m to n, if $source(e_1) = m$ and $dest(e_q) = n$. Additionally, $p[i, j]$, where $1 \leq i \leq j \leq q$, denotes the *subpath* $\langle e_i, \ldots, e_j \rangle$ of p. Finally, $\mathbf{P}[m, n]$ denotes the set of all finite paths from m to n. Without loss of generality we assume that every node $n \in N$ lies on a path from $\mathbf{s}$ to $\mathbf{e}$.

---

[6] Our approach is not limited to a setting with scalar variables. However, we do not consider subscripted variables here in order to avoid burdening the development by alias-analyses.

3 Semantic Code Motion

In essence, the reason making semantic CM much more intricate than syntactic CM is that in the semantic setting safety is not the sum of up-safety and down-safety (i.e., does not coincide with their disjunction). In order to illustrate this in more detail, we consider as in [17] *transparent equivalence* of terms, i.e., we fully treat the effect of assignments, but we do not exploit any particular properties of term operators.[7] Moreover, we essentially base our investigations on the semantic CM-algorithm of [20] consisting of two major phases:

- *Preprocess:* a) Computing transparent equivalences (cf. Section 3.1).

             b) Constructing the *value-flow graph* (cf. Section 3.1).
- *Main Process:* Eliminating semantic redundancies (cf. Section 4).

After computing the transparent equivalences of program terms for each program point, the preprocess globalizes this information according to the value flow of the program. The value-flow graph is just the syntactic representation for storing the global flow information. Based on this information the main process eliminates semantically redundant computations by appropriately placing the computations in the program. In the following section we sketch the preprocess as far as it is necessary for the development here, while we investigate the main process in full detail. In comparison to [20] it is completely redesigned.

3.1 The Preprocess: Constructing the Value-Flow Graph

The first step of the preprocess computes for every program point the set of all transparently equivalent program terms. The corresponding algorithm is fairly straightforward and matches the well-known pattern of Kildall's algorithm (cf. [10]).

As a result of this algorithm every program point is annotated by a *structured partition* (*SP*) *DAG* (cp. [9]), i.e., an ordered, directed, acyclic graph whose nodes are labeled with at most one operator or constant and a set 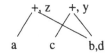 of variables. The SPDAG attached to a program point represents the set of all terms being transparently equivalent at this point: two terms are transparently equivalent iff they are represented by the same node of an SPDAG; e.g., the SPDAG on the right represents the term equivalences $[a \mid b, d \mid c \mid z, a+b, a+d \mid y, c+b, c+d]$.

Afterwards, the *value-flow graph* is constructed. Intuitively, it connects the nodes, i.e., the term equivalence classes of the SPDAG-annotation $\mathcal{D}$ computed in the previous step according to the data flow. Thus, its nodes are the classes of transparently equivalent terms, and its edges are the representations of the data flow: if two nodes ν and ν' of a value-flow graph are connected by a value-flow graph edge (ν, ν'), then the terms represented by ν' evaluate to the same value after executing the flow-graph edge e corresponding to (ν, ν') as the terms represented by ν before executing e (cf. Figure 7). This is made precise by

---

[7] In [20] transparent equivalence is therefore called *Herbrand equivalence* as it is induced by the Herbrand interpretation.

means of the relation $\overset{\delta}{\longleftarrow}$ defined next. To this end, let Γ denote the set of all nodes of the SPDAG-annotation $\mathcal{D}$. Moreover, let $Terms(\nu)$ denote the set of all terms represented by node ν of Γ, and let $\mathcal{N}(\nu)$ denote the flow-graph node ν is related to. Central is the definition of the *backward substitution* δ, which is defined for each flow-graph edge $e \equiv (x_1, \ldots, x_r) := (t_1, \ldots, t_r)$ by $\delta_e :$ $\mathbf{T} \to \mathbf{T}$, $\delta_e(t) =_{df} t[t_1, \ldots, t_r / x_1, \ldots, x_r]$, where $t[t_1, \ldots, t_r / x_1, \ldots, x_r]$ stands for the simultaneous replacement of all occurrences of x_i by t_i in t, $i \in \{1, \ldots, r\}$.[8] The relation $\overset{\delta}{\longleftarrow}$ on Γ is now defined by:

$$\forall (\nu, \nu') \in \Gamma. \; \nu \overset{\delta}{\longleftarrow} \nu' \Longleftrightarrow_{df} (\mathcal{N}(\nu), \mathcal{N}(\nu')) \in E \wedge Terms(\nu) \supseteq \delta_e(Terms(\nu'))$$

The value-flow graph for a SPDAG-designation $\mathcal{D}$ is then as follows:

Definition 1 (Value-Flow Graph). *The* value-flow graph *with respect to $\mathcal{D}$ is a pair* $VFG = (VFN, VFE)$ *consisting of*

- *a set of nodes* $VFN =_{df} \Gamma$ *called* abstract values *and*
- *a set of edges* $VFE \subseteq VFN \times VFN$ *with* $VFE =_{df} \overset{\delta}{\longleftarrow}$.

It is worth noting that the value-flow graph definition given above is technically much simpler than its original version of [20]. This is simply a consequence of representing procedures here by edge-labeled flow graphs instead of node-labeled flow graphs as in [20]. Predecessors, successors and finite paths in the value-flow graph are denoted by overloading the corresponding notions for flow graphs, e. g., $pred(\nu)$ addresses the predecessors of $\nu \in \Gamma$.

VFG-**Redundancies:** In order to define the notion of (partial) redundancies with respect to a value-flow graph VFG, we need to extend the local predicate $Comp$ for terms known from syntactic CM to the abstract values represented by value-flow graph nodes. In the syntactic setting $Comp_e$ expresses that a given term t under consideration is computed at edge e, i.e., t is a sub-term of some right-hand side term of the statement associated with e. Analogously, for every abstract value $\nu \in VFN$ the local predicate $Comp_\nu$ expresses that the statements of the corresponding outgoing flow-graph edges compute a term represented by ν:[9]

$$Comp_\nu \Longleftrightarrow_{df} (\forall e \in E. \; source(e) = \mathcal{N}(\nu) \Rightarrow Terms(\nu) \cap Terms(e) \neq \emptyset)$$

Here $Terms(e)$ denotes the set of all terms occurring on the right-hand side of the statement of edge e.

In addition, we need the notion of *correspondence* between value-flow graph paths and flow-graph paths. Let $p = \langle e_1, \ldots, e_q \rangle \in \mathbf{P}[m, n]$ be a path in the flow

---

[8] Note, for edges labeled by "skip" the function δ_e equals the identity on terms $Id_{\mathbf{T}}$.

[9] Recall that edges starting in nodes with more than one successor are labeled by "skip". Thus, we have: $\forall n \in N. \; |\{e \mid source(e) = n\}| > 1 \Rightarrow Terms(\{e \mid source(e) = n\}) = \emptyset$. Hence, the truth value of the predicate $Comp_\nu$ depends actually on a single flow-graph edge only.

graph G, and let $p' = (\varepsilon_1, \ldots, \varepsilon_r) \in \mathbf{P}[\nu, \mu]$ be a path in a value-flow graph VFG of G. Then p' is a *corresponding VFG-prefix* of p, if for all $i \in \{1, \ldots, r\}$ holds: $\mathcal{N}(source(\varepsilon_i)) = source(e_i)$ and $\mathcal{N}(dest(\varepsilon_i)) = dest(e_i)$. Analogously, the notion of a *corresponding VFG-postfix* p' of p is defined. We can now define:

Definition 2 (VFG-Redundancy). *Let VFG be a value-flow graph, let n be a node of G, and t be a term of* **T**. *Then t is*

1. *partially VFG-redundant at n, if there is a path $p = \langle e_1, \ldots, e_q \rangle \in \mathbf{P}[\mathbf{s}, n]$ with a corresponding VFG-postfix $p' = \langle \varepsilon_1, \ldots, \varepsilon_r \rangle \in \mathbf{P}[\nu, \mu]$ such that $Comp_\nu$ and $t \in Terms(\mu)$ holds.*
2. *(totally) VFG-redundant at n, if t is partially VFG-redundant along each path $p \in \mathbf{P}[\mathbf{s}, n]$.*

4   The Main Process: Eliminating Semantic Redundancies

The nodes of a value-flow graph represent semantic equivalences of terms *syntactically*. In the main process of eliminating semantic redundancies, they play the same role as the lexical term patterns in the elimination of syntactic redundancies by syntactic CM. We demonstrate this analogy in the following section.

4.1   The Straightforward Approach

In this section we extend the analyses underlying the syntactic CM-procedure to the semantic situation in a straightforward fashion. To this end let us recall the equation system characterizing up-safety in the syntactic setting first: up-safety of a term pattern t at a program point n means that t is computed on every program path reaching n without an intervening modification of some of its operands.[10]

Equation System 3 (Syntactic Up-Safety for a Term Pattern t)

$$\text{Syn-US}_n = (n \neq \mathbf{s}) \cdot \prod_{m \in pred(n)} (\text{Syn-US}_m + Comp_{(m,n)}) \cdot Transp_{(m,n)}$$

The corresponding equation system for *VFG*-up-safety is given next. Note that there is no predicate like "VFG-Transp" corresponding to the predicate *Transp*. In the syntactic setting, the transparency predicate $Transp_e$ is required for checking that the value of the term t under consideration is maintained along a flow-graph edge e, i.e., that none of its operands is modified. The essence of the value-flow graph is that transparency is modeled by the edges: two value-flow graph nodes are connected by a value-flow graph edge iff the value they represent is maintained along the corresponding flow-graph edge.

---

[10] As convenient, we use $\cdot$, $+$ and overlining for logical conjunction, disjunction and negation, respectively.

Equation System 4 (*VFG-Up-Safety*)

$$\text{VFG-US}_\nu = (\nu \notin VFN_{\mathbf{s}}) \cdot \prod_{\mu \in pred(\nu)} (\text{VFG-US}_\mu + Comp_\mu)$$

The roles of the start node and end node of the flow graph are here played by the "start nodes" and "end nodes" of the value-flow graph defined by:

$$VFN_{\mathbf{s}} =_{df} \{ \nu \mid \mathcal{N}(pred(\nu)) \neq pred(\mathcal{N}(\nu)) \vee \mathcal{N}(\nu) = \mathbf{s} \}$$
$$VFN_{\mathbf{e}} =_{df} \{ \nu \mid \mathcal{N}(succ(\nu)) \neq succ(\mathcal{N}(\nu)) \vee \mathcal{N}(\nu) = \mathbf{e} \}$$

Down-safety is the dual counterpart of up-safety. However, the equation system for the *VFG*-version of this property is technically more complicated, as we have two graph structures, the flow graph and the value-flow graph, which must both be taken separately into account: as in the syntactic setting (or for up-safety), we need safety universally along all flow-graph edges, which is reflected by a value-flow graph node ν being down-safe at the program point $\mathcal{N}(\nu)$, if a term represented by ν is computed on all *flow-graph* edges leaving $\mathcal{N}(\nu)$, or if it is down-safe at all successor points. However, we may justify safety along a flow-graph edge e by means of the *VFG* in *various* ways, as, in contrast to up-safety concerning the forward flow (or the syntactic setting), a value-flow graph node may have *several* successors corresponding to e (cf. Figure 7), and it suffices to have safety only along one of them. This is formally described by:

Equation System 5 (*VFG-Motion-Down-Safety*)

$$\text{VFG-MDS}_\nu = (\nu \notin VFN_{\mathbf{e}}) \cdot (Comp_\nu + \prod_{m \in succ(\mathcal{N}(\nu))} \sum_{\substack{\mu \in succ(\nu) \\ \mathcal{N}(\mu) = m}} \text{VFG-MDS}_\mu)$$

The Transformation (of the Straightforward Approach) Let VFG-US* and VFG-MDS* denote the greatest solutions of the Equation Systems 4 and 5. The analogy with the syntactic setting is continued by the specification of the semantic CM-transformation, called *Sem-CM$_{Strght}$*. It is essentially given by the set of insertion and replacement points. *Insertion* of an abstract value ν means to initialize a fresh temporary with a minimal representative t' of ν, i.e., containing a minimal number of operators, on the flow-graph edges leaving node $\mathcal{N}(\nu)$. *Replacement* means to replace an original computation by a reference to the temporary storing its value.

$$\text{Insert}_\nu \iff \text{VFG-MDS}_\nu^* \cdot ((\nu \in VFN_{\mathbf{s}}) + \sum_{\mu \in pred(\nu)} \overline{\text{VFG-MDS}_\mu^* + \text{VFG-US}_\mu^*})$$

$$\text{Replace}_\nu \iff Comp_\nu$$

Managing and reinitializing temporaries: In the syntactic setting, there is for every term pattern a unique temporary, and these temporaries are not interacting with each other: the values computed at their initialization sites are thus propagated to all their use sites, i.e., the program points containing an original occurrence of the corresponding term pattern, without requiring special care. In the semantic setting propagating these values requires usually to reset them at certain points to values of other temporaries as illustrated in Figure 2(b). The complete process including managing temporary names is accomplished by a straightforward analysis starting at the original computation sites and following the value-graph edges in the opposite direction to the insertion points. The details of this procedure are not recalled here as they are not essential for the point of this article. They can be found in [20, 21].

Second-Order Effects: In contrast to the syntactic setting, the straightforward semantic counterpart Sem-CM_{Strght} has second-order effects. This is illustrated in Figure 5: applying Sem-CM_{Strght} to the program of Figure 5(a) results in the program of Figure 5(b). Repeating the transformation again, results in the optimal program of Figure 5(c).

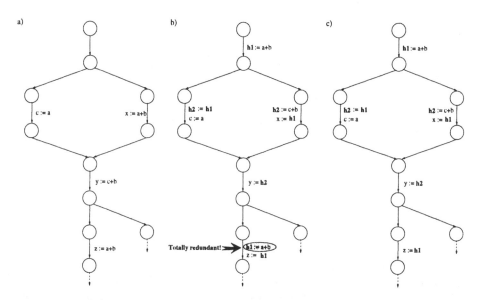

Fig. 5. Illustrating Second-Order Effects

Intuitively, the reason that Sem-CM_{Strght} has second-order effects is that safety is no longer the sum of up-safety and down-safety. Above, up-safety is only computed with respect to original computations. While this is sufficient in the syntactic case, it is not in the semantic one as it does not take into account that the placement of computations as a result of the transformation may make "new" values available, e.g. in the program of Figure 5(b) the value of $a + b$ becomes available at the end of the program fragment displayed. As a consequence, total redundancies like the one in Figure 5(b) can remain in the program. Eliminating them (TRE) as illustrated in Figure 5(c) is sufficient to capture the second-order effects completely. We have:

Theorem 3 ($Sem\text{-}CM_{Strght}$).

1. $Sem\text{-}CM_{Strght}$ *relies on only* two uni-directional analyses.
2. $Sem\text{-}CM_{Strght}$ has second-order effects.
3. $Sem\text{-}CM_{Strght}$ *followed by TRE achieves* computationally motion-optimal results wrt the Herbrand interpretation *like its bidirectional precursor of [20]*.

4.2 Avoiding Second-Order Effects: The Hierarchical Approach

The point of this section is to reestablish as a footing for the algorithm a notion of safety which can be characterized as the sum of up-safety and down-safety. The central result here is that a notion of safety tailored to capture the idea of "motion" (in contrast to "placement") can be characterized by down-safety together with the following hierarchical notion of up-safety:

Equation System 6 ("Hierarchical" *VFG*-Up-Safety)

$$\text{VFG-MUS}_\nu = \text{VFG-MDS}_\nu^* + (\nu \notin VFN_s) \cdot \prod_{\mu \in pred(\nu)} \text{VFG-MUS}_\mu$$

In fact, the phenomenon of second-order effects can now completely and elegantly be overcome by the following hierarchical procedure:[11]

1. Compute down-safety (cf. Equation System 5).
2. Compute the modified up-safety property on the basis of the down-safety computation (cf. Equation System 6).

The transformation $Sem\text{-}CM_{Hier}$ of the Hierarchical Approach is now defined as before except that VFG-MUS* is used instead of VFG-US*. Its results coincide with those of an exhaustive application of the CM-procedure proposed in Subsection 4.1, as well as of the original (bidirectional) CM-procedure of [20]. However, in contrast to the latter algorithm, which due to its bidirectionality required a complicated correctness argument, the transformation of the hierarchical approach allows a rather straightforward link to the Herbrand semantics, which drastically simplifies the correctness proof. Besides this conceptual improvement, the new algorithm is also easier to comprehend and to implement as it does not require any bidirectional analysis. We have:

Theorem 4 ($Sem\text{-}CM_{Hier}$).

1. $Sem\text{-}CM_{Hier}$ *relies on only* two uni-directional analyses sequentially ordered.
2. $Sem\text{-}CM_{Hier}$ *is* free of second-order effects.
3. $Sem\text{-}CM_{Hier}$ *achieves* computationally motion-optimal results wrt the Herbrand interpretation *like its bidirectional precursor of [20]*.

---

[11] The "down-safety/earliest" characterization of [12] was also already hierarchical. However, in the syntactic setting this is not relevant as it was shown in [13].

5 Semantic Code Placement

In this section we are concerned with crossing the frontier marked by semantic CM towards to semantic CP, and giving theoretical and practical reasons for the fact that no algorithm has gone beyond this frontier so far. On the theoretical side (I), we prove that computational optimality is impossible for semantic CP in general. On the practical side (II), we demonstrate that down-safety, the handle for correctly and profitably placing computations by syntactic and semantic CM, is inadequate for semantic CP.

(I) No Optimality in General: Semantic CP cannot be done "computationally placement-optimal" in general. This is a significant difference in comparison to syntactic and semantic CM, which have a least element with respect to the relation "computationally better" (cf. [13, 20]). In semantic CP, however, we are faced with the phenomenon of incomparable minima. This is illustrated in the example of Figure 6 showing a slight modification of the program of Figure 3. Both programs of Figure 6 are of incomparable quality, since the "right-most" path is improved by impairing the "left-most" one.

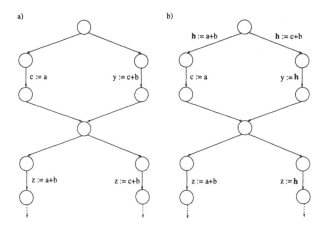

Fig. 6. No Optimality in General: An Incomparable Result due to CP

(II) Inadequateness of Down-safety: For syntactic and semantic CM, down-safe program points are always legal insertion points. Inserting a computation at a down-safe point guarantees that it can be used on every program continuation. This, however, does not hold for semantic CP. Before showing this in detail, we illustrate the difference between "placable" *VFG*-down-safety (*VFG-DownSafe*) and "movable" *VFG*-down-safety (*VFG-M-DownSafe*) by means of Figure 7 which shows the difference by means of the value-flow graph corresponding to the example of Figure 3.

We remark that the predicate *VFG-DownSafe* is decidable. However, the point to be demonstrated here is that this property is insufficient anyhow in

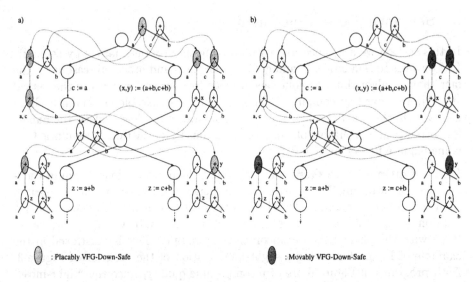

Fig. 7. The Corresponding Value-Flow Graph

order to (straightforwardly) arrive at an algorithm for semantic CP. This is illustrated by Figure 8 showing a slight modification of the program of Figure 6. Though the placement of $\mathbf{h} := a + b$ is perfectly down-safe, it cannot be used at all. Thus, impairing the program.

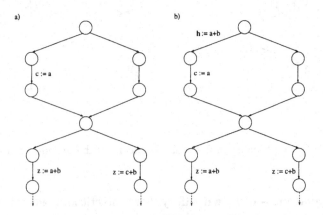

Fig. 8. Inadequateness of Down-Safety: Degradation through Naive CP

Summary: The examples of Figure 3 and of this section commonly share that they are invariant under semantic CM, since $a + b$ cannot safely be moved to (and hence not across) the join node in the mid part. However, $a + b$ can safely be placed in the left branch of the upper branch statement. In the example of Figure 3 this suffices to show that semantic CP is in general strictly more powerful than semantic CM. On the other hand, Figure 6 demonstrates that "computational optimality" for semantic CP is impossible in general. While this rules out the possibility of an algorithm for semantic CP being uniformly superior to every other semantic CP-algorithm, the inadequateness of down-safety revealed by the second example of this section gives reason for the lack even of heuristics for semantic CP: this is because down-safety, the magic wand of syntactic and semantic CM, loses its magic for semantic CP. In fact, straightforward adaptions of the semantic CM-procedure to semantic CP would be burdened with the placing anomalies of Figures 6 and 8. We conjecture that a satisfactory solution to these problems requires structural changes of the argument program. Summarizing, we have:

Theorem 5 (Semantic Code Placement).

1. *Semantic CP is strictly more powerful than semantic CM.*
2. *Computational placement-optimality is impossible in general.*
3. *Down-safety is inadeqate for semantic CP.*

6 Conclusion

We have re-investigated semantic CM under the perspective of the recent development of syntactic CM, which has clarified the essential difference between the syntactic and the semantic approach, and uncovered the difference of CM and CP in the semantic setting. Central for the understanding of this difference is the role of the notion of *safety* of a program point for some computation. Modification of the considered notion of safety is the key for obtaining a transfer of the syntactic algorithm to the semantic setting which captures the full potential of motion algorithms. However, in contrast to the syntactic setting, motion algorithms do not capture the full potential of code placement. Actually, we conjecture that there does not exist a satisfactory solution to the code placement problem, unless one is prepared to change the structure of the argument program.

References

1. B. Alpern, M. N. Wegman, and F. K. Zadeck. Detecting equality of variables in programs. In *Conf. Rec. 15th Symp. Principles of Prog. Lang. (POPL'88)*, pages 1 – 11. ACM, NY, 1988.
2. F. Chow. *A Portable Machine Independent Optimizer – Design and Measurements.* PhD thesis, Stanford Univ., Dept. of Electrical Eng., Stanford, CA, 1983. Publ. as Tech. Rep. 83-254, Comp. Syst. Lab., Stanford Univ.
3. C. Click. Global code motion/global value numbering. In *Proc. ACM SIGPLAN Conf. Prog. Lang. Design and Impl. (PLDI'95)*, volume *30,6* of *ACM SIGPLAN Not.*, pages 246–257, 1995.
4. J. Cocke and J. T. Schwartz. Programming languages and their compilers. Courant Inst. Math. Sciences, NY, 1970.

5. D. M. Dhamdhere. A fast algorithm for code movement optimization. *ACM SIGPLAN Not.*, 23(10):172 – 180, 1988.

6. D. M. Dhamdhere. Practical adaptation of the global optimization algorithm of Morel and Renvoise. *ACM Trans. Prog. Lang. Syst.*, 13(2):291 – 294, 1991. Tech. Corr.

7. D. M. Dhamdhere, B. K. Rosen, and F. K. Zadeck. How to analyze large programs efficiently and informatively. In *Proc. ACM SIGPLAN Conf. Prog. Lang. Design and Impl. (PLDI'92)*, volume 27,7 of *ACM SIGPLAN Not.*, pages 212 – 223, 1992.

8. K.-H. Drechsler and M. P. Stadel. A solution to a problem with Morel and Renvoise's "Global optimization by suppression of partial redundancies". *ACM Trans. Prog. Lang. Syst.*, 10(4):635 – 640, 1988. Tech. Corr.

9. A. Fong, J. B. Kam, and J. D. Ullman. Application of lattice algebra to loop optimization. In *Conf. Rec. 2nd Symp. Principles of Prog. Lang. (POPL'75)*, pages 1 – 9. ACM, NY, 1975.

10. G. A. Kildall. A unified approach to global program optimization. In *Conf. Rec. 1st Symp. Principles of Prog. Lang. (POPL'73)*, pages 194 – 206. ACM, NY, 1973.

11. J. Knoop, D. Koschützki, and B. Steffen. Basic-block graphs: Living dinosaurs? In *Proc. 7th Int. Conf. on Compiler Constr. (CC'98)*, LNCS, Springer-V., 1998.

12. J. Knoop, O. Rüthing, and B. Steffen. Lazy code motion. In *Proc. ACM SIGPLAN Conf. Prog. Lang. Design and Impl. (PLDI'92)*, volume 27,7 of *ACM SIGPLAN Not.*, pages 224 – 234, 1992.

13. J. Knoop, O. Rüthing, and B. Steffen. Optimal code motion: Theory and practice. *ACM Trans. Prog. Lang. Syst.*, 16(4):1117–1155, 1994.

14. J. Knoop, O. Rüthing, and B. Steffen. Code Motion and Code Placement: Just Synonyms? Technical Report MIP-9716, Fakultät für Mathematik und Informatik, Universität Passau, Germany, 1997.

15. E. Morel and C. Renvoise. Global optimization by suppression of partial redundancies. *Comm. ACM*, 22(2):96 – 103, 1979.

16. J. H. Reif and R. Lewis. Symbolic evaluation and the global value graph. In *Conf. Rec. 4th Symp. Principles of Prog. Lang. (POPL'77)*, pages 104 – 118. ACM, NY, 1977.

17. B. K. Rosen, M. N. Wegman, and F. K. Zadeck. Global value numbers and redundant computations. In *Conf. Rec. 15th Symp. Principles of Prog. Lang. (POPL'88)*, pages 2 – 27. ACM, NY, 1988.

18. A. Sorkin. Some comments on a solution to a problem with Morel and Renvoise's "Global optimization by suppression of partial redundancies". *ACM Trans. Prog. Lang. Syst.*, 11(4):666 – 668, 1989. Tech. Corr.

19. B. Steffen. Property-oriented expansion. In *Proc. 3rd Stat. Analysis Symp. (SAS'96)*, LNCS 1145, pages 22 – 41. Springer-V., 1996.

20. B. Steffen, J. Knoop, and O. Rüthing. The value flow graph: A program representation for optimal program transformations. In *Proc. 3rd Europ. Symp. Programming (ESOP'90)*, LNCS 432, pages 389 – 405. Springer-V., 1990.

21. B. Steffen, J. Knoop, and O. Rüthing. Efficient code motion and an adaption to strength reduction. In *Proc. 4th Int. Conf. Theory and Practice of Software Development (TAPSOFT'91)*, LNCS 494, pages 394 – 415. Springer-V., 1991.

Recursive Object Types
in a Logic of Object-Oriented Programs

K. Rustan M. Leino

Digital Equipment Corporation Systems Research Center
130 Lytton Ave., Palo Alto, CA 94301, U.S.A.
http://www.research.digital.com/SRC/people/Rustan_Leino

Abstract. This paper formalizes a small object-oriented programming notation. The notation features imperative commands where objects can be shared (aliased), and is rich enough to allow subtypes and recursive object types. The syntax, type checking rules, axiomatic semantics, and operational semantics of the notation are given. A soundness theorem showing the consistency between the axiomatic and operational semantics is also given. A simple corollary of the soundness theorem demonstrates the soundness of the type system. Because of the way types, fields, and methods are declared, no extra effort is required to handle recursive object types.

0   Introduction

It is well known that C.A.R. Hoare's logic of the basic commands of imperative, procedural languages [9] has been useful in understanding imperative languages. Object-oriented programming languages being all the rage, one is surprised that the literature has not produced a corresponding logic for modern object-oriented programs. The control structures of object-oriented programs are similar to those treated by Hoare, but the data structures of object-oriented programs are more complicated, mainly because objects are (possibly shared) references to data fields.

This paper presents a logic for an object-oriented programming notation. In an early attempt at such a logic, Leavens gave an axiomatic semantics for an object-oriented language [11]. However, the language he used differs from popular object-oriented languages in that it is functional rather than imperative, so the values of the fields of objects cannot be changed. America and de Boer have given a logic for the parallel language POOL [4]. This logic applies to imperative programs with object sharing (sometimes called aliasing), but without subtyping and method overriding. In a logic that I will refer to as logic AL, Abadi and I defined an axiomatic semantics for an imperative, object-oriented language with object sharing [2], but it does not permit recursive object types. Poetzsch-Heffter and Müller have defined (but not proved sound) a Hoare-style logic for object-oriented programs that remove many of the previous limitations [18]. However, instead of following the standard methodological discipline of letting the designer of a method define its specification and then checking that implementations meet the specification, the specification of a method in the Poetzsch-Heffter and Müller logic is derived from the method's known implementations. The present logic deals with imperative features, subtyping, and recursive object types.

The literature has paid much attention to the type systems of object-oriented languages. Such papers tend to define some notion of types, the commands of some language, the type rules and operational semantics for the commands, and a soundness theorem linking the type system with the operational semantics. (Several examples of this are found in Abadi and Cardelli's book on objects [1].) But after all that effort, one still doesn't know how to *reason* about the programs that can be written with the provided commands, since no axiomatic semantics is given. In addition to giving a programming notation and its axiomatic semantics, this paper, like the paper describing logic AL, gives an operational semantics and a soundness theorem that links the operational semantics with the axiomatic semantics. The soundness theorem directly implies the soundness of the type system.

A complication with type systems is that types can be *recursive*, that is, an object type T may contain a field of type T or a method whose return type is T. The literature commonly treats recursive data types by introducing some sort of fix-point operator into the type system, good examples of which are a paper by Amadio and Cardelli on recursive types and subtypes [3] and the book by Abadi and Cardelli. By treating types in a dramatically different way, the present logic supports recursive object types without the need for any special mechanism like fix-points. The inclusion of recursive object types is one main advantage of the present logic over logic AL, which does not allow them. (The other main advantage over logic AL is that the present logic can be used with any first-order theory.) Because the given soundness theorem implies the soundness of the type system, the present work contributes also to the world of type systems.

In difference to the paper by Amadio and Cardelli, which considers unrestricted recursive types, the type system in the present paper uses a restriction along the lines of name matching. In particular, types are simply identifiers, and the subtype relation is simply a given partial order among those identifiers. This is much like the classes in Java [8] or the branded object types in Modula-3 [17]. But in contrast to languages like Java or Modula-3, fields and methods are declared separately from types in the language considered in this paper. (This is also done in Cecil [5] and Ecstatic [13].) Not only does this simplify the treatment without loss of applicability to languages like Java and Modula-3, but it also makes explicit the separation of concerns. For example, as the logic shows, having to know all the fields of a particular object type is necessary only for the allocation of a new object.

Furthermore, when a field or method is declared at some type T, each subtype of T automatically acquires, or *inherits*, that field or method. Consequently, one gets behavioral subtyping for free, something that can also be achieved by the inheritance discipline considered by Dhara and Leavens [6]. In contrast, subtype relations frequently found in the literature (including the subtype relation used in logic AL), involves the fields and methods of types. In such treatments of types, one often encounters words like "co-variant"; there will be no further occurrence of such words in this paper.

The rest of this paper is organized as follows. Section 1 relates the present logic to some work that has influenced it. Section 2 describes the declarations that can be used in program environments, and Section 3 describes the commands: their syntax, axiomatic semantics, and operational semantics. Section 4 discusses an example program. Then,

Section 5 states the soundness theorem. Section 6 discusses some limitations of the logic, and the paper concludes with a brief summary.

1 Sources of Influence

My work with Abadi has inculcated the present logic with its style and machinery. The present logic also draws from other sources with which I am quite familiar: my thesis [12], my work on an object logic with Nelson [15], and the Ecstatic language [13]. This section compares the features of these sources of influence with the features of the present logic.

My thesis includes a translation of common object-oriented language constructs into Dijkstra's *guarded commands*, an imperative language whose well-known axiomatic semantics is given in terms of *weakest preconditions* [7]. My attempt at an object logic with Nelson is also based on guarded commands, and Ecstatic is a richer object-oriented programming language defined directly in terms of weakest preconditions. Types, fields, and methods in these three sources are declared in roughly the same way as in the present logic. While these sources do provide a way to reason about object-oriented programs, they take for granted the existence of an operational semantics that implements the axiomatic semantics. The present paper includes an operational semantics for the given commands, and establishes the correctness of the operational semantics with respect to the axiomatic semantics by proving a soundness theorem.

Like logic AL, the present logic has few and simple commands. Each command in logic AL operates on an object store and produces a value placed in a special register called r. In the present logic, commands are allowed to refer to the initial value of that register, which simplifies many of the rules. (It also makes the commands "cute".) Another difference is that the present logic splits logic AL's *let* command into two commands: sequential composition and binding. The separation works well because the initial value of register r can be used. Perhaps surprisingly, another consequence of using the initial value of r is that the present logic manages fine without Abadi and Cardelli's ς binder that appears in logic AL to bind a method's self parameter.

2 Environments

This section starts defining the logic by describing program environments and the declarations that a program environment can contain.

A *program environment* is a list of declarations. A declaration introduces a type, a field, or a method.

An identifier is said to be declared in an environment if it is introduced by a type, field, or method declaration in the environment, or if it is one of the built-in types. I write $x \notin E$ to denote that identifier x is not declared in environment E.

The judgement $E \vdash \diamond$ says that E is a well-formed environment. The empty list, written $\emptyset$, is a valid environment.

Empty Environment

$$\frac{}{\emptyset \vdash \diamond}$$

The next three subsections describe types, fields, and methods, and give the remaining rules for well-formed environments.

2.0 Types

A *type* is an identifier. There are two built-in types, *Boolean* and *Object*. (Other types, like integers, can easily be added, but I omit them for brevity.) Types other than *Boolean* are called *object types*. A new object type is introduced by a *subtyping pair*, which has the form $T <: U$, where T is identifier that names the new type, and U is an object type. Like in Java, *Object* denotes the root of the class hierarchy. The analogue of a subtyping pair $T <: U$ in Java is a class T declared as a subclass of a class U: *class T extends U { ... }*.

A type is said to be declared in an environment if it is *Boolean*, *Object*, or if it occurs as the first component of a subtyping pair. To express this formally, the judgement $E \vdash_{type} T$ says that T is a type in environment E, and the judgement $E \vdash_{obj} T$ says that T is an object type in E. The rules for these judgements are as follows. Here and throughout this paper, I use T and U, possibly subscripted, to denote types.

Types in Environments   **Declared Types** $(\vdash_{type}, \vdash_{obj})$

$$\frac{E \vdash_{obj} U \qquad T \notin E}{(E, T<:U) \vdash \diamond} \qquad \frac{E \vdash \diamond}{E \vdash_{obj} Object} \qquad \frac{(E, T<:U, E') \vdash \diamond}{(E, T<:U, E') \vdash_{obj} T}$$

$$\frac{E \vdash \diamond}{E \vdash_{type} Boolean} \qquad \frac{E \vdash_{obj} T}{E \vdash_{type} T}$$

The reflexive, transitive closure of the subtyping pairs forms a partial order called the *subtyping order*. The judgement $E \vdash T <: U$ says that T and U are types in E that are ordered by the subtyping order. Type T is then said to be a *subtype* of U. The rules are:

Subtyping Order $(\vdash <:)$

$$\frac{E \vdash_{type} T}{E \vdash T <: T} \qquad \frac{(E, T<:U, E') \vdash \diamond}{(E, T<:U, E') \vdash T <: U} \qquad \frac{E \vdash T_0 <: T_1 \qquad E \vdash T_1 <: T_2}{E \vdash T_0 <: T_2}$$

2.1 Fields

A field is a map from an object type to another type. A field f is introduced by a *field triple*, written $f: T \rightarrow U$, where f is the identifier that names the field, T is an object type called the *index type* of f, and U is a type called the *range type* of f. The analogue of a field triple $f: T \rightarrow U$ in Java is an instance variable f of type U declared in a class T: *class T { ... U f; ... }*.

An environment can contain field triples. A field f is said to be declared in an environment E if it occurs in some field triple $f: T \rightarrow U$ in E. This is expressed by the judgement $E \vdash_{field} f: T \rightarrow U$. The rules for these judgements are as follows. Here and throughout, I use f, possibly subscripted, to denote field names.

Fields in Environments **Declared Fields** $(\vdash_{field})$

$$\frac{E \vdash_{obj} T \quad E \vdash_{type} U \quad f \notin E}{(E, f\colon T \to U) \vdash \diamond}$$

$$\frac{(E, f\colon T \to U, E') \vdash \diamond}{(E, f\colon T \to U, E') \vdash_{field} f\colon T \to U}$$

For a type T_0 declared in an environment E, the *set of fields of T_0 in E*, written $Fields(T_0, E)$, is the set of all field triples $f\colon T \to U$ such that $E \vdash_{field} f\colon T \to U$ and $E \vdash T_0 <: T$.

2.2 Methods

A *method quadruple* has the form $m\colon T \to U : R$, where m is an identifier denoting a *method*, T is an object type, U is a type, and R is a *relation*. The analogue of a method quadruple $m\colon T \to U : R$ in Java is a method m with return type U declared in a class T and given a specification R: *class* $T \{ \ldots U \, m() \{\ldots\} \ldots \}$. Note that the Java language does not have a place to write down the specification of a method. In the present language, the declaration of a method includes a specification, which specifies the effect of the method as a relation on the pre- and post-state of each method invocation. Note also that methods take no parameters (other than the object on which the method is invoked, an object commonly referred to as *self*). This simplifies the logic without losing theoretical expressiveness, since parameters can be passed through fields.

An environment can contain method quadruples. A method m is said to be declared in an environment E if it occurs in some method quadruple $m\colon T \to U : R$ in E. This is expressed by the judgement $E \vdash_{method} m\colon T \to U : R$. Formally, the rules are as follows. I use m, possibly subscripted, to denote methods.

Methods in Environments **Declared Methods** $(\vdash_{method})$

$$\frac{\begin{array}{cc} E \vdash_{obj} T & E \vdash_{type} U \\ E, \emptyset \vdash_{rel} R & m \notin E \end{array}}{(E, m\colon T \to U : R) \vdash \diamond}$$

$$\frac{(E, m\colon T \to U : R, E') \vdash \diamond}{(E, m\colon T \to U : R, E') \vdash_{method} m\colon T \to U : R}$$

The judgement $E, \emptyset \vdash_{rel} R$, which will be described in more detail in Section 3.1, essentially says that R is a relation that may mention fields declared in E but doesn't mention any local program variables.

For a type T_0 declared in an environment E, the *set of methods of T_0 in E*, written $Methods(T_0, E)$, is the set of all method quadruples $m\colon T \to U : R$ such that $E \vdash_{method} m\colon T \to U : R$ and $E \vdash T_0 <: T$.

2.3 Relations

Methods are specified using *relations*. A relation is an untyped first-order predicate on a pre-state and a post-state. In order to make relations expressive, the present logic can be used with an *underlying logic*, which provides a set of function symbols and a set of first-order axioms about those function symbols. The example in Section 4 shows how an underlying logic may be used.

Syntactically, relations are made up only of:

- the constants *false*, *true*, and *nil*;
- constants for field names, and the special field alloc ;
- the special variables $\grave{r}$, $\acute{r}$, $\grave{\sigma}$, $\acute{\sigma}$;
- other variables (I will write v to denote a typical variable);
- equality between terms;
- applications of the functions *select* and *store* ;
- applications of the functions of the underlying logic;
- the usual logical connectives $\neg$, $\wedge$, and $\forall$.

The grammars for relations (R) and terms (e) are thus:

$$R ::= e_0 = e_1 \mid \neg R \mid R_0 \wedge R_1 \mid \langle \forall x :: R \rangle$$
$$e ::= false \mid true \mid nil \mid f \mid \grave{r} \mid \acute{r} \mid \grave{\sigma} \mid \acute{\sigma} \mid v$$
$$\mid select(e_0, e_1, e_2) \mid store(e_0, e_1, e_2, e_3)$$
$$\mid pa(e_0, \ldots, e_{ka-1}) \mid \cdots \mid pz(e_0, \ldots, e_{kz-1}) \quad ,$$

where $pa, \ldots, pz$ denote the function symbols of the underlying logic with arities $ka, \ldots, kz$, respectively. It will be convenient to also allow $\neq$, $\vee$, $\Rightarrow$, $\Leftarrow$, $\equiv$, and $\exists$ as the usual abbreviations of the operators above.

The semantics of a command (program statement) is defined in terms of a relation on a *register* and a *(data) store*, together called a *state*. The variables $\grave{r}$ and $\acute{r}$ denote the register in the pre- and post-states of the command, respectively, and $\grave{\sigma}$ and $\acute{\sigma}$ denote the store in those respective states. The value of a field f of an object e in a store σ is denoted $select(\sigma, e, f)$. The expression $store(\sigma, e_0, f, e_1)$ represents the store that results from setting the f field of object e_0 in store σ to the value e_1 . The relationship between *select* and *store* is defined as follows.

$$\langle \forall \sigma, e_0, e_1, f_0, f_1, e ::$$
$$select(store(\sigma, e_0, f_0, e), e_0, f_0) = e \wedge \tag{0}$$
$$(e_0 \neq e_1 \vee f_0 \neq f_1 \Rightarrow$$
$$select(store(\sigma, e_0, f_0, e), e_1, f_1) = select(\sigma, e_1, f_1)) \rangle$$

The special field alloc is used to record which objects in the data store have been allocated; the alloc field of an object is *false* until the object is allocated, and is *true* from there on.

As we shall see, the logic allows relations to be rewritten. A rewriting uses the rules of logic and some axioms. In particular, a rewriting may use as axioms the definition of *select* and *store* (0), the distinctness of the boolean values and the distinctness of field name constants:

$$false \neq true \tag{1}$$
$$\text{all field name constants (including alloc) are distinct} \tag{2}$$

and the axioms of the underlying logic.

3   Commands

This section describes commands: their syntax, their axiomatic semantics, and their operational semantics.

3.0 Syntax

A *command* has a form dictated by the following grammar.

$$
\begin{array}{ll}
a ::= c & \text{constant} \\
\quad | \ v & \text{local variable} \\
\quad | \ a_0 \Leftrightarrow a_1 & \text{conditional} \\
\quad | \ a_0 \ ; \ a_1 & \text{composition} \\
\quad | \ with \ v : T \ do \ a & \text{binding} \\
\quad | \ [T \colon f_i = c_i \ ^{i \in I}, \ m_j = a_j \ ^{j \in J}] & \text{object construction} \\
\quad | \ f & \text{field selection} \\
\quad | \ f := v & \text{field update} \\
\quad | \ m & \text{method invocation} \\
c ::= false \ | \ true \ | \ nil &
\end{array}
$$

Informally, the semantics of the language is as follows. (Recall from the previous section that commands operate on a register and a store.)

- The constants *false*, *true*, and *nil* evaluate to themselves. That is, they have the effect of setting the register to themselves.
- A local variable is an identifier introduced via a binding command. Every local variable is immutable: once bound (using *with*, see below), the value of a local variable cannot be changed. A local variable evaluates to its value.
- The conditional command evaluates a_0 if the register is initially *false*, and evaluates a_1 if the register is initially *true*. Note that the guard of the conditional is not shown explicitly in the command; rather, the initial value of the register is used as the guard.
- The sequential composition of a_0 and a_1 first evaluates a_0 and then evaluates a_1. The final values of the register and store in the evaluation of a_0 are used as the initial values of the register and store in the evaluation of a_1. Composition is usually written $a_0 \ ; \ a_1$, but to keep the language looking like popular object-oriented languages, I also allow the alternative syntax $a_0 . a_1$ (see examples below).
- The binding command *with v: T do a* introduces a local variable v for use in a. Its evaluation consists in evaluating a with v bound to the initial value of the register.
- The command $[T \colon f_i = c_i \ ^{i \in I}, \ m_j = a_j \ ^{j \in J}]$ constructs a new object of type T, and sets the register to (a reference to the fields and methods of) the object. The command must list every field f_i from the set of fields of T. The initial value for field f_i is the given constant c_i. The command must also list every method m_j from the set of methods of T. The implementation of method m_j for the new object is given as the command a_j, which receives self as the initial value of the register and returns the method result value as the final value of the register. The command a_j cannot reference local variables other than those it declares.
- A field can be selected (f) and updated (f := v). Both operate on the object referenced by the initial value of the register. Selection sets the register to the f field of the object. Update sets the f field of the object to the value of v, leaving the register unchanged.

– The method invocation m finds the implementation of method m for the object referenced by the initial value of the register, and then proceeds to evaluate that implementation. The evaluation of the implementation begins with the initial register and store values of the invocation, and the invocation ends with the final register and store values of the evaluation of the implementation. Other than the initial and final register values (which encode self and the result value, respectively), a method does not have explicit parameters; instead, parameters can be passed via the fields of the object.

Here are some examples that compare the present commands with programs written in other languages. The Modula-3 program statement *if b then S else T end* is written as the command $b ; (T \Leftrightarrow S)$. The Modula-3 expression $new(T, f := true).f$, where T is an object type with one field f and no methods, is written as the command $[T : f = true] ; f$, or with the alternative syntax for composition, the command is written $[T : f = true].f$. The Modula-3 program $x.f := true$ is written $true ; with v: Boolean do x.f := v$.

As an example of object sharing, the command

$$[T: f = c] ; with v: T do with w: T do (v.f := y ; w.f)$$

allocates a new T object whose f field is set to c, creates two references to the object (v and w), updates the object's f field via v, and reads f back via w, returning y.

The following example shows the construction of a T object whose method or computes the disjunction of fields x and y:

$$[T: x = false, y = false, or = with self: T do (x ; (self.y \Leftrightarrow true))]$$.

Note that although primitive, the programming notation is expressive enough to admit common object-oriented languages features like object construction, method invocation, and object sharing. The programming notation is kept minimal in order to simplify the associated rules.

3.1 Axiomatic Semantics

This subsection gives the axiomatic semantics of the commands. The judgement

$$E, V \vdash a : T \rightarrow U : R$$

says that command a in command environment (E, V) can be started in a state where the register contents has type T, and terminates in a state where the register contents has type U. The execution of a is such that its pre- and post-states satisfy the relation R. The rules of the axiomatic semantics double as type checking rules, because with a trivial R (such as $\dot{r} = \dot{r}$), the judgement expresses what it means for command a to be well-typed.

Before giving the axiomatic semantics, some other definitions and rules pertaining to constants, local variables, and command environments are in order.

There are three constants: *false*, *true*, and *nil*. The judgement $E \vdash_{const} c : T$ expresses that constant c has type T.

Type of Constants   ($\vdash_{const}$)

$$\frac{E \vdash \diamond}{E \vdash_{const} false: Boolean} \qquad \frac{E \vdash \diamond}{E \vdash_{const} true: Boolean} \qquad \frac{E \vdash_{obj} T}{E \vdash_{const} nil: T}$$

A *local variable declaration* has the form $v: T$, where v is an identifier denoting a *local variable* and T is a type. A *command environment* is a pair (E, V), where E is a program environment and V is a list of local variable declarations. A local variable v is said to be declared in a command environment (E, V) if it occurs in some local variable declaration $v: T$ in V. This is expressed by the judgement $E, V \vdash_{var} v: T$. Thus, in a command environment (E, V), E contains declarations of types, fields, and methods, whereas V contains declarations of local variables. This separation allows a simple characterization of a command environment without local variable declarations: $(E, \emptyset)$. We saw this in the "Methods in Environments" rule in Section 2.2, and we will see it in the "Object Construction" rule below and in Theorems 0, 1, and 2 in Section 5.

The judgement

$$E, V \vdash_{rel} R$$

says that R is a relation whose free variables are fields or local variables declared in (E, V), or are among the special fields and variables $alloc$, $\grave{r}$, $\acute{r}$, $\grave{\sigma}$, and $\acute{\sigma}$. The obvious formal rules for this judgement are omitted. Thus, the judgement $E, \emptyset \vdash_{rel} R$ used in the hypothesis of the "Methods in Environments" rule in Section 2.2 implies that R does not mention local variables.

I write $x \notin (E, V)$ to denote that identifier x is not declared in command environment (E, V). The formal rules of the above are then:

Well-formed Command Environment   **Declared Local Variables**   ($\vdash_{var}$)

$$\frac{E \vdash \diamond}{E, \emptyset \vdash \diamond} \qquad \frac{E, V \vdash \diamond \quad v \notin (E, V) \quad E \vdash_{type} T}{E, (V, v: T) \vdash \diamond} \qquad \frac{E, (V, v: T, V') \vdash \diamond}{E, (V, v: T, V') \vdash_{var} v: T}$$

Now for the rules of the axiomatic semantics. There is one rule for each command, and one subsumption rule.

Subsumption

$$\frac{E \vdash T_0 <: T_1 \quad E \vdash T_2 <: T_3 \quad \vdash_{fol} R \Rightarrow R' \quad E, V \vdash_{rel} R' \qquad E, V \vdash a : T_1 \rightarrow T_2 : R}{E, V \vdash a : T_0 \rightarrow T_3 : R'}$$

The judgement $\vdash_{fol} P$ represents provability in first-order logic, under axioms (0), (1), and (2) from Section 2.3 and the axioms of the underlying logic.

Constant   **Local Variable**

$$\frac{E, V \vdash \diamond \quad E \vdash_{const} c: T \quad E \vdash_{type} U}{E, V \vdash c : U \rightarrow T : \acute{r} = c \wedge \grave{\sigma} = \acute{\sigma}} \qquad \frac{E, V \vdash_{var} v: T \quad E \vdash_{type} U}{E, V \vdash v : U \rightarrow T : \acute{r} = v \wedge \grave{\sigma} = \acute{\sigma}}$$

Conditional

$$\frac{E, V \vdash a_0 : Boolean \rightarrow T : R_0 \quad E, V \vdash a_1 : Boolean \rightarrow T : R_1}{E, V \vdash a_0 \diamond a_1 : Boolean \rightarrow T : (\grave{r} = false \Rightarrow R_0) \wedge (\grave{r} = true \Rightarrow R_1)}$$

Composition

$$E, V \vdash a_0 : T_0 \to T_1 : R_0 \qquad E, V \vdash a_1 : T_1 \to T_2 : R_1$$
$$\check{r} \text{ and } \check{\sigma} \text{ do not occur free in } R_0 \text{ or } R_1$$

$$\overline{E, V \vdash a_0 \,; a_1 : T_0 \to T_2 : \langle \exists \check{r}, \check{\sigma} \,::\, R_0[\acute{r}, \acute{\sigma} := \check{r}, \check{\sigma}] \wedge R_1[\grave{r}, \grave{\sigma} := \check{r}, \check{\sigma}] \rangle}$$

Binding

$$\frac{E, (V, v{:}\, T) \vdash a : T \to U : R}{E, V \vdash with\ v{:}\, T\ do\ a : T \to U : R[v := \acute{r}]}$$

Object Construction

$$E, V \vdash \diamond \qquad E \vdash_{type} U \qquad E \vdash_{obj} T$$
$$\mathsf{f}_i : T_i \to U_i{}^{i \in I} \text{ are the elements of } Fields(T, E) \qquad E \vdash_{const} c_i : U_i{}^{i \in I}$$
$$\mathsf{m}_j : T_j \to U_j : R_j{}^{j \in J} \text{ are the elements of } Methods(T, E) \qquad E, \emptyset \vdash a_j : T \to U_j : R_j{}^{j \in J}$$

$$\overline{E, V \vdash [T{:}\ \mathsf{f}_i = c_i{}^{i \in I},\ \mathsf{m}_j = a_j{}^{j \in J}] : U \to T : \acute{r} \neq nil \wedge}$$
$$select(\grave{\sigma}, \acute{r}, \mathsf{alloc}) = false \wedge \acute{\sigma} = store(\cdots (store(\grave{\sigma}, \acute{r}, \mathsf{alloc}, true),\ \acute{r}, \mathsf{f}_i, c_i){}^{i \in I}$$

Field Selection

$$\frac{E, V \vdash \diamond \qquad E \vdash_{field} \mathsf{f} : T \to U}{E, V \vdash \mathsf{f} : T \to U :}$$
$$\acute{r} \neq nil \Rightarrow \acute{r} = select(\grave{\sigma}, \grave{r}, \mathsf{f}) \wedge \acute{\sigma} = \grave{\sigma}$$

Field Update

$$E \vdash_{field} \mathsf{f} : T_0 \to U_0 \quad E \vdash T_1 <: T_0$$
$$E, V \vdash_{var} v : U_1 \qquad E \vdash U_1 <: U_0$$
$$\overline{E, V \vdash \mathsf{f} := v : T_1 \to T_1 :}$$
$$\grave{r} \neq nil \Rightarrow \acute{r} = \grave{r} \wedge \acute{\sigma} = store(\grave{\sigma}, \grave{r}, \mathsf{f}, v)$$

Method Invocation

$$\frac{E, V \vdash \diamond \qquad E \vdash_{method} \mathsf{m} : T \to U : R}{E, V \vdash \mathsf{m} : T \to U : \grave{r} \neq nil \Rightarrow R}$$

3.2 Operational Semantics

The operational semantics is defined by the judgement

$$r, \sigma, \mu, S \vdash a \leadsto r', \sigma', \mu'$$.

It says that given an initial *operational state* (r, σ, μ) and *stack* S, executing command a terminates in operational state (r', σ', μ'). Operational states are triples whose first two components correspond to the register and data store components of states, as defined above. The third component is a *method store*. Let $\mathcal{H}$ denote a set of given *object names*. A *stack* is a partial function from local variables to $\mathcal{H} \cup \{false, true, nil\}$. A *method store* is a partial function μ from $\mathcal{H}$, such that

- $\mu(h)(\mathsf{type})$ is the allocated type of object h, and
- $\mu(h)(\mathsf{m})$, if defined, is the implementation of method m of object h.

A *store pair* is a pair (σ, μ) where σ is a data store and μ is a method store.

In addition to keeping the method implementations of objects, the method store keeps the allocated type of objects. The operational semantics records this information as it allocates a new object, but doesn't use it subsequently. The information is used only to state and prove the soundness theorem. By conveniently recording this information in the operational semantics, where it causes no harm, one avoids the use of a *store type* (*cf.* [2]). The result is a simpler statement and proof of soundness.

To save space, I omit the rules for the operational semantics. They can be found in a SRC Technical Note [14].

4 Example

In this section, I show an example of a program that can be proved in the logic.

Let us consider a linked-list type with a method that appends a list to another. Reasoning about a program with such a type requires reasoning about reachability among linked-list nodes. To this end, we assume the underlying logic to contain a function symbol *Reach* (adapted from Greg Nelson's reachability predicate [16]). Informally, $Reach(e_0, e_1, \sigma, f, e_2)$ is *true* whenever it is possible to reach from object e_0 to object e_1 via applications of f in σ, never going through object e_2.

The example in this section assumes that the underlying logic contains the following two axioms, which relate *Reach* to *select* and *store*, respectively.

$$\langle \forall e_0, e_1, \sigma, f, e_2 :: Reach(e_0, e_1, \sigma, f, e_2) = true \equiv \qquad (3)$$
$$e_0 = e_1 \vee (e_0 \neq e_2 \wedge Reach(select(\sigma, e_0, f), e_1, \sigma, f, e_2) = true) \rangle$$

$$\langle \forall e_0, e_1, \sigma, f_0, e_2, f_1, e_3, e_4 :: f_0 \neq f_1 \Rightarrow \qquad (4)$$
$$Reach(e_0, e_1, \sigma, f_0, e_2) = Reach(e_0, e_1, store(\sigma, e_3, f_1, e_4), f_0, e_2) \rangle$$

Axiom (3) resembles Nelson's axiom A1 and says that every object reaches itself, and that e_0 reaches e_1 if e_0 is not e_2 and $e_0.f$ reaches e_1. Axiom (4) says that whether or not e_0 reaches e_1 via f_0 is independent of the values of another field f_1.

The example uses the following environment, which I shall refer to as E:

$$Node <: Object \qquad \text{next}: Node \rightarrow Node$$
$$\text{appendArg}: Node \rightarrow Node \qquad \text{append}: Node \rightarrow Node : R$$

where R is the relation

$$\grave{r} \neq nil \Rightarrow Reach(\grave{r}, \acute{r}, \grave{\sigma}, \text{next}, nil) \wedge select(\grave{\sigma}, \acute{r}, \text{next}) = nil \wedge$$
$$select(\acute{\sigma}, \acute{r}, \text{next}) = select(\grave{\sigma}, \grave{r}, \text{appendArg}) \wedge$$
$$\langle \forall o, f :: select(\grave{\sigma}, o, f) = select(\acute{\sigma}, o, f) \vee$$
$$(o = \acute{r} \wedge f = \text{next}) \vee f = \text{appendArg} \rangle \quad.$$

Informally, this relation specifies that the method store its argument (which is passed in via the appendArg field) at the end of the list linked via field next. More precisely, the relation specifies that the method find an object $\acute{r}$ reachable from $\grave{r}$ (self) via the next field such that $\acute{r}$.next is *nil*. The method is to set $\acute{r}$.next to the given argument node. The method can modify $\acute{r}$.next and can modify the appendArg field of any object (since this field is used only as a way to pass a parameter to append anyway), but it is not allowed to modify the store in any other way.

To present the example code, I introduce a new command, *isnil*, which tests whether or not the register is *nil*.

Nil Test

$$\frac{E, V \vdash \diamond \qquad E \vdash_{obj} T}{\begin{array}{l} E, V \vdash isnil : T \to Boolean : \\ (\grave{r} = nil \Rightarrow \acute{r} = true) \wedge (\grave{r} \neq nil \Rightarrow \acute{r} = false) \wedge \acute{\sigma} = \grave{\sigma} \end{array}}$$

(Section 6 discusses expression commands such as *nil* tests.) To write the program text, I assume the following binding powers, from highest to lowest: := . ; ◇ *with ... do* . Now, consider the following command.

$$
\begin{aligned}
[Node:\; &\mathsf{next} = nil,\; \mathsf{appendArg} = nil, \\
&\mathsf{append} = with\; self : Node\; do\; \mathsf{appendArg}\;;\; with\; n : Node\; do \\
&\qquad self.\mathsf{next}\;;\; isnil\;; \\
&\qquad (\;\; self.\mathsf{next.appendArg} := n\;;\; \mathsf{append} \\
&\qquad \diamond\, self.\mathsf{next} := n\;;\; self\;\;)\;]
\end{aligned}
\tag{5}
$$

This command allocates and returns a *Node* object whose next and appendArg fields are initially *nil*. The implementation of append starts by giving names to the self object and the method's argument. Then it either calls append recursively on *self*.next or sets *self*.next to the given argument, depending on whether or not *self*.next is *nil*.

With axioms (3) and (4) in the underlying logic, one can prove the following judgement about the given allocation command.

$$E, \emptyset \vdash (5) : Object \to Node : \grave{r} = \acute{r} \tag{6}$$

Though the relation in this judgement ($\grave{r} = \acute{r}$) is trivial, establishing the judgement requires showing that the given implementation of append satisfies its declared specification. I omit the proof, which is straightforward.

I conclude the example with three remarks. First, remember that to reason about a call to a method, in particular the recursive call to append , one uses the specification of the method being called, not its implementation. This makes the reasoning independent of the actual implementation of the callee, which may in fact even be a different implementation than the one shown.

Second, remember that only partial correctness is proved. That is, judgement (6) says that *if* the method terminates, its pre- and post-states will satisfy the specified relation. Indeed, an invocation of method append on an object in a cyclic structure of *Node* objects will not terminate.

Third, the static type of the field *self*.next and the argument *self*.appendArg is *Node*, but the dynamic types of these objects in an execution may be any subtype of *Node*. Note, however, that judgement (6) is independent of the dynamic types of these objects. Indeed, having established judgement (6) means that the method works in every execution. This is because the logic is *sound*, as is shown in the next section.

5 Soundness

This section states a soundness theorem, which proves the correctness of the operational semantics with respect to the axiomatic semantics. I first motivate the soundness theorem, and then state it together with an informal explanation. Some additional formal definitions and the proof itself are found in a SRC Technical Note [14].

As a gentle step in presenting the full soundness theorem, consider the following theorem.

Theorem 0. If one can derive both $E, \emptyset \vdash a : Object \rightarrow Boolean : \acute{r} = true$ and $nil, \sigma_0, \emptyset, \emptyset \vdash a \rightsquigarrow r, \sigma, \mu$, then $r = true$.

Here and in the next two theorems, σ_0 denotes a data store that satisfies $\langle \forall h \in \mathcal{H} :: select(\sigma_0, h, \mathsf{alloc}) = false \rangle$, and $\emptyset$ denotes the partial function whose domain is empty. The theorem says that if in an environment E one can prove that a command a satisfies the transition relation $\acute{r} = true$, then any terminating execution of command a from a "reset" state ends with a register value of $true$.

A simple theorem about the result type of a command is the following.

Theorem 1. If one can derive $E, \emptyset \vdash a : Object \rightarrow T : R$ and $E \vdash_{obj} T$ and $nil, \sigma_0, \emptyset, \emptyset \vdash a \rightsquigarrow r, \sigma, \mu$, then the value r has type T, that is, either $r = nil$ or $E \vdash \mu(r)(\mathsf{type}) <: T$.

This theorem says that if one can prove, using the axiomatic semantics, that a command a has final type T, where T is an object type, and one can show that, operationally, the program terminates with a register value of r, then r is a value of type T (that is, it is nil or its allocated type is a subtype of T). This theorem shows the soundness of the type system's treatment of object types.

An interesting theorem that says something about the final object store of a program is the following.

Theorem 2. If one can derive both $E, \emptyset \vdash a : Object \rightarrow T : R$ and $nil, \sigma_0, \emptyset, \emptyset \vdash a \rightsquigarrow r, \sigma, \mu$, then $R[\grave{r}, \grave{\sigma}, \acute{r}, \acute{\sigma} := nil, \sigma_0, r, \sigma]$ holds as a first-order predicate.

This theorem says that if one can prove the two judgements about a, then relation R actually describes the relation between the initial and final states.

To prove the theorems above, one needs to prove something stronger. I call the stronger theorem, of which the theorems above are corollaries, the main theorem. The theorem is stated as follows.

Main Theorem. If (7) $E, V \vdash a : T \rightarrow U : R$, (8) $r, \sigma, \mu, S \vdash a \rightsquigarrow r', \sigma', \mu'$, (9) $E, \sigma, \mu \Vdash r : T$, (10) $E \Vdash \sigma, \mu$, and (11) $E, V, \sigma, \mu \Vdash S$; then (12) $r, \sigma, r', \sigma', S \Vdash R$, (13) $(\sigma, \mu) \preceq (\sigma', \mu')$, (14) $E, \sigma', \mu' \Vdash r' : U$, and (15) $E \Vdash \sigma', \mu'$.

In the antecedent of this theorem, (7) and (8) express the judgements that have been derived for some command a. One can hope to say something interesting in the conclusion of the theorem only if the execution under consideration is from a "reasonable" state (r, σ, μ) and uses a "reasonable" stack S. Therefore, judgement (9) states that r is a value of type T, judgement (10) says that store pair (σ, μ) *matches* the environment E, and judgement (11) says that S is a *well-typed stack*.

In the conclusion of the theorem, (12) expresses that R does indeed describe the relation between the initial and final states of the execution, and (14) expresses that r' has type U. In addition, to use the theorem as a sufficiently strong induction hypothesis in the proof, (13) says that (σ, μ) is *continued by* (σ', μ'). This property expresses a kind of monotonicity that holds between two store pairs, the first of which precedes the other in some execution. Also, judgement (15) says that (σ', μ'), like the initial store pair, matches the environment.

By removing (12) from the conclusion of the main theorem, one gets a corollary that expresses that the type system is sound with respect to the operational semantics. Such a corollary follows directly from the main theorem, but could also be proved directly in the same way the main theorem is.

6 Limitations of the Logic

The object construction command is rather awkward. Because it lists method implementations, a method cannot directly construct objects whose type and method implementations are the same as for self. Instead, one can declare object types representing classes, as is done, for example, by Abadi and Cardelli [1] (see SRC TN 1997-025 for an example [14]). One can consider modifying the present logic to remove the limitation from the object construction command. For example, like in common class-based object-oriented languages, one can extend the program environment to include method implementations. One must then have a "link-time" check that ensures that every method that may be called by the program at run-time has an implementation. Or, like in common object-based languages, one can add a construct for cloning objects or their method implementations.

Another omission from the present logic is the ability to compare objects for equality. Just like one would expect to add primitive types like integers to the present logic, one would expect to add more general expressions, including comparison expressions.

A logic of programs provides a connection between programs and their specifications. In the present logic, method declarations contain specifications that are given simply as transition relations. Transition relations are not practically suited for writing down method specifications, because they are painfully explicit. Specification features like modifies clauses and abstract fields would remedy the situation, but lie outside the scope of this paper. To mention some work in this area, Lano and Haughton [10] have surveyed object-oriented specifications, and my thesis [12] shows how to deal with modifies clauses and data abstraction in modular, object-oriented programs. The logic for POOL [4] includes some specification features that can be used to state properties of recursive data structures.

7 Summary

I have presented a sound logic for object-oriented programs whose commands are imperative and whose objects are references to data fields. The programming notation requires that types, fields, and methods be declared in the environment before they can be used in a program. The main contributions of the paper are the logic itself, the soundness theorem, and the way that types are handled, which makes the subtype relation and the admission of recursive object types trivial.

Acknowledgements. I am grateful to Martín Abadi, Luca Cardelli, Greg Nelson, and Raymie Stata for helpful comments on the logic and the presentation thereof.

References

1. Martín Abadi and Luca Cardelli. *A Theory of Objects.* Springer-Verlag, 1996.
2. Martín Abadi and K. Rustan M. Leino. A logic of object-oriented programs. In *Theory and Practice of Software Development: Proceedings / TAPSOFT '97, 7th International Joint Conference CAAP/FASE*, volume 1214 of *Lecture Notes in Computer Science*, pages 682–696. Springer, April 1997.
3. Roberto M. Amadio and Luca Cardelli. Subtyping recursive types. *ACM Transactions on Programming Languages and Systems*, 15(4):575–631, September 1993.
4. Pierre America and Frank de Boer. Reasoning about dynamically evolving process structures. *Formal Aspects of Computing*, 6(3):269–316, 1994.
5. Craig Chambers. The Cecil language: Specification & rationale, version 2.1, March 7, 1997. Available from `http://www.cs.washington.edu/research/projects/ce cil/www/Papers/cecil-spec.html`, 1997.
6. Krishna Kishore Dhara and Gary T. Leavens. Forcing behavioral subtyping through specification inheritance. Technical Report TR #95-20c, Iowa State University, Department of Computer Science, 1997.
7. Edsger W. Dijkstra. *A Discipline of Programming.* Prentice-Hall, Englewood Cliffs, NJ, 1976.
8. James Gosling, Bill Joy, and Guy Steele. *The Java™ Language Specification.* Addison-Wesley, 1996.
9. C. A. R. Hoare. An axiomatic basis for computer programming. *Communications of the ACM*, 12(10):576–580,583, October 1969.
10. Kevin Lano and Howard Haughton. *Object-Oriented Specification Case Studies.* Prentice Hall, New York, 1994.
11. Gary Todd Leavens. *Verifying Object-Oriented Programs that Use Subtypes.* PhD thesis, MIT Laboratory for Computer Science, February 1989. Available as Technical Report MIT/LCS/TR-439.
12. K. Rustan M. Leino. *Toward Reliable Modular Programs.* PhD thesis, California Institute of Technology, January 1995. Available as Technical Report Caltech-CS-TR-95-03.
13. K. Rustan M. Leino. Ecstatic: An object-oriented programming language with an axiomatic semantics. In *The Fourth International Workshop on Foundations of Object-Oriented Languages*, January 1997. Proceedings available from `http://www.cs.indiana.edu/hyplan/pierce/fool/`.
14. K. Rustan M. Leino. Recursive object types in a logic of oject-oriented programs. Technical Note 1997-025a, Digital Equipment Corporation Systems Research Center, January 1998.
15. K. Rustan M. Leino and Greg Nelson. Object-oriented guarded commands. Internal manuscript KRML 50, Digital Equipment Corporation Systems Research Center, March 1995.
16. Greg Nelson. Verifying reachability invariants of linked structures. *Conference Record of the Tenth Annual ACM Symposium on Principles of Programming Languages*, pages 38–47, January 1983.
17. Greg Nelson, editor. *Systems Programming with Modula-3.* Series in Innovative Technology. Prentice-Hall, Englewood Cliffs, NJ, 1991.
18. Arnd Poetzsch-Heffter and Peter Müller. A logic for the verification of object-oriented programs. In R. Berghammer and F. Simon, editors, *Programming Languages and Fundamentals of Programming*. Christian Albrechts-Universität Kiel, 1997.

Mode-Automata:
About Modes and States for Reactive Systems[*]

Florence Maraninchi and Yann Rémond

VERIMAG[**] – Centre Equation, 2 Av. de Vignate – F38610 GIERES
http://www.imag.fr/VERIMAG/PEOPLE/Florence.Maraninchi

Abstract. In the field of reactive system programming, dataflow synchronous languages like Lustre [BCH+85,CHPP87] or Signal [GBBG85] offer a syntax similar to block-diagrams, and can be efficiently compiled into C code, for instance. Designing a system that clearly exhibits several "independent" *running modes* is not difficult since the mode structure can be encoded explicitly with the available dataflow constructs. However the mode structure is no longer readable in the resulting program; modifying it is error prone, and it cannot be used to improve the quality of the generated code.

We propose to introduce a special construct devoted to the expression of a mode structure in a reactive system. We call it *mode-automaton*, for it is basically an automaton whose states are labeled by dataflow programs. We also propose a set of operations that allow the composition of several mode-automata (parallel and hierarchic compositions taken from Argos [Mar92]), and we study the properties of our model, like the existence of a congruence of mode-automata for instance, as well as implementation issues.

1 Introduction

The work on which we report here has been motivated by the need to talk about running modes in a dataflow synchronous language.

Dataflow languages like Lustre [BCH+85,CHPP87] or Signal [GBBG85] belong to the family of *synchronous* languages [BB91] devoted to the design, programming and validation of reactive systems. They have a formal semantics and can be efficiently compiled into C code, for instance.

The dataflow style is clearly appropriate when the behaviour of the system to be described has some regularity, like in signal-processing. Designing a system that clearly exhibits several "independent" *running modes* is not so difficult since the mode structure can be encoded explicitly with the available dataflow constructs. However the mode structure is no longer readable in the resulting program; modifying it is error prone, and it cannot be used to improve the

---

[*] This work has been partially supported by Esprit Long Term Research Project SYRF 22703

[**] Verimag is a joint laboratory of Université Joseph Fourier (Grenoble I), CNRS and INPG

quality of the generated code, decompose the proofs or at least serve as a guide in the analysis of the program.

In section 2 we propose a definition of a mode, in order to motivate our approach. Section 3 defines *mini-Lustre*, a small subset of Lustre which is sufficient for presenting our notion of mode-automata in section 4. Section 5 explains how to compose these mode-automata, with the operators of Argos, and Section 6 defines a congruence. Section 7 compares the approach to others, in which modes have been studied. Finally, section 8 gives some ideas for further work.

2 What is a Mode?

One (and perhaps the only one) way of facing the complexity of a system is to decompose it into several "independent" tasks. Of course the tasks are never completely independent, but it should be possible to find a decomposition in which the tasks are not too strongly connected with each other — i.e. in which the interface between tasks is relatively simple, compared to their internal structure. The tasks correspond to some abstractions of the global behaviour of the system, and they may be viewed as differents parts of this global behaviour, devoted to the treatment of distinct situations. Decomposing a system into tasks allows independent reasoning about the individual tasks.

Tasks may be *concurrent*, in which case the system has to be decomposed into concurrent and communicating components. The interface defines how the components communicate and synchronize with each other in order to reach a global goal.

Thinking in terms of *independent modes* is in some sense an orthogonal point of view, since a mode structure is rather *sequential* than concurrent. This is typically the case with the modes of an airplane, which can be as high level as "landing" mode, "take-off" mode, etc. The normal behaviour of the system is a sequence of modes. In a transition between modes, the source mode is designed to build and guarantee a given configuration of the parameters of the system, such that the target mode can be entered. On the other hand, modes may be divided into sub-modes.

Of course the mode structure may interfere with the concurrent structure, in which case each concurrent subsystem may have its own modes, and the global view of the system shows a Cartesian product of the sets of modes. Or the main view of the system may be a set of modes, and the description of each mode is further decomposed into concurrent tasks. Hence we need a richer notion of mode.

This seems to give something similar to the notion of mode we find in Modecharts [JM88], where modes are structured like in Statecharts [Har87] (an And/Or tree). However, see section 7 for more comments about Modecharts, and a comparison between Modecharts and our approach.

2.1 Modes and States

Technically, all systems can be viewed as a (possibly huge, or even infinite) set of elementary and completely detailed states, such that the knowledge about the current state is sufficient to determine the correct output, at any point in time. States are connected by *transitions*, whose firing depends on the inputs to the system. This complete model of the system behaviour may not be manageable, but it exists. We call its states and transitions *execution* states and transitions. Execution states are really concrete ones, related for instance to the content of the program memory during execution.

The question is: how can we define the modes of a system in terms of its execution states and transitions?

Since the state-transition view of a complex behaviour is intrinsically sequential, it seems that, in all cases, it should be possible to relate the abstract notion of mode to *collections* of execution states. The portion of behaviour corresponding to a mode is then defined as a set of execution states together with the attached transitions. Related questions are: are these collections disjoint? do they cover the whole set of states? S. Paynter [Pay96] suggests that these two questions are orthogonal, and defines *Real-Time Mode-Machines*, which describe exhaustive but not necessarily exclusive modes (see more comments on this paper in section 7). In fact, the only relevant question is that of exclusivity, since, for non exhaustive modes, one can always consider that the "missing" states form an additional mode.

2.2 Talking about Modes in a Programming Language

All the formalisms or languages defined for reactive systems offer a parallel composition, together with some synchronization and communication mechanism. This operation supports a conceptual decomposition in terms of concurrent tasks, and the parallel structure can be used for compositional proofs, generation of distributed code, etc.

The picture is not so clear for the decomposition into modes. The question here is how to use the mode structure of a complex system for programming it, i.e. what construct should we introduce in a language to express this view of the system? The mode structure should be as readable in a program as the concurrent structure is, thus making modifications easier; moreover, it should be usable to improve the quality of the generated code, or to serve as a guide for decomposing proofs.

The key point is that *it should be possible to project a program onto a given mode, and obtain the behaviour restricted to this mode* (as it is usually possible to project a parallel program onto one of its concurrent components, and get the behaviour restricted to this component).

2.3 Modes and Synchronous Languages

None of the existing synchronous languages can be considered as providing a construct for expressing the mode structure of a reactive system.

We are particularly interested in dataflow languages. When trying to think in terms of modes in a dataflow language, one has to face two problems: first, there should be a way to express that some parts of a program are not always active (and this is not easy); second, if these parts of the program represent different modes, there should be a way of describing how the modes are organized into the global behaviour of the system.

Several proposals have been made for introducing some *control* features in a dataflow program, and this has been tried for one language or another among the synchronous family: [RM95] to introduce in Signal a way to define *intervals* delimited by some properties of the inputs, and to which the activity of some subprograms can be attached; [JLMR94,MH96] propose to mix the automaton constructs of Argos with the dataflow style of Lustre: the refinement operation of Argos allows to refine a state of an automaton by a (possibly complex) subsystem. Hence the activity of subprograms is attached to states. Embedding Lustre nodes in an Esterel program is possible, and would have the same effect.

However, providing a full set of start-and-stop control structures for a dataflow language does not necessarily improve the way modes can be dealt with. It solves the first problem mentioned above, i.e. the control structures taken in the imperative style allow the specification of activity periods of some subprograms described in a dataflow declarative style. But it does little for the second problem: a control structure like the interrupt makes it easy to express that the system switches between different behaviours, losing information about the current state of the behaviour that is interrupted, and starting a new one in some initial configuration. Of course, some information may be transmitted from the behaviour that is killed to the one that is started, but this is not the default, and it has to be expressed explicitly, with the communication mechanism for instance. For switching between *modes*, we claim that the emphasis should be on what is *transmitted* from one mode to another. Transmitting the whole configuration reached by the system should be the default if we consider that the source mode is designed to build and guarantee a given configuration of the parameters of the system, such that the target mode can be entered.

2.4 A Proposal: Mode-Automata

We propose a programming model called *"mode-automata"*, made of: operations on automata taken from the definition of Argos [Mar92]; dataflow equations taken from Lustre [BCH+85]. We shall see that mode-automata can be considered as a discrete version of hybrid automata [MMP91], in which the states are labeled by systems of differential equations that describe how the continuous environment evolves. In our model, states represent the running *modes* of a system, and the equations associated with the states could be obtained by discretizing the control laws. Mode-automata have the property that a program may be projected onto one of its modes.

3 Mini-Lustre: a (very) Small Subset of Lustre

For the rest of the paper, we use a very small subset of Lustre. A program is a single node, and we avoid the complexity related to types as much as possible. In some sense, the mini-Lustre model we present below is closer to the DC [CS95] format used as an intermediate form in the Lustre, Esterel and Argos compilers.

Definition 1 (mini-Lustre programs). $N = (\mathcal{V}_i, \mathcal{V}_o, \mathcal{V}_l, f, I)$ where:
$\mathcal{V}_i, \mathcal{V}_o$ and $\mathcal{V}_l$ are pairwise disjoint sets of input, output and local variable names. I is a total function from $\mathcal{V}_o \cup \mathcal{V}_l$ to constants. f is a total function from $\mathcal{V}_o \cup \mathcal{V}_l$ to the set $Eq(\mathcal{V}_i \cup \mathcal{V}_o \cup \mathcal{V}_l)$ and $Eq(V)$ is the set of expressions with variables in V, defined by the following grammar: $e ::= c \mid x \mid op(e, ..., e) \mid pre(x)$. c stands for constants, x stands for a name in V, and op stands for all combinational operators. An interesting one is the conditional if e_1 then e_2 else e_3 where e_1 should be a Boolean expression, and e_2, e_3 should have the same type. $pre(x)$ stands for the previous value of the flow denoted by x. In case one needs $pre(x)$ at the first instant, $I(x)$ should be used. □

We restrict mini-Lustre to integer and Boolean values. All expressions are assumed to be typed correctly. As in Lustre, we require that the dependency graph between variables be acyclic. A dependency of X onto Y appears whenever there exists an equation of the form $X = ...Y...$ and Y does not appear inside a **pre** operator. In the syntax of mini-Lustre programs, it means that Y appears in the expression $f(X)$, not in a **pre** operator.

Definition 2 (Trace semantics of mini-Lustre). *Each variable name v in the mini-Lustre program describes a flow of values of its type, i.e. an infinite sequence $v_0, v_1, ...$ Given a sequence of inputs, i.e. the values v_n, for each $v \in \mathcal{V}_i$ and each $n \geq 0$, we describe below how to compute the sequences (or traces) of local and output flows of the program. The initialization function gives values to variables for the instant "before time starts", since it provides values in case $pre(x)$ is needed at instant 0. Hence we can call it x_{-1}:*

$$\forall v \in \mathcal{V}_o \cup \mathcal{V}_l. \quad v_{-1} = I(v)$$

For all instants in time, the value of an output or local variable is computed according to its definition as given by f:

$$\forall n \geq 0. \quad \forall v \in \mathcal{V}_o \cup \mathcal{V}_l. \quad v_n = f(v)[x_n/x][x_{n-1}/pre(x)]$$

We take the expression $f(v)$, in which we replace each variable name x by its current value x_n, and each occurrence of $pre(x)$ by the previous value x_{n-1}. This yields an expression in which combinational operators are applied to constants. The set of equations we obtain for defining the values of all the flows over time is acyclic, and is a sound definition. □

Definition 3 (Union of mini-Lustre nodes). *Provided they do not define the same outputs, i.e.* $\mathcal{V}_o^1 \cap \mathcal{V}_o^2 = \emptyset$, *we can put together two mini-Lustre programs. This operation consists in connecting the outputs of one of them to the inputs of the other, if they have the same name. These connecting variables should be removed from the inputs of the global program, since we now provide definitions for them. This corresponds to the usual dataflow connection of two nodes.*

$$(\mathcal{V}_i^1, \mathcal{V}_o^1, \mathcal{V}_l^1, f^1, I^1) \cup (\mathcal{V}_i^2, \mathcal{V}_o^2, \mathcal{V}_l^2, f^2, I^2) =$$
$$((\mathcal{V}_i^1 \cup \mathcal{V}_i^2) \setminus \mathcal{V}_o^1 \setminus \mathcal{V}_o^2, \quad \mathcal{V}_o^1 \cup \mathcal{V}_o^2, \quad \mathcal{V}_l^1 \cup \mathcal{V}_l^2,$$
$$\lambda x. \text{if } x \in \mathcal{V}_o^1 \cup \mathcal{V}_l^1 \text{ then } f^1(x) \text{ else } f^2(x),$$
$$\lambda x. \text{if } x \in \mathcal{V}_o^1 \text{ then } I^1(x) \text{ else } I^2(x))$$

Local variables should be disjoint also, but we can assume that a renaming is performed before two mini-Lustre programs are put together. Hence $\mathcal{V}_l^1 \cap \mathcal{V}_l^2 = \emptyset$ *is guaranteed. The union of sets of equations should still satisfy the acyclicity constraint.* □

Definition 4 (Trace equivalence for mini-Lustre). *Two programs* $L_1 = (\mathcal{V}_i, \mathcal{V}_o, \mathcal{V}_l^1, f^1, I^1)$ *and* $L_2 = (\mathcal{V}_i, \mathcal{V}_o, \mathcal{V}_l^2, f^2, I^2)$ *having the same input/output interface are trace-equivalent (denoted by* $L_1 \sim L_2$) *if and only if they give the same sequence of outputs when fed with the same sequence of inputs.* □

Definition 5 (Trace equivalence for mini-Lustre with no initial specification). *We consider mini-Lustre programs without initial specification, i.e. mini-Lustre programs without the function I that gives values for the flows "before time starts". Two such objects* $L_1 = (\mathcal{V}_i, \mathcal{V}_o, \mathcal{V}_l^1, f^1)$ *and* $L_2 = (\mathcal{V}_i, \mathcal{V}_o, \mathcal{V}_l^2, f^2)$ *having the same input/output interface are trace-equivalent (denoted by* $L_1 \approx L_2$) *if and only if, for all initial configuration I, they give the same sequence of outputs when fed with the same sequence of inputs.* □

Property 1 : Trace equivalence is preserved by union
$$L \sim L' \Longrightarrow L \cup M \sim L' \cup M$$
□

4 Mode-Automata

4.1 Example and Definition

The mode-automaton of figure 1 describes a program that outputs an integer X. The initial value is 0. Then, the program has two *modes*: an incrementing mode, and a decrementing one. Changing modes is done according to the value reached by variable X: when it reaches 10, the mode is switched to "decrementing"; when X reaches 0 again, the mode is switched to "incrementing".

For simplicity, we give the definition for a simple case where the equations define only *integer* variables. One could easily extend this framework to all types of variables.

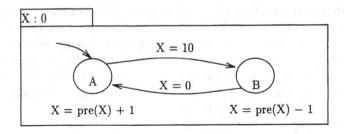

Fig. 1. Mode-automata: a simple example

Definition 6 (Mode-automata).
A mode-automaton is a tuple $(Q, q_0, \mathcal{V}_i, \mathcal{V}_o, \mathcal{I}, f, T)$ where:

- *Q is the set of states of the automaton part*
- *$q_0 \in Q$ is the initial state*
- *$\mathcal{V}_i$ and $\mathcal{V}_o$ are sets of names for input and output integer variables.*
- *$T \subseteq Q \times C(\mathcal{V}) \times Q$ is the set of transitions, labeled by conditions on the variables of $\mathcal{V} = \mathcal{V}_i \cup \mathcal{V}_o$*
- *$\mathcal{I} : \mathcal{V}_o \longrightarrow Z$ is a function defining the initial value of output variables*
- *$f : Q \longrightarrow \mathcal{V}_o \longrightarrow$ EqR defines the labeling of states by total functions from $\mathcal{V}_o$ to the set EqR$(\mathcal{V}_i \cup \mathcal{V}_o)$ of expressions that constitute the right parts of the equations defining the variables of $\mathcal{V}_o$.*

The expressions in EqR$(\mathcal{V}_i \cup \mathcal{V}_o)$ have the same syntax as in mini-Lustre nodes: $e ::= c \mid x \mid op(e, ..., e) \mid \mathbf{pre}(x)$, where c stands for constants, x stands for a name in $\mathcal{V}_i \cup \mathcal{V}_o$, and op stands for all combinational operators. The conditions in $C(\mathcal{V}_i \cup \mathcal{V}_o)$ are expressions of the same form, but without $\mathbf{pre}$ operators; the type of an expression serving as a condition is Boolean. □

Note that *Input* variables are used only in the right parts of the equations, or in the conditions. *Output* variables are used in the left parts of the equations, or in the conditions.
We require that the automaton part of a mode-automaton be *deterministic*, i.e., for each state $q \in Q$, if there exist two outgoing transitions (q, c_1, q_1) and (q, c_2, q_2), then $c_1 \wedge c_2$ is not satisfiable.
We also require that the automaton be *reactive*, i.e., for each state $q \in Q$, the formula $\bigvee_{(q,c,q') \in T} c$ is true.
With these definitions, the example of figure 1 is written as:

$$(\{A, B\}, A, \emptyset, \{X\}, I : X \rightarrow 0,$$
$$f(A) = \{ \; X \; = \; \mathbf{pre}(X) \; + \; 1 \; \}, f(B) = \{ \; X \; = \; \mathbf{pre}(X) \; - \; 1 \; \}),$$
$$\{(A, X \; = \; 10, B), (B, X \; = \; 0, A), (A, X \; \neq \; 10, A), (B, X \; \neq \; 0, B)\})$$

In the graphical notation of the example, we omitted the two loops $(A, X \neq 10, A)$ and $(B, X \neq 0, B)$.

4.2 Semantics by Translation into Mini-Lustre

The main idea is to translate the automaton structure of a mode-automaton into mini-Lustre, in a very classical and straightforward way. Then we gather all the sets of equations attached to states into a single conditional structure. We choose to encode each state by a Boolean variable. Arguments for a more efficient encoding exist, and such an encoding could be applied here, independently from the other part of the translation. However, it is sometimes desirable that the pure Lustre program obtained from mode-automata be *readable*; in this case, a clear (and one-to-one) relation between states in the mode-automaton, and variables in the Lustre program, is required.

The function $\mathcal{L}$ associates a mini-Lustre program with a mode-automaton. We associate a Boolean local variable with each state in $Q = \{q_0, q_1, ..., q_n\}$, with the same name. Hence:

$$\mathcal{L}((Q, q_0, \mathcal{V}_i, \mathcal{V}_o, \mathcal{I}, f, T)) = (\mathcal{V}_i, \mathcal{V}_o, Q, e, J)$$

The initial values of the variables in $\mathcal{V}_o$ are given by the initialization function $\mathcal{I}$ of the mode-automaton, hence $\forall x \in \mathcal{V}_o, \; J(x) = \mathcal{I}(x)$. For the local variables of the mini-Lustre program, which correspond to the states of the mode-automaton, we have: $J(q_0) = true$ and $J(q) = false, \forall q \neq q_0$.

The equation for a local variable q that encodes a state q expresses that we are in state q at a given instant if and only if we were in some state q', and a transition (q', c, q) could be taken. Note that, because the automaton is reactive, the system can always take a transition, in any state. A particular case is $q' = q$: staying in a state means taking a loop on that state, at each instant

$$\text{for } q \in Q, e(q) \text{ is the expression:} \quad \bigvee_{(q',c,q) \in T} \text{pre } (q' \wedge c)$$

For $x \in \mathcal{V}_o$, $e(x)$ is the expression :

$$\text{if } q_0 \text{ then } f(q_0) \text{else if } q_1 \text{ then } f(q_1)...\text{else if } q_n \text{ then } f(q_n)$$

The mini-Lustre program obtained for the example is the following (note that pre(A and X = 10) is the same as pre(A) and pre(X) = 10, hence the equations have the form required in the definition of mini-Lustre).

$\mathcal{V}_i = \emptyset \qquad \mathcal{V}_o = \{X\} \qquad \mathcal{V}_l = \{A, B\}$

```
f(X) : if A then pre(X)+1 else pre(X)-1
f(A) : pre (A and not X=10) or pre(B and X = 0)
f(B) : pre (B and not X=0) or pre(A and X = 10)
```

$I(X) = 0 \qquad I(A) = true \qquad I(B) = false$

5 Compositions of Mode-Automata

5.1 Parallel Composition with Shared Variables

A single mode-automaton is appropriate when the structure of the running modes is flat. Parallel composition of mode-automata is convenient whenever the modes can be split into at least two orthogonal sets, such that a set of modes is used for controlling some of the variables, and another set of modes is used for controlling other variables.

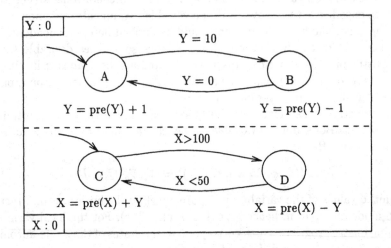

Fig. 2. Parallel composition of mode-automata, an example

Definition Provided $V^1_o \cap V^2_o = \emptyset$, we define the parallel composition of two mode-automata by :

$$(Q^1, q^1_0, T^1, V^1_i, V^1_o, \mathcal{I}^1, f^1) \| (Q^2, q^2_0, T^2, V^2_i, V^2_o, \mathcal{I}^2, f^2) =$$
$$(Q^1 \times Q^2, (q^1_0, q^2_0), (V^1_i \cup V^2_i) \setminus V^1_o \setminus V^2_o, V^1_o \cup V^2_o, \mathcal{I}, f)$$

Where:

$$f(q^1, q^2)(X) = \begin{cases} f^1(q^1)(X) \text{ if } X \in V^1_o \\ f^2(q^2)(X) \text{ otherwise, i.e. if } X \in V^2_o \end{cases}$$

Similarly:

$$\mathcal{I}(X) = \begin{cases} \mathcal{I}^1(X) \text{ if } X \in V^1_o \\ \mathcal{I}^2(X) \text{ if } X \in V^2_o \end{cases}$$

And the set T of global transitions is defined by:

$$(q^1, C^1, q'^1) \in T^1 \quad \wedge (q^2, C^2, q'^2) \in T^2 \quad \Longrightarrow \quad ((q^1, q^2), C^1 \wedge C^2, (q'^1, q'^2)) \in T$$

The following property establishes a relationship between the parallel composition defined for mode-automata as a synchronous product, and the intrinsic parallelism of Lustre programs, captured by the union of sets of equations:

Property 2
$$\mathcal{L}(M_1 \| M_2) \sim \mathcal{L}(M_1) \cup \mathcal{L}(M_2) \qquad \qquad \square$$

5.2 Ideas for Hierarchic Modes

A very common notion related to modes is that of *sub-modes*. In the hierarchic composition below, the equation X = pre(X) − 1 associated with state D is shared by the two submodes, while these submodes have been introduced for defining Y more precisely. Note that the scope of Y is the whole program, not only state D. Splitting state D for refining the definition of Y has something to do with equivalences of mode-automata (see below). Indeed, we would like the hierarchic composition to be defined in such a way that the program of figure 3 be "equivalent" to that of figure 4, where the program associated with state D uses a Boolean variable q. "Refining" (or exploding) the conditional definition of Y into the mode-automaton with states A, B of figure 3 is the work performed by the Lustre compiler, when building an interpreted automaton from a Lustre program.

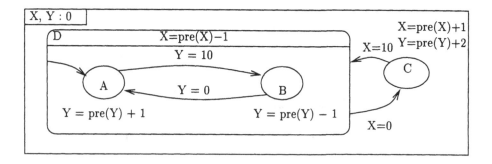

Fig. 3. Hierarchic composition of mode-automata, an example

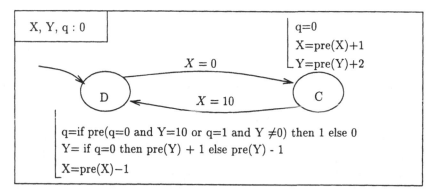

Fig. 4. Describing Y with a conditional program ($q = 0$ corresponds to A; $q = 1$ corresponds to B)

6 Congruences of Mode-Automata

We try to define an equivalence relation for mode-automata, to be a congruence for the parallel composition.

There are essentially two ways of defining such an equivalence : either as a relation induced by the existing trace equivalence of Lustre programs; or by an explicit definition on the structure of mode-automata, inspired by the trace equivalence of automata. The idea is that, if two states have equivalent sets of equations, then they can be identified.

Definition 7 (Induced equivalence of mode-automata).
$M_1 \equiv_i M_2 \iff \mathcal{L}(M_1) \sim \mathcal{L}(M_2)$ *(see definition 4 for $\sim$).*   □

Definition 8 (Direct equivalence of mode-automata). *The direct equivalence is a bisimulation, taking the labeling of states into account:*

$(Q^1, q_0^1, T^1, V_i^1, V_o^1, \mathcal{I}^1, f^1) \equiv_d (Q^2, q_0^2, T^2, V_i^2, V_o^2, \mathcal{I}^2, f^2) \iff$
$\exists R \subseteq R_s$ *such that:*
$(q_0^1, q_0^2) \in R \;\; \wedge$

$(q^1, q^2) \in R \implies \begin{cases} (q^1, c^1, q'^1) \in T^1 & \implies \quad \exists q'^2, c^2 \; s. \; t. \; (q^2, c^2, q'^2) \in T^2 \\ & \qquad \wedge (q'^1, q'^2) \in R \\ & \qquad \wedge c^1 = c^2 \\ \text{and conversely.} \end{cases}$

Where $R_s \subseteq Q^1 \times Q^2$ is the relation on states induced by the equivalence of the attached sets of equations: $(q^1, q^2) \in R_s \iff f^1(q^1) \approx f^2(q^2)$ (see definition 5 for $\approx$).   □

Note: the conditions labeling transitions are Boolean expressions with subexpressions of the form $a \# b$, where a and b are integer constants or variables, and $\#$ is a comparison operator yielding a Boolean result. We can always consider that these conditions are expressed as sums of monomials, and that a transition labeled by a sum $c \vee c'$ is replaced by two transitions labeled by c and c' (between the same states). Hence, in the equivalence relation defined above, we can require that the conditions c^1 and c^2 match. Since $c^1 = c^2$ is usually undecidable (it is not the syntactic identity), the above definition is not practical.

It is important to note that the two equivalences *do not* coincide: $M_1 \equiv_d M_2 \implies M_1 \equiv_i M_2$, but this is not an equivalence. Translating the mode-automaton into Lustre before testing for equivalence provides a global comparison of two mode-automata. On the contrary, the second definition of equivalence compares subprograms attached to states, and may fail in recognizing that two mode-automata describe the same global behaviour, when there is no way of establishing a correspondence between their states (see example below).

Example 1. Let us consider a program that outputs an integer X. X has three different behaviours, described by: $B_1 : X = pre(X) + 1$, $B_2 : X = pre(X) + 2$

and $B_3 : X = pre(X) - 1$. The transitions between these behaviours are triggered by conditions on X: C_{ij} is the condition for switching from B_i to B_j.

A mode-automaton M_1 describes B_1 and B_2 with a state q_{12}, and B_3 with another state q_3. Of course the program associated with q_{12} has a conditional structure, depending on C_{12}, C_{21} and a Boolean variable. The program associated with q_3 is B_3.

Now, consider the mode-automaton M_2 that describes B_1 with a state q_1', B_2 and B_3 with a state q_{23}'. In M_2, the program associated with q_{23}' has a conditional structure.

There is no relation R between the states of M_1 and the states of M_2 that would allow to recognize that they are equivalent. Translating them into mini-Lustre is a way of translating them into single-state mode-machines (with conditional associated programs), and it allows to show that they are indeed equivalent. On the other hand, if we are able to split q_{12} into two states, and q_{23}' into two states (as suggested in section 5.2) then the two machines have three states, and we can show that they are equivalent. □

Property 3 : Congruences of mode-automata

The two equivalences are congruences for parallel composition. □

7 Related Work and Comments on the Notion of *Mode*

We already explained in section 2.3 that there exists no construct dedicated to the expression of modes in the main synchronous programming languages. Mode-automata are a proposal for that. They allow to distinguish between *explicit* states (corresponding to modes, and described by the automaton part of the program) and *implicit* states (far more detailed and grouped into modes, described by the dataflow equational part of the program). This is an answer for people who argue that *modes* should not be related to *states*, because they are far more states than modes.

Other people argue that modes are not necessarily exclusive. The modes in one mode-automaton *are* exclusive. However, concurrent modes are elements of a Cartesian product, and can share something. Similarly, two submodes of a refined mode also share something. We tried to find a motivation for (and thus a definition of) *non-exclusive modes*.

Modecharts have recently joined the synchronous community, and we can find an Esterel-like semantics in [PSM96]. In this paper, modes are simply hierarchical and concurrent states like in Argos [Mar92]. It is mentioned that *"the actual interaction with the environment is produced by the operations associated with entry and exit events"*. Hence the *modes* are not dealt with in the language itself; the language allows to describe a complex control structure, and an external activity can be attached to a composed state. It seems that the activity is not necessarily killed when the state is left; hence the activities associated with exclusive states are not necessarily exclusive. This seems to be the motivation for non-exclusive modes. Activities are similar to the external tasks of Esterel but, in Esterel, the way tasks interfere with the control struture is well defined in the language itself.

Real-time mode-machines have been proposed in [Pay96]. In this paper, modes are collections of states, in the sense recalled above (section 2.1). These collections are exhaustive but not exclusive. However, it seems that this requirement for non-exclusivity is related to *pipelining* of the execution: part of the system is still busy with a given piece of data, while another part is already using the next piece of data. The question is whether pipelining has anything to do with *overlapping* or *non-exclusive modes*. In software pipelining, there may be two components running in parallel and corresponding to the *same piece of source program*; if this portion of source describes modes, it may be the case that the two execution instances of it are in different modes at the same time, because one of them starts treating some piece of data, while the other one finishes treating another piece of data. Each instance is in exactly one mode at a given instant; should this phenomenon be called "non-exclusive modes"?

We are still searching for examples of *non-exclusive modes* in reactive systems.

8 Implementation and Further Work

We presented mode-automata, a way to deal with modes in a synchronous language. Parallel composition is well defined, and we also have a congruence of mode-automata, w.r.t. this operation. We still have to study the hierarchic composition, following the lines of [HMP95] (in this paper we proposed an extension of Argos dedicated to hybrid systems, as a description language for the tool Polka [HPR97], in which hybrid automata may be composed using the Argos operators. In particular, hierarchic composition in HybridArgos is a way to express that a set of states share the same description of the environment). We shall also extend the language of mode-automata by allowing full Lustre in the equations labeling the states (clocks, node calls, external functions or procedures...). Mode-automata composed in parallel are already available as a language, compiled into pure Lustre, thus benefiting from all the lustre tools.

We said in section 2 that *"It should be possible to project a program onto a given mode, and obtain the behaviour restricted to this mode"*. How can we do that for programs made of mode-automata? When a program is reduced to a single mode-automaton, the mode is a state, and extracting the subprogram of this mode consists in taking the equations associated with this state. The object we obtain is a mini-Lustre program without initial state. When the program is something more complex, we are still able to extract a non-initialized mini-Lustre program for a given composed mode; for instance the program of a parallel mode (q, q') is the union of the programs attached to q and q'.

Projecting the complete program onto its modes may be useful for generating efficient sequential code. Indeed, the mode-structure clearly identifies which parts of a program are active at a given instant. In the SCADE (Safety Critical

Application Development Environment) tool sold by Verilog S.A. (based upon a commercial Lustre compiler), designers use an *activation condition* if they want to express that some part of the dataflow program should not be computed at each instant. It is a low level mechanism, which has to be used carefully: the activation condition for subprogram P is a Boolean flow computed elsewhere in the dataflow program. Our mode structure is a higher level generalization of this simple mechanism. It is a real language feature, and it can be used for better code generation.

Another interesting point about the mode-structure of a program is the possibility of decomposing proofs. For the decomposition of a problem into concurrent tasks, and the usual parallel compositions that support this design, people have proposed *compositional* proof rules, for instance the assume-guarantee scheme. The idea is to prove properties separately for the components, and to infer some property of the global system. We claim that the decomposition into several modes — provided the language allows to deal with modes explicitly, i.e. to project a global program onto a given mode — should have a corresponding compositional proof rule. At least, a mode-automaton is a way of identifying a control structure in a complex program. It can be used for splitting the work in analysis tools like Polka [HPR97].

References

[BB91]   A. Benveniste and G. Berry. Another look at real-time programming. *Special Section of the Proceedings of the IEEE*, 79(9), September 1991.

[BCH+85] J-L. Bergerand, P. Caspi, N. Halbwachs, D. Pilaud, and E. Pilaud. Outline of a real time data-flow language. In *Real Time Systems Symposium*, San Diego, September 1985.

[CHPP87] P. Caspi, N. Halbwachs, D. Pilaud, and J. Plaice. LUSTRE, a declarative language for programming synchronous systems. In *14th Symposium on Principles of Programming Languages*, Munich, January 1987.

[CS95]   C2A-SYNCHRON. The common format of synchronous languages – The declarative code DC version 1.0. Technical report, SYNCHRON project, October 1995.

[GBBG85] P. Le Guernic, A. Benveniste, P. Bournai, and T. Gauthier. Signal: A data flow oriented language for signal processing. Technical report, IRISA report 246, IRISA, Rennes, France, 1985.

[Har87]   D. Harel. Statecharts : A visual approach to complex systems. *Science of Computer Programming*, 8:231–275, 1987.

[HMP95] N. Halbwachs, F. Maraninchi, and Y. E. Proy. The railroad crossing problem, modeling with hybrid argos - analysis with polka. In *Second European Workshop on Real-Time and Hybrid Systems*, Grenoble (France), June 1995.

[HPR97]   N. Halbwachs, Y.E. Proy, and P. Roumanoff. Verification of real-time systems using linear relation analysis. *Formal Methods in System Design*, 11(2):157–185, August 1997.

[JLMR94] M. Jourdan, F. Lagnier, F. Maraninchi, and P. Raymond. A multiparadigm language for reactive systems. In *In 5th IEEE International Conference on Computer Languages*, Toulouse, May 1994. IEEE Computer Society Press.

[JM88]   Farnam Jahanian and Aloysius Mok. Modechart: A specification language
           for real-time systems. *IEEE Transactions on Software Engineering*, 14,
           1988.

[Mar92]   F. Maraninchi. Operational and compositional semantics of synchronous
           automaton compositions. In *CONCUR*. LNCS 630, Springer Verlag, August
           1992.

[MH96]   F. Maraninchi and N. Halbwachs. Compiling argos into boolean equations.
           In *Formal Techniques for Real-Time and Fault Tolerance (FTRTFT)*, Up-
           psala (Sweden), September 1996. Springer verlag, LNCS 1135.

[MMP91]   O. Maler, Z. Manna, and A. Pnueli. From timed to hybrid systems. In REX
           Workshop on Real-Time: Theory in Practice, DePlasmolen (Netherlands),
           June 1991. LNCS 600, Springer Verlag.

[Pay96]   S. Paynter. Real-time mode-machines. In *Formal Techniques for Real-Time
           and Fault Tolerance (FTRTFT)*, pages 90–109. LNCS 1135, Springer Verlag,
           1996.

[PSM96]   Carlos Puchol, Douglas Stuart, and Aloysius K. Mok. An operational se-
           mantics and a compiler for modechart specificiations. Technical Report
           CS-TR-95-37, University of Texas, Austin, July 1, 1996.

[RM95]   E. Rutten and F. Martinez. SIGNALGTI, implementing task preemption
           and time interval in the synchronous data-flow language SIGNAL. In *7th
           Euromicro Workshop on Real Time Systems*, Odense (Denmark), June 1995.

From Classes to Objects via Subtyping

Didier Rémy

INRIA-Rocquencourt*

Abstract. We extend the Abadi-Cardelli calculus of primitive objects with object extension. We enrich object types with a more precise, uniform, and flexible type structure. This enables to type object extension under both width and depth subtyping. Objects may also have extend-only or virtual contra-variant methods and read-only co-variant methods. The resulting subtyping relation is richer, and types of objects can be weaken progressively from a class level to a more traditional object level along the subtype relationship.

1 Introduction

Object extension has long been considered unsound when combined with subtyping. The problem may be explained as follows: in an object built with two methods ℓ_1 and ℓ_2 of types τ_1 and τ_2, the method ℓ_1 may require ℓ_2 to be of type τ_2. Forgetting the method ℓ_2 by subtyping would result in the possible redefinition of method ℓ_2 with another, incompatible type τ_3. Then, the invocation of ℓ_1 may fail.

Indeed, the first strongly-typed object-based languages that have been proposed provided either subtyping [1] or object extension [21] to circumvent the problem described above. However, each proposal was missing an important feature supported by the other one.

Both of them were improved later following the same principle: At an earlier stage, object components were assembled in prototypes [20] or classes [2], relying on some extension mechanism to provide inheritance. Objects were formed in a second, atomic step, immediately losing their extension capabilities for ever, to the benefit of subtyping.

In contrast to the previous work, we allow both extension and subtyping at the level of objects, avoiding stratification. Our solution is based on the enrichment of the structure of object types. Thus, our type-system rejects the above counter-example while keeping many other useful programs. In our proposal, an object and its class are unified and can be considered as two different perspectives on the same value: the type of an object is a supertype of the type of its class. Fine grain subtyping allows type information to be lost gradually, both width-wise and depth-wise, slowly fading classes into objects. As is well-known, when more type information is exposed, more operations can be performed (class

---

* BP 105, 78153 Le Chesnay Cedex, France. Email: `Didier.Remy@inria.fr`

perspective). On the contrary, hiding a sufficient amount of type information allows for more object interchangeability, but permits fewer operations (object perspective).

We add object extension to the object calculus of Abadi and Cardelli [3]. We adapt their typing rules to our enriched object types. In particular, we force methods to be parametric in self, that is, polymorphic over all possible extensions of the respective object. In this sense, our proposal is not a strict extension of theirs.

In addition to object extension, the enriched type structure has other benefits. We can allow virtual methods in objects (*i.e.* methods that are required by some other method but that have not been defined yet) since we are able to described them in types. Using co-variant subtyping forbids further re-definition of the corresponding method, as in [3]. Since classes are objects, such methods are in fact final methods. Final methods can only be accessed but no more redefined (except, indirectly, by the invocation of a previously defined method).

Virtual methods are useful because they allow objects to be built progressively, component by component, rather than all at once. They also improve security, since they sometime avoid the artificial use of dangerous default methods. While final methods are co-variant, virtual methods, are naturally contra-variant.

The rest of the paper is organized as follows. In the next section, we describe our solution informally. The following section is dedicated to the formal presentation. In section 4, we show some properties of the type system, in particular the type soundness property. Section 5 illustrates the gain in security and flexibility of our proposal by running a few examples. To a large extend, these examples can be understood intuitively and may also be read simultaneously with or immediately after the informal presentation. In section 6 we discuss possible extensions and variations of our proposal, as well as further meta-theoretical developments. A brief comparison with other works is done in section 7 before concluding.

2   Informal presentation

Technically, our first goal is to provide method extension, while preserving some form of subtyping. The counter-example given above does not imply that both method extension and width subtyping are in contradiction. It only shows that combining two existing typing rules would allow to write unsafe programs. Thus, if ever possible, a type system with both method extension and subtyping should clearly impose restrictions when combining them. Our solution is to enrich types so that subtyping becomes traceable, and so that extension can be limited to those fields whose exact type is known.

We first recall record types with symmetric type information. Using a similar structure for object types, some safe uses of subtyping and object extension can be typed, while the counter-example given in the introduction is rejected.

Record types

Record values are partial functions with finite domains that map labels to values. Traditionally, the types of records are also partial functions with finite domains that map labels to types. They are represented as records of types, that is, $\{\ell_i : \tau_i \, {}^{i \in I}\}$. This type says that fields ℓ_i's are defined with values of type τ_i's. However, it does not imply anything about other fields.

Another richer, more symmetric structure has also been used for record types, originally to allow type inference for records in ML [23, 24]. There, record types are treated as total functions mapping labels to field types, with the restriction that all but a finite number of labels have isomorphic images (*i.e.* are equal modulo renaming). Thus, record types can still be represented finitely by listing all significant labels with their corresponding field types and then adding an extra field-type acting as a template for all other labels.

In their simplest form, field types are either P τ (read *present* with type τ) or A (read *absent*). For instance, a record with two fields ℓ_1 of type τ_1 and ℓ_2 of type τ_2 is given type $\langle \ell_1 : \text{P } \tau_1 \, ; \, \ell_2 : \text{P } \tau_2 \, ; \, \text{A} \rangle$. It could also, equivalently, be given type $\langle \ell_1 : \text{P } \tau_1 \, ; \, \ell_2 : \text{P } \tau_2 \, ; \, \ell : \text{A} \, ; \, \text{A} \rangle$ where ℓ is distinct from ℓ_1 and ℓ_2.

In the absence of subtyping, standard types for records $\{\ell_i : \tau_i \, {}^{i \in I}\}$ can indeed be seen as a special case of record types, where field variables are disallowed; their standard subtyping relation then corresponds to the one generated by the axiom P $\tau <: \text{A}$ (and obvious structural rules). The type $\{\ell_1 : \tau_1; ..\ell_n : \tau_n\}$ becomes an abbreviation for $\langle \ell_1 : \text{P } \tau_1 \, ; \, ..\ell_n : \text{P } \tau_n \, ; \, \text{A} \rangle$. However, record types are much more flexible. For instance, they inherently and symmetrically express negative information. Before we added subtyping, a field ℓ of type A was known to be absent in the corresponding record. This is quite different from the absence of information about field ℓ. Such precise information is sometimes essential; a well-known example is record concatenation [16]. Instead of breaking the symmetry with the subtyping axiom P $\tau <: \text{A}$, we might have introduced a new field U (read *unknown*), with two axioms P $\tau <: \text{U}$ and A $<: \text{U}$. This would preserve the property that a field of type A is known to be absent, still allowing present and absent field to be interchanged but at their common supertype U.

Field variables and row variables also increase the expressiveness of record types. However, for simplicity, we do not take this direction here. Below, we use meta-variables for rows. This is just a notational convenience. It does not add any power.

Object types

In their simplest form, objects are just records, thus object types mimic record types. We write object types with $[\rho]$ instead of $\langle \rho \rangle$ to avoid confusion. An object with type $[\ell_1 : \text{P } \tau_1 \, ; \, \ell_2 : \text{P } \tau_2 \, ; \, \text{A}]$ possesses two methods ℓ_1 and ℓ_2 of respective types τ_1 and τ_2. Intuitively, an object $[\ell_1 = a_i \, {}^{i \in I}]$ can be given type $[\ell_i : \text{P } \tau_i \, {}^{i \in I} \, ; \, \text{A}]$ provided methods a_i's have type τ_i's.

However, objects soon differ from records by their ability to send messages to themselves, or to return themselves in response to a method call. More generally, objects are of the form $[\ell_i = \varsigma(x_i)a_i]$. Here, x_i is a variable that is bound to the object itself when the method ℓ_i is invoked. Consistently, the expression a_i must be typed in a context where x_i is assumed of the so-called "mytype", represented by some type variable χ equal to the object type τ. The following typing rule is a variant of the one used in [3].

$$\frac{\tau \equiv \varsigma(\chi)[\ell_i : P \; \tau_i{}^{i \in I} \; ; \; A] \qquad A, \chi = \tau, x_i : \chi \vdash a_i : \tau_i}{A \vdash \varsigma(\chi, \tau)[\ell_i = \varsigma(x_i)a_i{}^{i \in I}] : \tau}$$

(The type annotation (χ, τ) in the object expression binds the name of mytype locally and specifies the type of the object.)

An extendible object v may also be used to build a new object v' with more methods than v and thus of a different type, say τ'. The type τ' of self in v' is different from the type τ of self in v. In order to remain well-typed in v', the methods of v, should have been typed in a context where the type of self could have been τ' as well as τ. This applies to any possible extension v' of v. In other words, methods of an object of type τ should be parametric in all possible types of all possible successive extensions of an object of type τ. This condition can actually be expressed with subtyping by $\chi <: \#\tau$, where $\#\tau$ is called the *extension type* of τ (also called the internal type of the object). That is, the least upper bound of all exact[1] types of complete extensions (extensions in which no virtual method remains) of objects of external type τ.

A field of type A can be overridden with methods of arbitrary types. Thus, the best type for that field in the self parameter is U, *i.e.* we choose $\#A$ to be U. Symmetrically, we choose $\#(P \; \tau)$ to be U. This makes methods of type $P \; \tau$ internally unaccessible. Fields of type $P \; \tau$ are known to be present externally, but are not assumed to be so internally. Thus, fields of type $P \; \tau$ can be overridden with methods of arbitrary types, such as fields of type A. To recover the ability to send messages to self, we introduce a new type field $R \; \tau$ (read *required* of type τ). A field of type $R \; \tau$ is defined with a method of type τ, and is required to remain of at least type τ, internally. Such a field can only be overridden with a method of type τ. Therefore, self can also view it as a field that is, and will remain, of type τ. In math, $\#R \; \tau$ is $R \; \tau$. A field of type $P \; \tau$, can safely be considered as a field of type $R \; \tau$. Thus, we assume $P \; \tau <: R \; \tau$. We also assume $R \; \tau$ to be a subtype of U. As an example, $\# \varsigma(\chi)[\ell_1 : R \; \tau_1 \; ; \; \ell_2 : P \; \tau_2 \; ; \; \ell_3 : U \; ; \; A]$ is $\varsigma(\chi)[\ell_1 : R \; \tau_1 \; ; \; \ell_2 : U \; ; \; \ell_3 : U \; ; \; U]$, or shortly $\varsigma(\chi)[\ell_1 : R \; \tau \; ; \; U]$.

The extension of a field with a method of type τ requires that field to be either of type A or $R \; \tau$ in the original record (the field may also be of type $P \; \tau$, which is a subtype of $R \; \tau$.) It is possible to factor the two cases by introducing a new field type $M \; \tau$ (read *maybe* of type τ), and the axioms $R \; \tau <: M \; \tau$, $A <: M \; \tau$, and $M \; \tau <: U$. Intuitively, $M \; \tau$ is the union type $R \; \tau \cup A$. This allows, in a first step, to ignore the presence of a method while retaining its type, and, in a second step, to forget the type itself. The type of object extension becomes more uniform.

---

[1] The exact type of an object is the type with which the methods can initially be typed. The external type of an object may be a supertype of the exact type.

Roughly, if the original object has type $[\ell_1\!:\!\mathtt{M}\,\tau_1\;;\tau_2]$ and the new method ℓ_1 has type τ_1 then the resulting object has type $[\ell_1\!:\!\mathtt{R}\,\tau_1\;;\tau_2]$.

A field of type $\mathtt{M}\,\tau$ may later be defined or redefined with some method of type τ, becoming of type $\mathtt{R}\,\tau$, which is a subtype of $\mathtt{M}\,\tau$. It may also be left unchanged and thus remain of type $\mathtt{M}\,\tau$. Thus, a field of type $\mathtt{M}\,\tau$ will always remain of a subtype of $\mathtt{M}\,\tau$. That is, $\#(\mathtt{M}\,\tau)$ is $\mathtt{M}\,\tau$.

Deep subtyping

Subtyping rules described so far allow for width subtyping but not for depth subtyping, since all constructors have been left invariant. The only constructor that could be made covariant without breaking type-soundness is P. Making R covariant would be unsafe. However, we can safely introduce a new field type $\mathtt{R}^+\,\tau$ to tell that a method is defined and required to be of a subtype of τ, provided that a field of type $\mathtt{R}^+\,\tau$ is never overridden. On the other hand, a method ℓ_1 can safely be invoked on any object of type $[\ell_1\!:\!\mathtt{R}^+\,\tau_1\;;\mathtt{U}]$, which returns an expression of type τ_1. Of course, we also add $\mathtt{R}\,\tau <: \mathtt{R}^+\,\tau$ to just forget the fact that we are revealing the exact type information.

Symmetrically, a field ℓ of type $\mathtt{M}\,\tau$ cannot be accessed, but it can be redefined with a method of a subtype of τ. Still, it would be unsound to make $\mathtt{M}\,\tau$ contravariant. By contradiction, consider an object p of type $\zeta(\chi)[\ell\!:\!\mathtt{R}\,\tau\;;\ell'\!:\!\mathtt{P}\,\chi\;;\mathtt{A}]$ where calling method ℓ' overrides ℓ in self with a new method of type τ. By subtyping p_0 could be given type $\zeta(\chi)[\ell\!:\!\mathtt{M}\,\tau_0\;;\ell'\!:\!\mathtt{P}\,\chi\;;\mathtt{A}]$ where τ_0 is a subtype of τ. Then let p_2 of type $\zeta(\chi)[\ell\!:\!\mathtt{M}\,\tau_0\;;\ell'\!:\!\mathtt{P}\,\chi\;;\ell''\!:\!\mathtt{P}\,\mathtt{unit}\;;\mathtt{A}]$ be the extension of p_1 with a new method ℓ'' that requires ℓ of type τ_0. Calling method ℓ' of p_2 restore field ℓ of p_2 to some method of type τ and returns an object p_3. However, calling method ℓ'' of p_3 expects a method ℓ of type τ_0 but finds one of type τ.

We can still introduce a contra-variant symbol $\mathtt{M}^-$ with the axiom $\mathtt{M}\,\tau <: \mathtt{M}^-\,\tau$. Then, a method $\mathtt{M}^-\,\tau$ can be redefined, but the method in the resulting object remains of type $\mathtt{M}^-\,\tau$ and is thus unaccessible. This is still useful in situations where contra-variance is mandatory or to enforce protection against accidental access (see sections 5.6, 5.2 and [3].)

Virtual methods

A method ℓ is *virtual* with type τ (which we write $\mathtt{V}\,\tau$) if other methods have assumed ℓ to be of type $\mathtt{R}\,\tau$, while the method itself might not have been defined yet. When an object has a virtual method, no other method of that object can be invoked. Thus, $\mathtt{V}\,\tau$ should not be a subtype of $\mathtt{U}$. A method of type $\mathtt{V}\,\tau$ can be extended as a method of type $\mathtt{R}\,\tau$. Virtual methods may also be contra-variant. We use another symbol $\mathtt{V}^-\,\tau$ to indicate that deep subtyping has been used. A contra-variant virtual method can be extended, but it must remain contra-variant after its extension, *i.e.* of type $\mathtt{M}^-\,\tau$, and thus inaccessible. This may be surprising at first. The intuition if that $\#(\mathtt{V}^-\,\tau)$ should be $\mathtt{R}^-\,\tau$. However, a method of field-type $\mathtt{R}^-\,\tau$ would be inaccessible, since its best type is unknown. Thus $\mathtt{R}^-\,\tau$ has been identified with $\mathtt{M}^-\,\tau$.

For convenience, we also introduce a new constant F that is a top type for fields. That is, we assume $V^- \tau <: F$ and $U <: F$ (all other relations hold by transitivity).

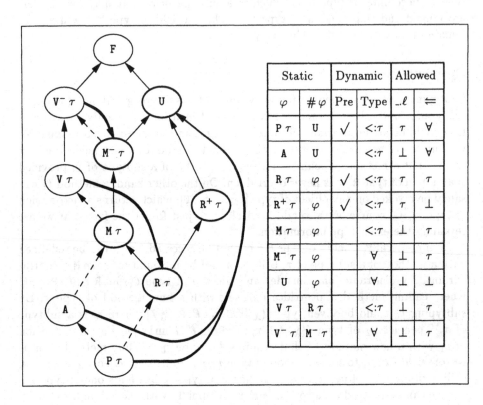

Figure table:

Static		Dynamic		Allowed	
φ	$\#\varphi$	Pre	Type	$\_\ell$	$\Leftarrow$
$P\,\tau$	U	✓	$<:\tau$	τ	$\forall$
A	U		$<:\tau$	$\bot$	$\forall$
$R\,\tau$	φ	✓	$<:\tau$	τ	τ
$R^+\,\tau$	φ	✓	$<:\tau$	τ	$\bot$
$M\,\tau$	φ		$<:\tau$	$\bot$	τ
$M^-\,\tau$	φ		$\forall$	$\bot$	τ
U	φ		$\forall$	$\bot$	$\bot$
$V\,\tau$	$R\,\tau$		$<:\tau$	$\bot$	τ
$V^-\,\tau$	$M^-\,\tau$		$\forall$	$\bot$	τ

Fig. 1. Structure of field types

The final structure of field types and subtyping axioms are summarized in figure 1. Thick arrows represent the function #. Thick nodes are used instead of reflexive thick arrows, that is, thick nodes are left invariant by #. Thin arrows represent subtyping. We added a redundant but useful distinction between continuous and dashed thin arrows. They are respectively covariant and contravariant by type-extension: when a continuous arrow connects τ_1 and τ_2, then $\#\,\tau_1$ is also a subtype of $\#\,\tau_2$; the inverse applies to dashed arrows.

Although it is easy to give intuitions for parts of the hierarchy taken alone (variances, virtual methods, idempotent field-types), we are not able to propose a good intuition for the whole hierarchy. The different components are modular technically, but their intuitive, thus approximative descriptions, cannot be composed here. We think that the field-type hierarchy should be understood locally, and then considered as such.

The table on the right is a summary of field types and their properties. The entry φ in the first column indicates the static external type. The second column $\# \varphi$ is its extension type, *i.e.* the static internal type. The two following columns tell whether the field is guaranteed to be present ($\sqrt{}$ sign) and its type if present. The reason for having $<:\tau$ instead of τ is the covariance of P. The symbol $\forall$ means any possible type. The last two columns describe access and overriding capabilities ($\perp$ means disallowed).

3 Formal developments

3.1 Types

We assume given a denumerable collection of type variables, written α, β, or χ. Type expressions, written with letter τ, are type variables, object types, or the top type T. An object type $\zeta(\chi)[\ell_i : \varphi_i{}^{i \in I} ; \varphi]$ is composed of a finite sequence of fields $\ell_i : \varphi_i$, without repetition, and a template φ for fields that are not explicitly mentioned. Variable χ is bound in the object type, and should only appear positively in φ_i's as in φ.

$$\tau ::= \alpha \mid \zeta(\alpha)[\ell_i : \varphi_i{}^{i \in I} ; \varphi] \mid T$$
$$\varphi ::= A \mid P\,\tau \mid R\,\tau \mid M\,\tau \mid V\,\tau \mid R^+\,\tau \mid M^-\,\tau \mid V^-\,\tau \mid U \mid F$$

The variance of an occurrence is defined in the usual way: it is the parity of the number of times a variable crosses a contra-variant position (*i.e.*, the number of symbols V^- or M^-) on that path from the root to that occurrence. The set of free variables of τ is $fv(\tau)$. We write $fv^-(\tau)$ the subset of those variables that occurs negatively at least once.

Object types are considered equal modulo reordering of fields. They are also equal modulo expansion, that is, by extracting a field from the template:

$$\zeta(\chi)[\ell_i : \varphi_i{}^{i \in I} ; \varphi] = \zeta(\chi)[\ell_i : \varphi_i{}^{i \in I} ; \ell : \varphi ; \varphi] \qquad \ell \neq \ell_i, \forall i \in I$$

Rules for the formation of types will be defined jointly with subtyping rules in figure 2 and are described below.

Notation For convenience and brevity of notation, we use meta-variables ρ for rows of fields, that is, syntactic expressions of the form $(\ell_i : \varphi_i{}^{i \in I} ; \varphi_0)$, where φ_i's and I are left implicit. We write $\rho(\ell)$ the value of ρ in ℓ, that is, φ_i if ℓ is one of the ℓ_i's, or φ_0 otherwise. We write $\rho \backslash \ell$ for $(\ell_i : \varphi_i{}^{i \in I, \ell_i \neq \ell} ; \varphi_0)$. and $\ell : \varphi; \rho$ for $(\ell : \varphi ; \ell_i : \varphi_i{}^{i \in I, \ell_i \neq \ell} ; \varphi_0)$. If $\mathcal{R}$ is a relation, we write $\rho \,\mathcal{R}\, \rho'$ for $\forall \ell, \rho(\ell) \,\mathcal{R}\, \rho'(\ell)$.

This is just a meta-notation that is not part of the language of types. It can always be expanded unambiguously into the more explicit notation $(\ell_i : \varphi_i{}^{i \in I} ; \varphi)$.

3.2 Type extension

We define the *extension* of field type φ, written $\# \varphi$ by the two first columns of the table 1. Type extension is lifted to object types homomorphically, *i.e.*, $\# \zeta(\chi)[\rho]$ is $\zeta(\chi)[\# \rho]$. The extension is not defined for type variables, nor for F. Note that the extension is idempotent, that is $\#(\# \tau)$ is always equal to $\# \tau$.

Well-formation of environments

$$(\text{Env } \emptyset) \qquad \frac{(\text{Env } x)}{E \vdash \tau <: \text{T} \qquad x \notin dom(E)}{E, x : \tau \vdash \diamond} \qquad \frac{(\text{Env } \alpha)}{E \vdash \tau <: \text{T} \qquad \alpha \notin dom(E)}{E, \alpha <: \tau \vdash \diamond}$$

$$\frac{}{\emptyset \vdash \diamond}$$

General subtyping

$$(\text{Sub Var}) \qquad (\text{Sub Ref F}) \qquad (\text{Sub Ref T})$$

$$\frac{E, \alpha <: \tau, E' \vdash \diamond}{E, \alpha <: \tau, E' \vdash \alpha <: \tau} \qquad \frac{E \vdash \varphi <: \text{F}}{E \vdash \varphi <: \varphi} \qquad \frac{E \vdash \tau <: \text{T}}{E \vdash \tau <: \tau}$$

$$(\text{Sub Trans T}) \qquad\qquad (\text{Sub Trans F})$$

$$\frac{E \vdash \tau_1 <: \tau_2 \qquad E \vdash \tau_2 <: \tau_3}{E \vdash \tau_1 <: \tau_3} \qquad \frac{E \vdash \varphi_1 <: \varphi_2 \qquad E \vdash \varphi_2 <: \varphi_3}{E \vdash \varphi_1 <: \varphi_3}$$

Field subtyping (assuming $E \vdash \tau <: \text{T}$)

$$(\text{Sub PA}) \qquad (\text{Sub PR}) \qquad (\text{Sub AM}) \qquad (\text{Sub UF})$$

$$\frac{}{E \vdash \text{P}\,\tau <: \text{A}} \qquad \frac{}{E \vdash \text{P}\,\tau <: \text{R}\,\tau} \qquad \frac{}{E \vdash \text{A} <: \text{M}\,\tau} \qquad \frac{}{E \vdash \text{U} <: \text{F}}$$

$$(\text{Sub RR}^+) \qquad (\text{Sub RM}) \qquad (\text{Sub R}^+\text{U}) \qquad (\text{Sub MV})$$

$$\frac{}{E \vdash \text{R}\,\tau <: \text{R}^+\,\tau} \qquad \frac{}{E \vdash \text{R}\,\tau <: \text{M}\,\tau} \qquad \frac{}{E \vdash \text{R}^+\,\tau <: \text{U}} \qquad \frac{}{E \vdash \text{M}\,\tau <: \text{V}\,\tau}$$

$$(\text{Sub MM}^-) \qquad (\text{Sub M}^-\text{U}) \qquad (\text{Sub VV}^-) \qquad (\text{Sub V}^-\text{F})$$

$$\frac{}{E \vdash \text{M}\,\tau <: \text{M}^-\,\tau} \qquad \frac{}{E \vdash \text{M}\,\tau <: \text{U}} \qquad \frac{}{E \vdash \text{V}\,\tau <: \text{V}^-\,\tau} \qquad \frac{}{E \vdash \text{V}^-\,\tau <: \text{F}}$$

$$(\text{Sub PP}) \qquad (\text{Sub R}^+\text{R}^+) \qquad (\text{Sub M}^-\text{M}^-) \qquad (\text{Sub V}^-\text{V}^-)$$

$$\frac{E \vdash \tau <: \tau'}{E \vdash \text{P}\,\tau <: \text{P}\,\tau'} \qquad \frac{E \vdash \tau <: \tau'}{E \vdash \text{R}^+\,\tau <: \text{R}^+\,\tau'} \qquad \frac{E \vdash \tau <: \tau'}{E \vdash \text{M}^-\,\tau' <: \text{M}^-\,\tau} \qquad \frac{E \vdash \tau <: \tau'}{E \vdash \text{V}^-\,\tau' <: \text{V}^-\,\tau}$$

Object subtyping

$$(\text{Sub TT}) \qquad (\text{Sub Obj})$$

$$\frac{E \vdash \diamond}{E \vdash \text{T} <: \text{T}} \qquad \frac{E, \chi <: \text{T} \vdash \rho <: \text{F} \qquad \chi \notin fv^-(\rho)}{E \vdash \varsigma(\chi)[\rho] <: \text{T}}$$

$$(\text{Sub Obj Deep}) \ (\tau \equiv \varsigma(\chi)[\rho],\ \tau' \equiv \varsigma(\chi)[\rho'])$$

$$\frac{E \vdash \tau <: \text{T} \qquad E \vdash \tau' <: \text{T}}{E, \chi <: \#\tau \vdash \rho <: \rho' \qquad E, \chi <: \#\tau \vdash \#\rho <: \#\rho'}{E \vdash \tau <: \tau'}$$

Fig. 2. Types and Subtypes

3.3 Expressions

Expressions are variables, objects, method invocation, and method overriding.

$$a ::= x \mid \varsigma(\chi, \tau)[\ell_i : \varsigma(x_i)a_i] \mid a.\ell \mid a.\ell \Leftarrow \varsigma(\chi, \tau)\varsigma(x)a$$

The expression $a.\ell \Leftarrow \varsigma(\chi,\tau)\varsigma(x)a_\ell$ is the extension of a on field ℓ with a method $\varsigma(x)a_\ell$. The expression (χ,τ) binds χ to the type of self in a_ℓ and indicates that the resulting type of the extension should be τ. This information is important so that types do not have to be inferred but only checked. Field update is just a special case of object extension. This is more general, since the selection between update and extension is resolved dynamically.

3.4 Well formation of types and subtyping

Typing environments are sequences of bindings written with letter E. There are free kinds of judgments (the second and third ones are similar):

$E ::= \emptyset \mid \alpha <: \tau \mid x : \tau$	Typing environments
$E \vdash \diamond$	Environment E is well-formed
$E \vdash \tau <: \tau'$	Regular type τ is a subtype of τ' in E
$E \vdash \varphi <: \varphi'$	Field type φ is a subtype of φ' in E
$E \vdash a : \tau$	Expression a has type τ in E

The subtyping judgment $E \vdash \tau <: \mathsf{T}$ is used to mean that τ is a well-formed regular type in E, while $E \vdash \varphi <: \mathsf{F}$ means that φ is a well-formed field-type in E. Thus, T and F also play a role of kinds. For sake of simplicity, we do not allow field variables $\alpha <: \mathsf{F}$ in environments. We have used different meta-variables τ and φ for regular types and field-types for sake of readability, although this is redundant with the constraint enforced by the well-formation rules. The formation of environments is recursively defined with rules for the formation of types and subtyping rules given in figure 2.

The subtyping rules are quite standard. Most of the rules are dedicated to field subtyping; they formally described the relation that was drawn in figure 1. A few facts are worth noticing. First we cannot derive $E \vdash F <: F$. Thus F is only used in $E \vdash \varphi <: \mathsf{F}$ to tell that φ is a well-formed field type. It prevents using F in object types. The typing rule SUB PA is also worth consideration. By transitivity with other rules, it allows $\mathsf{P}\ \tau$ to be a subtype of $\mathsf{M}\ \tau'$, even if types τ and τ' are incompatible. However, it remains true, and this is essential, that $\mathsf{P}\ \tau$ is a subtype of $\mathsf{R}\ \tau'$ if and only if τ is a subtype of τ'.

The most interesting rule SUB OBJ DEEP describes subtyping for object types. As explained above, row variables are just a meta-notation; thus, the judgment $E \vdash \rho <: \rho'$ is just a short hand for $E \vdash \rho(\ell) <: \rho'(\ell)$ for any label ℓ, which only involves a finite number of them. The simpler, but weaker rule below would keep mytype invariant during subtyping.

$$(\text{SUB OBJ INVARIANT})\ (\tau \equiv \varsigma(\chi)[\rho], \tau' \equiv \varsigma(\chi)[\rho'])$$

$$\frac{E \vdash \tau <: \mathsf{T} \qquad E \vdash \tau' <: \mathsf{T} \qquad E, \chi <: \mathsf{T} \vdash \rho <: \rho'}{E \vdash \tau <: \tau'}$$

This would prevent (positive) occurrences of self to be replaced by $\#\tau$ where τ is the current type of the object. Replacing in SUB OBJ INVARIANT the bound

T of χ by $\#\tau$ would actually not behave well with respect to transitivity. The additional premise in rule SUB OBJ DEEP restores the correct behavior with respect to transitivity. Namely, the application of a rule SUB TRANS between two object types, can be replaced by SUB OBJ DEEP and applications of SUB TRANS to the bounds of the premises.

(EXPR SUBSUMPTION)
$$\frac{E \vdash a : \tau \qquad E \vdash \tau <: \tau'}{E \vdash a : \tau'}$$

(EXPR VAR)
$$\frac{E, x : \tau, E' \vdash \diamond}{E, x : \tau, E' \vdash x : \tau}$$

(EXPR OBJECT) $(\tau \equiv \varsigma(\chi)[\rho])$
$$\frac{E, \chi <: \#\tau, x_i : \chi \vdash a_i : \tau_i, i \in I \qquad E, \chi <: \#\tau \vdash (\text{P } \tau_i{}^{i \in I}; \text{A}) <: \rho}{E \vdash \varsigma(\chi, \tau)[\ell_i = \varsigma(x_i)a_i{}^{i \in I}] : \tau}$$

(EXPR SELECT)
$$\frac{E \vdash a : \tau \qquad E \vdash \tau <: \varsigma(\chi)[\ell : \text{R}^+ \tau_\ell \; ; \text{U}]}{E \vdash a.\ell : \tau_\ell\{\tau/\alpha\}}$$

(EXPR UPDATE)
$$\frac{E \vdash a : \tau \qquad E \vdash \tau <: \varsigma(\chi)[\ell : \text{R } \tau_\ell \; ; \rho_0] \qquad E, \chi <: \#\tau, x : \chi \vdash a_\ell : \tau_\ell}{E \vdash a.\ell \Leftarrow \varsigma(\chi, \tau)\varsigma(x)a_\ell : \tau}$$

(EXPR EXTEND) $(\tau \equiv \varsigma(\chi)[\rho])$
$$\frac{(\varphi_0, \rho(\ell)) \in \{(\text{A}, \text{P } \tau_\ell), (\text{V } \tau_\ell, \text{R } \tau_\ell), (\text{V}^- \tau_\ell, \text{M}^- \tau_\ell)\}}{E \vdash a : \varsigma(\chi)[\ell : \varphi_0 \; ; \rho \setminus \ell] \qquad E, \chi <: \#\tau, x : \chi \vdash a_\ell : \tau_\ell}{E \vdash a.\ell \Leftarrow \varsigma(\chi, \tau)\varsigma(x)a_\ell : \tau}$$

Fig. 3. Typing rules

3.5 Typing rules

Typing rules are given in figure 3. The rules for subsumption, variables, and method invocation are quite standard.

Rule EXPR OBJECT has been discussed earlier. The last premise says that the fields ℓ_i may actually be super-types of P τ_i in ρ and other fields may also be super types of A. One cannot simply require that ρ be $(\ell_i : \text{P } \tau_i{}^{i \in I}; \text{A})$ and later use subsumption, since the assumption made on the type of x_i while typing a_i could then be too weak.

Rule EXPR UPDATE is similar to the overriding rule in [3]. This rule is important since it permits both internal and external updates: the result type of the object is exactly the same as the one before the update.

On the contrary, rule EXPR EXTEND is intended to add new methods that were not necessarily defined before, and thus change the type of the object.

Let ℓ and $\ell_i{}^{i \in I}$ be distinct labels, j in I,
and v be of the form $\zeta(\chi, \tau)[\ell_i = \varsigma(x_i)a_i{}^{i \in I}]$.

$$v.\ell_j \longrightarrow a_j\{\tau/\chi\}\{v/x\} \qquad\qquad (\text{SELECT})$$

$$v.\ell_j \Leftarrow \zeta(\chi, \tau')\varsigma(x)a \longrightarrow \zeta(\chi, \tau \Leftarrow \tau')[\ell_i = \varsigma(x_i)a_i{}^{i \in I-j}, \ell_j = \varsigma(x)a] \qquad (\text{UPDATE})$$

$$v.\ell \Leftarrow \zeta(\chi, \tau')\varsigma(x_0)a_0 \longrightarrow \zeta(\chi, \tau \Leftarrow \tau')[\ell_i = \varsigma(x_i)a_i{}^{i \in I}, \ell = \varsigma(x)a] \qquad (\text{EXTEND})$$

$$\text{if } a_1 \longrightarrow a_2 \text{ then } C\{a_1\} \longrightarrow C\{a_2\} \qquad\qquad (\text{CONTEXT})$$

Fig. 4. Reduction rules

There are three different sub-cases in rule EXPR EXTEND; the one that applies is uniquely determined by the given type τ. Then the type of field ℓ in the argument is deduced from the small table.

Rules EXPR EXTEND and EXPR UPDATE both apply only when τ is of the form $\zeta(\chi)[\ell: P \, \tau_\ell \, ; \rho]$ or $\zeta(\chi)[\ell: R \, \tau_\ell \, ; \rho]$. Then, the requirements on the type of a are the same (letting the premise of SUB EXTEND be preceded by a subsumption rule). Thus, different derivations lead to the same judgment. It would also be possible to syntactically distinguish between object extension and method update, as well as to separate the extension between three different primitive corresponding to each of the three typing cases.

3.6 Operational semantics

We give a reduction semantics for a call-by-value strategy. Values are reduced to objects. A leftmost outermost evaluation strategy is enforced by the evaluation contexts C.

$$v ::= \zeta(\chi, \tau)[\ell_i = \varsigma(x_i)a_i{}^{i \in I}] \qquad C ::= \{\} \mid C.\ell \mid C.\ell \Leftarrow \zeta(\tau, \chi)\varsigma(x)a$$

The reduction rules are given in figure 4. Since programs are explicitly typed, the reduction must also manipulate types in order to maintain programs both well-formed and well-typed, even though it is not type-driven. In fact, the reduction uses an auxiliary binary operation on types $\varphi \Leftarrow \varphi'$, to recompute the witness type of object values during object extension. It is defined in figure 5. The function $\varphi \Leftarrow \varphi'$ is extended to object types homomorphically, *i.e.*, $\zeta(\chi)[\rho] \Leftarrow \zeta(\chi)[\rho']$ is $\zeta(\chi)[\rho \Leftarrow \rho']$. There is some flexibility in defining type reduction. As explained in the next section, it is only necessary that type-extension validates lemma 4.

⇐	φ_2			
φ_1	$P\,\tau',\ A,\ U,\ V^-\,\tau'$	$R\,\tau',\ R^+\,\tau'$	$M\,\tau',\ M^-\,\tau'$	$V\,\tau'$
$P\,\tau,\ A$	φ_2	φ_2	φ_2	φ_2
$R\,\tau,\ R^+\,\tau,\ U,\ M^-\,\tau$	φ_1	φ_1	φ_1	φ_1
$M\,\tau$	φ_1	$R\,\tau$	φ_1	$V\,\tau$
$V\,\tau$	φ_1	$R\,\tau$	$R\,\tau$	φ_1
$V^-\,\tau$	φ_1	φ_1	$M^-\,\tau$	φ_1

Fig. 5. Type reduction $\varphi_1 \Leftarrow \varphi_2$

4 Soundness of the typing rules

The soundness of the typing rules results from a combination of subject reduction and canonical forms. The proof of subject reduction is standard (see [3] for instance). A few classical lemmas help simplifying the main proof.

Lemma 1 (Bound weakening). *If $E \vdash \tau <: \tau'$ and $E, \alpha <: \tau', E' \vdash \mathcal{J}$, then $E, \alpha <: \tau, E' \vdash \mathcal{J}$.*

Lemma 2 (Substitution).

1. *If $E, \alpha <: \tau, E' \vdash \mathcal{J}$ and $E \vdash \tau' <: \tau$, then $E, E'\{\tau'/\alpha\} \vdash \mathcal{J}\{\tau'/\alpha\}$.*
2. *If $E, x : \tau, E' \vdash \mathcal{J}$ and $E \vdash a : \tau$, then $E, E' \vdash \mathcal{J}\{a/x\}$.*

Lemma 3 (Structural subtyping).

1. *If $\tau \equiv \zeta(\chi)[\rho]$ and $E \vdash \tau <: \tau'$, then τ' is either T or of the form $\zeta(\chi)[\rho']$ and $E, \chi <: \#\tau \vdash \rho <: \rho'$.*
2. *If $E \vdash \varphi <: R\,\tau_l$, then φ is either $R\,\tau_l$ or $P\,\tau_0$ where $E \vdash \tau_0 <: \tau_l$.*
3. *If $E \vdash \varphi <: R^+\,\tau_l$, then φ is either $P\,\tau_0$, $R\,\tau_0$, or $R^+\,\tau_0$ where $E \vdash \tau_0 <: \varphi_l$.*
4. *If $E \vdash \varphi <: P\,\tau_l$, then φ is $P\,\tau_0$ where $E \vdash \tau_0 <: \tau_l$.*
   Etc.

The proof of subject reduction also uses an essential lemma that relates computation on types to subtyping. Actually, the proof does not depend on the particular definition of $\#$, but only on the following lemma.

Lemma 4 (Type computation). *Let τ and τ' be two object types $\zeta(\chi)[\rho]$ and $\zeta(\chi)[\rho']$. Assume that there exists a row ρ'' such that $E, \chi <: \#\tau \vdash \rho <: \rho''$ and for each label ℓ, the pair $(\rho''(\ell), \rho'(\ell))$ is one of the four forms $(A, P\,\tau_\ell)$, $(V\,\tau_\ell, R\,\tau_\ell)$, $(V^-\,\tau_\ell, M^-\,\tau_\ell)$, or (φ, φ). Let $\hat{\tau}$ be $\tau \Leftarrow \tau'$ and $\hat{\rho}$ be $\rho \Leftarrow \rho'$. Then,*

$$E \vdash \hat{\tau} <: \tau' \qquad E \vdash \#\hat{\tau} <: \#\tau' \qquad E \vdash \#\hat{\tau} <: \#\tau'$$

Moreover, if $E, \chi <: \#\tau \vdash \rho(\ell) <: \rho'(\ell)$, then $E, \chi <: \#\tau \vdash \rho(\ell) <: \hat{\rho}(\ell)$; otherwise $E, \chi <: \#\tau \vdash P\,\tau_\ell <: \hat{\rho}(\ell)$.

Lemma 5 (Virtual methods). *If $E \vdash \tau <: \zeta(\chi)[U]$, then $E \vdash \tau <: \#\tau$.*

Theorem 1 (Subject Reduction). *Typings are preserved by reduction. If $E \vdash a : \tau_a$ and $a \longrightarrow a'$ then $E \vdash a' : \tau_a$.*

Theorem 2 (Canonical Forms). *Well-typed expressions that cannot be reduced are values. If $\emptyset \vdash a : \tau$ and there exists no a' such that $a \longrightarrow a'$, then a is a value.*

5 Examples

For simplicity, we assume that the core calculus has been extended with abstraction and application. This extension could either be primitive or derived from the encoding given in section 5.6. For brievity, we write $a.\ell \Leftarrow a'$ instead of $a.\ell \Leftarrow \zeta(\chi, \tau)\varsigma(z)a'$ when a' does not depend on the self parameter z. In practice, other abbreviations could be made, but we avoid them here to reduce confusion.

We consider the simple example of points and colored points. These objects can of course already be written in [3]. The expressiveness of our calculus is not so much its capability to write new forms of complete objects but to provide new means of defining them. This provides more flexibility, increases security in several ways , and removes the complexity of the encoding of classes into objects.

5.1 Objects

A point object p_0 can be defined as follows:

$$\zeta(\chi, \text{point})[x = 0 \; ; \; mv = \varsigma(z)\lambda y.(z.x \Leftarrow y) \; ; \; print = \varsigma(z)print\_int \; z.x]$$

where point is $\zeta(\chi)[x : \text{R int} \; ; \; mv : \text{P int} \to \chi \; ; \; print : \text{P unit} \; ; \; A]$. As in [3], new points can be created using method update as in $p_0.x \Leftarrow \zeta(\chi, \text{point})\varsigma(z)1$. Moreover, colored points can be defined inheriting from points:

$$\text{cpoint} \stackrel{\triangle}{=} \zeta(\chi)[x : \text{R int} \; ; \; c : \text{R bool} \; ; \; mv : \text{P int} \to \chi \; ; \; print : \text{P unit} \; ; \; A]$$

$$cp \stackrel{\triangle}{=} (p_0.c \Leftarrow \zeta(\chi, \text{cpoint})\varsigma(z)\text{true}).print$$
$$\Leftarrow \zeta(\chi, \text{cpoint})\varsigma(z)\text{if } z.c \text{ then } print\_int \; z.x$$

When two values of different types have a common super-type τ, they can be interchanged at type τ. Here, cpoint is not a subtype of point, since both types carry too precise type information. However, they admit the common super-type $\zeta(\chi)[x : \text{R int} \; ; \; c : U \; ; \; mv : \text{P int} \to \chi \; ; \; print : \text{P unit} \; ; \; A]..$

5.2 Abstraction via subtyping

Subtyping can also be used to enforce security. For instance, field x may be hidden by weakening its type to U. Similarly, method mv may be protected against further redefinition by weakening its type to $R^+ \tau$. That is, by giving p_0 the type $\zeta(\chi)[mv\colon R^+ \text{int} \to \chi \; ; print\colon R \text{ unit} \; ; U]$. While method mv can no longer be directly redefined, there is still a possibility for indirect redefinition. For instance, method $print$ could have been written so that it overrides method mv before printing. To ensure that a method can never be redefined, directly or indirectly, it must be given type $R^+ \tau$ at its creation.

5.3 Virtual methods

The creation of new points by updating the field of an already existing point is not quite satisfactory since it requires the use of default methods to represent the undefined state, which are often arbitrary and may be a source of errors. Indeed, a class of points can be seen as a virtual point lacking its field components.

$$\texttt{POINT} \overset{\triangle}{=} \zeta(\chi)[x\colon V \text{ int} \; ; mv\colon P \text{ int} \to \chi \; ; print\colon P \text{ unit} \; ; A]$$

$$P \overset{\triangle}{=} \zeta(\chi, \texttt{POINT})[mv = \varsigma(z)\lambda y.(z.x \Leftarrow y) \; ; print = \varsigma(z)print\_int \; z.x]$$

New points are then created by filling in the missing fields:

$$\texttt{new\_point} \overset{\triangle}{=} \lambda y.(P.x \Leftarrow \zeta(\chi, \texttt{point})\varsigma(z)y) \qquad p_1 \overset{\triangle}{=} \texttt{new\_point } 0$$

5.4 Traditional class-based perspective

To keep closer to the traditional approach, we may by default choose to hide both fields corresponding to instance variables and the extendible capabilities of the remaining methods. For instance, treating x as an instance variable, and mv and $print$ as "regular" methods, we choose $\zeta(\chi)[mv\colon R^+\text{int} \to \chi \; ; print\colon R^+\text{unit} \; ; U]$ for point. Intuitively, the object-type point hides all information that is not necessary to increase security. Conversely, the class-type POINT remains as precise as possible, to keep expressiveness. Indeed, a class of points is still an object. However, as opposed to the previous section, we adopt some uniform, more structured style, treating "real" objects differently from those representing classes.

In colored points, we may choose to leave field c readable and overridable, as if we defined two methods set_c and get_c.

$$\texttt{cpoint} \overset{\triangle}{=} \zeta(\chi)[c\colon R \text{ bool} \; ; mv\colon R^+\text{int} \to \chi \; ; print\colon R^+\text{unit} \; ; U]$$

Single inheritance is obtained by class extension:

$$\texttt{CPOINT} \overset{\triangle}{=} \zeta(\chi)[x\colon V \text{ int} \; ; c\colon V \text{ bool} \; ; mv\colon P \text{ int} \to \chi \; ; print\colon P \text{ unit} \; ; A]$$

$$CP \overset{\triangle}{=} (P.print \Leftarrow \zeta(\chi, \texttt{CPOINT})\varsigma(z)\text{if } z.c \text{ then } print\_int \; z.x)$$

$$\texttt{new\_cpoint} \overset{\triangle}{=} \lambda y.\lambda w.(CP.x \Leftarrow \zeta(\chi, \texttt{cpoint})\varsigma(z)y).c \Leftarrow \zeta(\chi, \texttt{cpoint})\varsigma(z)w$$

While CPOINT is not a subtype of POINT at the class level, we recover the usual relationship that cpoint is a subtype of point at the object level. Moreover, at the object level, types are invariant by #. Thus, we also recover the subtyping relation of [3]. In particular, object types can be unfolded.

5.5   An advanced example

A colorable point p' is a point prepared to be colored without actually being colored. It can be obtained by adding to the point p_0 an extra method paint that when called with an argument y returns the colored point obtained by adding the color field c with value y and by updating the print method of p_0.

$$p' \overset{\triangle}{=} p_0.paint \Leftarrow \varsigma(z, \texttt{point}')\lambda y.$$
$$((z.c \Leftarrow y).print \Leftarrow \zeta(\chi, \texttt{cpoint})\varsigma(z)\texttt{if } z.c \texttt{ then } print\_int \ z.x)$$

where point' is

$$\zeta(\chi)[x\!:\!\texttt{R int} \ ; \ ...print\!:\!\texttt{R unit} \ ; \ paint\!:\!\texttt{P bool} \rightarrow \texttt{cpoint} \ ; \ c\!:\!\texttt{M bool} \ ; \ \texttt{U}]$$

This example may be seen as the installation (method *paint*) of a new behavior (method *print*) that interacts with the existing state x and adds some new state c. The above solution becomes more interesting if each installation involves many methods, and especially if several installation are either different fields of the same objects or the same field of different objects. Then, the installation procedure can be selected dynamically by message invocation instead of manually by applying an external function to the object.

5.6   Encoding of the lambda-calculus

This part improves the encoding proposed in [3]. It also illustrates the use of virtual methods and variances. The untyped encoding of the lambda-calculus into objects in [3] is the following[2]:

$$\langle\!\langle x \rangle\!\rangle \overset{\triangle}{=} x.\texttt{arg} \qquad \langle\!\langle \lambda x.M \rangle\!\rangle \overset{\triangle}{=} [\texttt{arg} = \varsigma(x)x.\texttt{arg} \ ; \ \texttt{val} = \varsigma(x).\langle\!\langle M \rangle\!\rangle]$$

$$\langle\!\langle M \ M' \rangle\!\rangle \overset{\triangle}{=} (\langle\!\langle M \rangle\!\rangle.\texttt{arg} \Leftarrow \varsigma(x)\langle\!\langle M' \rangle\!\rangle).\texttt{val}$$

A function is encoded as an object with a diverging method arg. The encoding of an application overrides the method arg of the encoding of the function with the encoding of the argument and invokes the method val of the resulting object. Programs obtained by the translation of functional programs will never call val before loading the argument. However, if the encoding is used as a programming style, the type system will not provide as much safety as a type system with primitive function types would. The method val could also be called, accidently, before the field arg has been overridden. In general, this will, in turn, call the method arg and diverge. The use of default diverging methods is a hack that palliates the absence of virtual methods. It can be assimilated to a "method not understood" type error and one could argue that the encoding of [3] is not strongly typed.

---

[2] If both functions and objects co-exist, one should actually mark variables introduced by the encoding of functions so as to leave the other variables unchanged.

The encoding can be improved using object extension to treat a function $\lambda x.M$ as an object $[\mathtt{val} = \varsigma(x).\langle\!\langle M \rangle\!\rangle]$ with a virtual method $\mathtt{arg}$ (remember that $x.\mathtt{arg}$ may appear in $\langle\!\langle M \rangle\!\rangle$). The type-system will then prevent the method $\mathtt{val}$ to be called before the argument has been loaded. More precisely, let us consider the simply typed lambda-calculus:

$$t ::= \alpha \mid t \to t \qquad\qquad M ::= x \mid \lambda x : t.M \mid M\ M$$

Functional types are encoded as follows:

$$\langle\!\langle \alpha \rangle\!\rangle \triangleq \alpha \qquad\qquad \langle\!\langle t \to t' \rangle\!\rangle \triangleq \varsigma(\chi)[\mathtt{arg}\colon \mathtt{V}^- \langle\!\langle t \rangle\!\rangle \ ; \ \mathtt{val}\colon \mathtt{R}^+ \langle\!\langle t' \rangle\!\rangle \ ; \ \mathtt{U}]$$

This naturally induces a subtyping relation between function types that is contra-variant on the domain and covariant on the co-domain. The typed encoding is given by the following inference rules:

$$\frac{x : t \in A}{A \vdash x : t \Rightarrow x.\mathtt{arg}} \qquad \frac{A, x : t \vdash M : t' \Rightarrow a \qquad x \notin dom\,(A)}{A \vdash \lambda x : t.M : t \to t' \Rightarrow \varsigma(\chi, \langle\!\langle t \to t' \rangle\!\rangle)[\mathtt{val} = \varsigma(x).a]}$$

$$\frac{A \vdash M : t' \to t \Rightarrow a \qquad A \vdash M' : t' \Rightarrow a'}{A \vdash M\ M' : t \Rightarrow (a.\mathtt{arg} \Leftarrow \varsigma(\chi, \#\langle\!\langle t \to t' \rangle\!\rangle)\varsigma(x)a').\mathtt{val}}$$

It is easy to see that the translation transforms well-typed judgments $\emptyset \vdash M : t$ into well-typed judgments $\emptyset \vdash \langle\!\langle M \rangle\!\rangle : \langle\!\langle t \rangle\!\rangle$.

As in [3], the translation provides a call-by-name operational semantics for the lambda-calculus. The encoding of [3] also provides an equational theory for the object calculus and, thefore, for the lambda calculus, via translation, which we do not.

6 Discussion

6.1 Variations

Several variations can be made by consistently modifying field-types, their subtyping relationship, and the typing rule for object extension. The easiest is to drop some subtyping asumption (such as SUB PP, or SUB PA) or drop the field-type P τ altogether. This weakens the type system (some examples are not typable any longer), but it retains the essential features. More significant simplifications can be made at the price of a higher restriction of expressiveness. For instance, virtual field-types could be removed.

Some extensions or modifications to the type hierarchy are also possible. For instance, one could introduce fields of type $\dagger$P τ that do no depend on any other method. These methods would be dual of those of type P τ on which no other method depend. Methods of type $\dagger$P τ could always be called even if the object is virtual. This extends to field-types $\dagger$R τ and $\dagger$ R$^+$ τ similarly.

6.2 Extensions

Imperative update is an orthogonal issue to the one studied here, and it could be added without any problem. Object extension should, of course, remain functional.

Equational theory We see no difficulty in adding an equational theory to our calculus, but this remains to be investigated. Treating object extension as a commutative operator would allow to reduce object construction to a sequence of object extensions of the empty object (virtual methods would be crucial here).

Higher-order types As shown above, our objects are sufficiently powerful to represent classes. As opposed to [3], this does not necessitate higher-order polymorphism because methods are already required to be parametric in all possible extensions of self.

The addition of higher-order polymorphism might still be useful, in particular to enable parametric classes. We believe that there is no problem in constraining type abstraction by some supertype bound, written $\alpha <: \tau$ as in $F_{<:}$. However, it would also be useful to introduce #-bounds of the form $\alpha <: \# \tau$. This might require more investigation.

Row variables and binary methods We have used row variables only as a meta-notation for simplifying the presentation. It would be interesting to really allow row variables in types. This would probably augment the expressiveness of the language, since it should provide some form of matching that revealed quite useful, especially for binary methods [11, 9, 26].

Actually, it remains to investigate how the presented calculus could be extended to cope with binary methods. Row variables might not be sufficient to express matching, and some new form of matching might have to be found. It is unclear whether the known solutions [10] could be adapted to our calculus.

7 Comparison with other works

Our proposal is built on the calculus of objects of Abadi and Cardelli [3], which is invoked throughout this paper. Our use of variance annotations is in principle similar to theirs. By attaching variance annotations to field-types rather than to fields themselves, we eliminate some useless types such as $M^+ \tau$. Indeed, such a field could not be overriden, nor accessed, and thus it could be just given type U. (Our use of variances also eliminate the ability to specify the type of a field without specifying its variance, which may cause problem with type inference [22].) An essential imported tool is the structure of record-types of [23], which was originally designed for type inference in ML [24]. The use of a richer structure of record types has previously been proposed for type checking records [15, 16, 13, 12]. To our knowledge, the benefits of symmetric information were first transfered from record types to object types in [25]. There, first-order typing rules for objects with extension and both deep and width subtyping were roughly drafted without any formal treatment.

A similar approach has also been independently proposed by Bono, Liquori and others. Their first related work [6] has later lead to many closely related proposals [8, 7, 4, 18, 17, 19]. Most of these are extensions of the Fisher-Honsel calculus of objects [20]. The differences between their approach and the one of [3] (which is also ours) are not always significant but they make a close comparisson more difficult. Only two of these works [19, 18] are extensions of the Abadi-Cardelli calculus of objects [3] and are thus more connected to our proposal. The first-order version [19], is subsumed by both [25] (which also covers deep subtyping) and [18] (which also addresses self types.) Our proposal extends both [25] and [18].

The most interesting comparison can be made with [18]. The main motivation and the key idea behind both proposals are similar: they integrate object subtyping and object extension, using a richer type structure to preserve type soundness. Saturated *vs* diamond types correspond to our object-types with a field template U *vs* A, respectively. Our treatment seems more uniform. We only have one kind of object types. We distinguish between the "saturation" and "diamond" properties in fields instead of objects. As a result, we can write an object type that is saturated, except for a few particular fields. Our proposal also includes several additional features: it addresses deep subtyping and virtual methods; it uses a more powerful subtyping rule for object types; it also allows methods to extend self. Moreover, in our proposal, the subtyping relationship is structural for object types. Additionally, subtyping axioms are only given at the level of fields, each one of them treating a different important subtyping capability. As a result, object types have a more regular structure, and can easily be adapted to further extensions. We think this is easier to understand, to modify, and to manipulate.

An alternative to virtual methods has also been studied in [4], using a quite different approach, which consists in annotating each method with the list of all other methods they depend on. Thus, each method has a different view of self. Their approach to incomplete objects is, in principle, more powerful that ours; in particular, they can type programs that even traditional class-based languages would reject. We found their types of objects too detailed, and thus their proposal less practical than ours. (Tracing dependencies is closer to some form of program analysis than to standard type systems.) In fact, we intendedly restricted our type system so that methods have a uniform view of self. In practice, our solution is sufficient to capture common forms of inheritance.

In [20], pre-objects have pro-types and can be turned into objects with obj-types by subtyping. Pro-types and obj-types are similar to our object types $\zeta(\chi)[\ell_i : R\ \tau_i{}^{i \in I}\ ;\ A]$ and $\zeta(\chi)[\ell_i : R^+\ \tau_i{}^{i \in I}\ ;\ U]$. One difference is that, in our case, subtyping is defined and permitted field by field rather than all at once. Fisher and Mitchell also studied the relationship between objects and classes in [14]. They use bounded existential quantification to hide some of the structure of the object in the *public* interface. This still allows public methods to be called, while *private* methods become innaccessible. In our calculus, the richer structure of objects permits to use subtyping instead of bounded existential quantification to provide a similar abstraction. This is not suprising, theoretically, since subtyping, as existential quantification, is a lost of type information. However, this is practically a significant difference, since subtyping allows more explicit type information but is less expressive. Another difference is that using the standard record types they had to introduce record sorts to express negative type information. As pointed out in a more recent paper [5], the design of the language of kinds becomes important for modularity. In particular, [5] improves over [14] by changing default kinds from unknown (U in our setting) to absent (A). Instead, our record types express positive and negative information symmetrically and are viewed as total functions from fields to types, which avoids the somehow *ad hoc* language of sorts.

In a recent paper, Riecke and Stone have circumvented the problem of merging extension with deep and width subtyping by changing the semantics of objects [27]. In fact, their semantics remain in correspondance with the standard semantics of objects in the general case, but the semantics of extension is changed so that the counter example becomes sound in the new semantics. They distinguish between method update and object extension. Then, a field that is already defined is automatically renamed by extension into an anonymous field that becomes externally inaccessible.

With their semantics, some of our enriched type information would become obsolete for ensuring type soundness, but it might remain useful for compile-time optimizations. Other pieces of information, e.g. virtual types, would remain quite pertinent.

8 Conclusion

We have proposed a uniform and flexible method for enriching type systems of object calculi by refining the field structure of object types, so that they carry more precise type information.

Applying our approach to the object calculus of Abadi and Cardelli, we have integrated object extension and depth and width subtyping, with covariant final methods and contra-variant virtual methods, in a type-safe calculus. When sufficient type information is revealed, objects may represent classes. Type information may also be hidden progressively, until objects can be used and interchanged in a traditional fashion.

An important gain is to avoid the encoding of classes as records of premethods. Instead, we provide a more uniform, direct approach. Another benefit of this integration is to allow mixed formed of classes and objects. The use of richer object types also increases both safety by capturing more dynamic misbehavior as static type errors and security by allowing more privacy via subtyping. Moreover, our approach subsumes several other unrelated proposals, and it might provide a unified framework for studying or comparing new proposals. Some extensions and variations are clearly possible, provided the operations on objects, their types and the subtyping hierarchy are changed consistently.

More investigation still remains to be done. Adding an equational theory to the calculus, would simplify our primitives, since objects could always be built field by field using object extension only. This might also be a first step towards a better integration of record-based and delegation-based object calculi. In the future, we would also like to study the potential increase of expressiveness that field and row variables could provide. Of course, investigating binary methods remains one of the most important issues.

Classes can be viewed as objects. We hope that an even richer type structure would finally enable to see objects for what they really are —records of functions— in the (yet untyped) self-application interpretation.

References

1. Martín Abadi and Luca Cardelli. A theory of primitive objects: Untyped and first-order systems. In *Theoretical Aspects of Computer Software*, pages 296–320. Springer-Verlag, April 1994.

2. Martín Abadi and Luca Cardelli. A theory of primitive objects: Second-order systems. *Science of Computer Programming*, 25(2-3):81–116, December 1995. Preliminary version appeared in D. Sanella, editor, Proceedings of European Symposium on Programming, pages 1-24. Springer-Verlag, April 1994.

3. Martín Abadi and Luca Cardelli. *A theory of objects*. Springer, 1996.

4. V. Bono, M. Bugliesi, M. Dezani-Ciancaglini, and L. Liquori. Subtyping Constraints for Incomplete Objects. In *Proceedings of TAPSOFT-CAAP-97, International Joint Conference on the Theory and Practice of Software Development*, Lecture Notes in Computer Science. Springer-Verlag, 1997.

5. V. Bono and K. Fisher. An imperative, first-order calculus with object extension. In *Informal Proceedings of the FOOL 5 workshop on Foundations of Object Oriented Programming*, Sans Diego, CA, January 1998. To appear.

6. V. Bono and L. Liquori. A subtyping for the fisher-honsell-mitchell lambda calculus of object. In *Proc. of CSL-94, International Conference of Computer Science Logic*, volume 933 of *Lecture Notes in Computer Science*, pages 16–30. Springer-Verlag, 1995.

7. Viviana Bono and Michele Bugliesi. A lambda calculus of incomplete objects. In *Proceedings of Mathematical Foundations of Computer Science(MFCS)*, number 1113 in Lecture Notes in Computer Science, pages 218–229, 1996.

8. Viviana Bono and Michele Bugliesi. Matching constraints for the lambda calculus of objects. In *Proceedings of (MFCS)*, 1997.

9. Kim B. Bruce. Typing in object-oriented languages: Achieving expressibility and safety. Revised version to appear in Computing Surveys, November 1995.

10. Kim B. Bruce, Luca Cardelli, Giuseppe Castagna, Valery Trifonov) the Hopkins Objects Group (Jonathan Eifrig, Scott Smith, Gary T. Leavens, and Benjamin Pierce. On binary methods. *Theory and Practice of Object Systems*, 1(3):221–242, 1996.

11. Kim B. Bruce, Angela Schuett, and Robert van Gent. Polytoil: A type-safe polymorphic object-oriented language. In *ECOOP*, number 952 in LNCS, pages 27–51. Springer Verlag, 1995.

12. Luca Cardelli. Extensible records in a pure calculus of subtyping. In Carl A. Gunter and John C. Mitchell, editors, *Theoretical Aspects Of Object-Oriented Programming. Types, Semantics and Language Design*, pages 373–425. MIT Press, 1994.

13. Luca Cardelli and John C. Mitchell. Operations on records. In *Fifth International Conference on Mathematical Foundations of Programming Semantics*, 1989.

14. K. Fisher and J. C. Mitchell. On the relationship between classes, objects and data abstraction. *Theoretical And Practice of Objects Systems*, To appear, 1998. A preliminary version appeared in the proceedings of the International Summer School on Mathematics of Program Construction, Marktoberdorf, Germany, Springer LNCS, 1997.

15. Robert W. Harper and Benjamin C. Pierce. Extensible records without subsumption. Technical Report CMU-CS-90-102, Carnegie Mellon University, Pittsburg, Pensylvania, February 1990.

16. Robert W. Harper and Benjamin C. Pierce. A record calculus based on symmetric concatenation. Technical Report CMU-CS-90-157, Carnegie Mellon University, Pittsburg, Pensylvania, February 1990.

17. L. Liquori and G. Castagna. A Typed Lambda Calculus of Objects. In *Proc. of ASIAN-96, International Asian Computing Science Conference*, volume 1212 of *Lecture Notes in Computer Science*. Springer-Verlag, 1996.

18. Luigi Liquori. Bounded polymorphism for extensible objects. Technical Report CS-24-96, Dipartimento di Informatica, Universita' di Torino, 1997.

19. Luigi Liquori. An Extended Theory of Primitive Objects: First Order System. In *Proceedings of ECOOP-97, International European Conference on Object Oriented Programming*, Lecture Notes in Computer Science. Springer-Verlag, 1997.

20. John C. Mitchell and Kathleen Fisher. A delegation-based object calculus with subtyping. In *Fundamentals of Computation Theory*, number 965 in LNCS, pages 42–61. Springer, 1995.

21. John C. Mitchell, Furio Honsell, and Kathleen Fisher. A lambda calculus of objects and method specialization. In *IEEE Symposium on Logic in Computer Science*, pages 26–38, June 1993.

22. Jens Palsberg and Trevor Jim. Type inference of object types with variances. Private Discussion, 1996.

23. Didier Rémy. Syntactic theories and the algebra of record terms. Research Report 1869, Institut National de Recherche en Informatique et Automatisme, Rocquencourt, BP 105, 78 153 Le Chesnay Cedex, France, 1993.

24. Didier Rémy. Type inference for records in a natural extension of ML. In Carl A. Gunter and John C. Mitchell, editors, *Theoretical Aspects Of Object-Oriented Programming. Types, Semantics and Language Design*. MIT Press, 1993.

25. Didier Rémy. Better subtypes and row variables for record types. Presented at the workshop on Advances in types for computer science at the Newton Institute, Cambridge, UK, August 1995.

26. Didier Rémy and Jérôme Vouillon. Objective ML: An effective object-oriented extension to ML. *Theoretical And Practice of Objects Systems*, To appear, 1998. A preliminary version appeared in the proceedings of the 24th ACM Conference on Principles of Programming Languages, 1997.

27. Jon G. Riecke and Christopher A. Stone. Privacy via subsumption. In *Informal Proceedings of the FOOL 5 workshop on Foundations of Object Oriented Programming*, Sans Diego, CA, January 1998. To appear.

Building a Bridge between Pointer Aliases and Program Dependences *

John L. Ross[1] and Mooly Sagiv[2]

[1] University of Chicago, e-mail: johnross@cs.uchicago.edu
[2] Tel-Aviv University, e-mail: sagiv@math.tau.ac.il

Abstract. In this paper we present a surprisingly simple reduction of the program dependence problem to the may-alias problem. While both problems are undecidable, providing a bridge between them has great practical importance. Program dependence information is used extensively in compiler optimizations, automatic program parallelizations, code scheduling in super-scalar machines, and in software engineering tools such as code slicers. When working with languages that support pointers and references, these systems are forced to make very conservative assumptions. This leads to many superfluous program dependences and limits compiler performance and the usability of software engineering tools. Fortunately, there are many algorithms for computing conservative approximations to the may-alias problem. The reduction has the important property of always computing conservative program dependences when used with a conservative may-alias algorithm. We believe that the simplicity of the reduction and the fact that it takes linear time may make it practical for realistic applications.

1 Introduction

It is well known that programs with pointers are hard to understand, debug, and optimize. In recent years many interesting algorithms that conservatively analyze programs with pointers have been published. Roughly speaking, these algorithms [19, 20, 25, 5, 16, 17, 23, 8, 6, 9, 14, 27, 13, 28] conservatively solve the may-alias problem, i.e., the algorithms are sometimes able to show that two pointer access paths never refer to the same memory location at a given program point.

However, may-alias information is insufficient for compiler optimizations, automatic code parallelizations, instruction scheduling for super-scalar machines, and software engineering tools such as code slicers. In these systems, information about the program dependences between *different* program points is required. Such dependences can be uniformly modeled by the program dependence graph (see [21, 26, 12]).

In this paper we propose a simple yet powerful approach for finding program dependences for programs with pointers:

---

* Partially supported by Binational Science Foundation grant No. 9600337

Given a program $\mathcal{P}$, we generate a program $\mathcal{P}'$ (hereafter also referred to as the *instrumented* version of $\mathcal{P}$) which simulates $\mathcal{P}$. The program dependences of $\mathcal{P}$ can be computed by applying an arbitrary conservative may-alias algorithm to $\mathcal{P}'$.

We are reducing the program dependence problem, a problem of great practical importance, to the may-alias problem, a problem with many competing solutions. The reduction has the property that as long as the may-alias algorithm is conservative, the dependences computed are also conservative. Furthermore, there is no loss of precision beyond that introduced by the chosen may-alias algorithm. Since the reduction is quite efficient (linear in the program size), it should be possible to integrate our method into compilers, program slicers, and other software tools.

1.1 Main Results and Related Work

The major results in this paper are:

- The unification of the concepts of program dependences and may-aliases. While these concepts are seemingly different, we provide linear reductions between them. Thus may-aliases can be used to find program dependences and program dependences can be used to find may-aliases.
- A solution to the previously open question about the ability to use "store-less" (see [8–10]) may-alias algorithms such as [9, 27] to find dependences. One of the simplest store-less may alias algorithm is due to Gao and Hendren [14]. In [15], the algorithm was generalized to compute dependences by introducing new names. Our solution implies that there is no need to re-develop a new algorithm for every may-alias algorithm. Furthermore, we believe that our reduction is actually simpler to understand than the names introduced in [15] since we are proving program properties instead of modifying a particular approximation algorithm.
- Our limited experience with the reduction that indicates that store-less may-alias algorithms such as [9, 27] yield quite precise dependence information.
- The provision of a method to compare the time and precision of different may-alias algorithms by measuring the number of program dependences reported. This metric is far more interesting than just comparing the number of may-aliases as done in [23, 11, 31, 30, 29].

Our program instrumentation closely resembles the "instrumented semantics" of Horwitz, Pfeiffer, and Reps [18]. They propose to change the program semantics so that the interpreter will carry-around program statements. We instrument the program itself to locally record statement information. Thus, an arbitrary may-alias algorithm can be used on the instrumented program without modification. In contrast, Horwitz, Pfeiffer, and Reps proposed modifications to the specific store based may-alias algorithm of Jones and Muchnick [19] (which is imprecise and doubly exponential in space).

An additional benefit of our shift from semantics instrumentation into a program transformation is that it is easier to understand and to prove correct. For example, Horwitz, Pfeiffer, and Reps, need to show the equivalence between the original and the instrumented program semantics and the instrumentation properties. In contrast, we show that the instrumented program simulates the original program and the properties of the instrumentation.

Finally, program dependences can also be conservatively computed by combining side-effect analysis [4, 7, 22, 6] with reaching definitions [2] or by combining conflict analysis [25] with reaching definitions as done in [24]. However, these techniques are extremely imprecise when recursive data structures are manipulated. The main reason is that it is hard to distinguish between occurrences of the same heap allocated run-time location (see [6, Section 6.2] for an interesting discussion).

1.2   Outline of the rest of this paper

In Section 2.1, we describe the simple Lisp-like language that is used throughout this paper. The main features of this language are its dynamic memory, pointers, and destructive assignment. The use of a Lisp-like language, as opposed to C, simplifies the presentation by avoiding types and the need to handle some of the difficult aspects of C, such as pointer arithmetic and casting.

In Section 2.2, we recall the definition of flow dependences. In Section 2.3 the may-alias problem is defined.

In Section 3 we define the instrumentation. We show that the instrumented program simulates the execution of the original program. We also show that for every run-time location of the original program the instrumented program maintains the history of the statements that last wrote into that location. These two properties allow us to prove that may-aliases in the instrumented program precisely determine the flow dependences in the original program.

In Section 4, we discuss the program dependences computed by some may-alias algorithms on instrumented programs. Finally, Section 5, contains some concluding remarks.

2   Preliminaries

2.1   Programs

Our illustrative language (following [19, 5]) combines an Algol-like language for control flow and functions, Lisp-like memory access, and explicit destructive assignment statements. The atomic statements of this language are shown in Table 1. Memory access paths are represented by ⟨*Access*⟩. Valid expressions are represented by ⟨*Exp*⟩. We allow arbitrary control flow statements using conditions ⟨*Cond*⟩[1]. Additionally all statements are labeled.

---

[1] Arbitrary expressions and procedures can be allowed as long as it is not possible to observe actual run-time locations.

Figure 1 shows a program in our language that is used throughout this paper as a running example. This program reads atoms and builds them into a list by destructively updating the *cdr* of the tail of the list.

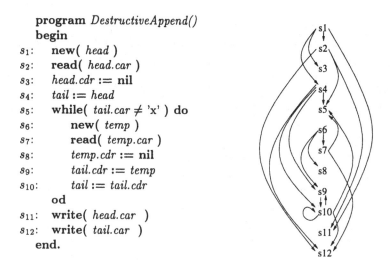

```
program DestructiveAppend()
    begin
s₁:     new( head )
s₂:     read( head.car )
s₃:     head.cdr := nil
s₄:     tail := head
s₅:     while( tail.car ≠ 'x' ) do
s₆:         new( temp )
s₇:         read( temp.car )
s₈:         temp.cdr := nil
s₉:         tail.cdr := temp
s₁₀:        tail := tail.cdr
        od
s₁₁:    write( head.car )
s₁₂:    write( tail.car )
    end.
```

Fig. 1. A program that builds a list by destructively appending elements to *tail* and its flow dependences.

2.2   The Program Dependence Problem

Program dependences can be grouped into flow dependences (def-use), output dependences (def-def), and anti-dependences (use-def) [21, 12]. In this paper, we focus on flow dependences between program statements. The other dependences are easily handled with only minor modifications to our method.

Table 1. An illustrative language with dynamic memory and destructive updates.

$\langle St \rangle ::= s_i : \langle Access \rangle := \langle Exp \rangle$
$\langle St \rangle ::= s_i : \textbf{new}(\langle Access \rangle)$
$\langle St \rangle ::= s_i : \textbf{read}(\langle Access \rangle)$
$\langle St \rangle ::= s_i : \textbf{write}(\langle Exp \rangle)$
$\langle Access \rangle ::= variable \mid \langle Access \rangle . \langle Sel \rangle$
$\langle Exp \rangle ::= \langle Access \rangle \mid atom \mid \textbf{nil}$
$\langle Sel \rangle ::= car \mid cdr$
$\langle Cond \rangle ::= \langle Exp \rangle = \langle Exp \rangle$
$\langle Cond \rangle ::= \langle Exp \rangle \neq \langle Exp \rangle$

Our language allows programs to explicitly modify their store through pointers. Because of this we must phrase the definition of flow dependence in terms of memory *locations* (cons-cells) and not variable names. We shall borrow the following definition for flow dependence:

Definition 1 ([18]). *Program point q has a flow dependence on program point p if p writes into memory location loc that q reads, and there is no intervening write into loc along an execution path by which q is reached from p.*

Figure 1 also shows the flow dependences for the running example program. Notice that s_{11} is flow dependent on only s_1 and s_2, while s_{12} is flow dependent on s_2, s_4, s_7, and s_{10}. This information could be used by slicing tools to find that the loop need not be executed to print *head.car* in s_{11}, or by an instruction scheduler to reschedule s_{11} for anytime after s_2. Also, s_3 and s_8 have no statements dependent on them, making them candidates for elimination. Thus, even in this simple example, knowing the flow dependences would potentially allow several code transformations.

Since determining the exact flow dependences in an arbitrary program is undecidable, approximation algorithms must be used. A flow dependence approximation algorithm is *conservative* if it always finds a superset of the true flow dependences.

2.3 The May-Alias Problem

The may-alias problem is to determine whether two access-paths, at a given program point, could denote the same cons-cell.

Definition 2. *Two access-paths are may-aliases at program point p, if there exists an execution path to program point p where both denote the same cons-cell.*

In the running example program, *head.cdr.cdr* and *tail* are may-aliases at s_6 since before the third iteration these access paths denote the same cons-cell. However, *tail.cdr.cdr* is not a may-alias to *head* since they can never denote the same cons-cell.

Since the may-alias problem is undecidable, approximation algorithms must be used. A may-alias approximation algorithm is *conservative* if it always finds a superset of the true may-aliases.

3 The Instrumentation

In this section the instrumentation is defined. For notational simplicity, $\mathcal{P}$ stands for an arbitrary fixed program, and $\mathcal{P}'$ stands for its instrumented version.

3.1 The Main Idea

The program $\mathcal{P}'$ simulates all the execution sequences of $\mathcal{P}$. Additionally, the "observable" properties of $\mathcal{P}$ are preserved.

Most importantly, $\mathcal{P}'$ records for every variable v, the statement from $\mathcal{P}$ that last wrote into v. This "instrumentation information" is recorded in $v.car$ (while storing the original content of v in $v.cdr$). This "totally static" instrumentation[2] allows program dependences to be recovered by may-alias queries on $\mathcal{P}'$.

More specifically, for every statement in $\mathcal{P}$ there is an associated cons-cell in $\mathcal{P}'$. We refer to these as *statement* cons-cells. Whenever a statement s_i assigns a value into a variable v, $\mathcal{P}'$ allocates a cons-cell that we refer to as an *instrumentation* cons-cell. The *car* of this instrumentation cons-cell always points to the statement cons-cell associated with s_i. Thus there is a flow dependence from a statement p to q: $x := y$ in $\mathcal{P}$ if and only if $y.car$ can point to the statement cons-cell associated with p in $\mathcal{P}'$. Finally, we refer to the *cdr* of the instrumentation cons-cell as the *data* cons-cell. The data cons-cell is inductively defined:

- If s_i is an assignment $s_i\colon v := A$ for an atom, A, then the data cell is A.
- If s_i is an assignment $s_i\colon v := v'$ then the data cell denotes $v'.cdr$.
- If the statement is $s_i\colon new(v)$, then the data cons-cell denotes a newly allocated cons-cell. Thus $\mathcal{P}'$ allocates two cons-cells for this statement.

In general, there is an inductive syntax directed definition of the data cells formally defined by the function *txe* defined in Table 3.

3.2 The Instrumentation of the Running Example

To make this discussion concrete, Figure 2 shows the beginning of the running example program and its instrumented version. Figure 3 shows the stores of both the programs just before the loop (on the input beginning with 'A'). The cons-cells in this figure are labeled for readability only.

The instrumented program begins by allocating one statement cons-cell for each statement in the original program. Then, for every statement in the original program, the instrumented statement block in the instrumented program records the last wrote-statement and the data. The variable _rhs is used as a temporary to store the right-hand side of an assignment to allow the same variable to be used on both sides of an assignment.

Let us now illustrate this for the statements s_1 through s_4 in Figure 3.

- In the original program, after s_1, *head* points a new uninitialized cons-cell, c_1. In the instrumented program, after the block of statements labeled by s_1, *head* points to an instrumentation cons-cell, i_1, *head.car* points to the statement cell for s_1, and *head.cdr* points to c_1'.

---

[2] In contrast to dynamic program slicing algorithms that record similar information using hash functions, e.g., [1].

- In the original program, after s_2, *head.car* points to the atom A. In the instrumented program, after the block of statements labeled by s_2, *head.cdr.car* points to an instrumentation cons-cell, i_2, *head.cdr.car.car* points to the statement cell for s_2, and *head.cdr.car.cdr* points to A.
- In the original program, after s_3, *head.cdr* points to nil. In the instrumented program, after the block of statements labeled by s_3, *head.cdr.cdr* points to an instrumentation cons-cell, i_3, *head.cdr.cdr.car* points to the statement cell for s_3, and *head.cdr.cdr.cdr* points to nil.
- In the original program, after s_4, *tail* points to the cons-cell c_1. In the instrumented program, after the block of statements labeled by s_4, *tail* points to an instrumentation cons-cell, i_4, *tail.car* points to the statement cell for s_4, and *tail.cdr* points to c_1'. Notice how the sharing of the r-values of *head* and *tail* is preserved by the transformation.

3.3 A Formal Definition of the Instrumentation

Formally, we define the instrumentation as follows:

Definition 3. *Let P be a program in the form defined in Table 1. Let $s_1, s_2, \ldots, s_n$ be the statement labels in P. The instrumented program P' is obtained from P starting with a prolog of the form* **new**(ps_i) *where $i = 1, 2 \ldots n$. After the prolog, we rewrite P according to the translation rules shown in Table 2 and Table 3.*

Example 4. In the running example program (Figure 2), in P, s_{11} writes *head.car* and in P', s_{11} writes *head.cdr.car.cdr*. This follows from:
$txe(head.car) = txa(head.car).cdr = txa(head).cdr.car.cdr = head.cdr.car.cdr$

3.4 Properties of the Instrumentation

In this section we show that the instrumentation has reduced the flow dependence problem to the may-alias problem. First the simulation of P by P' is shown in the Simulation Theorem. This implies that the instrumentation does not introduce any imprecision into the flow dependence analysis. We also show the Last Wrote Lemma which states that the instrumentation maintains the needed invariants. Because of the Simulation Theorem, and the Last Wrote Lemma, we are able to conclude that:

1. exactly all the flow dependences in P are found using a may-alias oracle on P'.
2. using any conservative may-alias algorithm on P' always results in conservative flow dependences for P.

Intuitively, by simulation, we mean that at every label of P and P', all the "observable properties" are preserved in P', given the same input. In our case, observable properties are:

- r-values printed by the write statements

```
program DestructiveAppend()              program InstrumentedDestructiveAppend()
begin                                    begin
                                             new( psᵢ ) ∀i ∈ {1, 2, ..., 12}
s₁:   new( head )                        s₁:   new( head )
                                               head.car := ps₁
                                               new( head.cdr )
s₂:   read( head.car )                   s₂:   new( head.cdr.car )
                                               head.cdr.car.car := ps₂
                                               read( head.cdr.car.cdr)
s₃:   head.cdr := nil                    s₃:   _rhs := nil
                                               new( head.cdr.cdr )
                                               head.cdr.cdr.car := ps₃
                                               head.cdr.cdr.cdr := _rhs
s₄:   tail := head                       s₄:   _rhs := head.cdr
                                               new( tail )
                                               tail.car := ps₄
                                               tail.cdr := _rhs
s₅:   while( tail.car ≠ 'x' ) do         s₅:   while( tail.cdr.car.cdr ≠ 'x' ) do
```

Fig. 2. The beginning of the example program and its corresponding instrumented program.

Table 2. The translation rules that define the instrumentation excluding the prolog. For simplicity, every assignment allocates a new instrumentation cons-cell. The variable _rhs is used as a temporary to store the right-hand side of an assignment to allow the same variable to be used on both sides of an assignment.

$s_i: \langle Access\rangle := \langle Exp\rangle \implies$	$s_i:$ _rhs $:= txe(\langle Exp\rangle)$
	$\mathbf{new}(txa(\langle Access\rangle))$
	$txa(\langle Access\rangle).car := ps_i$
	$txa(\langle Access\rangle).cdr := $ _rhs
$s_i: \mathbf{new}(\langle Access\rangle) \implies$	$s_i: \mathbf{new}(txa(\langle Access\rangle))$
	$txa(\langle Access\rangle).car := ps_i$
	$\mathbf{new}(txa(\langle Access\rangle).cdr)$
$s_i: \mathbf{read}(\langle Access\rangle) \implies$	$s_i: \mathbf{new}(txa(\langle Access\rangle))$
	$txa(\langle Access\rangle).car := ps_i$
	$\mathbf{read}(txa(\langle Access\rangle).cdr)$
$s_i: \mathbf{write}(\langle Exp\rangle) \implies$	$s_i: \mathbf{write}(txa(\langle Exp\rangle))$
$\langle Exp_1\rangle = \langle Exp_2\rangle \implies$	$txe(\langle Exp_1\rangle) = txe(\langle Exp_2\rangle)$
$\langle Exp_1\rangle \neq \langle Exp_2\rangle \implies$	$txe(\langle Exp_1\rangle) \neq txe(\langle Exp_2\rangle)$

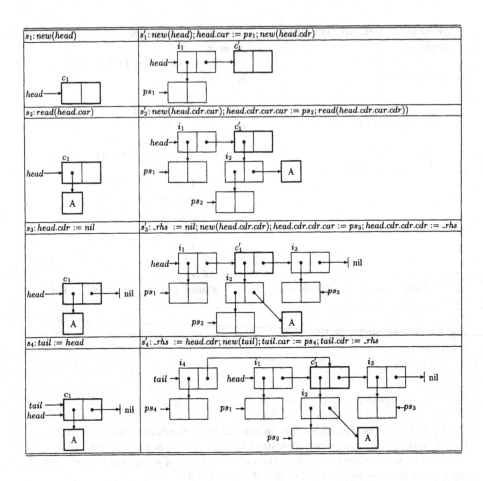

Fig. 3. The store of the original and the instrumented running example programs just before the loop on an input list starting with 'A'. For visual clarity, statement cons-cells not pointed to by an instrumentation cons-cell are not shown. Also, cons-cells are labeled and highlighted to show the correspondence between the stores of the original and instrumented programs.

Table 3. The function *txa* which maps an access path in the original program into the corresponding access path in the instrumented program. The function *txe* maps an expression into the corresponding expression in the instrumented program.

$txa(variable)$	$= variable$
$txa(\langle Access\rangle.\langle Sel\rangle)$	$= txa(\langle Access\rangle).cdr.\langle Sel\rangle$
$txe(\langle Access\rangle)$	$= txa(\langle Access\rangle).cdr$
$txe(atom)$	$= atom$
$txe(nil)$	$= nil$

– equalities of r-values

In particular, the execution sequences of $\mathcal{P}$ and $\mathcal{P}'$ at every label are the same. This discussion motivates the following definition:

Definition 5. *Let S be an arbitrary sequence of statement labels in $\mathcal{P}$ e_1, e_2 be expressions, and I be an input vector. We denote by $I, S \overset{\mathcal{P}}{\models} e_1 = e_2$ the fact that the input I causes S to be executed in $\mathcal{P}$, and in the store after S, the r-values of e_1 and e_2 are equal.*

Example 6. In the running example, *head.cdr.cdr* and *tail* denote the same cons-cell before the third iteration for inputs lengths of four or more. Therefore,

$$I, [s_1, s_2, s_3, s_4, s_5]([s_6, s_7, s_8, s_9, s_{10}])^2 \overset{\mathcal{P}}{\models} head.cdr.cdr = tail$$

Theorem 7. (Simulation Theorem) *Given input I, expressions e_1 and e_2, and sequence of statement labels S:*

$$I, S \overset{\mathcal{P}}{\models} e_1 = e_2 \iff I, S \overset{\mathcal{P}'}{\models} txe(e_1) = txe(e_2)$$

Example 8. In the running example, before the first iteration, in the last box of Figure 3, *head* and *tail* denote the same cons-cell and *head.cdr* and *tail.cdr* denote the same cons-cell. Also, in the instrumented program, *head.cdr.cdr.cdr.cdr* and *tail.cdr* denote the same cons-cell before the third iteration for inputs of length four or more. Therefore, as expected from Example 6,

$$I, [s_1, s_2, s_3, s_4, s_5]([s_6, s_7, s_8, s_9, s_{10}])^2 \overset{\mathcal{P}'}{\models} txe(head.cdr.cdr) = txe(tail)$$

The utility of the instrumentation is captured in the following lemma.

Lemma 9. (Last Wrote Lemma) *Given input I, sequence of statement labels S, and an access path a, the input I leads to the execution of S in $\mathcal{P}$ in which the last statement that wrote into a is s_i if and only if*

$$I, S \overset{\mathcal{P}'}{\models} txa(a).car = ps_i.$$

Example 10. In the running example, before the first iteration, in the last box of Figure 3, we have $I, [s_1, s_2, s_3, s_4, s_5] \overset{\mathcal{P}'}{\models} txa(head).car = ps_1$ since s_1 is the statement that last wrote into *head*. Also, for input list $I = ['A', 'x']$, we have: $I, [s_1, s_2, s_3, s_4, s_5, s_{11}, s_{12}] \overset{\mathcal{P}'}{\models} txa(tail.car).car = ps_2$ since for such input s_2 last wrote into *tail.car* (through the assignment to *head.car*).

A single statement in our language can read from many memory locations. For example, in the running example program, statement s_5 reads from *tail* and *tail.car*. The complete read-sets for the statements in our language are shown in Tables 4 and 5.

We are now able to state the main result.

Table 4. Read-sets for the statements in our language.

$s_i: \langle Access \rangle := \langle Exp \rangle$	$rsa(\langle Access \rangle) \cup rse(\langle Exp \rangle)$
$s_i: \mathbf{new}(\langle Access \rangle)$	$rsa(\langle Access \rangle)$
$s_i: \mathbf{read}(\langle Access \rangle)$	$rse(\langle Access \rangle)$
$s_i: \mathbf{write}(\langle Exp \rangle)$	$rse(\langle Exp \rangle)$
$\langle Exp_1 \rangle = \langle Exp_2 \rangle$	$rse(\langle Exp_1 \rangle) \cup rse(\langle Exp_2 \rangle)$
$\langle Exp_1 \rangle \neq \langle Exp_2 \rangle$	$rse(\langle Exp_1 \rangle) \cup rse(\langle Exp_2 \rangle)$

Table 5. An inductive definition of rsa, the read-set for access-paths, and rse, the read-set for expressions.

$rsa(variable)$	$= \emptyset$
$rsa(\langle Access \rangle.\langle Sel \rangle)$	$= rsa(\langle Access \rangle) \cup \{\langle Access \rangle\}$
$rse(variable)$	$= \{variable\}$
$rse(\langle Access \rangle.\langle Sel \rangle)$	$= rse(\langle Access \rangle) \cup \{\langle Access \rangle.\langle Sel \rangle\}$
$rse(atom)$	$= \emptyset$
$rse(nil)$	$= \emptyset$

Theorem 11. (Flow Dependence Reduction) *Given program $\mathcal{P}$, its instrumented version $\mathcal{P}'$, and any two statement labels p and q. There is a flow dependence from p to q (in $\mathcal{P}$) if and only if there exists an access path, a, in the read-set of q, s.t. ps_p is a may-alias of $txa(a).car$ at q in $\mathcal{P}'$.*

Example 12. To find the flow dependences of s_5 in the running example:
$s_5 : while(tail.car \neq `x')$
First Tables 4 and 5 are used to determine the read-set of s_5:
$rse(\langle Exp_1 \rangle) \cup rse(\langle Exp_2 \rangle) = rse(tail.car) \cup rse(`x') = rse(tail) \cup \{tail.car\} \cup \emptyset$
$$= \{tail\} \cup \{tail.car\} = \{tail, tail.car\}.$$
Then $txa(a).car$ is calculated for each a in the read-set:
$txa(tail).car = tail.car$
$txa(tail.car).car = txa(tail).cdr.car.car = tail.cdr.car.car$
Next the may-aliases to $tail.car$ and $tail.cdr.car.car$ are calculated by any may-aliases algorithm. Finally s_5 is flow dependent on the statements associated with the statement cons-cells that are among the may-aliases found to $tail.car$ and $tail.cdr.car.car$.

The Read-Sets and May-Aliases for the running example are summarized in Table 6.

From a complexity viewpoint our method can be very inexpensive. The program transformation time and space are linear in the size of the original program. In applying Theorem 11 the number of times the may-alias algorithm is invoked is also linear in the size of the original program, or more specifically, proportional

Table 6. Flow dependence analysis of the running example using a may-alias oracle.

Stmt	Read-Set	May-Aliases
s_1	$\emptyset$	$\emptyset$
s_2	$\{head\}$	$\{(head.car, ps_1)\}$
s_3	$\{head\}$	$\{(head.car, ps_1)\}$
s_4	$\{head\}$	$\{(head.car, ps_1)\}$
s_5	$\{tail, tail.car\}$	$\{(tail.car, ps_4), (tail.car, ps_{10}),$ $(tail.cdr.car.car, ps_2), (tail.cdr.car.car, ps_7)\}$
s_6	$\emptyset$	$\emptyset$
s_7	$\{temp\}$	$\{(temp.car, ps_6)\}$
s_8	$\{temp\}$	$\{(temp.car, ps_6)\}$
s_9	$\{tail, temp\}$	$\{(tail.car, ps_4), (tail.car, ps_{10}), (temp.car, ps_6)\}$
s_{10}	$\{tail, tail.cdr\}$	$\{(tail.car, ps_4), (tail.car, ps_{10}), (tail.cdr.cdr.car, ps_9)\}$
s_{11}	$\{head, head.car\}$	$\{(head.car, ps_1), (head.cdr.car.car, ps_2)\}$
s_{12}	$\{tail, tail.car\}$	$\{(tail.car, ps_4), (tail.car, ps_{10}),$ $(tail.cdr.car.car, ps_2), (tail.cdr.car.car, ps_7)\}$

to the size of the read-sets. It is most likely that the complexity of the may-alias algorithm itself is the dominant cost.

4 Plug and Play

An important corollary of Theorem 11 is that an arbitrary conservative may-alias algorithm on $\mathcal{P}'$ yields a conservative solution to the flow dependence problem on $\mathcal{P}$. Since existing may-alias algorithms often yield results which are difficult to compare, it is instructive to consider the flow dependences computed by various algorithms on the running example program.

- The algorithm of [9] yields the may-aliases shown in column 3 of Table 6. Therefore, on this program, this algorithm yields the exact flow dependences shown in Figure 1.
- The more efficient may-alias algorithms of [23, 14, 30, 29] are useful to find flow dependences in programs with disjoint data structures. However, in programs with recursive data structures such as the running example, they normally yield many superfluous may-aliases leading to superfluous flow dependences. For example, [23] is not able to identify that *tail* points to an acyclic list. Therefore, it yields that *head.car* and ps_7 are may-aliases at s_{11}. Therefore, it will conclude that the value of *head.car* read at s_{11} may be written inside the loop (at statement s_7).
- The algorithm of [27] finds, in addition to the correct dependences, superfluous flow dependences in the running example. For example, it finds that s_5 has a flow dependence on s_8. This inaccuracy is attributable to the anonymous nature of the second cons-cell allocated with each new statement. There are two possible ways to remedy this inaccuracy:

- Modify the algorithm so that it is 2-bounded, i.e., also keeps track of *car* and *cdr* fields of variables. Indeed, this may be an adequate solution for general k-bounded approaches, e.g., [19] by increasing k to $2k$.
- Modify the transformation to assign unique names to these cons-cells. We have implemented this solution, and tested it using the PAG [3] implementation of the [27] algorithm[3] and found exactly all the flow dependences in the running example.

5 Conclusions

In this paper, we showed that may-alias algorithms can be used, without any modification, to compute program dependences. We are hoping that this will lead to more research in finding practical may-alias algorithms to compute good approximations for flow dependences.

For simplicity, we did not optimize the memory usage of the instrumented program. In particular, for every executed instance of a statement in the original program that writes to the store, the instrumented program creates a new instrumentation cons-cell. This extra memory usage is harmless to may-alias algorithms (for some algorithms it can even improve the accuracy of the analysis, e.g., [5]). In cases where the instrumented program is intended to be executed, it is possible to drastically reduce the memory usage through cons-cell reuse.

Finally, it is worthwhile to note that flow dependences can be also used to find may-aliases. Therefore, may-aliases are necessary in order to compute flow dependences. For example, Figure 4 contains a program fragment that provides the instrumentation to "check" if two program variables v_1 and v_2 are may aliases at program point p. This instrumentation preserves the meaning of the original program and has the property that v_1 and v_2 are may-aliases at p if and only if s_2 has a flow dependence on s_1.

p: **if** $v_1 \neq nil$ **then**
    s_1: $v_1.cdr := v_1.cdr$ **fi**
    if $v_2 \neq nil$ **then**
        s_2: $write(v_2.cdr)$ **fi**

Fig. 4. A program fragment such that v_1 and v_2 are may-aliases at p if and only if s_2 has a flow dependence on s_1.

Acknowledgments

We are grateful for the helpful comments of Thomas Ball, Michael Benedikt, Thomas Reps, and Reinhard Wilhelm for their comments that led to substantial

---

[3] On a SPARCstation 20, PAG used 0.53 seconds of cpu time.

improvements of this paper. We also would like to thank Martin Alt and Florian Martin for PAG, and their PAG implementation of [27] for a C subset.

References

1. H. Agrawal and J.R. Horgan. Dynamic program slicing. In *SIGPLAN Conference on Programming Languages Design and Implementation*, volume 25 of *ACM SIGPLAN Notices*, pages 246–256, White Plains, New York, June 1990.

2. A.V. Aho, R. Sethi, and J.D. Ullman. *Compilers: Principles, Techniques and Tools*. Addison-Wesley, 1985.

3. M. Alt and F. Martin. Generation of efficient interprocedural analyzers with PAG. In *SAS'95, Static Analysis*, number 983 in Lecture Notes in Computer Science, pages 33–50. Springer-Verlag, 1995.

4. J.P. Banning. An efficient way to find the side effects of procedure calls and the aliases of variables. In *ACM Symposium on Principles of Programming Languages*, pages 29–41, New York, NY, 1979. ACM Press.

5. D.R. Chase, M. Wegman, and F. Zadeck. Analysis of pointers and structures. In *SIGPLAN Conference on Programming Languages Design and Implementation*, pages 296–310, New York, NY, 1990. ACM Press.

6. J.D. Choi, M. Burke, and P. Carini. Efficient flow-sensitive interprocedural computation of pointer-induced aliases and side-effects. In *ACM Symposium on Principles of Programming Languages*, pages 232–245, New York, NY, 1993. ACM Press.

7. K.D. Cooper and K. Kennedy. Interprocedural side-effect analysis in linear time. In *SIGPLAN Conference on Programming Languages Design and Implementation*, pages 57–66, New York, NY, 1988. ACM Press.

8. A. Deutsch. A storeless model for aliasing and its abstractions using finite representations of right-regular equivalence relations. In *IEEE International Conference on Computer Languages*, pages 2–13, Washington, DC, 1992. IEEE Press.

9. A. Deutsch. Interprocedural may-alias analysis for pointers: Beyond k-limiting. In *SIGPLAN Conference on Programming Languages Design and Implementation*, pages 230–241, New York, NY, 1994. ACM Press.

10. A. Deutsch. Semantic models and abstract interpretation for inductive data structures and pointers. In *Proc. of ACM Symposium on Partial Evaluation and Semantics-Based Program Manipulation, PEPM'95*, pages 226–228, New York, NY, June 1995. ACM Press.

11. M. Emami, R. Ghiya, and L. Hendren. Context-sensitive interprocedural points-to analysis in the presence of function pointers. In *SIGPLAN Conference on Programming Languages Design and Implementation*, New York, NY, 1994. ACM Press.

12. J. Ferrante, K. Ottenstein, and J. Warren. The program dependence graph and its use in optimization. *ACM Transactions on Programming Languages and Systems*, 3(9):319–349, 1987.

13. R. Ghiya and L.J. Hendren. Is it a tree, a dag, or a cyclic graph? In *ACM Symposium on Principles of Programming Languages*, New York, NY, January 1996. ACM Press.

14. R. Ghiya and L.J. Hendren. Connection analysis: A practical interprocedural heap analysis for c. In *Proc. of the 8th Intl. Work. on Languages and Compilers for Parallel Computing*, number 1033 in Lecture Notes in Computer Science, pages 515–534, Columbus, Ohio, August 1995. Springer-Verlag.

15. R. Ghiya and L.J. Hendren. Putting pointer analysis to work. In *ACM Symposium on Principles of Programming Languages*. ACM, New York, January 1998.

16. L. Hendren. *Parallelizing Programs with Recursive Data Structures*. PhD thesis, Cornell University, Ithaca, N.Y., Jan 1990.

17. L. Hendren and A. Nicolau. Parallelizing programs with recursive data structures. *IEEE Transactions on Parallel and Distributed Systems*, 1(1):35–47, January 1990.

18. S. Horwitz, P. Pfeiffer, and T. Reps. Dependence analysis for pointer variables. In *SIGPLAN Conference on Programming Languages Design and Implementation*, volume 24 of *ACM SIGPLAN Notices*, pages 28–40, Portland, Oregon, June 1989. ACM Press.

19. N.D. Jones and S.S. Muchnick. Flow analysis and optimization of Lisp-like structures. In S.S. Muchnick and N.D. Jones, editors, *Program Flow Analysis: Theory and Applications*, chapter 4, pages 102–131. Prentice-Hall, Englewood Cliffs, NJ, 1981.

20. N.D. Jones and S.S. Muchnick. A flexible approach to interprocedural data flow analysis and programs with recursive data structures. In *ACM Symposium on Principles of Programming Languages*, pages 66–74, New York, NY, 1982. ACM Press.

21. D.J. Kuck, R.H. Kuhn, B. Leasure, D.A. Padua, and M. Wolfe. Dependence graphs and compiler optimizations. In *ACM Symposium on Principles of Programming Languages*, pages 207–218, New York, NY, 1981. ACM Press.

22. W. Land, B.G. Ryder, and S. Zhang. Interprocedural modification side effect analysis with pointer aliasing. In *Proc. of the ACM SIGPLAN '93 Conf. on Programming Language Design and Implementation*, pages 56–67, 1993.

23. W. Landi and B.G. Ryder. Pointer induced aliasing: A problem classification. In *ACM Symposium on Principles of Programming Languages*, pages 93–103, New York, NY, January 1991. ACM Press.

24. J.R. Larus. Refining and classifying data dependences. Unpublished extended abstract, Berkeley, CA, November 1988.

25. J.R. Larus and P.N. Hilfinger. Detecting conflicts between structure accesses. In *SIGPLAN Conference on Programming Languages Design and Implementation*, pages 21–34, New York, NY, 1988. ACM Press.

26. K.J. Ottenstein and L.M. Ottenstein. The program dependence graph in a software development environment. In *Proceedings of the ACM SIGSOFT/SIGPLAN Software Engineering Symposium on Practical Software Development Environments*, pages 177–184, New York, NY, 1984. ACM Press.

27. M. Sagiv, T. Reps, and R. Wilhelm. Solving shape-analysis problems in languages with destructive updating. In *ACM Symposium on Principles of Programming Languages*, New York, NY, January 1996. ACM Press.

28. M. Sagiv, T. Reps, and R. Wilhelm. Solving shape-analysis problems in languages with destructive updating. *ACM Transactions on Programming Languages and Systems*, 1997. To Appear.

29. M. Shapiro and S. Horwitz. Fast and accurate flow-insensitive points-to analysis. In *ACM Symposium on Principles of Programming Languages*, 1997.

30. B. Steengaard. Points-to analysis in linear time. In *ACM Symposium on Principles of Programming Languages*. ACM, New York, January 1996.

31. R.P. Willson and M.S. Lam. Efficient context-sensitive pointer analysis for c programs. In *SIGPLAN Conference on Programming Languages Design and Implementation*, pages 1–12, La Jolla, CA, June 18-21 1995. ACM Press.

A Complete Declarative Debugger
of Missing Answers

Salvatore Ruggieri

Dipartimento di Informatica, Università di Pisa
Corso Italia 40, 56125 Pisa, Italy
e-mail: `ruggieri@di.unipi.it`

Abstract. We propose two declarative debuggers of missing answers with respect to C- and S-semantics. The debuggers are proved correct for every logic program. Moreover, they are complete and terminating with respect to a large class of programs, namely acceptable logic programs. The debuggers enhance existing proposals, which suffer from a problem due to the implementation of negation as failure. The proposed solution exploits decision procedures for C- and S-semantics introduced in [9].

Keywords. Logic programming, Declarative Debugging, Error Diagnosis, Missing Answers, Acceptable Logic Programs.

1   Introduction

Declarative debugging is concerned with finding errors that cause anomalies during the execution of a program starting from some information on the intended semantics of the program. In logic programming systems, a query which is valid in the intended meaning of a program but that is not in its actual semantics is an anomaly called *missing answer*. A missing answer originates from a "failure" in the construction of a proof tree for a valid query. The reason of such a failure is the presence of *uncovered atoms*, i.e. of atoms A in the intended interpretation of the program, for which there is no clause instance whose head is A and whose body is true in the intended interpretation. In other words, there is no immediate justification in the program in order to deduce A.

The role of a declarative debugger is to find out uncovered atoms starting from missing answers, which are usually detected during the testing phase, and from the intended semantics of the program. In this paper, we concentrate on the C-semantics of Falaschi et al. [5] (or least term model semantics of Clark [3]) and on the S-semantics of Falaschi et al. [6].

Many debuggers in the literature find uncovered atoms starting from missing answers that have a *finitely failed SLD-tree*. As we will point out, the assumption that missing answers have finitely failed SLD-trees is restrictive in some cases, and it is due to a well-known limitation of the *negation as failure* rule. We show that restriction in the case of Shapiro's debugger [10] [8, Debugger S.I].

In this paper, we propose two declarative debuggers of missing answers for C- and S-semantics that are correct for any program, and complete and terminating for a large class of logic programs, namely acceptable programs [2]. The implementations of the debuggers rely on decidability procedures for C- and S-semantics which are adapted from [9].

Compared with Shapiro's approach, the debugger for C-semantics relaxes the assumption that the missing answers in input have finitely failed SLD-trees. In addition, we show that a smaller search space is considered.

The debugger for S-semantics is derived by applying the insights underlying the construction of that for C-semantics to the theory of S-semantics. The only approach on debugging of missing answers with respect to S-semantics is due to Comini et al. [4]. They introduce a method for finding all uncovered atoms starting from the intended interpretation of an acceptable program. However, their approach is effective iff the intended interpretation is a finite set, whilst we make a weaker assumption.

Preliminaries We use in this paper the standard notation of Apt [1], when not specified otherwise. In particular, we use queries instead of goals. We denote by L the underlying language a program is defined on. $Atom_L$ denotes the set of atoms on L, B_L the Herbrand base on L. Usually, one considers $L = L_P$. $ground_L(P)$ denotes the set of ground instances of clauses from P. LD-resolution is SLD-resolution together the leftmost selection rule. An atom is called *pure* if it is of the form $p(x_1, \ldots, x_n)$ where $x_1, \ldots, x_n$ are different variables. N is the set of natural numbers. For a ground term t, $ll(t) = ll(t1) + 1$ if $t = [t2|t1]$ and $ll(t) = 0$ otherwise, i.e. ll is the list-length function.

2   Program Semantics and Missing Answers

Several declarative semantics have been considered as alternatives to the standard least Herbrand model. We focus on two of them, namely C-semantics of Falaschi et al. [5] (also known as the least term model of Clark [3]) and S-semantics of Falaschi et al. [6].

Definition 1. For a logic program P we define

$$C(P) = \{ A \in Atom_L \mid P \models A \}$$
$$S(P) = \{ A \in Atom_L \mid A \text{ is a computed instance of a pure atom } \}. \qquad \square$$

By correctness of SLD-resolution, we observe that $S(P) \subseteq C(P)$. To each semantics is associated a continuous *immediate consequence operator*. For a program P, the least fixpoint of T_P^C, $C(P)$, and the upward ordinal closure $T_P^C \uparrow \omega$ coincide [5]. Similarly, the least fixpoint of T_P^S, $S(P)$, and the upward ordinal closure $T_P^S \uparrow \omega$ coincide [6].

Definition 2. For a logic program P we define the following functions from sets of atoms into set of atoms:

$$T_P^C(I) = \{ \ A\theta \in Atom_L \mid \exists \ A \leftarrow B_1, \dots, B_n \ \in P,$$
$$\{B_1\theta, \dots, B_n\theta\} \subseteq I \ \}$$
$$T_P^S(I) = \{ \ A\theta \in Atom_L \mid \exists \ A \leftarrow B_1, \dots, B_n \ \in P,$$
$$B_1', \dots, B_n' \ \text{variants of atoms in } I \ \text{and renamed apart}$$
$$\exists \ \theta = mgu((B_1, \dots, B_n), (B_1', \dots, B_n')) \ \} \qquad \square$$

An intended interpretation of a program w.r.t. a semantics is a set of atoms which, in the intentions of the programmer, is supposed to be the actual semantics of the program. Starting points of the debugging analysis are *missing answers*.

Definition 3. We say that a query is in a set of atoms if every atom of the query is in the set. Let $\mathcal{F}$ be the $\mathcal{C}$- or $\mathcal{S}$-semantics, and $\mathcal{I}$ be the intended interpretation of a program P w.r.t. $\mathcal{F}$. A *missing answer* w.r.t. $\mathcal{F}$ is any query which is in $\mathcal{I}$ but that is not in $\mathcal{F}(P)$. $\qquad \square$

Missing answer are caused by *uncovered atoms*, i.e. atoms valid in the intended meaning of a program that have no immediate justification in the program.

Definition 4. An atom A is uncovered if $A \in \mathcal{I}$ and $A \notin T_P^{\mathcal{F}}(\mathcal{I})$. $\qquad \square$

3 Shapiro's Debugger

Consider the semantics of correct instances of logic programs, i.e. $\mathcal{C}$-semantics. A query Q which is supposed to be a logical consequence of the program, "fails" if it is not. However, by saying that a query Q "fails" it is often meant Q *finitely fails*. This stronger assumptions is due a well-known limitation of the *negation as failure* rule, and it affects several declarative debuggers in the literature. Let us consider the Shapiro's debugger [10] [8, Debugger S.I] as an example. Let P be the program under analysis.

```
miss([A | B], Goal) ←
    not( call(A) ),
    miss(A, Goal).
miss([A | B], Goal) ←
    call(A),
    miss(B, Goal).
miss(A, Goal) ←
    user_pred(A),
    clause(A, B),
    valid(B),
    miss(B, Goal).
miss(A, A) ←
```

```
user_pred(A),
not(
  (clause(A, B),
  valid(B))
).
```

clause(A, [B_1, ..., B_n]).   *for every $A \leftarrow B_1, \ldots, B_n \in P$*
augmented by P.

Program 1

user_pred characterizes user-defined predicates, and it is a collection of facts user_pred(p(X1, ..., Xn)) for every predicate symbol p of arity n. valid is an oracle defining the intended meaning of P. It may be implemented either by queries to the programmer or by using some specification of the program. Consider now the program:

```
s.
p(X) ←q(Y), r(Y,X).
q(a).
% q(b). % missing
r(a, c).
r(b, X).
```

Program 2

Shapiro's debugger correctly works when the missing answer in input has a finitely failed tree. On the other hand, the query p(X),s is a missing answer, since p(X) is not a logical consequence of the program, but there is no finitely failed tree, since there is a successful derivation that instantiates X to c. A call miss([p(X),s], A) to the Shapiro's debugger fails to return that q(b) is uncovered. The need for the hypothesis of finite failure lies in the use of negation in clauses such as:

miss([A | B], Goal) ←not(call(A)), miss(A, Goal).

where the debugger tries to prove not(call(A)). Due to well-known limitations of the negation as failure rule, not(call(A)) succeeds if $P \models \neg \exists A$, i.e. if there is a finitely-failed SLD-tree. Instead, the intended use of not(call(A)) is to prove $P \models \neg \forall A$, i.e. that A is not a logical consequence of P. A form of completeness has been shown for Ferrand's debugger [7], [8, Debugger F.1], which is obtained from *Program 1* by removing the literals not(call(A)) and call(A). As an example, the uncovered atom q(b) of *Program 2* is detected by Ferrand's debugger. However, Ferrand's approach differs from ours in the fact that it considers *impossible* atoms instead of uncovered atoms. A is impossible if no instance of A is uncovered. Let us consider the following incorrect EAppend version of the Append program:

```
append( [], Xs, Xs ).
append( [X|Xs], Ys, [X|Zs] ) ←
  append( Ys, Ys, Zs ). % should be append(Xs, Ys, Zs).
```

Program 3

The query $Q = $ append([X], Ys, [X|Ys]) is a missing answer, since it is in the intended interpretation, and it is not a logical consequence of EAppend. However, Shapiro's debugger is not able to find out that Q is an uncovered atom, since Q has not a finitely failed tree. On the other hand, Ferrand's debugger does not show that Q is uncovered, due to the fact that there exists an instance of Q which is covered, namely append([X], [], [X]), and then Q is not an impossible atom. Finally, it is worth noting that both debuggers ask the oracle for a valid instance of append(Ys, Ys, Ys). Consequently, the call miss(append([], [], []), Goal) is made, where append([], [], []) is not a missing answer. In general, unnecessary questions are addressed to the oracle, in the sense that the search space includes queries that are not missing answers, and then cannot lead to an uncovered atom.

4 Acceptable programs

In this section, we introduce acceptable logic programs, a well-known large class for which we provide a decision procedure for C- and S-semantics.

4.1 The Framework

First, we recall the definition of level mappings [2].

Definition 5. A *level mapping* is a function $| \, | : B_L \to N$ of ground atoms to natural numbers. For $A \in B_L$, $| \, A \, |$ is called the level of A. □

We are now in the position to recall the definition of acceptable logic programs, introduced by Apt and Pedreschi [2]. Intuitively, the definition of acceptability requires that for every clause, the level of the head of any of its ground instances is greater than the level of each atom in the body which might be selected further in a LD-derivation.

Definition 6. A program P is *acceptable by* $| \, | : B_L \to N$ *and a Herbrand interpretation I iff* I is a model of P, and for every $A \leftarrow B_1, \ldots, B_n$ in $ground_L(P)$:

$$\text{for } i \in [1, n] \quad I \models B_1, \ldots, B_{i-1} \quad implies \quad | \, A \, | \; > | \, B_i \, | .$$

P is *acceptable* if it is acceptable by some $| \, |$ and I. □

Consider the following program PREORDER for preorder traversals of binary trees.

```
(p1)    preorder(nil, [] ).
(p2)    preorder(leaf(X), [X] ).
(p3)    preorder(tree(X, Left, Right), Ls) ←
            preorder(Left, As),
            preorder(Right, Bs),
            append([X|As], Bs, Ls).
```

```
append( [], Xs, Xs ).
append( [X|Xs], Ys, [X|Zs] ) ←
    append( Xs, Ys, Zs ).
```

Program 4

PREORDER is acceptable by $|\ |$ and I, where

$$|\texttt{preorder}(t,\ ls)| = nodes(t) + 1$$
$$|\texttt{append}(xs,\ ys,\ zs)| = ll(xs)$$
$$I = \{\ \texttt{append}(xs,\ ys,\ zs)\ |\ ll(zs) = ll(xs) + ll(ys)\ \} \cup$$
$$\cup\ \{\ \texttt{preorder}(t,\ ls)\ |\ ll(ls) = nodes(t)\ \}$$

where $nodes(t)$ is 1 if $t = \texttt{leaf}(s)$; it is $1 + nodes(l) + nodes(r)$ if $t = \texttt{tree}(s, l, r)$; and it is 0 otherwise.

Suppose now that the variable X in clause *(p2)* has been erroneously typed in lower case, and let PREORDER$'$ be PREORDER where *(p2)* is replaced by:

(p2')   `preorder(leaf(x), [x] ).`

PREORDER$'$ is still acceptable by the same $|\ |$ and I. Note that `preorder(tree(E, leaf(X), leaf(Y)), [E, X, Y])` is a missing answer w.r.t. C and S-semantics. However, the query has no finitely failed SLD-tree. In particular, Shapiro's debugger is not able to find an uncovered atom starting from it. Other examples of acceptable programs are *Program 2* and *Program 3*.

4.2   Decision Procedures

We sum up the decidability properties of acceptable programs we are interested in by means of the following Lemma reported from [9].

Theorem 7. *Let P be an acceptable program.*
Every LD-derivation for P and any ground query (in any language) is finite.
Moreover, $C(P)$ and $S(P)$ are decidable sets.   □

The decision procedure for C- and S-semantics will be the crucial in the debugging approach of this paper. Interestingly, they have a natural implementation in the logic programming paradigm itself as Prolog meta-programs. The procedures are provided in [9] for observable decidability. Here we specialize them for semantics decidability.

We assume that the predicate `freeze` introduced in [12, Section 10.3] is available. A call to `freeze(A,B)` replaces every variable of A with new distinct constants to obtain B. Unfortunately, as described by Sterling and Shapiro, `freeze` is not present in existing Prolog implementations. In fact, in [9] `freeze` is approximated by a predicate `constants` that replaces every variable in Q by new distinct constants. The approximation works until a fixed maximum number of new constants is reached, and the results are parametric to that number. Here, we abstract away from such a parameterization and assume that `freeze` and its dual `melt` are available. Given a term B, `melt(`B`, A)` replaces every constants of B introduced by freezing some term by the original variable to obtain A. For instance `freeze(p(X), Y)` succeeds by instantiating Y to `p(`a_X`)`, where a_X is a fresh constant representing the frozen variable X. The following is the decision procedure for S-semantics.

```
in_s(A) ←
    freeze(A, A1),
    pure(A, B),
    demo([A1],[B]),
    variants(A, B).

demo([], []).

demo([A|As], [B|Bs]) ←
    clause(A, Ls, Id),
    demo(Ls, L1s),
    demo(As, Bs),
    clause(B, L1s, Id).

pure(p(X₁, ..., Xₙ), p(Y₁, ..., Yₙ)).
```
for every predicate symbol p *of arity* n

```
clause(A, [B₁, ..., Bₙ], k).
```
for every $C_k = A \leftarrow B_1,\ldots,B_n \in P$

augmented by the definition of `variants` [12, Program 11.7].

Program 5

`variants(A, A1)` is an extra-logical predicate that succeeds iff A and $A1$ are variants. `pure(A, B)` computes a pure atom for the predicate symbol of a given atom. `clause(`A`, [B], `k`)` models the clause $C_k = A \leftarrow \mathbf{B}$ of P. A distinct identifier k is assigned to every clause of P. Finally, as a corollary of the results reported in [9], given a program P, we have that for an atom A, `in_s(`A`)` succeeds iff $A \in \mathcal{S}(P)$. Moreover, if P is acceptable then every LD-derivation of `in_s(`A`)` is finite.

Next we present the procedure for $\mathcal{C}$-semantics. Given a program P and an atom A, `in_c(`A`)` succeeds iff $A \in \mathcal{C}(P)$. Moreover, if P is acceptable then every LD-derivation of `in_c(`A`)` is finite.

```
in_c(A) ←
    freeze(A, A1),
    call(A1).
```

augmented by P.

Program 6

5 Declarative Debuggers

5.1 $\mathcal{C}$-semantics

We revise the Shapiro's debugger, by integrating the decision procedure in_c within it.

```
(o)    missing_answers_c(Q, Goal) ←
           miss(Q, Goal1),
           melt(Goal1, Goal).
(i)    miss([A | B], Goal) ←
           not( in_c(A) ),
           miss(A, Goal).
(ii)   miss([A | B], Goal) ←
           in_c(A),
           miss(B, Goal).
(iii)  miss(A, Goal) ←
           user_pred(A),
           freeze(A, A1),
           clause(A1, B),
           valid_c(B),
           miss(B, Goal).
(iv)   miss(A, A1) ←
           user_pred(A),
           freeze(A, A1),
           not(
             (clause(A1, B),
             valid_c(B))
           ).
```

clause$(A, [B_1, \ldots, B_n])$.   *for every* $A \leftarrow B_1, \ldots, B_n \in P$

augmented by *Program 6*.

Program 7

valid_c is an oracle describing the queries in the intended interpretation $\mathcal{I}$. Formally, called V the definition of valid_c, an atom valid_c([B]) is in $\mathcal{C}(V)$ iff **B** is in $\mathcal{I}$. Consider now *Program 2*. We have the following definitions of user_pred and valid_c:

```
user_pred(s).
user_pred(p(X)).
user_pred(q(X)).
user_pred(r(X, Y)).

valid_c(s).
valid_c(p(X)).
valid_c(q(a)).
valid_c(q(b)).
valid_c(r(a,c)).
valid_c(r(b,X)).
```

```
valid_c([A|B]) ←
    valid_c(A), valid_c(B).
valid_c([]).
```

A call missing_answers_c([p(X),s], A) has a finite LD-tree, and computes the uncovered atom $A = $ q(b). The computation progresses as follows. First p(X) is found to be not a logical consequence of the program. Then the clause p(X) ← q(Y), r(Y,X) is instantiated by Y = b in order to find a valid body. Note that the instance Y = a, X = c cannot be considered as X is frozen. Finally, q(b) is found to be an uncovered atom.

Consider PREORDER' and the missing answer

$$Q = \text{preorder(tree(E, leaf(X), leaf(Y)), [E, X, Y]).}$$

A call missing_answers_c([Q], A) computes $A = $ preorder(leaf(X),[X]), which is indeed the correctly typed clause *(p2)*.

Consider now *Program 3*, i.e. EAppend, and the missing answer $Q = $ append([X], Ys, [X|Ys]). The proposed debugger shows that Q is an uncovered atom. The only query to the oracle during the computation is valid_c(append(Ys, Ys, Ys)) with Ys frozen. In other words, the oracle is asked whether append(Ys, Ys, Ys) is valid in the intended meaning of EAppend, which is obviously false.

The debugger is correct for every logic program.

Theorem 8 ($\mathcal{C}$-Correctness). *Let P be a program, and Q a missing answer w.r.t. $\mathcal{C}$-semantics. If missing_answers_c([Q], Goal) has a LD-computed instance missing_answers_c([Q], Goal) then Goal is an uncovered atom.*

Proof. First of all, we consider a language L' obtained by adding to L sufficiently many new constants, which are employed by the predicate freeze. Let us show that we are in the hypotheses of the Theorem considering L' instead of L, and

$$\mathcal{I}' = \{ A\theta \in Atom_{L'} \mid A \in Atom_L \land A \in \mathcal{I} \}$$

instead of $\mathcal{I}$. Since Q is a missing answer w.r.t. $\mathcal{I}$, then Q is in $\mathcal{I}'$ and $P \not\models Q$, i.e. Q is a missing answer w.r.t. $\mathcal{I}'$. Moreover the definition V of valid_c is an oracle w.r.t. $\mathcal{I}'$. In fact, consider any query Q in L'. Q can be written as $Q'\theta$, where Q' is in L and θ replaces some variables of Q' with distinct constants not in L. Then, we have that Q is in $\mathcal{I}'$ iff Q' is in $\mathcal{I}$, and then, since V is an oracle, iff $V \models $ valid_c([Q']). By the Theorem on Constants (see e.g. [11]), $V \models $ valid_c([Q']) iff $V \models $ valid_c([Q'])θ, when θ is of the considered form. This implies, that Q is in $\mathcal{I}'$ iff $V \models $ valid_c([Q]), i.e. that V is an oracle w.r.t. $\mathcal{I}'$. We now show that any computed instance of miss([Q], Goal) returns an uncovered atom on L'.

The proof proceeds by induction on the number n of calls to miss in a refutation.

(n = 1). Goal can be only instantiated by applying rule *(iv)*. Then there is no clause instance $A1 \leftarrow \mathbf{B}$ whose body is in $\mathcal{I}'$, i.e. $A1 \notin T_P^{\mathcal{C}}(\mathcal{I}')$, and $A1$ is obtained by freezing A, hence $A1$ in $\mathcal{I}'$. Then Goal is instantiated by an uncovered atom.

$(n > 1)$. We show that the hypothesis of the theorem holds for calls to miss in clauses *(i, ii, iii)*.

(i) Since not(in_c(A)) succeeds, A is not in $\mathcal{C}(P)$ albeit by hypothesis it is in $\mathcal{I}'$. Therefore, A is a missing answer.

(ii) Since in_c(A) succeeds, A is in $\mathcal{C}(P)$. Therefore, B must be a missing answer.

(iii) $A1 \leftarrow \mathbf{B}$ is a clause instance such that $A1$ is obtained by freezing A and $\mathbf{B}$ is in $\mathcal{I}'$. By the Theorem on Constants, A is not in $\mathcal{C}(P)$ implies $A1$ not in $\mathcal{C}(P)$. As a consequence $\mathbf{B}$ is not in $\mathcal{C}(P)$. Otherwise, by Definition 2, $A1$ would be in $T_P^{\mathcal{C}}(\mathcal{C}(P)) = \mathcal{C}(P)$. Therefore, the call miss($\mathbf{B}$, Goal) satisfies the inductive hypothesis, i.e. $\mathbf{B}$ is a missing answer.

In conclusion, the call miss(Q, Goal1) in *(o)* instantiates Goal1 with an uncovered atom $Goal1$ on L'. By melting the frozen variables of $Goal1$, we obtain an atom $Goal$ on L such that $Goal$ is in $\mathcal{I}$ (since $Goal1$ is in $\mathcal{I}'$) but not in $T_P^{\mathcal{C}}(\mathcal{I})$ (otherwise $Goal1$ would be in $T_P^{\mathcal{C}}(\mathcal{I}')$, i.e. $Goal$ is uncovered. $\square$

Restricting the attention to acceptable programs, we are in the position to show completeness of the debugger.

We make the further hypothesis that there are finitely many oracle's answers for Q, i.e that there are finitely many LD-derivations for every call to valid_c during a LD-derivation for missing_answers_c([Q], Goal).

Theorem 9 ($\mathcal{C}$-Completeness). *Let P be an acceptable program, and Q a missing answer w.r.t. $\mathcal{C}$-semantics such that there are finitely many oracle's answers for Q.*
Then there exists a LD-computed instance of missing_answers_c([Q], Goal).

Proof. Reasoning as in the proof of Theorem 8, we can assume a language with infinitely many constants.

We observe that every prefix ξ of a LD-derivation for Q is finite if the variables of Q are never instantiated along ξ. In fact, let θ be a substitution of the variables of Q with new distinct constants. If there is an infinite prefix ξ of a LD-derivation for Q such that the variables of Q are never instantiated along ξ, then $\xi\theta$ would be an infinite prefix of a LD-derivation for $Q\theta$. This is impossible by Theorem 7, since $Q\theta$ is ground. We denote by d_Q the maximum length of a prefix of a LD-derivation for Q that does not instantiate any variable of Q.

The proof proceeds by induction on d_Q.

$(d_Q = 1)$. Let A be the leftmost atom in Q. We claim that $A \notin \mathcal{C}(P)$. Otherwise, by strong completeness of SLD-resolution, there exists a LD-refutation for A that does not instantiate any variable of A. As a consequence, $d_Q > 1$.

Therefore, A is a missing answer. By applying clause *(i)* the query miss(A, Goal) is resolved. We now distinguish two cases: either A is or not a variant of the head of a clause instance $A1 \leftarrow \mathbf{B}$ such that $\mathbf{B}$ is in the intended interpretation $\mathcal{I}$. In the latter case, by resolving miss(A, Goal) with clause *(iv)* we get a refutation, since there are finitely many oracle answers.

In the former case, A unifies with a clause head without instantiating its variables, and then $d_A > 1$ and $d_Q > 1$. In conclusion, the former case is impossible.

$(d_Q > 1)$. Let A be the leftmost atom in $Q = \mathbf{D}, A, \mathbf{E}$ such that $A \notin \mathcal{C}(P)$. By repeatedly applying clauses *(i, ii)* the query miss$(A,$ Goal$)$ is eventually resolved, since for acceptable programs the calls to in_c terminate. Moreover, since $\mathbf{D}$ is in $\mathcal{C}(P)$ then by strong completeness of SLD-resolution, there exists a LD-refutation for $\mathbf{D}$ that does not instantiate any variable of $\mathbf{D}$, hence $d_Q \geq d_A$.

Again, we distinguish two cases: either A is or not a variant of the head a clause instance of P such that the body is in the intended interpretation $\mathcal{I}$. In the latter case, by resolving miss$(A,$ Goal$)$ with clause *(iv)* we get a refutation, since there are finitely many oracle answers.

In the former case, clause *(iii)* is applicable and a query miss$(\mathbf{B},$ Goal$)$ is eventually resolved where $A1 \leftarrow \mathbf{B}$ is an instance of a clause c from P such that $A1$ is obtained by freezing A (i.e., $A1 = A\mu$ for μ substituting variables with fresh constants) and $\mathbf{B}$ is in $\mathcal{I}$. As shown in the proof of Theorem 8, $\mathbf{B}$ cannot be in $\mathcal{C}(P)$, otherwise A would be. Therefore, $\mathbf{B}$ is a missing answer. It is readily checked that $d_A = d_{A1}$. We claim that $d_{A1} > d_{\mathbf{B}}$. In fact, let ξ be the prefix of a LD-derivation for P and $\mathbf{B}$ that does not instantiate any variable of $\mathbf{B}$. We observe that the LD-resolvent of $A1$ and c is more general than $\mathbf{B}$. Therefore, there exists ξ' prefix of a LD-derivation for $A1$ longer than ξ. Summarizing, $d_{A1} > d_{\mathbf{B}}$. As a consequence, $\mathbf{B}$ is a missing answer and $d_Q \geq d_A = d_{A1} > d_{\mathbf{B}}$. Therefore we can apply the inductive hypothesis on $\mathbf{B}$ to obtain the conclusion of the Theorem. $\qquad\square$

Finally, we have termination of the debugger.

Theorem 10 ($\mathcal{C}$-Termination). *Let P be an acceptable program, and Q a query such that there are finitely many oracle's answers for Q. Then the LD-tree of* missing_answers_c$([Q],$ Goal$)$ *is finite.*

Proof. Suppose there is an infinite LD-derivation. Since calls to in_c and valid_c terminate, then it necessarily happens that clause *(iii)* is called infinitely many times: miss$(A_1,$ Goal$)$, ..., miss$(A_n,$ Goal$)$, ... By reasoning as in the proof of Theorem 9, we have that $d_{A_1}, \ldots, d_{A_n}, \ldots$ is an infinite decreasing chain of naturals. This is impossible since naturals are well-founded. $\qquad\square$

5.2 $\mathcal{S}$-semantics

We observe that clauses *(iii, iv)* of *Program 7* followed directly from the definition of uncovered atoms (Definition 4) and the definition of $T_P^{\mathcal{C}}$ (Definition 2). We derive the debugger for $\mathcal{S}$-semantics similarly, but considering now $T_P^{\mathcal{S}}$.

(o)   missing_answers_s(Q, Goal) ←
         miss(Q, Goal).

(i)   miss([A | B], Goal) ←
         not(in_s(A)),
         miss(A, Goal).

(ii)
```
miss([A | B], Goal) ←
    in_s(A),
    miss(B, Goal).
```
(iii)
```
miss(A, Goal) ←
    user_pred(A),
    pure(A, A1),
    clause(A1, B),
    valid_s(B, C),
    variants(A, A1),
    miss(C, Goal).
```
(iv)
```
miss(A, A) ←
    user_pred(A),
    pure(A, A1),
    not(
      (clause(A1, B),
       valid_s(B, _),
       variants(A, A1))
    ).
```

$$\text{clause}(A, [B_1, \ldots, B_n]). \quad \text{for every } A \leftarrow B_1, \ldots, B_n \in P$$

augmented by *Program 5*.

Program 8

valid_s is an oracle describing the queries in the intended interpretation $\mathcal{I}$. Formally, called V the definition of valid_s, an atom valid_s([**B**],[**C**]) is in $S(V)$ iff **B** and **C** are queries whose atoms are in $\mathcal{I}$ and variable disjoint, and **C** is a variant of **B**. By [6, Theorems 7.1 and 7.7], a call valid_s(**B**, C) has a computed instance valid_s(**B**, C)θ iff for some renamed apart atom B in $S(V)$, $\mu = mgu(\text{valid\_s}(\mathbf{B}, \text{C}), B)$ and valid_s(**B**, C)θ = valid_s(**B**, C)μ. Therefore, for an atom A the query

```
pure(A, A1), clause(A1, B), valid_s(B, C), variants(A, A1)
```

has a LD-refutation iff there exists a renamed apart clause $A1 \leftarrow \mathbf{B}$ such that $\theta = mgu(\mathbf{B}, \mathbf{C})$ for some **C** in $\mathcal{I}$ and $A1\theta$ is a variant of A, i.e. iff $A \in T_P^S(\mathcal{I})$.

Consider now, as an example, the following variant of *Program 2*.

```
s.
p(X) ← q(Y), r(Y,X).
% q(a). % missing
q(b).
r(a, c).
r(b, X).
```

We have the following definition of valid_s:

```
valid_s(s, s).
valid_s(p(X), p(Y)).
valid_s(p(c), p(c)).
```

```
valid_s(q(a), q(a)).
valid_s(q(b), q(b)).
valid_s(r(a,c), r(a,c)).
valid_s(r(b,X), r(b,Y)).
valid_s([A|As], [B|Bs]) ←
    valid_s(A, B),
    valid_s(As, Bs).
valid_s([], []).
```

A call missing_answers_s([p(c),s], A) has a finite LD-tree, and returns the uncovered atom q(a). The debugger is correct for every logic program.

Theorem 11 (S-Correctness). *Let P be a program, and Q a missing answer w.r.t. S-semantics. If missing_answers_s([Q], Goal) has a LD-computed instance missing_answers_s([Q], Goal) then Goal is an uncovered atom.*

Proof. The proof is by induction on the number n of calls to miss in a refutation.

($n = 1$). Goal can be only instantiated by applying rule *(iv)*, i.e. if Q is an atom and there is no clause $A1 \leftarrow \mathbf{B}$ whose body unifies with a query in the intended interpretation $\mathcal{I}$ with mgu θ and $A1\theta$ is a variant of Q, namely if $Q \notin T_P^S(\mathcal{I})$.

($n > 1$). We show that the hypothesis of the theorem holds for calls to miss in clauses *(i, ii, iii)*.

(i) Since not(in_s(A)) succeeds, A is not in $S(P)$ albeit by hypothesis it is in $\mathcal{I}$. Therefore, A is a missing answer.

(ii) Since in_s(A) succeeds, A is in $S(P)$. Therefore, B must be a missing answer.

(iii) Assume that

```
pure(A, A1), clause(A1, B), valid_s(B, C), variants(A, A1)
```

succeeds. Then there exists a renamed apart clause $A1 \leftarrow \mathbf{B}$ such that $\theta = mgu(\mathbf{B}, \mathbf{C})$ for some $\mathbf{C}$ in I and $A1\theta$ is a variant of A. Since A is not in $S(P)$, then $\mathbf{C}$ is not in in $S(P)$. Otherwise, by Definition 2, A would be in $T_P^S(S(P)) = S(P)$. Summarizing, by definition of valid_s $\mathbf{C}$ is in $\mathcal{I}$, and we showed that $\mathbf{C}$ is not in $S(P)$. Therefore, the call miss($\mathbf{C}$, Goal) satisfies the inductive hypothesis, i.e. $\mathbf{C}$ is a missing answer. □

Restricting the attention to acceptable programs, we are in the position to show completeness of the debugger. Also, we assume that there are finitely many oracle's answers. Formally, we say that *there are finitely many oracle's answers for Q* iff there are finitely many LD-derivations for every call to valid_s during a LD-derivation for missing_answers_s([Q], Goal).

Theorem 12 (S-Completeness). *Let P be an acceptable program, and Q a missing answer w.r.t. S-semantics such that there are finitely many oracle's answers. Then there exists a LD-computed instance of missing_answers_s([Q], Goal).*

Proof. As shown in the proof of Theorem 9, every prefix ξ of a LD-derivation for Q is finite if the variables of Q are never instantiated along ξ. We denote by d_Q the maximum length of a prefix of a LD-derivation for Q that does not instantiate any variable of Q. The proof proceeds by induction on d_Q.

$(d_Q = 1)$. Let A be the leftmost atom in Q. We claim that $A \notin S(P)$. Otherwise $A \in C(P)$. Then by strong completeness of SLD-resolution, there exists a LD-refutation for A that does not instantiate any variable of A. As a consequence, $d_Q > 1$.

Therefore, A is a missing answer. By applying clause *(i)* the query miss(A, Goal) is resolved. We now distinguish two cases: either A is or not a variant of $A1\mu$ where $A1 \leftarrow \mathbf{B}$ is a clause of P and $\mu = mgu(\mathbf{B}, \mathbf{C})$ for some $\mathbf{C}$ in $\mathcal{I}$. In the latter case, we observe that by resolving miss(A, Goal) with clause *(iv)* we get a refutation, since there are finitely many oracle answers. In the former case, A unifies with a clause head without instantiating its variables, and then $d_A > 1$ and $d_Q > 1$. In conclusion, the latter case is impossible.

$(d_Q > 1)$. Let A be the leftmost atom in $Q = \mathbf{D}, A, \mathbf{E}$ such that $A \notin S(P)$. By repeatedly applying clauses *(i, ii)* the query miss(A, Goal) is eventually resolved, since for acceptable programs the calls to in_s terminate. Moreover, since $S(P) \subseteq C(P)$, then by strong completeness of SLD-resolution, there exists a LD-refutation for $\mathbf{D}$ that does not instantiate any variable of $\mathbf{D}$, hence $d_Q \geq d_A$.

Again, we distinguish two cases: either A is or not a variant of $A1\mu$ where $c : A1 \leftarrow \mathbf{B}$ is a clause of P and $\mu = mgu(\mathbf{B}, \mathbf{C})$ for some $\mathbf{C}$ in $\mathcal{I}$. In the latter case, we observe that by resolving miss(A, Goal) with clause *(iv)* we get a refutation, since there are finitely many oracle answers.

In the former case, clause *(iii)* is applicable and miss($\mathbf{C}$, Goal) is eventually resolved. In fact, by definition of valid_s, the query pure(A, A1), clause(A1, B), valid_s(B, C), variants(A, A1) succeeds under the stated hypothesis. As shown in the proof of Theorem 8, $\mathbf{C}$ cannot be in $S(P)$, otherwise A would be in $S(P)$, and then $\mathbf{C}$ is a missing answer. We claim that $d_A > d_{\mathbf{C}}$.

Let ξ be the prefix of a LD-derivation for P and $\mathbf{C}$ that does not instantiate any variable of $\mathbf{C}$. Since A and $A1\mu$ are variants, then there exists a renaming substitution σ such that $A = A1\mu\sigma$. Moreover, $A \leftarrow \mathbf{C}\mu\sigma$ is an instance of c. Let θ be a substitution mapping all variables of $A \leftarrow \mathbf{C}\mu\sigma$ into distinct fresh constants. Since no variable of $\mathbf{C}$ is instantiated in ξ, then there exists a prefix ξ' of a LD-derivation for $\mathbf{C}\mu\sigma\theta$ of the same length of ξ.

We observe that the LD-resolvent of $A\theta$ and c is more general than $\mathbf{C}\mu\sigma\theta$, since $A\theta \leftarrow \mathbf{C}\mu\sigma\theta$ is an instance of c. Therefore, there exists a prefix ξ'' of a LD-derivation for $A\theta$ longer than ξ'. By substituting in ξ'', every fresh constant introduced by θ with the variable it replaced, we get a prefix of a LD-derivation for P and A that does not instantiate any variable of A and whose length is greater than that of ξ. Summarizing, $\mathbf{C}$ is a missing answer and $d_Q \geq d_A > d_{\mathbf{C}}$. Therefore we can apply the inductive hypothesis on $\mathbf{C}$ to obtain the conclusion of the Theorem. □

Finally, we have termination of the debugger.

Theorem 13 (S-Termination). *Let P be an acceptable program, and Q a query such that there are finitely many oracle's answers for Q. Then the LD-tree of* missing_answers_s([Q], Goal) *is finite.* □

Observe that the hypothesis that there are finitely many oracle's answers is rather restrictive in the case of S-semantics. Looking at *Program 8*, we quickly realize that clauses *(iii,iv)* call valid_s(B, C) with B instantiated by the body of some program clause. In the case of a simple program such as Append, the resulting query valid_s([append(Xs, Ys, Zs)], C) has infinitely many LD-derivations. In general, we have that *"finitely many oracle's answers"* actually requires that $\mathcal{I}$ is a finite set. However, by noting that variants(A, A1) must succeed, a weaker assumption can be made by defining an oracle valid_s(B, C, A, A1) that stops a LD-derivation if A1 becomes more instantiated than A (or some sufficient condition that implies that, e.g. by checking that the size of A1 remains lower or equal than the size of A). By such an enhanced oracle, we have that the assumption of *"finitely many oracle's answers"* is less restrictive, and allows for reasoning on intended interpretations that are infinite sets. As an example, starting from the missing answer append([X], Ys, [X|Ys]) for *Program 3*, the debugger finds out that it is an uncovered atom, when valid_s is as described above.

6 Discussion

A Completeness Result The following result is an immediate consequence of Theorems 9 and 12.

Theorem 14. *Let P be an acceptable program. If there is a missing answer Q w.r.t. C-semantics (resp., S-semantics) and there are finitely many oracle's answers for Q then there exists an uncovered atom.* □

A non-constructive proof has been established by Comini et al. [4] also in the case that there are not finitely many oracle's answers. Indeed, the proofs of Theorems 9 and 12 (non-constructively) show that result if we remove the hypothesis that there are finitely many oracle's answers.

Bounded Programs A declarative characterization of a class larger than acceptable programs is considered in [9], namely the class of *bounded logic programs*, and a decision procedure is provided with respect to C- and S-semantics. Unfortunately, the overall approach presented in this paper cannot be extended to bounded programs. The main problem is that Theorem 14 does not hold for bounded program, in general. As an example, p is a missing answer for the following (bounded) program, but there is no uncovered atom.

```
p ← p
%p   % missing
```

Future work is aimed at extending the ideas and the results presented here to larger classes of logic programs, by investigating subclasses of bounded programs.

Conclusions We presented two declarative debuggers of missing answers with respect to $\mathcal{C}$- and $\mathcal{S}$-semantics. They are correct for any program, and complete and terminating for a large class of logic programs. The implementations of the debuggers rely on decidability procedures for $\mathcal{C}$- and $\mathcal{S}$-semantics which are adapted from [9].

The results presented in this paper improve on Shapiro's and Ferrand's proposals for completeness and termination. Moreover, efficiency is improved in the following sense. As shown in Theorem 8, only calls miss([Q], Goal) where Q is a missing answer are made. On the contrary, from the example *Program 3*, we realize that Shapiro's and Ferrand's debuggers search space include queries that are not missing answers, and then cannot lead to uncovered atoms.

Also, we introduced a debugger for $\mathcal{S}$-semantics. The only approach to debugging of missing answers w.r.t. $\mathcal{S}$-semantics is due to Comini et al. [4]. They present a method for finding all uncovered atoms starting from the intended interpretation $\mathcal{I}$ of an acceptable program. However, the approach of Comini et al. is effective iff $\mathcal{I}$ is a finite set, whilst we require a weaker condition, namely that there are finitely many oracle's answers.

References

1. K.R. Apt. Logic programming. In J. van Leeuwen, editor, *Handbook of Theoretical Computer Science*, volume B, pages 493–574. Elsevier, 1990.
2. K.R. Apt and D. Pedreschi. Reasoning about termination of pure prolog programs. *Information and computation*, 106(1):109–157, 1993.
3. K.L. Clark. Predicate logic as a computational formalism. Technical Report DOC 79/59, Imperial College, Dept. of Computing, 1979.
4. M. Comini, G. Levi, and G. Vitiello. Declarative Diagnosis Revisited. In J. W. Lloyd, editor, *Proceedings of the 1995 International Logic Programming Symposium*, pages 275–287. The MIT Press, 1995.
5. M. Falaschi, G. Levi, M. Martelli, and C. Palamidessi. A Model-Theoretic Reconstruction of the Operational Semantics of Logic Programs. *Information and Computation*, 103(1):86–113, 1993.
6. M. Falaschi, G. Levi, C. Palamidessi, and M. Martelli. Declarative Modeling of the Operational Behaviour of Logic Languages. *Theoretical Computer Science*, 69(3):289–318, December 1989.
7. G. Ferrand. Error Diagnosis in Logic Programming, an Adaption of E. Y. Shapiro's Method. *Journal of Logic Programming*, 4(3):177–198, 1987.
8. L. Naish. Declarative Diagnosis of Missing Answers. *New Generation Computing*, 10(3):255–285, 1991.
9. S. Ruggieri. Decidability of Logic Program Semantics and Applications to Testing. In *Proc. of PLILP'96*, volume 1140 of *Lecture Notes in Computer Science*, pages 347–362. Springer-Verlag, Berlin, 1996.
10. E. Shapiro. *Algorithmic program debugging*. The MIT Press, 1983.
11. J. Shoenfield. *Mathematical logic*. Addison Wesdley, Reading, 1967.
12. L. Sterling and E. Shapiro. *The Art of Prolog*. The MIT Press, second edition, 1994.

Systematic Change of Data Representation: Program Manipulations and a Case Study

William L. Scherlis *

School of Computer Science, Carnegie Mellon University, Pittsburgh, PA 15213

Abstract. We present a set of semantics-based program manipulation techniques to assist in restructuring software encapsulation boundaries and making systematic changes to data representations. These techniques adapt abstraction structure and data representations without altering program functionality. The techniques are intended to be embodied in source-level analysis and manipulation tools used interactively by programmers, rather than in fully automatic tools and compilers.

The approach involves combining techniques for adapting and specializing encapsulated data types (classes) and for eliminating redundant operations that are distributed among multiple methods in a class (functions in a data type) with techniques for cloning classes to facilitate specialization and for moving computation across class boundaries. The combined set of techniques is intended to facilitate revision of structural design decisions such as the design of a class hierarchy or an internal component interface.

The paper introduces new techniques, provides soundness proofs, and gives details of case study involving production Java code.

1 Introduction

Semantics-based program manipulation techniques can be used to support the evolution of configurations of program components and associated internal interfaces. Revision of these abstraction boundaries is a principal challenge in software reengineering. While structural decisions usually must be made early in the software development process, the consequences of these decisions are not fully appreciated until later, when it is costly and risky to revise them. Program

---

* This material is based upon work supported by the National Science Foundation under Grant No. CCR-9504339 and by the Defense Advanced Research Projects Agency and Rome Laboratory, Air Force Materiel Command, USAF, under agreement number F30602-97-2-0241. The U.S. Government is authorized to reproduce and distribute reprints for Governmental purposes notwithstanding any copyright annotation thereon. The views and conclusions contained herein are those of the authors and should not be interpreted as necessarily representing the official policies or endorsements, either expressed or implied, of the Defense Advanced Research Projects Agency, Rome Laboratory, the National Science Foundation, or the U.S. Government. Author email: scherlis@cs.cmu.edu.

manipulation techniques can potentially support the evolution of internal interface and encapsulation structure, offering greater flexibility in the management of encapsulation structure.

This paper focuses on data representation optimizations that are enabled by structural manipulations. It presents three new results: First, it introduces two new program manipulation techniques, *idempotency* and *projection*. Second, it provides proofs for the two techniques and for a related third technique, *shift*, that was previously described without proof [S86,S94]. Finally, a scenario of software evolution involving production Java code is presented to illustrate how the techniques combine with related structural manipulations to accomplish representation change. The case study is an account of how the classes `java.lang.String`, for immutable strings, and `java.lang.StringBuffer`, for mutable strings, could have been derived through a series of structural manipulations starting with a single class implementing C-style strings. The intent of this research is to make the evolution of data representations a more systematic and, from a software engineering point of view, low-risk activity that can be supported by interactive source-level program analysis and manipulation tools. Source-level program manipulation presents challenges unlike those for automatic systems such as compilers and partial evaluators. The sections below introduce the program manipulation techniques, sketch their proofs, and give an account of the evolutionary case study.

2 Program Manipulation

Most modern programming languages support information-hiding encapsulations such as Java classes, Standard ML structures and functors, Ada packages, and Modula-3 modules. In this paper, we use a simplified form of encapsulation based on Java classes but with no inheritance (all classes are *final*), full static typing, and only private non-static fields (i.e., the data components, or *instance variables*, of abstract objects).

The internal representation of an abstract object thus corresponds to a record containing the instance variables. In Standard ML terminology, these classes correspond to `abstypes` or simplified `structures`. We use the term *abstraction boundary* to refer informally to the interface between the class and its clients (the `signature` in Standard ML), including any associated abstract specifications. When the scope of access by clients to a class is bounded and its contents can be fully analyzed, then adjustment and specialization of the class *interface* (and its clients) becomes possible. For larger systems and libraries, this scope is effectively unbounded, however, and other techniques, such as cloning of classes (described below), may need to be used to artifically limit access scopes.

Language. We describe the manipulation techniques in a language-independent manner, though we adapt them for use on Java classes in the case study. We can think of an object being "unwrapped" as it passes into the internal scope of its controlling class, and "wrapped" as it passes out of the scope. It is convenient in this presentation to follow the example of the early Edinburgh ML and make this transit of the abstraction boundary explicit through functions **Abs** and **Rep**, which wrap and unwrap respectively. That is, **Rep** translates an encapsulated abstract object into an object of its data representation type, which in Java is a record containing the object's instance variables. For example, if an abstract **Pixel** consists of a 2-D coordinate pair together with some abstract intensity information, then Rep : Pixel $\rightarrow$ Int $*$ Int $*$ Intensity and Abs : Int $*$ Int $*$ Intensity $\rightarrow$ Pixel. Here "$*$" denotes product of types. The two key restrictions are that **Rep** and **Abs** (which are implicitly indexed on type names) can be called only within the internal scope of the controlling class and they are the only functions that can directly construct and deconstruct abstract values.

Manipulations. Manipulation of class boundaries and exploitation of specialized contexts of use are common operations at all stages of program development. We employ two general collections of meaning-preserving techniques to support this. The first collection, called *class* manipulations, is the focus of this paper. Class manipulations make systematic changes to data representations in classes. They can alter performance and other attributes but, with respect to overall class functionality (barring covert channels), the changes are invisible to clients. That is, class manipulations do not alter signatures (and external invariants), but they do change computation and representation.

The second class of manipulations are the boundary manipulations, which alter signatures, but do not change computation and representation. Boundary manipulations move computation into or out of classes, and they merge, clone, and split classes. The simplest boundary manipulations are *operation migration* manipulations, which move methods into and out of classes. Preconditions for these manipulation rules are mostly related to names, scopes, and types. A more interesting set of boundary manipulations are the *cloning manipulations*, which separate a class into distinct copies, without a need to fully partition the data space. Cloning manipulations introduce a type distinction and require analyses of types and use of object identity to assure that the client space can be partitioned—potentially with the introduction of explicit "conversion" points.

Boundary (and class) manipulations are used to juxtapose pertinent program elements, so they can be further manipulated as an aggregate, either mechanically or manually. Boundary manipulations are briefly introduced in [S94] and are not detailed here. It is worth noting, however, that many classical source-level transformation techniques [BD77] can be understood as techniques to juxtapose related program elements so simplifications can be made. Two familiar trivial examples illustrate: The derivation of a linear-space list reversal function from the quadratic form relies on transformation steps whose sole purpose is to juxtapose the two calls to list *append*, enabling them to be associated to the right, rather than the left association that is tacit in the recursion structure of the initial program. The derivation of the linear Fibonacci from exponential relies on juxtaposing two separate calls to $F(x-2)$ from separate recursive invocations. Various strategies for achieving this juxtaposition have been developed such as tupling, composition, and deforestation [P84,S80,W88].

Class manipulations. The *class* manipulations adjust representations and their associated invariants while preserving the overall meaning of a class. Details of these techniques and proofs are in the next two sections.

The *shift* transformation, in object-oriented terms, systematically moves computation among the method definitions within a class definition while preserving the abstract semantics presented to clients of a class. Shift operates by transferring a common computation fragment uniformly from *all* wrapping sites to *all* unwrapping sites (or vice versa). In the case study later in this paper, *shift* is used several times to make changes to the string representations. Shifts enable frequency reduction and localizing computation for later optimization. For example, in database design, the relative execution frequencies, use of space, and other considerations determine which computations are done when data is stored and which are done when data is retrieved. Shifts are also useful to accomplish representation change. For example, suppose a function `Magnitude : Int * Int → Real` calculates the distance from a point to the origin. If magnitudes are calculated when pixels are accessed, *shift* can be used to move these calls to wrapping sites. The representation of pixels thus changes from `Int * Int` to `Int * Int * Real`, with distances being calculated only when pixels are created or changed, not every time they are accessed.

The *project* transformation enables "lossy" specialization of representations, eliminating instance variables and associated computation. For example, in a specialized case where intensity information is calculated and maintained but not ultimately used by class clients, *project* could be used to simplify pixels from `Rep : Pixel → Int * Int * Intensity` to `Rep' : Pixel → Int * Int` and eliminate intensity-related calculations.

The *idempotency* transformation eliminates subcomputations that are idempotent and redundant *across* method definitions in a class. Idempotency is a surprisingly common property among program operations. Most integrity checks, cache building operations, and invariant maintaining operations such as tree balancing are idempotent.

3   Class manipulation techniques

Class manipulations exploit the information hiding associated with instance variables in a class (in Standard ML, variables of types whose data constructors are hidden in a **structure** or **abstype**). Significant changes can be made to the internal structure of a class, including introduction and elimination of instance variables, without effect on client-level semantics. Class manipulations are based on Hoare's venerable idea of relating abstraction and representation in data types.

Shift. The *shift* rule has two symmetrical variants. As noted above, the `Rep` and `Abs` functions are used to manage access to the data representation. A requirement on *all* instances of `Rep` or `Abs` (which are easy to find, since they are all within the syntactic scope of the class) thus has the effect of a universal requirement on all instances where an encapsulated data object is constructed or selected. Let T be the class (abstract) type of encapsulated objects and V be the type of their representations. In the steps below, a portion of the internal computation of all methods that operate on T objects is identified and abstracted into a function called *Span* that operates on V objects. Note, in a Java class definition V would be an aggregate of the instance variables (non-static fields) of the class. For our presentation purposes, we adapt the usual object-oriented notational convention to make the aggregate of instance variables an explicit value of type V. In the case study we make a similar adaptation for Java. This means we can require the fragment of shifted computation, abstracted as *Span*, can be a simple function, allowing a more natural functional style in the presentation of the technique. The effect of *Shift* is to move a common computation from all program points in a class where objects are unwrapped to program points where objects are wrapped (and vice-versa):

1. By other manipulations, local within each operation definition, establish that *all* sites of Rep : $T \rightarrow V$ appear in the context of a call to *Span*,

$$Span \circ Rep : T \rightarrow V'$$

where *Span* : $V \rightarrow V'$. That is, there is some common functional portion of computation of every method that occurs at object unwrapping. If this is not possible, the transformation cannot be carried out. Abstract all instances of this computation into calls to *Span*.

2. Replace Abs and Rep as follows. *All* instances of

$$Abs : V \rightarrow T \quad become \quad Abs' \circ Span : V \rightarrow T'$$

where Abs' : $V' \rightarrow T'$. *All* instances of Rep as

$$Span \circ Rep : T \rightarrow V' \quad become \quad Rep' : T' \rightarrow V'$$

3. It is now established that *all* sites of Abs' : $V' \rightarrow T'$ are in the context of a call to *Span*,

$$Abs' \circ Span : V \rightarrow T'$$

The *shift* rule, intuitively, advances computation from object unwrapping to object wrapping. The variant of *shift* is to reverse these three steps and the operations in them, thus delaying the *Span* computation from object wrapping to subsequent object unwrapping.

Although the universal requirement of the first step may seem difficult to achieve, but it can be accomplished trivially in those cases where *Span* is feasibly invertible by inserting $Span^{-1} \circ Span$ in specific method definitions. The *Span* operation is then relocated using the rule above. Later manipulations may then be able to unfold and simplify away the calls to $Span^{-1}$.

Project. The *project* manipulation rule eliminates code and fields in a class that has become dead, for example as a result of specialization of the class interface. The rule can be used when the "death" of code can be deduced only by analysis encompassing the entire class. Suppose the representation type V can be written as $V_1 * V_2$ for some V_1 and V_2. This could correspond to a partitioning of the instance variables (represented here as a composite type V) into two sets. If the conditions below are met, then *project* can be used to eliminate the V_2 portion of the representation type and associated computations. The rule is as follows:

1. Define **Rep** as **Rep**: $T \rightarrow V_1 * V_2$ and **Abs** as **Abs**: $V_1 * V_2 \rightarrow T$.
2. Represent the concrete computation of *each* method **op** that operates on any portion of the internal representation V as

$$\textbf{op}: V_1 * V_2 * U \rightarrow V_1 * V_2 * W$$

   where U and W are other types (representing non-encapsulated inputs and outputs). Then, by other manipulations, redefine **op** to calculate its result using two separate operations that calculate separate portions of the result,[1]

$$\textbf{op}_1: V_1 * U \rightarrow V_1 * W$$
$$\textbf{op}_2: V_1 * V_2 * U \rightarrow V_2$$

   Do this analogously for all operations **op** on internal representations $V_1 * V_2$. If this cannot be done for all such operations involving V_1 and V_2, then the rule cannot be applied.
3. Replace all operations **op** within the class by the new operations **op**$_1$.
4. Simultaneously, replace all instances of **Abs** and **Rep** by new versions **Rep'**: $T \rightarrow V_1$ and **Abs'**: $V_1 \rightarrow T$.

The effect of *project* is to eliminate the V_2 portion of the overall object representation and all the computations associated with it. In Java, for example, V_2 would be a subset of the instance variables of a class. The *project* manipulation generally becomes a candidate for application after boundary manipulations have eliminated or separated all methods that depend on the particular instance variables corresponding to V_2. It is possible to think of *shift* and *project* as introduction and elimination rules for instance variables in the specific sense that, among its uses, *shift* can be used to introduce new fields and computations that could later be eliminated using *project*.

Idempotency. The *idempotency* rule is used to eliminate certain instances of idempotent computations such as integrity checks, caching, or invariant-maintaining operations. When an idempotent operation is executed multiple times on the same data object, even as it is passed among different methods, then all but one of the calls can be eliminated.

1. Define an idempotent *Span* function of type $V \rightarrow V$.

$$Span \circ Span = Span$$

2. Establish that each call of **Abs** appears in context **Abs** $\circ$ *Span* or, alternatively, establish that each call to **Rep** appears in context *Span* $\circ$ **Rep**. (These variants are analogous to the two variants of *shift*.)

---

[1] $\textbf{op}(v_1, v_2, u) = [let\ (v_1', w) = \textbf{op}_1(v_1, u)\ and\ v_2' = \textbf{op}_2(v_1, v_2, u)\ in\ (v_1', v_2', w)\ end]$

3. For one or more particular operation (method) definitions, establish in each that the call to *Span* can be commuted with the entire remaining portion of the definition.

$$op = Span \circ op' = op' \circ Span$$

4. In each of the cases satisfying this commutativity requirement, replace op by op'. That is, replace the calls to *Span* by the identity function.

Examples: Performance-oriented calculations (spread over multiple operations) such as rebalancing search trees or rebuilding database indexes can be eliminated or delayed when their results are not needed for the immediate operation. An integrity check involving a proper subset of the instance variables can be eliminated from operations that do not employ those variables (i.e., delayed until a later operation that involves a variable in that subset). Note that this integrity check example depends on a liberal treatment of exceptions in the definition of program equivalence.

4   Correctness of Class Manipulations

The class manipulations alter data representations and method definitions in a class. Establishing correctness of the manipulations amounts to proving behavioral equivalence of the original and transformed class definitions. Since encapsulated objects are only unwrapped by methods within the class, the external behavior of a class can be construed entirely in terms of sequences of incoming and outgoing "exposed" values (to use Larch terminology) [G93]. This external class behavior is usually related to the internal definition of the class (i.e., the definitions of the instance variables and methods) through an explicit abstraction mapping, as originally suggested by Hoare [H72].

In the proofs below (as in the descriptions of the manipulations above), we employ a functional style in which methods are functional and objects are pure values. The set of instance variables of a Java class, which can be thought of as an implicit aggregate parameter and result, are made explicit in our rendering as new parameters and results of type T. This simple translation is possible (in our limited Java subset) because objects are pure values—i.e., there is no use of "object identity." Suppose, for example, that T is the abstract type of a class, U and W are other types, and there are four methods in the class, which are functional and have the following signatures: $op_1 : U \rightarrow T$, $op_2 : T * T \rightarrow T$, $op_3 : T \rightarrow U$, and $op_4 : T \rightarrow T * W$. Thus, for example, op_1 is a constructor and op_3 does not alter or create T objects.

Properties of objects in a class are expressed using an *invariant* $I(t, v)$ that relates abstract values t (of type T above) to representation (instance variables) v of type V. Behavioral correctness *of a class* is defined in terms of preconditions on incoming exposed values, postconditions on outgoing exposed values, and a predicate I that is an invariant and that relates abstract values with representations. If an abstract specification of the class is not needed, the proof can be obtained without reference to the abstract values t.

If op_i is a method, let $\overline{op}_i$ be the implementation of the method, typed accordingly. For example, if $op_i : U * T \to T * W$ then $\overline{op}_i : U * V \to V * W$. Let pre_i be a precondition on values of the exposed inputs to op_i and $post_i$ be a postcondition on the values of the exposed outputs from op_i. For the invariant I to hold for the class above (op_1 through op_4), the following four properties of I must hold:

$$pre_1(u) \Rightarrow I(op_1(u), \overline{op}_1(u))$$
$$I(t_1, v_1) \wedge I(t_2, v_2) \Rightarrow I(op_2(t_1, t_2), \overline{op}_2(v_1, v_2))$$
$$I(t, v) \Rightarrow post_3(\overline{op}_3(v))$$
$$I(t, v) \Rightarrow I(op_4(t), \overline{op}_4(v)) \wedge post_4(\overline{op}_4(v))$$

Behavioral correctness. Establishing behavioral correctness of a *manipulation rule* operating on a class definition amounts to showing that the relationships among pre_i and $post_j$ values remain unchanged, even as the definition of I changes in the course of transformation.

Correctness of shift. Let $I(t, v)$ be an invariant that holds for all methods in class T prior to carrying out the transformation. The effect of *shift* is to create a new invariant $I'(t, v')$ that relates the new representation values v' to the abstract values t. The proof proceeds by defining I', showing it is invariant in the transformed class, and showing that it captures the same relationships between preconditions and postconditions as does I. We prove the first variant of *shift*; the proof for the second variant is essentially identical.

For a method $op : T \to T$, for example, the *Span* precondition of the definition of the *shift* manipulation guarantees for some residual computation r that

$$I(t, v) \Rightarrow I(op(t), \overline{op}(v))$$
$$\Rightarrow I(op(t), (r \circ Span)(v))$$

Define the post-manipulation invariant $I'(t, v') \equiv I(t, v) \wedge v' = Span(v)$. Now,

$$
\begin{array}{ll}
I'(t, v') \equiv I(t, v) \wedge v' = Span(v) & \text{Definition of } I' \\
\Rightarrow I(op(t), (r \circ Span)(v)) \wedge v' = Span(v) & \text{Invariance property of } I \\
\Rightarrow I(op(t), r(v')) & \\
\Rightarrow I'(op(t), (Span \circ r)(v')) & \text{Definition of } I' \\
\Rightarrow I'(op(t), \overline{op}(v')) & \text{Definition of } shift
\end{array}
$$

This establishes that I' is invariant for the operation op in the class definition *after* it has been subject to the manipulation.

To understand the effect on postconditions, we consider the case of op_3.

$$
\begin{array}{ll}
I(t, v) \Rightarrow post_3(\overline{op}_3(v)) & \text{Assumed} \\
I(t, v) \Rightarrow post_3(r(Span(v)) & \text{Precondition of } shift \\
I'(t, Span(v)) \Rightarrow post_3(r(Span(v)) & \text{Definition of } I' \\
I'(t, Span(v)) \Rightarrow post_3(\overline{op}_3'(Span(v)) & \text{Definition of } I' \\
(\exists v)(v' = Span(v)) \wedge I'(t, v') \Rightarrow post_3(\overline{op}_3'(v'))
\end{array}
$$

This is sufficient, since in the modified class definition, all outputs of methods are in the codomain of *Span*. These arguments are easily generalized to methods that include additional parameters and results.

Correctness of idempotency. There are two variants of the *idempotency* manipulation. We prove one, in which the second precondition (in the description of the technique) assures that for any t, $I(op(t), v) \Rightarrow (\exists v')(v = (Span \circ \hat{r})(v'))$ for some residual function r. Consider the case $\mathsf{op} : T \to T$. Because of the second precondition of the idempotency rule, op preserves the invariant,

$$I(t, v) \Rightarrow I(\mathsf{op}(t), \overline{\mathsf{op}}(v))$$
$$\Rightarrow I(\mathsf{op}(t), (Span \circ \overline{\mathsf{op}}')(v))$$

For each method in which *Span* commutes (and in which *Span* can therefore be eliminated by the transformation), we need to show that the invariant is maintained, that is $I(t, v) \Rightarrow I(\mathsf{op}(t), \overline{\mathsf{op}}'(v))$. Assume inductively that invariant $I(t, v)$ holds for all class operations on type T prior to carrying out the transformation. We proceed as follows:

$$
\begin{aligned}
I(t, v) &\Rightarrow (\exists v')\ I(t, v)\ \wedge\ v = (Span \circ r)(v') && \textit{idempotency precondition} \\
&\Rightarrow (\exists v')\ I(\mathsf{op}(t), (Span \circ \overline{\mathsf{op}}' \circ Span \circ r)(v')) && \text{Invariant for } \mathsf{op} \\
&\Rightarrow (\exists v')\ I(\mathsf{op}(t), (\overline{\mathsf{op}}' \circ Span \circ Span \circ r)(v')) && \text{Commutativity} \\
&\Rightarrow (\exists v')\ I(\mathsf{op}(t), (\overline{\mathsf{op}}' \circ Span \circ r)(v')) && \text{Idempotency of } Span \\
&\Rightarrow I(\mathsf{op}(t), \overline{\mathsf{op}}'(v)) && \text{Definition of } v
\end{aligned}
$$

Correctness of project. The proof for the *project* manipulation is similar, and is omitted.

5 Strings in Java

We now present a modest-scale case study, which is a hypothetical re-creation of the evolution of early versions of the two Java classes used for strings, `String` and `StringBuffer`.[2] Java `Strings` are meant to be immutable and efficiently represented with minimal copying. For example, substring operations on `Strings` manipulate pointers and do not involve any copying. `StringBuffers`, on the other hand, are mutable and flexible, at a modest incremental performance cost. The typical use scenario is that strings are created and altered as `StringBuffers` and then searched and shared as `Strings`, with conversion operations between

---

[2] These two classes are part of an early version of the released Java Development Kit 1.0Beta from Sun Microsystems. Java is a trademark of Sun Microsystems. Since fragments of the code (string 1.51 and stringbuffer 1.21) are quoted in this paper, we include the following license text associated with the code: "Copyright (c) 1994 Sun Microsystems, Inc. All Rights Reserved. Permission to use, copy, modify, and distribute this software and its documentation for non-commercial purposes and without fee is hereby granted provided that this copyright notice appears in all copies. Please refer to the file "copyright.html" for further important copyright and licensing information. Sun makes no representations or warranties about the suitability of the software, either express or implied, including but not limited to the implied warranties of merchantability, fitness for a particular purpose, or non-infringement. Sun shall not be liable for any damages suffered by licensee as a result of using, modifying or distributing this software or its derivatives."

them. The data representations used in both classes facilitate this conversion by delaying or minimizing copying of structure. In particular, conversions from StringBuffer to String do not always result in copying of the character array data structure.

Both classes represent strings as character arrays called **value**. Both have an integer field called **count**, which is the length of the string in the array. The String class also maintains an additional integer field called **offset**, which is the initial character position in the array. Since Strings are immutable, this enables substrings to be represented by creating new String objects that *share* the character array and modify **count** and **offset**.

The StringBuffer class, which is used for mutable strings, has three fields. In addition to **value** and **count**, there is a boolean **shared** that is used to help delay or avoid array copy operations when StringBuffer objects are converted into Strings. The method used for this conversion does not copy **value**, but it does record the loss of exclusive access to the array **value** by setting the **shared** flag. If the flag is set, then a copy is done immediately prior to the next mutation, at which point the flag is reset. If no mutation is done, no copy is made. A simpler but less efficient scheme would always copy.

Selected steps of the evolutionary account are summarized below. The initial steps, omitted here, establish the initial string class, called Str, which manages mutable strings represented as null-terminated arrays, as in C. Str always copies character arrays passed to and from operations. (All boundary and class manipulation steps below have been manually carried out using our techniques, and one of these is examined more closely in the following section.)

1. Introduce **count**. In the initial class Str, trade space for time by using *shift* to replace uses of the null character by adding the private instance variable **count**. Simplifications following the shift eliminate all reference to and storage of null terminating characters.

2. Separate Str into String and StringBuffer. Label all Str variables in the scope in which Str is accessible as either String or StringBuffer, and introduce two methods to convert between them (both initially the identity function with a type cast). Since copy operations are done at every step, object identity cannot be relied upon, and this is a safe step. This process would normally be iterative, using type analysis and programmer-guided selection of conversion points. Those Str variables that are subject to mutating operations, such as **append**, **insert**, and **setCharAt** are typed as **StringBuffer**. Those Str variables that are subject to selection operations, such as **substring** and **regionMatches**, are typed as **String**. Common operations such as **length** and **charAt** are in both clones. Because copying is done at every step, conversion operations can always do an additional copy of mutable structures (i.e., **value**). This approach to allocating variables to the two clones enables use of boundary manipulations to remove mutating operations such as **setCharAt**, for example, from **String**. At this point, the two clones have different client variables, different sets of operations, but identical representations and representation invariants.

3. Introduce **offset**. Since **Strings** are immutable, **substring** does not need to copy **value**. But elimination of copying requires changing the representation to include offsets as well as length. Use *shift* to accomplish the representation change preparatory to eliminating the copying. (This is the step that is detailed below.)

4. Introduce **shared**. In **StringBuffer**, **value** is copied prior to passing it to the **String** constructor. This is necessary because **value** would otherwise be aliased and subject to subsequent mutation, which would violate the mutability invariant of **String**. In fact, the copying needs to be done only if **value** is subsequently mutated, and could be delayed until then. Use *shift* to relocate the copying to whatever **StringBuffer** method immediately follows the conversion, adding the **shared** flag. This delays the copy by "one step." Then use *idempotency* to delay that copying "multiple steps" (by commuting it within all calls to non-mutating access methods) until a **StringBuffer** operation that actually does mutation.

5. Add specialized methods. Identify conversion functions from various other common types to **char[]**. For both string classes, use boundary shifts to compose these conversion functions with the constructors and with commonly used functions such as **append** and **insert**. Then use additional boundary shifts to relocate these composed functions as public methods, naming them appropriately (mostly through overloading). Then, unfold (inline) the type conversion calls contained in these methods and specialize accordingly. (This introduces many of the large number of methods defined in the two classes.)

6 (hypothetical). Eliminate **value**. Suppose that in some context only the lengths of **StringBuffers** were needed, but not their contents. That is, after a series of calls to methods such as **insert**, **append**, **setCharAt**, **reverse**, and **setLength**, the only accessor method called is **length**. *Clone* and *project* can be used to create a specialized class for this case.

6 A Closer Look at Offsets in Class String

We now consider more closely step 3 above, which introduces the **offset** instance variable as an alternative to copying when substrings are calculated. This step must include, for example, modification of all character access operations to index from **offset**. This account illustrates how *shift* can be employed to introduce offsets into the string representation. An initial Java version of **substring** in class **String** could look like this:

```
public String substring (int b, int e) {
    // b is first char position; e-1 is last character position.
    if ((b < 0) || (e > count) || (b > e))
        {throw new IndexOutOfBoundsException (endi); }
    int ncount = e - b;
    char res[] = new char[ncount];
    ArrayCopy (value, b, res, 0, ncount);
    return new String (res, ncount);
}
```

ArrayCopy copies **ncount** characters from **value** to **res** starting at offsets **b** and 0 respectively.

To facilitate presentation consistent with the manipulation rules, the code below explicitly mentions in special brackets those (- instance variables -) that are referenced or changed. This allows a more functional treatment of methods. We also usually abbreviate {- integrity checks -}. Thus the code above could be rendered more succinctly as:

```
public String substring (int b, int e) (- value, count -) {
  {- Check (b, e, count) -}
  int ncount = e - b;
  char res[] = new char[ncount];
  ArrayCopy (value, b, res, 0, ncount);
  return new String (res, ncount);        }
```

The principal steps for *shift*, recall, are (1) defining a suitable *Span* function, (2) adapting code so it appears in all the required places, and (3) carrying out the *shift* transformation by relocating the *Span* calls. We then (4) simplify results.
(1) Define Span. The motivating observation is that the array copying is unnecessary when a substring is extracted. We therefore abstract the instances of array copy code into a new method definition and use that as *Span*. The original code sites will be replaced by calls.

```
private (char[],int) Span (- char[] nvalue, int ncount, int noffset -) {
  char res[] = new char[ncount];
  ArrayCopy (nvalue, noffset, res, 0, ncount);
  return (res,ncount);     }
```

(An additional notational liberty we take is to allow functions to return a *tuple* of results. For this variant of *shift*, the parameters of *Span* are exactly the new set of instance variables, and the results are the old instance variables.
(2) Call Span. The method abstraction step needs to be done in a way that introduces *Span* calls into all methods that construct or mutate string values (i.e., alter **value** or **count**). Note that **substring** does *not* mutate or construct string values directly; it uses a **String** constructor:

```
public String (nvalue, ncount) (- value, count -)  {
  value = new char[ncount];
  count = ncount;
  ArrayCopy (nvalue, 0, value, 0 count);        }
```

After *Span* is abstracted:

```
public String (nvalue, ncount) (- value, count -)  {
  (value, count) = Span (nvalue, ncount, 0);     }
```

When *Span* has an easily computed inverse function, then *Span* can always be introduced trivially into otherwise less tractable cases as part of a composition with the inverse. But this will likely necessitate later code simplification.
(3) Do the Shift. Once all the *Span* calls have been inserted, doing the *shift* is a mechanical operation. The effect is as follows:

- The class now has three private instance variables, **nvalue**, **ncount**, and **noffset**, corresponding to the parameters of *Span*.
- All *Span* calls are replaced by (simultaneous) assignments to the new instance variables of the actual parameters.
- In each method that accesses instance variables, the first operation becomes a call to *Span* that computes **value** and **count** (now ordinary local variables) in terms of the instance variables.

For example, here is the transformed definition of **substring**:

```
public String substring (int b, int e) (- nvalue, ncount, noffset -) {
   (char value[], int count) = Span (nvalue, ncount, noffset);
   {- Check (b, e, count) -}
   int c = e - b;
   char res[] = new char[c];
   ArrayCopy (value, b, res, 0, c);
   return new String (res, c);        }
```

(4) Simplify. Unfolding *Span* and simplifying:

```
public String substring (int b, int e) (- nvalue, ncount, noffset -) {
   {- Check (b, e, ncount) -}
   int c = e - b;
   char res[] = new char[c];
   ArrayCopy (nvalue, noffset, res, 0, c);
   ArrayCopy (res, b, res, 0, c);
   return new String (res, c);        }
```

This motivates our introducing a new string constructor that can take an offset, **public String(nvalue,ncount,noffset)**. This is done by abstracting the last two lines of **substring** and exploiting the idempotency of array copying. After simplifications:

```
public String substring (int b, int e) (- nvalue, ncount, noffset -) {
   {- Check (b, e, ncount) -}
   return new String (nvalue, e - b, b + noffset); }
```

In the case of the **charAt** method in **String**, we start with:

```
public char charAt(int i) (- value, count -) {
   {- Check (i, count) -}
   return value[i];        }
```

This does not create or modify the instance variables, so no call to *Span* is needed before the shift. It does, however, access instance variables, so *shift* inserts an initial call to *Span*:

```
public char charAt(int i) (- nvalue, ncount, noffset -) {
   (char value[], int count) = Span (nvalue, ncount, noffset);
   {- Check (i, count) -}
   return value[i];        }
```

Simplification entails unfolding *Span*, eliminating the array copy operation, and simplifying:

```
public char charAt(int i) (- nvalue, ncount, noffset -) {
  {- Check (i, ncount) -}
  return nvalue[i + noffset];        }
```

7 Background and Conclusion

Background. There is significant previous work on synthesizing and reasoning about encapsulated abstract data types. Class manipulations are most obviously influenced by Hoare's early work [H72]. Most related work focuses either on synthesizing type implementations from algebraic specifications or on refinement of data representations into more concrete forms [D80,MG90,W93]. But evolution does not always involve synthesis or refinement, and the techniques introduced here are meant to alter (and not necessarily refine) both structure and (internal) meaning.

Ideas for boundary manipulations appear in Burstall and Goguen's work on theory operations [BG77]. Wile developed some of these ideas into informally-described manipulations on types that he used to provide an account of the heapsort algorithm [W81]. He used a system of manipulating flag bits to record whether values have been computed yet in order to achieve the effect of a primitive class manipulation. For boundary manipulations, we build on several recent efforts which have developed and applied concepts analogous to the *operation migration* techniques [GN93,JF88,O92].

Early versions of the boundary manipulation and *shift* techniques were defined (without proof) and applied to introduce destructive operations in programs [JS87,S86] and in a larger case study in which a complex data structure for the text buffer of an interactive text editor was developed [NLS90].

The program manipulation techniques we introduce for classes and other encapsulations are meant to complement other manipulation and specialization techniques for achieving local restructuring and optimizations that do not involve manipulating encapsulations.

Conclusion. The techniques described in this paper are source-level techniques meant to be embodied in interactive tools used with programmer guidance to develop and evolve software. The intent is to achieve a more flexible and exploratory approach to the design, configuration, implementation, and adaptation of encapsulated abstractions. Manipulation techniques such as these can decrease the coupling between a programmer decision to perform a particular computation and the related decision of where the computation should be placed with respect to class and internal interface structure.

Acknowledgements. Thanks to John Boyland and Edwin Chan, who contributed valuable insights. Thanks also to the anonymous referees for helpful comments.

References

[BG94]   R.W.Bowdidge and W.G. Griswold, Automated Support for Encapsulating Abstract Data Types. ACM SIGSOFT Symposium Foundations of Software Engineering, 1994.

[BD77]   R.M. Burstall and J. Darlington, A transformation system for developing recursive programs. JACM 24, pp.44-67, 1977.

[BG77]   R.M. Burstall and J. Goguen, Putting theories together to make specifications. IJCAI, 1977.

[D80]   J. Darlington, The synthesis of implementations for abstract data types. Imperial College Report, 1980.

[GN93]   W.G. Griswold and D. Notkin, Automated assistance for program restructuring. ACM TOSEM 2:3, 1993.

[G93]   J.V. Guttag and J. J. Horning, et al., Larch: Languages and Tools for Formal Specification, Springer-Verlag, 1993.

[H72]   C.A.R. Hoare, Proof of correctness of data representations. Acta Informatica 1, pp. 271-281, 1972.

[JF88]   R. Johnson and B. Foote, Designing reusable classes. Journal of Object-Oriented Programming, June/July 1988.

[JS87]   U. Jørring and W. Scherlis, Deriving and using destructive data types. Program Specification and Transformation, Elsevier, 1987.

[K96]   G. Kiczales, Beyond the Black Box: Open Implementation, IEEE Software, January 1996.

[MG90]   Carroll Morgan and P.H.B. Gardiner, Data refinement by calculation. Acta Informatica 27 (1990).

[MG95]   J.D. Morgenthaler and W.G. Griswold, Program analysis for practical program restructuring. ICSE-17 Workshop on Program Transformation for Software Evolution, 1995.

[NLS90]   R.L. Nord, P. Lee, and W. Scherlis, Formal manipulation of modular software systems. ACM/SIGSOFT Formal methods in software development, 1990.

[O92]   W. Opdyke, Refactoring Object-Oriented Frameworks. PhD Thesis, University of Illinois, 1992.

[P86]   R. Paige, Programming with invariants. IEEE Software 3:1, 1986.

[P84]   A. Pettorossi, A powerful stragey for deriving efficient programs by transformation. ACM Symposium on Lisp and Functional Programming, 1984.

[S80]   W. Scherlis, Expression procedures and program derivation. Stanford University technical report, 1980.

[S86]   W. Scherlis, Abstract data types, specialization, and program reuse. Advanced programming environments, Springer, 1986.

[S94]   W. Scherlis, Boundary and path manipulations on abstract data types. IFIP 94, North-Holland, 1994.

[W88]   P. Wadler, Deforestation: Transforming programs to eliminate trees. European Symposium on Programming, Springer, 1988.

[W81]   D.S. Wile, Type transformations. IEEE TSE SE-7, pp.32-39, 1981.

[W93]   K.R. Wood, A practical approach to software engineering using Z and the refinement calculus. ACM SIGSOFT Symposium on the Foundations of Software Engineering, 1993.

A Generic Framework for Specialization (Abridged Version)

Peter Thiemann[*]

Universität Tübingen
`thiemann@informatik.uni-tuebingen.de`

Abstract. We present a generic framework for specifying and implementing offline partial evaluators. The framework provides the infrastructure for specializing higher-order programs with computational effects specified through a monad. It performs sound specialization for all monadic instances and is evaluation-order independent. It subsumes most previously published partial evaluators for higher-order functional programming languages in the sense that they are instances of the generic framework with respect to a particular monad.

Keywords: higher-order programming, program transformation, partial evaluation, computational effects

1   Introduction

A *partial evaluator* [10, 23] specializes a program with respect to a known part of its input. The resulting specialized program takes the rest of the input and delivers the same result as the original program applied to the whole input. The specialized program usually runs faster than the original one.

One particular flavor of partial evaluation is *offline* partial evaluation. In its first stage, a *binding-time analysis* annotates all phrases of a program that only depend on the known input as executable at specialization time. The execution of the remaining phrases is deferred to the run time of the specialized program. In the second stage, a *static reducer* interprets the annotated program. It evaluates all phrases annotated as executable and generates code for the remaining phrases.

The goal of this work is to present a generic framework to specify and implement the static reducer. The framework unifies the existing specifications of static reducers and it provides a sound basis to implement reducers that execute and generate code with computational effects. It goes beyond existing specializers in that it allows for experimentation with various effects in a modular way.

To achieve this modularity, the framework is parameterized over a monad. The choice of a monad fixes a particular computational effect. Monads have been used in the context of programming languages to structure denotational

---

[*] Author's present address: Department of Computer Science, University of Nottingham, University Park, Nottingham NG7 2RD, England

semantics [30], to structure functional programs [39,40], and to equip pure functional languages with side-effecting operations like I/O and mutable state [24,32]. Closely related to structuring denotational semantics is the construction of modular interpreters [18,28]. There are also recent theoretical approaches to formalize partial evaluation using monads [21,26].

1.1 Four Ways to Static Reduction

In the past, four different approaches have been used to implement static reducers dealing with a particular computational effect. All of them rest on denotational specifications of specialization, or—from a programmer's point of view—on viewing the static reducer as an interpreter for an annotated language. The implementation languages of these interpreters (the metalanguages of the specifications) range from applied lambda calculus to ML with control operators. By factoring these specifications over an annotated variant of Moggi's computational metalanguage [21,30], we demonstrate that all of them are composed from the same set of building blocks, the sole difference being the staging of computation at specialization time. Here is the set of building blocks:

$eval_v$ an evaluation function for a pure call-by-value lambda calculus;
$\mathcal{B}$ a binding-time analysis that maps terms to annotated terms;
$\mathcal{S}_v$ a specializer for applied lambda calculus written in lambda calculus (e.g., Lambdamix [19]);
$\mathcal{M}$ a *monadic expansion* translation that maps the computational metalanguage to applied lambda calculus by expanding the monadic operators to lambda terms according to the definition of the monad;
$\mathcal{E}_v$ a call-by-value *explication* that translates from the (annotated) source language to the (annotated) metalanguage, encoding a call-by-value evaluation strategy.

As an example for the different approaches consider a call-by-value language $\lambda_!$ with some computational effect and specialize a program p to r with respect to known data s. We assume access to the program text of all functions mentioned above: $\lceil \mathcal{S}_v \rceil$ is the lambda term denoting the function $\mathcal{S}_v = eval_v \lceil \mathcal{S}_v \rceil$, $\lceil p\ s \rceil$ is the textual application of p to s, and so on.

Transform Source Program to Expanded Monadic Style Applying $\mathcal{M} \circ \mathcal{E}_v$ to $\lceil p\ s \rceil$ yields an effect-free lambda term. This term can now be analyzed and statically reduced with a specializer for the lambda calculus [8,19].

$$\mathcal{S}_v\ (\mathcal{B}\ (\mathcal{M}\ (\mathcal{E}_v(\lceil p\ s \rceil)))) = \mathcal{M}\ (\mathcal{E}_v(\lceil r \rceil)) \tag{1}$$

This approach is viable [9,31,37], but it suffers from a number of drawbacks.

– Monadic expansion typically introduces many new abstractions. This increase in program size slows down the analysis $\mathcal{B}$ and the static reduction.

- The expanded term can be hard to read for the user of the partial evaluator. It provides no useful feedback from the annotated term on how to change the source program to achieve better specialization.
- The straightforward expansion often does not lead to satisfactory results from the binding-time analysis. For example, sophisticated state-passing translations have been designed to obtain better results [31,37].
- The specialized program is also in expanded monadic style (for example, in continuation-passing style [9]), which requires an inverse translation (for example, a direct style translation [13]) to obtain readable results.

Specializer in Expanded Monadic Style At the cost of moving to a more sophisticated binding-time analysis $\mathcal{B}_!$, which takes computational effects into account (e.g., [37]), equation (1) can be rewritten to

$$
\begin{aligned}
\mathcal{S}_v \left(\mathcal{M} \left(\mathcal{E}_v(\mathcal{B}_!\lceil p\ s\rceil)\right)\right) &= \mathcal{M} \left(\mathcal{E}_v\lceil r\rceil\right) \\
\text{hence} \quad (\mathcal{S}_v \circ \mathcal{M} \circ \mathcal{E}_v)\ (\mathcal{B}_!\lceil p\ s\rceil) &= (\mathcal{M} \circ \mathcal{E}_v)\ \lceil r\rceil \\
\text{hence} \quad (\mathcal{E}_v^{-1} \circ \mathcal{M}^{-1} \circ \mathcal{S}_v \circ \mathcal{M} \circ \mathcal{E}_v)\ (\mathcal{B}_!\lceil p\ s\rceil) &= \lceil r\rceil
\end{aligned}
$$

Changing the staging by symbolically composing the specializer with the monadic expansion and the explication and their inverses yields

$$
\text{eval}_v\ \lceil \mathcal{E}_v^{-1} \circ \mathcal{M}^{-1} \circ \mathcal{S}_v \circ \mathcal{M} \circ \mathcal{E}_v \rceil\ \mathcal{B}_!\lceil p\ s\rceil = \lceil r\rceil \tag{2}
$$

There are a number of advantages in return for this complication.

- The source program does not undergo any translation.
- The binding-time analysis applies directly to the source program p and can transmit useful feedback to the user of the system.
- The specialized program is built from pieces of the original source program. The inverse translation is hard-wired into the specializer.

Examples of this approach are Bondorf's specializer in extended continuation-passing style [4] and a specializer for call-by-value lambda calculus with first-class references in extended continuation-passing store-passing style [17].

Specializer in Direct Style with Monadic Operators Here we depart from writing the specializer in a pure language and use a meta-interpreter $\text{eval}_! = (\text{eval}_v \circ \mathcal{M} \circ \mathcal{E}_v)$ for $\lambda_!$ with the monad in question built in. On top of that we write a direct style specializer $\mathcal{S}_!$ in $\lambda_!$ using the built-in monadic operations. For example, if $\mathcal{S}_!$ was written in ML it could make use of exceptions, state, and control operations.

This approach has the same advantages as the previous approach. Additionally, it is usually more efficient since $\text{eval}_!$ can employ machine-level implementations of the monadic operations. Now we can reason as follows:

$$
\begin{aligned}
\lceil r\rceil &= \text{eval}_!\ \lceil \mathcal{S}_! \rceil\ (\mathcal{B}_!\lceil p\ s\rceil) \\
&= (\text{eval}_v \circ \mathcal{M} \circ \mathcal{E}_v)\ \lceil \mathcal{S}_! \rceil\ (\mathcal{B}_!\lceil p\ s\rceil) \\
&= \text{eval}_v\ (\mathcal{M}(\mathcal{E}_v\lceil \mathcal{S}_! \rceil))\ (\mathcal{B}_!\lceil p\ s\rceil)
\end{aligned}
$$

Lawall and Danvy [25] have followed exactly this path (for the continuation monad) to construct an efficient implementation of Bondorf's specializer in direct style with control operators. Their work exploits the built-in continuation monad of Scheme and ML.

Since $\mathcal{S}_!$ simply interprets unannotated pure terms, it follows that

$$\mathcal{M}(\mathcal{E}_v \lceil \mathcal{S}_! \rceil) = \lceil \mathcal{S}_! \circ \mathcal{M} \circ \mathcal{E}_v \rceil$$

This generalizes a result of Lawall and Danvy [25], namely $\lceil \mathcal{S}_c \rceil = \mathcal{C}_v \lceil \mathcal{S}_! \rceil$ where

$\mathcal{C}_v$ is a translation to extended continuation-passing style, encoding call-by-value evaluation; it holds [20] that $\mathcal{C}_v = \mathcal{M}_c \circ \mathcal{E}_v$ (where $\mathcal{M}_c$ is the monadic expansion for the continuation monad, see Sec. 5);

$\mathcal{S}_c$ is a continuation-based specializer in CPS; it holds that $\mathcal{S}_c = \mathcal{S}_v \circ \mathcal{C}_v$.

Define a Specializer for the Metalanguage Hatcliff and Danvy [21] translate p to the metalanguage via $\mathcal{E}_v$ and then define the binding-time analysis $\mathcal{B}_{ML}$ and the specializer $\mathcal{S}_{ML}$ for the metalanguage.

$$\mathcal{S}_{ML} \ (\mathcal{B}_{ML}[\![\mathcal{E}_v(\lceil p\ s\rceil)]\!]) = \mathcal{E}_v(\lceil r\rceil)$$

The specialized program is also written in the metalanguage and may have to be translated back into $\lambda_!$.

1.2 The Design Space

Figure 1 shows the design space of specialization for languages with computational effects. Again, $\lambda_!$ is an impure lambda calculus with some "built-in" effects, λ_{ML} is an enrichment of Moggi's computational metalanguage, and λ is a pure (but applied) lambda calculus. The underlined variants are the respective annotated versions of the calculi. They are connected via binding-time analyses $\mathcal{B}$ for the respective calculi. The annotated programs are mapped to their specialized versions by the respective specializer $\mathcal{S}$. The diagram should convey the idea that—ideally—the order of the transformations should not matter for the results. Paths in the diagram correspond to design choices in constructing a specializer, as exemplified before. Clearly, if the path to the specialized program does not end in the lower left of the diagram, we need inverse transformations for $\mathcal{E}$ and (possibly) $\mathcal{M}$ to get a specialized program in the source language.

The diagram suggests that a specializer has to map the annotated version of a calculus to its standard version. As a counterexample, consider the specializer $\mathcal{M}^{-1} \circ \mathcal{S}_!$ that maps $\underline{\lambda}_!$ to λ_{ML}.

1.3 Our Approach

We distinguish three languages, the annotated source language $\underline{\lambda}_!$, the annotated computational metalanguage $\underline{\lambda}_{ML}$, and an *implementation language* λimpl, which

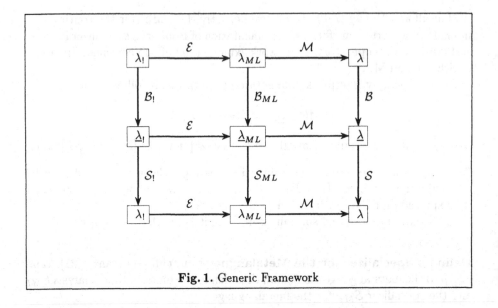

Fig. 1. Generic Framework

is a functional programming language equipped with a particular monad T . All of them are defined in Sec. 2. In Sec. 3, we define a monadic semantics for the annotated source language in terms of an explication translation from $\underline{\lambda}_!$ to $\underline{\lambda}_{ML}$. The actual specializer maps $\underline{\lambda}_{ML}$ programs to $\lambda_!$ programs. This has two advantages: the binding-time analysis and the explication of the evaluation order are left to the frontend and an inverse of the explication translation is not required. The first stage of specialization, $\mathcal{G}$, maps $\underline{\lambda}_{ML}$ programs to λimpl programs. $\mathcal{G}$ is generalized from a continuation interpretation for $\underline{\lambda}_{ML}$ in Sec. 4. Evaluation of the λimpl program yields the specialized program in $\lambda_!$. Subsequently, we instantiate T with various monads and discuss the outcome: the continuation monad yields continuation-based partial evaluation (Sec. 5), the identity monad yields Gomard and Jones's specializer for the lambda calculus (Sec. 6), a combination of the continuation monad and the store monad yields a specializer for core ML with references (Sec. 7), a combination of the continuation monad and the exception monad yields a specializer that can process exceptions at specialization time (Sec. 8). For each choice of monad T we give a specification $\mathcal{G}_T$ of the monadic operators in terms of λ. The composition $\mathcal{G}_T \circ \mathcal{G}$ plays the role of $\mathcal{M}$ in the diagram. As outlined in 1.1 above, any implementation of the operators will do, as long as it obeys the specification.

2 Notation

2.1 Annotated Lambda Calculus

The source language is a simply typed annotated lambda calculus $\underline{\lambda}$. It will be extended later to $\underline{\lambda}_!$ to demonstrate the treatment of monadic effects like state and exceptions. It is straightforward to extend both with the usual programming constructs. The typing rules are standard.

$$\text{terms } E ::= x \mid \lambda x.E \mid E@E \mid \underline{\lambda} x.E \mid E\underline{@}E$$
$$\text{types } \tau ::= \iota \mid \tau \to \tau \mid \underline{\iota} \mid \tau \underline{\to} \tau$$

The type ι is the type of integers, and $\tau \to \tau'$ is the type of functions that map τ to τ'. In the implementation, the underlined (dynamic) types are subsumed in the type Code. Beta reduction of static terms is the only rule of computation.

We use standard notational conventions: application associates to the left, the scope of a λ goes as far to the right as possible, and we can merge lambda abstractions as in $\lambda xy.E$. As usual, $\Rightarrow$ is single step reduction, $\Rightarrow\!\!\Rightarrow$ is the reflexive transitive closure of $\Rightarrow$, and $=$ is the reflexive, transitive, and symmetric closure of $\Rightarrow$.

2.2 Annotated Computational Metalanguage

The computational metalanguage [30] is an extended lambda calculus that makes the introduction and composition of computations explicit. Here is the syntax of its annotated version [21]:

$$\text{terms } M ::= x \mid \lambda x.M \mid M@M \mid \text{unit}(M) \mid \text{let } x \Leftarrow M \text{ in } M$$
$$\mid \underline{\lambda} x.M \mid M\underline{@}M \mid \underline{\text{unit}}(M) \mid \underline{\text{let }} x \Leftarrow M \underline{\text{ in }} M$$
$$\text{types } \tau ::= \iota \mid \tau \to \tau \mid T\,\tau \mid \underline{\iota} \mid \tau \underline{\to} \tau \mid \underline{T}\,\tau$$

Intuitively, $\text{unit}(M)$ denotes a trivial computation that returns the value of M. The *monadic let* let $x \Leftarrow M_1$ in M_2 expresses the sequential composition of computations: first, M_1 is performed and then M_2 with x bound to the value returned by M_1. We augment beta reduction and the monadic reduction rules

$$\text{let } x \Leftarrow (\text{let } y \Leftarrow M_1 \text{ in } M_2) \text{ in } M_3 \to \text{let } y \Leftarrow M_1 \text{ in let } x \Leftarrow M_2 \text{ in } M_3 \quad (3)$$
$$\text{let } x \Leftarrow M \text{ in unit}(x) \to M \quad (4)$$
$$\text{let } x \Leftarrow \text{unit}(M_1) \text{ in } M_2 \to M_2[x := M_1] \quad (5)$$

by rules that reorganize underlined let expressions, too.

$$\text{let } x \Leftarrow (\underline{\text{let }} y \Leftarrow M_1 \underline{\text{ in }} M_2) \text{ in } M_3 \to \underline{\text{let }} y \Leftarrow M_1 \underline{\text{ in }} \text{let } x \Leftarrow M_2 \text{ in } M_3 \quad (6)$$
$$\underline{\text{let }} x \Leftarrow (\text{let } y \Leftarrow M_1 \text{ in } M_2) \underline{\text{ in }} M_3 \to \text{let } y \Leftarrow M_1 \text{ in } \underline{\text{let }} x \Leftarrow M_2 \underline{\text{ in }} M_3 \quad (7)$$
$$\underline{\text{let }} x \Leftarrow (\underline{\text{let }} y \Leftarrow M_1 \underline{\text{ in }} M_2) \underline{\text{ in }} M_3 \to \underline{\text{let }} y \Leftarrow M_1 \underline{\text{ in }} \underline{\text{let }} x \Leftarrow M_2 \underline{\text{ in }} M_3 \quad (8)$$

2.3 Implementation Language

The implementation language λimpl is a lambda-calculus extended with the monadic constructs and some special operators. The special operators include the binary syntax constructors $\hat{\lambda}(,)$ and $\hat{@}(,)$. Furthermore, there are operators specific to the currently used monad (see below for examples). The implementation language is no longer a true annotated language, since $\hat{\lambda}(,)$ and $\hat{@}(,)$ are merely constructors for the datatype Code. The implementation language is purposefully close to existing functional programming languages so that its programs are easily transcribed.

3 Explication

The explication translation performs the first part of the work. It maps the (annotated) source language $\lambda_!$ into the (annotated) metalanguage λ_{ML} and makes a particular evaluation order explicit. We only consider $\mathcal{E}_v()$ which fixes left-to-right call-by-value evaluation.

$$\begin{aligned}
\mathcal{E}_v(x) &\equiv \text{unit}(x) \\
\mathcal{E}_v(\lambda x.E) &\equiv \text{unit}(\lambda x.\mathcal{E}_v(E)) \\
\mathcal{E}_v(E_1 @ E_2) &\equiv \text{let } x_1 \Leftarrow \mathcal{E}_v(E_1) \text{ in let } x_2 \Leftarrow \mathcal{E}_v(E_2) \text{ in } x_1 @ x_2 \\
\mathcal{E}_v(\underline{\lambda} x.E) &\equiv \underline{\text{unit}}(\underline{\lambda} x.\mathcal{E}_v(E)) \\
\mathcal{E}_v(E_1 \underline{@} E_2) &\equiv \underline{\text{let }} x_1 \Leftarrow \mathcal{E}_v(E_1) \underline{\text{ in }} \text{let } x_2 \Leftarrow \mathcal{E}_v(E_2) \underline{\text{ in }} x_1 \underline{@} x_2
\end{aligned}$$

The translation of the underlined constructs mirrors the translation of the static constructs exactly, which in turn is standard [20]. This will always be the case for the explication translation. It is easy to show that the translation preserves typing.

Lemma 1. *Suppose* $\Gamma \vdash E : \tau$. *Then* $\mathcal{M}_v[\![\Gamma]\!] \vdash \mathcal{E}_v(E) : \mathcal{M}_{cv}[\![\tau]\!]$ *where*

$$\begin{aligned}
\mathcal{M}_{cv}[\![\tau]\!] &= \text{T } \mathcal{M}_v[\![\tau]\!] \\
\mathcal{M}_v[\![\iota]\!] &= \iota & \mathcal{M}_v[\![\tau_2 \to \tau_1]\!] &= \mathcal{M}_v[\![\tau_2]\!] \to \mathcal{M}_{cv}[\![\tau_1]\!] & \mathcal{M}_v[\![\text{Code}]\!] &= \text{Code} \\
\mathcal{M}_v[\![\{\}]\!] &= \{\} & \mathcal{M}_v[\![\Gamma\{x : \tau\}]\!] &= \mathcal{M}_v[\![\Gamma]\!]\{x : \mathcal{M}_v[\![\tau]\!]\}
\end{aligned}$$

This approach is similar to that of Hatcliff and Danvy [21]. They translate the source language to the metalanguage in the very beginning and perform the binding-time analysis on terms of the metalanguage. We can accommodate this setup, but we also support a translation from the annotated source language (after binding-time analysis) to the annotated metalanguage. Both metalanguages have in common the existence of reductions involving the underlined constructs. The language considered by Hatcliff and Danvy excludes rules (7) and (8) [21, fig. 10]. This is merely a different design choice as explained by Lawall and Thiemann [26]. The crucial point is the following theorem [21].

Theorem 1. λ_{ML} *reduction preserves operational equivalence.*

4 Semantics for λ_{ML}

The language λ_{ML} contains non-standard reductions, namely the reorganizing rules for let expressions. Hence we develop a CPS translation that maps λ_{ML} to λ in such a way that reduction in λ_{ML} is simulated by reduction in λimpl. Figure 2 defines the translation using $\widehat{\text{let}}(x, E_1, E_2)$ as syntactic sugar for $\hat{@}((\hat{\lambda}(x, E_2)), E_1)$.

Lemma 2. *Suppose* $M_1 \Rrightarrow_{ML} M_2$ *then* $\mathcal{M}_c[\![M_1]\!] =_{\lambda impl} \mathcal{M}_c[\![M_2]\!]$.

Recall that we promised a generic implementation scheme parameterized over a monad. So far, we have only produced one implementation for a particular instance, the continuation monad. Let us now abstract from this instance

$$
\begin{aligned}
\mathcal{M}_c[\![x]\!] &\equiv x \\
\mathcal{M}_c[\![\lambda x.M]\!] &\equiv \lambda x.\mathcal{M}_c[\![M]\!] \\
\mathcal{M}_c[\![M_1 @ M_2]\!] &\equiv \lambda k.\mathcal{M}_c[\![M_1]\!] @ \mathcal{M}_c[\![M_2]\!] @ k \\
\mathcal{M}_c[\![\mathrm{unit}(M)]\!] &\equiv \lambda k.k @ \mathcal{M}_c[\![M]\!] \\
\mathcal{M}_c[\![\mathrm{let}\ x \Leftarrow M_1\ \mathrm{in}\ M_2]\!] &\equiv \lambda k.\mathcal{M}_c[\![M_1]\!] @ \lambda x.\mathcal{M}_c[\![M_2]\!] @ k \\
\mathcal{M}_c[\![\underline{\lambda} x.M]\!] &\equiv \hat{\lambda}(x, \mathcal{M}_c[\![M]\!] @ \lambda z.z) \\
\mathcal{M}_c[\![M_1 \underline{@} M_2]\!] &\equiv \lambda k.k @ (\hat{@}(\mathcal{M}_c[\![M_1]\!], (\mathcal{M}_c[\![M_2]\!] @ \lambda z.z))) \ \text{if } M_2 : \underline{\mathrm{T}}\ \tau \\
&\equiv \lambda k.k @ (\hat{@}(\mathcal{M}_c[\![M_1]\!], \mathcal{M}_c[\![M_2]\!])) \\
\mathcal{M}_c[\![\underline{\mathrm{unit}}(M)]\!] &\equiv \lambda k.k @ \mathcal{M}_c[\![M]\!] \\
\mathcal{M}_c[\![\underline{\mathrm{let}}\ x \Leftarrow M_1\ \underline{\mathrm{in}}\ M_2]\!] &\equiv \lambda k.\mathcal{M}_c[\![M_1]\!] @ \lambda z.\widehat{\mathrm{let}}(x, z, \mathcal{M}_c[\![M_2]\!] @ k)
\end{aligned}
$$

Fig. 2. Annotated continuation introduction

$$
\begin{aligned}
\mathcal{G}[\![x]\!] &\equiv x \\
\mathcal{G}[\![\lambda x.M]\!] &\equiv \lambda x.\mathcal{G}[\![M]\!] \\
\mathcal{G}[\![M_1 @ M_2]\!] &\equiv \mathrm{apply}\ \mathcal{G}[\![M_1]\!]\ \mathcal{G}[\![M_2]\!] \\
\mathcal{G}[\![\mathrm{unit}(M)]\!] &\equiv \mathrm{unit}(\mathcal{G}[\![M]\!]) \\
\mathcal{G}[\![\mathrm{let}\ x \Leftarrow M_1\ \mathrm{in}\ M_2]\!] &\equiv \mathrm{let}\ x \Leftarrow \mathcal{G}[\![M_1]\!]\ \mathrm{in}\ \mathcal{G}[\![M_2]\!] \\
\mathcal{G}[\![\underline{\lambda} x.M]\!] &\equiv \hat{\lambda}(x, \sharp_{\mathrm{Code}}(\mathcal{G}[\![M]\!])) \\
\mathcal{G}[\![M_1 \underline{@} M_2]\!] &\equiv \mathrm{unit}(\hat{@}(\mathcal{G}[\![M_1]\!], \sharp_{\mathrm{Code}}(\mathcal{G}[\![M_2]\!]))) \ \text{if } M_2 : \underline{\mathrm{T}}\ \tau \\
&\equiv \mathrm{unit}(\hat{@}(\mathcal{G}[\![M_1]\!], \mathcal{G}[\![M_2]\!])) \ \text{otherwise} \\
\mathcal{G}[\![\underline{\mathrm{unit}}(M)]\!] &\equiv \mathrm{unit}(\mathcal{G}[\![M]\!]) \\
\mathcal{G}[\![\underline{\mathrm{let}}\ x \Leftarrow M_1\ \underline{\mathrm{in}}\ M_2]\!] &\equiv \mathrm{shift}_{\mathrm{Code}}\ w.\ \mathrm{let}\ z \Leftarrow \mathcal{G}[\![M_1]\!]\ \mathrm{in} \\
&\qquad\qquad \mathrm{unit}(\widehat{\mathrm{let}}(x, z, \sharp_{\mathrm{Code}}(w @ \mathcal{G}[\![M_2]\!])))
\end{aligned}
$$

Fig. 3. Translation to the implementation language

by rewriting—in the implementation language—the right sides of $\mathcal{M}_c$ such that we obtain the original definition of $\mathcal{M}_c$ by monadic expansion, i.e., CPS transformation.

Figure 3 defines the translation. It might seem like nothing has happened in this transformation. However, we have taken an important conceptual step. We have gotten rid of the annotated language with non-standard reductions in favor of a standard functional language with monadic operators. In other words, we have an implementation.

There are two non-standard constructs in the translated terms. $\sharp_{\mathrm{Code}}(M)$ denotes an effect delimiter. It runs the computation M (which may involve effects), discards all effects, and returns the result, provided that M terminates. $\mathrm{shift}_{\mathrm{Code}}\ x.M$ grabs the context of the computation up to the next enclosing $\sharp_{\mathrm{Code}}(M')$, discards it, and binds it as a function to x. The standard implementation of these operators in terms of continuations is given in the next section 5.

These operators are restricted so that shift$_{\text{Code}}$ $x.M$ only abstracts contexts that return Code. Otherwise, type soundness could not be guaranteed.

5 Continuation-Based Specialization

We obtain sound continuation-based specialization [26] from the generic specification $\mathcal{G}$ by substituting the continuation monad $T\,\tau = (\tau \to \text{Code}) \to \text{Code}$ in the implementation language.

The monadic expansion translation boils down to defining the operators apply $M\ M$, unit(M), let $x \Leftarrow M$ in M, $\sharp_{\text{Code}}(M)$, and shift$_{\text{Code}}$ $x.M$.

$$
\begin{aligned}
\mathcal{G}_c[\![x]\!] &\equiv x \\
\mathcal{G}_c[\![\lambda x.M]\!] &\equiv \lambda x.\mathcal{G}_c[\![M]\!] \\
\mathcal{G}_c[\![\text{apply } M_1\ M_2]\!] &\equiv \lambda k.\mathcal{G}_c[\![M_1]\!]@\mathcal{G}_c[\![M_2]\!]@k \\
\mathcal{G}_c[\![\hat{\lambda}(x, M)]\!] &\equiv \hat{\lambda}(x, \mathcal{G}_c[\![M]\!]) \\
\mathcal{G}_c[\![\hat{@}(M_1, M_2)]\!] &\equiv \hat{@}(\mathcal{G}_c[\![M_1]\!], \mathcal{G}_c[\![M_2]\!]) \\
\mathcal{G}_c[\![\text{unit}(M)]\!] &\equiv \lambda k.k@\mathcal{G}_c[\![M]\!] \\
\mathcal{G}_c[\![\text{let } x \Leftarrow M_1 \text{ in } M_2]\!] &\equiv \lambda k.\mathcal{G}_c[\![M_1]\!]@\lambda x.\mathcal{G}_c[\![M_2]\!]@k \\
\mathcal{G}_c[\![\sharp_{\text{Code}}(M)]\!] &\equiv \mathcal{G}_c[\![M]\!]@\lambda x.x \\
\mathcal{G}_c[\![\text{shift}_{\text{Code}}\ x.M]\!] &\equiv \lambda k.(\lambda x.\mathcal{G}_c[\![M]\!]@\lambda z.z)@\lambda y.\lambda k'.k'@(k@y)
\end{aligned}
$$

Here is the connection to $\mathcal{M}_c$ with $\circ$ denoting composition.

Lemma 3. $\mathcal{G}_c \circ \mathcal{G} \Rrightarrow_\beta \mathcal{M}_c$.

For the specializer $\mathcal{S}_c$ of Lawall and Thiemann [26] we find:

Lemma 4. $(\mathcal{G}_c \circ \mathcal{G} \circ \mathcal{E}_v) \Rrightarrow_\beta \mathcal{S}_c$.

There are specifications of continuation-based specialization in direct style [25] that employ the control operators shift and reset [14]. In contrast to reset, $\sharp_{\text{Code}}()$ is a general effect delimiter that runs an encapsulated computation, extracts its results, and hides all its effects. The difference is visible in the computation type of "reset(M)".

6 Specialization for the Lambda Calculus

Gomard's specializer Lambdamix [19] is targeted towards an applied lambda calculus. It results from setting $T\,\tau = \tau$, the identity monad.

$$
\begin{aligned}
\mathcal{G}_i[\![x]\!] &\equiv x & \mathcal{G}_i[\![\text{unit}(M)]\!] &\equiv \mathcal{G}_i[\![M]\!] \\
\mathcal{G}_i[\![\lambda x.M]\!] &\equiv \lambda x.\mathcal{G}_i[\![M]\!] & \mathcal{G}_i[\![\text{let } x \Leftarrow M_1 \text{ in } M_2]\!] &\equiv (\lambda x.\mathcal{G}_i[\![M_2]\!])@\mathcal{G}_i[\![M_1]\!] \\
\mathcal{G}_i[\![\text{apply } M_1\ M_2]\!] &\equiv \mathcal{G}_i[\![M_1]\!]@\mathcal{G}_i[\![M_2]\!] & \mathcal{G}_i[\![\sharp_{\text{Code}}(M)]\!] &\equiv \mathcal{G}_i[\![M]\!] \\
\mathcal{G}_i[\![\hat{\lambda}(x, M)]\!] &\equiv \hat{\lambda}(x, \mathcal{G}_i[\![M]\!]) & \mathcal{G}_i[\![\text{shift}_{\text{Code}}\ x.M]\!] &\equiv (\lambda x.\mathcal{G}_i[\![M]\!])@(\lambda z.z) \\
\mathcal{G}_i[\![\hat{@}(M_1, M_2)]\!] &\equiv \hat{@}(\mathcal{G}_i[\![M_1]\!], \mathcal{G}_i[\![M_2]\!]) & &
\end{aligned}
$$

Calling Lambdamix $\mathcal{S}_i$ we have the following connection (see also [38]):

Lemma 5. $(\mathcal{G}_i \circ \mathcal{E}_n) \Rrightarrow_\beta \mathcal{S}_i$

7 Specialization with Mutable Store

If we set $T\ \tau = (\tau \times \text{Store} \to \text{Code} \times \text{Store}) \to \text{Store} \to \text{Code} \times \text{Store}$ (a continuation-passing and store-passing monad) we obtain a specializer for a language with mutable store [17]. The expansion now reads as follows (using $(,)$ for pairing and π_i for projection).

$$
\begin{aligned}
\mathcal{G}_s[\![x]\!] &\equiv x \\
\mathcal{G}_s[\![\lambda x.M]\!] &\equiv \lambda x.\mathcal{G}_s[\![M]\!] \\
\mathcal{G}_s[\![\text{apply } M_1\ M_2]\!] &\equiv \lambda ks.\mathcal{G}_s[\![M_1]\!]@\mathcal{G}_s[\![M_2]\!]@k@s \\
\mathcal{G}_s[\![\hat{\lambda}(x,M)]\!] &\equiv \hat{\lambda}(x,\mathcal{G}_s[\![M]\!]) \\
\mathcal{G}_s[\![\hat{@}(M_1,M_2)]\!] &\equiv \hat{@}(\mathcal{G}_s[\![M_1]\!],\mathcal{G}_s[\![M_2]\!]) \\
\mathcal{G}_s[\![\text{unit}(M)]\!] &\equiv \lambda ks.k@(\mathcal{G}_s[\![M]\!],s) \\
\mathcal{G}_s[\![\text{let } x \Leftarrow M_1 \text{ in } M_2]\!] &\equiv \lambda ks.\mathcal{G}_s[\![M_1]\!]@(\lambda(x,s').\mathcal{G}_s[\![M_2]\!]@k@s')@s \\
\mathcal{G}_s[\![\sharp_{\text{Code}}(M)]\!] &\equiv \pi_1(\mathcal{G}_s[\![M]\!]@(\lambda(x,s).(x,s))@s_{\text{empty}}) \\
\mathcal{G}_s[\![\text{shift}_{\text{Code}}\ x.M]\!] &\equiv \lambda ks.(\lambda x.\mathcal{G}_s[\![M]\!]@(\lambda(z,s').(z,s'))@s)@\lambda y.\lambda k's'.k'@(k@(y,s'))
\end{aligned}
$$

The only problematic cases are $\sharp_{\text{Code}}(M)$ and $\text{shift}_{\text{Code}}\ x.M$. The $\sharp_{\text{Code}}(M)$ case shows that the standard reset operator is not sufficient here. The computation M is applied to the empty continuation $\lambda(x,s).(x,s)$ and the empty store s_{empty}. In the end the Store component is discarded and only the value returned. An implementation of reset would have to thread the store through the computation.

Since $\sharp_{\text{Code}}(M)$ discards the static store, the binding-time analysis *must guarantee* that each reference, whose lifetime crosses the effect delimiter, is dynamic. We have developed such an analysis elsewhere [37].

To understand the implementation of $\text{shift}_{\text{Code}}\ x.M$ observe that the computation M is applied to the empty continuation and to the current store s. In the translated term, each occurrence of x stands for a function that accepts a value y, a continuation k', and a store s'. The function applies the captured continuation k to (y, s') to obtain the result of k paired with the resulting store. Both are passed to k' to produce the result of the computation.

Specialization with a store is not very interesting without any operations on it. We add the standard set of primitive operations, to allocate, read, and update references, to the source language.

$$
\begin{aligned}
E &::= \ldots \mid \text{ref } E \mid !\ E \mid E := E \mid \underline{\text{ref}}\ E \mid \underline{!}\ E \mid E \underline{:=} E \\
\tau &::= \ldots \mid \text{ref } \tau \mid \underline{\text{ref}}\ \tau
\end{aligned}
$$

The typing rules and operational semantics are again standard (similar to ML). The metalanguage and the implementation language are extended by the same set of operators, but the result type of all these operations is a computation type, i.e., we consider Store an abstract datatype with operations $\text{mkref} : \mathcal{M}_v[\![\tau \to \text{ref } \tau]\!]$, $\text{rdref} : \mathcal{M}_v[\![\text{ref } \tau \to \tau]\!]$, and $\text{wrref} : \text{ref } \tau \to \mathcal{M}_v[\![\tau \to \tau]\!]$. Extending the explication is standard:

$$
\begin{aligned}
\mathcal{E}_v(\text{ref } E) &\equiv \text{let } x \Leftarrow \mathcal{E}_v(E) \text{ in ref } x \\
\mathcal{E}_v(!\ E) &\equiv \text{let } x \Leftarrow \mathcal{E}_v(E) \text{ in }!\ x \\
\mathcal{E}_v(E_1 := E_2) &\equiv \text{let } x_1 \Leftarrow \mathcal{E}_v(E_1) \text{ in let } x_2 \Leftarrow \mathcal{E}_v(E_2) \text{ in } x_1 := x_2
\end{aligned}
$$

$\mathcal{G}$ requires some more care.

$$\mathcal{G}[\![\text{ref } M]\!] \equiv \text{ref } \mathcal{G}[\![M]\!] \qquad\qquad \mathcal{G}[\![\underline{\text{ref }} M]\!] \quad \equiv \text{unit}(\widehat{\text{ref}}(\sharp_{\text{Code}}(\mathcal{G}[\![M]\!]))) \text{ if } M : \underline{T}\,\tau$$
$$\mathcal{G}[\![! M]\!] \quad \equiv \,! \,\mathcal{G}[\![M]\!] \qquad\qquad\qquad\quad\;\; \equiv \text{unit}(\widehat{\text{ref}}(\mathcal{G}[\![M]\!])) \text{ otherwise}$$
$$\mathcal{G}[\![\underline{!} M]\!] \quad \equiv \text{unit}(\widehat{!}(\mathcal{G}[\![M]\!])) \quad \mathcal{G}[\![M_1 := M_2]\!] \equiv \mathcal{G}[\![M_1]\!] := \mathcal{G}[\![M_2]\!]$$
$$\mathcal{G}[\![M_1 \underline{:=} M_2]\!] \equiv \text{unit}(\widehat{:=}(\mathcal{G}[\![M_1]\!], \sharp_{\text{Code}}(\mathcal{G}[\![M_2]\!]))) \text{ if } M_2 : \underline{T}\,\tau$$
$$\equiv \text{unit}(\widehat{:=}(\mathcal{G}[\![M_1]\!], \mathcal{G}[\![M_2]\!])) \text{ otherwise}$$

The translation depends on the type of terms. In the image of the call-by-name translation, the argument of $\underline{\text{ref}}$ and the second argument of $\underline{:=}$ have computation type. The placement of the delimiter $\sharp_{\text{Code}}()$ is required to preserve type correctness. Since each effect delimiter causes less effects to be performed at specialization time, it is obvious that in a call-by-name language with effects less computations are performed in a known context. The monadic expansion to the implementation language is straightforward.

$$\mathcal{G}_s[\![\text{ref } M]\!] \quad \equiv \lambda ks.\text{mkref } \mathcal{G}_s[\![M]\!] \; ks \qquad \mathcal{G}_s[\![\underline{\text{ref}}(M)]\!] \quad \equiv \widehat{\text{ref}}(\mathcal{G}_s[\![M]\!])$$
$$\mathcal{G}_s[\![! M]\!] \quad \equiv \lambda ks.\text{rdref } \mathcal{G}_s[\![M]\!] \; ks \qquad\quad \mathcal{G}_s[\![\underline{!}(M)]\!] \quad \equiv \widehat{!}(\mathcal{G}_s[\![M]\!])$$
$$\mathcal{G}_s[\![M_1 := M_2]\!] \equiv \lambda ks.\text{wrref } \mathcal{G}_s[\![M_1]\!] \; \mathcal{G}_s[\![M_2]\!] \; ks \qquad \mathcal{G}_s[\![\underline{:=}(M_1, M_2)]\!] \equiv \widehat{:=}(\mathcal{G}_s[\![M_1]\!], \mathcal{G}_s[\![M_2]\!])$$

8 Specialization with Exceptions

Finally, we embark on processing exceptions at specialization time. We use a model of exceptions with "raise E" and "E_1 handle E_2" constructs to raise and intercept exceptions and one fixed type "Exception" of exceptions. We assume that E_2 is a function that maps Exception to the same type as E_1.

$$E ::= \ldots \mid \text{raise } E \mid E \text{ handle } E \mid \underline{\text{raise }} E \mid E \;\underline{\text{handle }} E$$

The extension of the explication translation is standard:

$$\mathcal{E}_v(\text{raise } E) \qquad = \text{let } x \Leftarrow \mathcal{E}_v(E) \text{ in raise } x$$
$$\mathcal{E}_v(E_1 \text{ handle } E_2) = \mathcal{E}_v(E) \text{ handle } \lambda x.\mathcal{E}_v(E_2@x)$$

The interesting part is the translation $\mathcal{G}$.

$$\mathcal{G}[\![\text{raise } M]\!] \qquad\quad = \text{raise } \mathcal{G}[\![M]\!]$$
$$\mathcal{G}[\![M_1 \text{ handle } M_2]\!] = \mathcal{G}[\![M_1]\!] \text{ handle } \mathcal{G}[\![M_2]\!]$$
$$\mathcal{G}[\![\underline{\text{raise }} M]\!] \qquad\quad = \widehat{\text{raise}}(\mathcal{G}[\![M]\!])$$
$$\mathcal{G}[\![M_1 \;\underline{\text{handle }} M_2]\!] = \widehat{\text{handle}}(\sharp_{\text{Code}}(\mathcal{G}[\![M_1]\!]), \mathcal{G}[\![M_2]\!])$$

In the definition of the monadic expansion $\mathcal{M}_e$ for the exception monad, we write $[f, g] : (A + B) \to C$ if $f : A \to C$ and $g : B \to C$. We use standard notation for the injection functions $\text{inl} : A \to A + B$ and $\text{inr} : B \to A + B$. We do not use the straightforward exception monad, but a composition with the continuation monad, which is required to define a sound call-by-value specializer with exceptions.

$$\text{T}\,\tau = ((\tau + \text{Exception}) \to (\text{Code} + \text{Exception})) \to (\text{Code} + \text{Exception})$$

$$\mathcal{G}_e[\![x]\!] \equiv x$$
$$\mathcal{G}_e[\![\lambda x.M]\!] \equiv \lambda x.\mathcal{G}_e[\![M]\!]$$
$$\mathcal{G}_e[\![M_1 @ M_2]\!] \equiv \lambda k.\mathcal{G}_e[\![M_1]\!]@\mathcal{G}_e[\![M_2]\!]@k$$
$$\mathcal{G}_e[\![\hat{\lambda}(x, M)]\!] \equiv \hat{\lambda}(x, \mathcal{G}_e[\![M]\!])$$
$$\mathcal{G}_e[\![\hat{@}(M_1, M_2)]\!] \equiv \hat{@}(\mathcal{G}_e[\![M_1]\!], \mathcal{G}_e[\![M_2]\!])$$
$$\mathcal{G}_e[\![\mathrm{unit}(M)]\!] \equiv \lambda k.k@(\mathrm{inl}\ \mathcal{G}_e[\![M]\!])$$
$$\mathcal{G}_e[\![\mathrm{let}\ x \Leftarrow M_1\ \mathrm{in}\ M_2]\!] \equiv \lambda k.\mathcal{G}_e[\![M_1]\!]@[\lambda x.\mathcal{G}_e[\![M_2]\!]@k, \lambda y.k@\mathrm{inr}\ y]$$
$$\mathcal{G}_e[\![\sharp_{\mathrm{Code}}(M)]\!] \equiv \mathcal{G}_e[\![M]\!]@[\lambda x.x, \lambda y.\hat{\lambda}(z, z)]$$
$$\mathcal{G}_e[\![\mathrm{shift}_{\mathrm{Code}}\ x.M]\!] \equiv \lambda k.(\lambda x.\mathcal{G}_e[\![M]\!]@[\lambda z.\mathrm{inl}\ z, \lambda z.\mathrm{inr}\ z])@\lambda y.\lambda k'.k'@(k@(\mathrm{inl}\ y))$$
$$\mathcal{G}_e[\![\mathrm{raise}\ M]\!] \equiv \lambda k.k@(\mathrm{inr}\ \mathcal{G}_e[\![M]\!])$$
$$\mathcal{G}_e[\![\widehat{\mathrm{raise}}(M)]\!] \equiv \widehat{\mathrm{raise}}(\mathcal{G}_e[\![M]\!])$$
$$\mathcal{G}_e[\![M_1\ \mathrm{handle}\ M_2]\!] \equiv \lambda k.\mathcal{G}_e[\![M_1]\!]@[\lambda x.k@(\mathrm{inl}\ x), \mathcal{G}_e[\![M_2]\!]@k]$$
$$\mathcal{G}_e[\![M_1\ \mathrm{handle}\ M_2]\!] \equiv \mathcal{G}_e[\![M_1]\!]\ \mathrm{handle}\ \mathcal{G}_e[\![M_2]\!]$$

Again, the placement of $\sharp_{\mathrm{Code}}(M)$ restricts the binding-time analysis. All exceptions that may cross the effect delimiter must be dynamic.

9 Related Work

There are two formalizations of partial evaluation using Moggi's work [30]. Hatcliff and Danvy [21] define a binding-time analysis and specialization for an annotated version of the monadic metalanguage. Their specializer exploits the monadic law 3 to "flatten" nested let expressions. To obtain an executable specification of the specializer they define a separate operational semantics (close to an abstract machine) that they prove equivalent to their first definition of specialization. Lawall and Thiemann [26] define an annotated version of Moggi's computational lambda calculus and show that it is implementable through a annotated CPS translation. This translation forms a reflection in a annotated lambda calculus of the annotated computational lambda calculus. Thus they show that a particular flavor of continuation-based partial evaluation is sound for all monadic models, thereby establishing firm ground for the development of specializers with computational effects expressed through monads.

In contrast to these works, the present work continues the work on monadic interpreters [18, 28, 40] in that it shows how to use monads to structure specializers in functional programming languages. Hence, the focus is on directly executable specifications. Our specifications implement the flattening transformation (the monad law 3) using special operations of the monad used to implement the specializer. Incidentally, these operations correspond to effect delimiters, control operators, and store operators [22]. We rely on the two above works [21, 26] for the soundness of this approach.

Effect delimiters have been considered by a number of researchers for varying purposes. Riecke and Viswanathan [35, 36] construct fully abstract denotational semantics for languages with monadic effects. Launchbury and Peyton Jones [24] define an effect delimiter for the state monad with a second order polymorphic type to encapsulate state-based computations. Similar operators have been used by Dussart et al [16] in order to get satisfactory results in a type specializer for the monadic metalanguage extended with mutable store (as in Sec.7).

There are offline partial evaluators for first-order imperative languages [1, 5, 7, 11, 12] and for higher-order languages [2, 3, 8, 29]. However, most partial evaluators for higher-order imperative languages [2, 3, 6] defer all computational effects to run time [5]. Realistic partial evaluators for higher-order languages with side effects must be able to perform side effects at specialization time. The only partial evaluator so far capable of this has been specified for a subset of Scheme by Thiemann and Dussart [17]. That work defines the specializer in extended continuation-passing store-passing style, it defines a binding-time analysis (which is proved correct elsewhere [37]), and considers pragmatic aspects such as efficient management of the store at specialization time and specialization of named program points. In contrast, the present work identifies a general scheme underlying the construction of specializers that address languages with computational effects. It does so in an evaluation-order independent framework and is built around monads in order to achieve maximum flexibility.

Birkedal and Welinder [2] developed an ad hoc scheme to deal with exceptions in their specializer for ML. It needs a separate correctness proof, because it is not based on the monadic metalanguage.

10 Conclusion

We have specified a generic framework for partial evaluation and demonstrated that it subsumes many existing algorithms for partial evaluation. The framework is correct for all monadic instances since it only performs reductions which are sound in the computational metalanguage.

In addition, we have investigated the construction of a generic binding-time analysis for languages with arbitrary effects, the construction of program generators instead of specializers, and the construction of specializers in direct style. These are reported in the full version of this paper [38] which also considers the call-by-name explication and some further language constructs, namely numbers and primitive operations, conditionals, and recursion.

References

1. Lars Ole Andersen. *Program Analysis and Specialization for the C Programming Language*. PhD thesis, DIKU, University of Copenhagen, May 1994. (DIKU report 94/19).
2. Lars Birkedal and Morten Welinder. Partial evaluation of Standard ML. Rapport 93/22, DIKU, University of Copenhagen, 1993.
3. Anders Bondorf. Automatic autoprojection of higher order recursive equations. *Science of Programming*, 17:3–34, 1991.
4. Anders Bondorf. Improving binding times without explicit CPS-conversion. In *Proc. 1992 ACM Conference on Lisp and Functional Programming*, pages 1–10, San Francisco, California, USA, June 1992.

5. Anders Bondorf and Olivier Danvy. Automatic autoprojection of recursive equations with global variables and abstract data types. *Science of Programming*, 16(2):151–195, 1991.

6. Anders Bondorf and Jesper Jørgensen. Efficient analysis for realistic off-line partial evaluation. *Journal of Functional Programming*, 3(3):315–346, July 1993.

7. Mikhail A. Bulyonkov and Dmitrij V. Kochetov. Practical aspects of specialization of Algol-like programs. In Danvy et al. [15], pages 17–32.

8. Charles Consel. Polyvariant binding-time analysis for applicative languages. In David Schmidt, editor, *Proc. ACM SIGPLAN Symposium on Partial Evaluation and Semantics-Based Program Manipulation PEPM '93*, pages 66–77, Copenhagen, Denmark, June 1993. ACM Press.

9. Charles Consel and Olivier Danvy. For a better support of static data flow. In John Hughes, editor, *Proc. Functional Programming Languages and Computer Architecture 1991*, volume 523 of *Lecture Notes in Computer Science*, pages 496–519, Cambridge, MA, 1991. Springer-Verlag.

10. Charles Consel and Olivier Danvy. Tutorial notes on partial evaluation. In POPL1993 [33], pages 493–501.

11. Charles Consel, Luke Hornof, François Noël, Jacques Noyé, and Nicolae Volanschi. A uniform approach for compile-time and run-time specialization. In Danvy et al. [15], pages 54–72.

12. Charles Consel and Francois Noël. A general approach for run-time specialization and its application to C. In *Proc. 23rd Annual ACM Symposium on Principles of Programming Languages*, pages 145–156, St. Petersburg, Fla., January 1996. ACM Press.

13. Olivier Danvy. Back to direct style. *Science of Programming*, 22:183–195, 1994.

14. Olivier Danvy and Andrzej Filinski. Abstracting control. In LFP 1990 [27], pages 151–160.

15. Olivier Danvy, Robert Glück, and Peter Thiemann, editors. *Dagstuhl Seminar on Partial Evaluation 1996*, volume 1110 of *Lecture Notes in Computer Science*, Schloß Dagstuhl, Germany, February 1996. Springer-Verlag.

16. Dirk Dussart, John Hughes, and Peter Thiemann. Type specialisation for imperative languages. In Mads Tofte, editor, *Proc. International Conference on Functional Programming 1997*, pages 204–216, Amsterdam, The Netherlands, June 1997. ACM Press, New York.

17. Dirk Dussart and Peter Thiemann. Partial evaluation for higher-order languages with state. Berichte des Wilhelm-Schickard-Instituts WSI-97-XX, Universität Tübingen, April 1997.

18. David Espinosa. Building interpreters by transforming stratified monads. ftp://altdorf.ai.mit.edu/pub/dae, June 1994.

19. Carsten K. Gomard and Neil D. Jones. Compiler generation by partial evaluation: A case study. *Structured Programming*, 12:123–144, 1991.

20. John Hatcliff and Olivier Danvy. A generic account of continuation-passing styles. In *Proc. 21st Annual ACM Symposium on Principles of Programming Languages*, pages 458–471, Portland, OG, January 1994. ACM Press.

21. John Hatcliff and Olivier Danvy. A computational formalization for partial evaluation. *Mathematical Structures in Computer Science*, 7(5):507–542, 1997.

22. G. F. Johnson and Dominic Duggan. Stores and partial continuations as first-class objects in a language and its environment. In *Proc. 15th Annual ACM Symposium on Principles of Programming Languages*, pages 158–168, San Diego, California, January 1988. ACM Press.

23. Neil D. Jones, Carsten K. Gomard, and Peter Sestoft. *Partial Evaluation and Automatic Program Generation*. Prentice-Hall, 1993.
24. John Launchbury and Simon L. Peyton Jones. Lazy functional state threads. In *Proc. of the ACM SIGPLAN '94 Conference on Programming Language Design and Implementation*, pages 24–35, Orlando, Fla, USA, June 1994. ACM Press.
25. Julia Lawall and Olivier Danvy. Continuation-based partial evaluation. In *Proc. 1994 ACM Conference on Lisp and Functional Programming*, pages 227–238, Orlando, Florida, USA, June 1994. ACM Press.
26. Julia Lawall and Peter Thiemann. Sound specialization in the presence of computational effects. In *Proc. Theoretical Aspects of Computer Software*, volume 1281 of *Lecture Notes in Computer Science*, pages 165–190, Sendai, Japan, September 1997. Springer-Verlag.
27. *Proc. 1990 ACM Conference on Lisp and Functional Programming*, Nice, France, 1990. ACM Press.
28. Sheng Liang, Paul Hudak, and Mark Jones. Monad transformers and modular interpreters. In POPL1995 [34], pages 333–343.
29. Karoline Malmkjær, Nevin Heintze, and Olivier Danvy. ML partial evaluation using set-based analysis. In *Record of the 1994 ACM SIGPLAN Workshop on ML and its Applications*, number 2265 in INRIA Research Report, pages 112–119, Orlando, Florida, June 1994.
30. Eugenio Moggi. Notions of computations and monads. *Information and Computation*, 93:55–92, 1991.
31. Bàrbara Moura, Charles Consel, and Julia Lawall. Bridging the gap between functional and imperative languages. Publication interne 1027, Irisa, Rennes, France, July 1996.
32. Simon L. Peyton Jones and Philip L. Wadler. Imperative functional programming. In POPL1993 [33], pages 71–84.
33. *Proc. 20th Annual ACM Symposium on Principles of Programming Languages*, Charleston, South Carolina, January 1993. ACM Press.
34. *Proc. 22nd Annual ACM Symposium on Principles of Programming Languages*, San Francisco, CA, January 1995. ACM Press.
35. John Riecke. Delimiting the scope of effects. In Arvind, editor, *Proc. Functional Programming Languages and Computer Architecture 1993*, pages 146–155, Copenhagen, Denmark, June 1993. ACM Press, New York.
36. John Riecke and Ramesh Viswanathan. Isolating side effects in sequential languages. In POPL1995 [34], pages 1–12.
37. Peter Thiemann. Correctness of a region-based binding-time analysis. In *Proc. Mathematical Foundations of Programming Semantics, Thirteenth Annual Conference*, volume 6 of *Electronic Notes in Theoretical Computer Science*, page 26, Pittsburgh, PA, March 1997. Carnegie Mellon University, Elsevier Science BV. URL: http://www.elsevier.nl/locate/entcs/volume6.html.
38. Peter Thiemann. A generic framework for specialization. Berichte des Wilhelm-Schickard-Instituts WSI-97-XXX, Universität Tübingen, October 1997.
39. Philip L. Wadler. Comprehending monads. In LFP 1990 [27], pages 61–78.
40. Philip L. Wadler. The essence of functional programming. In *Proc. 19th Annual ACM Symposium on Principles of Programming Languages*, pages 1–14, Albuquerque, New Mexico, January 1992. ACM Press.

Author Index

M. Abadi	12		K. R. M. Leino	170
			M. Leuschel	27
M. Bruynooghe	27			
			F. Maraninchi	185
L. Caires	42		L. Monteiro	42
R. Chatterjee	57			
W.-N. Chin	75		Y. Rémond	185
			D. Rémy	200
C. Fecht	90		J. L. Ross	221
			S. Ruggieri	236
A. D. Gordon	12		O. Rüthing	154
			B. G. Ryder	57
U. Hensel	105			
K. Honda	122		M. Sagiv	221
M. Huisman	105		K. Sagonas	27
			W. L. Scherlis	252
B. Jacobs	105		H. Seidl	90
C. B. Jay	139		G. Smolka	1
			P. A. Steckler	139
S.-C. Khoo	75		B. Steffen	154
J. Knoop	154			
M. Kubo	122		H. Tews	105
			P. Thiemann	267
W. A. Landi	57			
T.-W. Lee	75		V. T. Vasconcelos	122

Lecture Notes in Computer Science

For information about Vols. 1–1300

please contact your bookseller or Springer-Verlag

Vol. 1301: M. Jazayeri, H. Schauer (Eds.), Software Engineering - ESEC/FSE'97. Proceedings, 1997. XIII, 532 pages. 1997.

Vol. 1302: P. Van Hentenryck (Ed.), Static Analysis. Proceedings, 1997. X, 413 pages. 1997.

Vol. 1303: G. Brewka, C. Habel, B. Nebel (Eds.), KI-97: Advances in Artificial Intelligence. Proceedings, 1997. XI, 413 pages. 1997. (Subseries LNAI).

Vol. 1304: W. Luk, P.Y.K. Cheung, M. Glesner (Eds.), Field-Programmable Logic and Applications. Proceedings, 1997. XI, 503 pages. 1997.

Vol. 1305: D. Corne, J.L. Shapiro (Eds.), Evolutionary Computing. Proceedings, 1997. X, 307 pages. 1997.

Vol. 1306: C. Leung (Ed.), Visual Information Systems. X, 274 pages. 1997.

Vol. 1307: R. Kompe, Prosody in Speech Understanding Systems. XIX, 357 pages. 1997. (Subseries LNAI).

Vol. 1308: A. Hameurlain, A M. Tjoa (Eds.), Database and Expert Systems Applications. Proceedings, 1997. XVII, 688 pages. 1997.

Vol. 1309: R. Steinmetz, L.C. Wolf (Eds.), Interactive Distributed Multimedia Systems and Telecommunication Services. Proceedings, 1997. XIII, 466 pages. 1997.

Vol. 1310: A. Del Bimbo (Ed.), Image Analysis and Processing. Proceedings, 1997. Volume I. XXII, 722 pages. 1997.

Vol. 1311: A. Del Bimbo (Ed.), Image Analysis and Processing. Proceedings, 1997. Volume II. XXII, 794 pages. 1997.

Vol. 1312: A. Geppert, M. Berndtsson (Eds.), Rules in Database Systems. Proceedings, 1997. VII, 214 pages. 1997.

Vol. 1313: J. Fitzgerald, C.B. Jones, P. Lucas (Eds.), FME '97: Industrial Applications and Strengthened Foundations of Formal Methods. Proceedings, 1997. XIII, 685 pages. 1997.

Vol. 1314: S. Muggleton (Ed.), Inductive Logic Programming. Proceedings, 1996. VIII, 397 pages. 1997. (Subseries LNAI).

Vol. 1315: G. Sommer, J.J. Koenderink (Eds.), Algebraic Frames for the Perception-Action Cycle. Proceedings. 1997. VIII, 395 pages. 1997.

Vol. 1316: M. Li, A. Maruoka (Eds.), Algorithmic Learning Theory. Proceedings, 1997. XI, 461 pages. 1997. (Subseries LNAI).

Vol. 1317: M. Leman (Ed.), Music, Gestalt, and Computing. IX, 524 pages. 1997. (Subseries LNAI).

Vol. 1318: R. Hirschfeld (Ed.), Financial Cryptography. Proceedings, 1997. XI, 409 pages. 1997.

Vol. 1319: E. Plaza, R. Benjamins (Eds.), Knowledge Acquisition, Modeling and Management. Proceedings, 1997. XI, 389 pages. 1997. (Subseries LNAI).

Vol. 1320: M. Mavronicolas, P. Tsigas (Eds.), Distributed Algorithms. Proceedings, 1997. X, 333 pages. 1997.

Vol. 1321: M. Lenzerini (Ed.), AI*IA 97: Advances in Artificial Intelligence. Proceedings, 1997. XII, 459 pages. 1997. (Subseries LNAI).

Vol. 1322: H. Hußmann, Formal Foundations for Software Engineering Methods. X, 286 pages. 1997.

Vol. 1323: E. Costa, A. Cardoso (Eds.), Progress in Artificial Intelligence. Proceedings, 1997. XIV, 393 pages. 1997. (Subseries LNAI).

Vol. 1324: C. Peters, C. Thanos (Eds.), Research and Advanced Technology for Digital Libraries. Proceedings, 1997. X, 423 pages. 1997.

Vol. 1325: Z.W. Raś, A. Skowron (Eds.), Foundations of Intelligent Systems. Proceedings, 1997. XI, 630 pages. 1997. (Subseries LNAI).

Vol. 1326: C. Nicholas, J. Mayfield (Eds.), Intelligent Hypertext. XIV, 182 pages. 1997.

Vol. 1327: W. Gerstner, A. Germond, M. Hasler, J.-D. Nicoud (Eds.), Artificial Neural Networks – ICANN '97. Proceedings, 1997. XIX, 1274 pages. 1997.

Vol. 1328: C. Retoré (Ed.), Logical Aspects of Computational Linguistics. Proceedings, 1996. VIII, 435 pages. 1997. (Subseries LNAI).

Vol. 1329: S.C. Hirtle, A.U. Frank (Eds.), Spatial Information Theory. Proceedings, 1997. XIV, 511 pages. 1997.

Vol. 1330: G. Smolka (Ed.), Principles and Practice of Constraint Programming – CP 97. Proceedings, 1997. XII, 563 pages. 1997.

Vol. 1331: D. W. Embley, R. C. Goldstein (Eds.), Conceptual Modeling – ER '97. Proceedings, 1997. XV, 479 pages. 1997.

Vol. 1332: M. Bubak, J. Dongarra, J. Waśniewski (Eds.), Recent Advances in Parallel Virtual Machine and Message Passing Interface. Proceedings, 1997. XV, 518 pages. 1997.

Vol. 1333: F. Pichler. R.Moreno-Díaz (Eds.), Computer Aided Systems Theory – EUROCAST'97. Proceedings, 1997. XII, 626 pages. 1997.

Vol. 1334: Y. Han, T. Okamoto, S. Qing (Eds.), Information and Communications Security. Proceedings, 1997. X, 484 pages. 1997.

Vol. 1335: R.H. Möhring (Ed.), Graph-Theoretic Concepts in Computer Science. Proceedings, 1997. X, 376 pages. 1997.

Vol. 1336: C. Polychronopoulos, K. Joe, K. Araki, M. Amamiya (Eds.), High Performance Computing. Proceedings, 1997. XII, 416 pages. 1997.

Vol. 1337: C. Freksa, M. Jantzen, R. Valk (Eds.), Foundations of Computer Science. XII, 515 pages. 1997.

Vol. 1338: F. Plášil, K.G. Jeffery (Eds.), SOFSEM'97: Theory and Practice of Informatics. Proceedings, 1997. XIV, 571 pages. 1997.

Vol. 1339: N.A. Murshed, F. Bortolozzi (Eds.), Advances in Document Image Analysis. Proceedings, 1997. IX, 345 pages. 1997.

Vol. 1340: M. van Kreveld, J. Nievergelt, T. Roos, P. Widmayer (Eds.), Algorithmic Foundations of Geographic Information Systems. XIV, 287 pages. 1997.

Vol. 1341: F. Bry, R. Ramakrishnan, K. Ramamohanarao (Eds.), Deductive and Object-Oriented Databases. Proceedings, 1997. XIV, 430 pages. 1997.

Vol. 1342: A. Sattar (Ed.), Advanced Topics in Artificial Intelligence. Proceedings, 1997. XVII, 516 pages. 1997. (Subseries LNAI).

Vol. 1343: Y. Ishikawa, R.R. Oldehoeft, J.V.W. Reynders, M. Tholburn (Eds.), Scientific Computing in Object-Oriented Parallel Environments. Proceedings, 1997. XI, 295 pages. 1997.

Vol. 1344: C. Ausnit-Hood, K.A. Johnson, R.G. Pettit, IV, S.B. Opdahl (Eds.), Ada 95 – Quality and Style. XV, 292 pages. 1997.

Vol. 1345: R.K. Shyamasundar, K. Ueda (Eds.), Advances in Computing Science - ASIAN'97. Proceedings, 1997. XIII, 387 pages. 1997.

Vol. 1346: S. Ramesh, G. Sivakumar (Eds.), Foundations of Software Technology and Theoretical Computer Science. Proceedings, 1997. XI, 343 pages. 1997.

Vol. 1347: E. Ahronovitz, C. Fiorio (Eds.), Discrete Geometry for Computer Imagery. Proceedings, 1997. X, 255 pages. 1997.

Vol. 1348: S. Steel, R. Alami (Eds.), Recent Advances in AI Planning. Proceedings, 1997. IX, 454 pages. 1997. (Subseries LNAI).

Vol. 1349: M. Johnson (Ed.), Algebraic Methodology and Software Technology. Proceedings, 1997. X, 594 pages. 1997.

Vol. 1350: H.W. Leong, H. Imai, S. Jain (Eds.), Algorithms and Computation. Proceedings, 1997. XV, 426 pages. 1997.

Vol. 1351: R. Chin, T.-C. Pong (Eds.), Computer Vision – ACCV'98. Proceedings Vol. I, 1998. XXIV, 761 pages. 1997.

Vol. 1352: R. Chin, T.-C. Pong (Eds.), Computer Vision – ACCV'98. Proceedings Vol. II, 1998. XXIV, 757 pages. 1997.

Vol. 1353: G. BiBattista (Ed.), Graph Drawing. Proceedings, 1997. XII, 448 pages. 1997.

Vol. 1354: O. Burkart, Automatic Verification of Sequential Infinite-State Processes. X, 163 pages. 1997.

Vol. 1355: M. Darnell (Ed.), Cryptography and Coding. Proceedings, 1997. IX, 335 pages. 1997.

Vol. 1356: A. Danthine, Ch. Diot (Eds.), From Multimedia Services to Network Services. Proceedings, 1997. XII, 180 pages. 1997.

Vol. 1357: J. Bosch, S. Mitchell (Eds.), Object-Oriented Technology. Proceedings, 1997. XIV, 555 pages. 1998.

Vol. 1358: B. Thalheim, L. Libkin (Eds.), Semantics in Databases. XI, 265 pages. 1998.

Vol. 1360: D. Wang (Ed.), Automated Deduction in Geometry. Proceedings, 1996. VII, 235 pages. 1998. (Subseries LNAI).

Vol. 1361: B. Christianson, B. Crispo, M. Lomas, M. Roe (Eds.), Security Protocols. Proceedings, 1997. VIII, 217 pages. 1998.

Vol. 1362: D.K. Panda, C.B. Stunkel (Eds.), Network-Based Parallel Computing. Proceedings, 1998. X, 247 pages. 1998.

Vol. 1363: J.-K. Hao, E. Lutton, E. Ronald, M. Schoenauer, D. Snyers (Eds.), Artificial Evolution. XI, 349 pages. 1998.

Vol. 1364: W. Conen, G. Neumann (Eds.), Coordination Technology for Collaborative Applications. VIII, 282 pages. 1998.

Vol. 1365: M.P. Singh, A. Rao, M.J. Wooldridge (Eds.), Intelligent Agents IV. Proceedings, 1997. XII, 351 pages. 1998. (Subseries LNAI).

Vol. 1367: E.W. Mayr, H.J. Prömel, A. Steger (Eds.), Lectures on Proof Verification and Approximation Algorithms. XII, 344 pages. 1998.

Vol. 1368: Y. Masunaga, T. Katayama, M. Tsukamoto (Eds.), Worldwide Computing and Its Applications — WWCA'98. Proceedings, 1998. XIV, 473 pages. 1998.

Vol. 1370: N.A. Streitz, S. Konomi, H.-J. Burkhardt (Eds.), Cooperative Buildings. Proceedings, 1998. XI, 267 pages. 1998.

Vol. 1372: S. Vaudenay (Ed.), Fast Software Encryption. Proceedings, 1998. VIII, 297 pages. 1998.

Vol. 1373: M. Morvan, C. Meinel, D. Krob (Eds.), STACS 98. Proceedings, 1998. XV, 630 pages. 1998.

Vol. 1375: R. D. Hersch, J. André, H. Brown (Eds.), Electronic Publishing, Artistic Imaging, and Digital Typography. Proceedings, 1998. XIII, 575 pages. 1998.

Vol. 1376: F. Parisi Presicce (Ed.), Recent Trends in Algebraic Development Techniques. Proceedings, 1997. VIII, 435 pages. 1998.

Vol. 1377: H.-J. Schek, F. Saltor, I. Ramos, G. Alonso (Eds.), Advances in Database Technology – EDBT'98. Proceedings, 1998. XII, 515 pages. 1998.

Vol. 1378: M. Nivat (Ed.), Foundations of Software Science and Computation Structures. Proceedings, 1998. X, 289 pages. 1998.

Vol. 1379: T. Nipkow (Ed.), Rewriting Techniques and Applications. Proceedings, 1998. X, 343 pages. 1998.

Vol. 1380: C.L. Lucchesi, A.V. Moura (Eds.), LATIN'98: Theoretical Informatics. Proceedings, 1998. XI, 391 pages. 1998.

Vol. 1381: C. Hankin (Ed.), Programming Languages and Systems. Proceedings, 1998. X, 283 pages. 1998.

Vol. 1382: E. Astesiano (Ed.), Fundamental Approaches to Software Engineering. Proceedings, 1998. XII, 331 pages. 1998.

Vol. 1383: K. Koskimies (Ed.), Compiler Construction. Proceedings, 1998. X, 309 pages. 1998.